DISTRIBUTION INVENTORY MANAGEMENT
FOR THE 1990s!

DISTRIBUTION INVENTORY MANAGEMENT

FOR THE 1990s!

GORDON GRAHAM

INVENTORY MANAGEMENT PRESS
Richardson, Texas

Illustration Credits: Graphics used with permission of *Distributor* magazine, published by Technical Reporting Corp. and *Construction Equipment Distribution* magazine, published by the Associated Equipment Dealers.

This book was designed and typeset by Publications Development Company, Crockett, Texas.
Designer: James W. Land
Production Manager: Jean Brasher
Production Editor: Peggy Hayes

For more information or additional copies contact
Inventory Management Press
P.O. Box 832795,
Richardson, Texas 75083

Library of Congress Cataloging in Publication Data available.

Copyright © 1987 by Gordon Graham.
This book may not be reproduced by any means without written permission from the publisher.

Printing *(last digit):* 9 8 7

Printed in the United States of America

DEDICATION

To my Lord and Savior, Jesus Christ
Who is both a light to the Gentiles and
for the Jews,
the Messiah,
the long-awaited "Anointed One."

CONTENTS

Introduction   xiii

1. **Must You Have a Computer to Control Inventories?**   1

    There Were Other Helpful Conditions • The Big Turn-Around • The Effect of the Turn-Around • A Computer Is Needed for Today's Inventory Management! • How about Sales Features? • The Computer Touches Everything You Do! • Avoid the Traps! • Avoid the "Field/Tent" Syndrome! • The Bass-Ackward System-Selection Sequence

2. **System Planning: What Does a Good System Do Today?**   9

    One More Look at the Two Traps • What's a "Me,Too" System? • 1. Does the System Make a Team out of the Computer and Your People? • 2. Is the System On-Line? • 3. Can You Expect Inventory "Tracking" or Inventory Management? • 4. Are There Safeguards on How Branch Transfers Are Handled? • 5. Does the System Provide Exception Reports for Buying? • 6. Are Non-Stock Items Controlled from Ordering to Shipment? • 7. How about Dead Stock? Does the System Help You Find It? • 8. Will Your Salesmen Be Crippled by a Menu-Driven System? • 9. Does the System Offer Up-to-Date "IQ" Capability? • Summary

CONTENTS

3. How a Computer Makes Your Salesmen Look Good! . . . And Eases Their Minds While Keeping Inventories Down! 23

The Good Old Days Are Gone • But What Does This Have to Do with Inventory Management? • OtherReasons: Surprise Stock, Lost Customers, Protected Stock • Why So Much Emphasis on Telephone Sales? • Interchanges, Superseded Parts, and Customer Part Numbers • Non-Stock Item Processing and Control • An Occasional Need to Handle Stock Items Like Non-Stock • Ship-Complete and Tag & Hold Orders • Future Orders • Direct-Ship Orders • "Pick-up-on-the-Way-to-the-Customer" Sales • Quotations • Summary

4. Converting the System 45

What Are We Really Like? • Mechanics Change . . . But So Does Your Inventory Philosophy! • The Four Stages of a System Change • System Degeneration • Inspection . . . Not Expectation! • Assign Someone Full-Time to "Bird-Dog" Your Installation • Summary

5. Planning for the Future: New Attitudes and Organization! 59

The Uncertain Future • Why? What Does It Have to Do with Inventory Control? • The President's Role in Computer Planning • The Place for Data Processing in the Organization • Summary

6. Usage—The Most Important Element of Information! 65

Forecasting Usage . . . One of the More Hazardous Tasks! • Outguessing the Future • Usage • Types of Usage • Transfer Usage • How Much of the Past Is Important? • Use the Last Six Months to Develop a Usage Rate per Month • Seasonal Items • Qualifying the History • Conditions That Should Cause History

CONTENTS ix

Disqualification • Unusual Sales or Transfers • Extended Stockouts • Single or Dominate-Customer Item • Items with Very Low Sales • What Does All This Accomplish? • Usage—The Vital Decision

7. More Information Required for Good Inventory Control . . . And Efficient Use of People   89

Human Work-Time Is Valuable . . . Don't Waste It! • Information Classifications • The Cost of Carrying Inventory Percentage ("K" Factor) • The Cost of a Replenishment Cycle ("R" Cost) • Supplier Lead Times • Master Inventory Records • Manufacturer-Supplier (Vendor) Records • Customer Records • Customers' Special Prices File • Sales Order Records • Purchase Order Records • Summary

8. Your Service Control: When to Order!   113

The Most Misunderstood Aspect of Inventory Management • The Order Point • The Order Point Formula • The Safety Allowance Computation • The Exceptions • Summary

9. Solving the "Line Buying" Problem   129

The Way It's Always Been Done • Line Points • Review Cycles • Dangerous Product Lines • Interrupting the Normal Review Cycle • Summary

10. Your Turnover Control: How Much to Buy?   143

Be Aware of Past Confusion • The Outgoing Cost Concept • Achieving the Lowest Outgoing Cost • The Economic Order Quantity (EOQ) Calculation • Where and When to Use EOQ . . . and When Not To! • An Alternate Approach: Buying by Inventory Class! • What to Do When the Supplier Offers a Price Break by the Item • Summary

11. Special Ordering Situations 161

A Time-Tested Inventory Principle to Remember • Total-Order Discounts • Buying Ahead of Price Increases • Promotions • Summary

12. Replenishment Action: When "Control" Is Exercised! 177

Reports Designed to Maximize What's Already Been Done! • Recommended Replenishment Action Report • Replenishment Options • Discontinue the Item as "Stock" • Surplus Material in Other Locations • Consider Using Alternate Brands • Ease of Purchasing or Transferring-In Merchandise . . . Important! • Expediting and the Expedite Report • Summary

13. Reference Information and the Query Feature 199

The Need for "Backup" Reports • The Query Feature . . . A New Approach to Reports • Summary

14. Physical Control: The Foundation of Your System! 205

Physical Control • What Undergirds Your Ordering Decisions? • Don't Chase the Causes First! • Cycle Counting: The First Step! • The Goal: Get the Available-for-Sale Balance Right! • Remove the Paper Float with "A-Day's-Work-in-a-Day!" • Cycle Count in the "Gap" • Use the Block Method • How Many Items per Night?

15. Dead Stock: The Profit and Control System Crippler! 223

When Inventory "Control" Is Exercised • The Four-Part Dead Stock Program • Summary

16. Branch Inventory Disciplines and Control 245

Non-Recurring Transfers • "Authorized-Path-of-Replenishment" • Rules and Codes • Restrictions on When One Branch Can Use Another's Inventory • The Slow-Moving Stock Item . . . Companywide!

• Different Replenishment Controls for Branches •
A New Method for Setting Branch Replenishment
Quantities • Hand-to-Mouth Ordering Out of
the Warehouse • Summary

17. Kits, Assemblies and Family-Grouped Items   263

What's the Problem? • What's the Correct Recordkeeping
Process? • Are Family-Grouped Items Related to This
Discussion? • Summary: And You Thought the Computer
Would Solve All Your Problems?

18. Monitors, Measures, Modification, and Motivation   273

The Need for "Gauges" and Steering Mechanisms
• Inventory Turnover • Turn & Earn . . . . And
Some Wrong Conclusions • Service Level • Shocking
the System with Extra Merchandise • Other Warning
Signs • The Inventory "Budget" • Motivation . . . An
Incentive Plan for Buyers • Summary

19. The Wrap-Up   299

It's Time Now for Filtering • A Good Way to Start
• The Search for a System Is Tough

Glossary   308

Index   327

INTRODUCTION

My earlier book about computerized inventory management for distributors was written between 1976 and 1979 . . . to be published in 1980. I certainly had no thoughts then that the book covered the subject in a comprehensive manner, nor that the concepts were timeless. There just wasn't much published material to guide a wholesale distributor out of the manual-system era into the computer age. There was even less help in the area of inventory management. The 1980 book seemed to meet a need.

But this is a dynamic world. Have you noticed the faster pace of technological change? How fast knowledge boundaries are being pushed back? The improvement in transportation and communication? The enhancements in computerized systems? The intensity seems to be increasing. The momentum has picked up. Old barriers are being left behind every month. Things you couldn't do (or afford) ten years ago in a computerized system are now commonplace and the hardware costs have come *way* down!

INVENTORY MANAGEMENT HAS CHANGED ALSO

In a relatively new profession like "Distribution Inventory Management," there have been similar changes and breakthroughs. The computer's magnificent capabilities allow new ways to capture and use information, remove the "grunt" work from dreaded activity of years past, and permit new levels of profits. No longer does a distributor have to make a 30 percent gross margin (as in the 50s or 60s) to survive. The computer offers methods for asset management that allow a "lean & hungry" approach to business . . . survival when economic times are bad; solid profits when competition operates in a "Buy-the-Business" mode; and the ability to swallow less-efficient outfits when the time and price is right.

SOME CONCEPTS DO STAND THE TEST OF TIME

The computer hasn't changed everything in Inventory Management. Oh yes, the old manual systems are just about gone. You'll find almost no mention of manual systems in this book, but certain other principles, concepts, formulas, and disciplines are still valid. The purpose of this book is to flesh out these important basics in more depth than my 1980 effort, while incorporating a host of newer developments all along the way. Where a better idea has surfaced, you should know about it. Where an old standby hasn't yet been topped, you should know that too. There's much more detail this time. You should be able to design a system, if you can stay awake, because the subjects are handled in more scope and depth.

BE CAUTIOUS OF INVENTORY EXPERIMENTATION

There are always the inventory "experimenters," especially where the computer's power can be employed, and there's nothing wrong with that. But just like diesel-engine automobiles . . . you'd better wait a while to see how they perform before junking the proven performers. The revolutionary inventory management concept may not last either. The programmer's "whole new theory" or a new software package's "21st Century Controls" might best be postponed until about then. Like the old hammer, some tools have been around for a long time, they're hard to improve on . . . and there's a good reason. Try to avoid being some systems designer's "pioneer." Pioneers are easy to spot. They're the guys with arrows in the back!

BE WARY OF THE CRITIC FROM ANOTHER BUSINESS!

If you adopt the suggestions of this book, you may be identified with me . . . pretty basic, favoring the simple approach, and unwavering in a push for new levels of discipline and accuracy in distribution! There are those who think I'm way behind the times, don't permit the computer to do as much as it can, and shy away from magnificent mathematical gyrations, but interestingly enough, nearly all those critics come out of a manufacturing or processing background. They've never worked in wholesale distribution or have been involved just briefly. There's a pretty good crowd of distributors who identify with my solutions. They recognize the unique characteristics of distribution that are different from manufacturing.

INTRODUCTION xv

BUT WATCH OUT FOR OLD HABITS TOO

Some distributors know 20 times what I do about this business, and they think perhaps I'm too demanding. I expect too much from Management, too much from the people, and too much from the computerized system. I want to see higher pay scales for administrative and warehouse personnel and then I want them to perform at levels far beyond what we've seen in the past. Yes, I admit that the ideas, suggestions, and concepts of this book will push you. You'll feel pressure. If you're in Management, there'll be those who say: "Hey Boss, you need to read this chapter! Graham says we ought to do _____." . . . or maybe the Boss will be the one who corners *you* with some highlighted segment.

You can get defensive. You can assume a "pride of authorship" attitude about your current system, organization, or procedures. You can dismiss these concepts and exhortations as irrelevant. . . . but you'll see 'em again. Next time, it'll be in the way your competitor operates, the information he uses, his financial power. It may be in the methods and system of the company who buys you out! Don't fall in love with ". . . the way we've always done it." In Inventory Management today, if you're still operating the way you did in the 1970s or even part of the 80s, you're in trouble.

As you read this book, fight like a tiger to keep an open mind. Nothing you'll read is theoretical. It's *ALL* being done somewhere, by some distributor, in some software package! . . . and it works. That's the most important point. Sure, all manner of changes were necessary before many of the ideas became reality and the benefits followed. Attitudes, facilities, organizations, sometimes people, and certainly bank accounts had to change before conditions brightened. Move into this book more like a "sponge" than a piece of "steel," and you should soak up enough ideas to pay for your computerized system . . . and maybe even a new warehouse!

1

MUST YOU HAVE A COMPUTER TO CONTROL INVENTORIES?

In my earlier book from 1980, the opening chapter asked the question: "Why Automate?" It was a valid question . . . then! There was a time when distributors could do reasonably well controlling their inventory investment in a manual mode. Good ol' Charlie had been doing all the buying for 20 years. He knew all the customers, most of the part numbers by heart, and had a terrific feel for which items sold well and which didn't. The best total-order discounts, seasonal items, lead times to expect, items that were part of kits . . . shoot, ol' Charlie handled them all smoothly. He relied almost totally on "SWAG" (Scientific, Wild-Ass Guessing) in deciding when and how much to order, but Charlie was good at it. His SWAG was pretty effective. His years of experience helped immensely.

Reliable ol' Agnes worked the kardex. She, too, had been around for a long time, and nothing slipped by her. She corrected bad part numbers or incomplete descriptions, caught improper units of measure, often found prices that were too low, and even knew when the wrong item had been put on the order by a new salesman. "That customer never orders the 50 lb. size! He *always* buys this item in 100 lb. boxes." . . . and Agnes would call, check, and then change the sales order. She had eyes like a hawk for stuff like this.

When Receiving was a bit slow checking in a shipment, Agnes compensated. "Hmmm . . . the warehouse seems to be shipping stock we don't have. I'll bet our outstanding P. O. has come in!" She skipped a line on the kardex card and continued to post the sales orders anyway, showing no balance. When the receiving paperwork finally arrived, Agnes went back and made an entry on the skipped line and then straightened out all the balances.

THERE WERE OTHER HELPFUL CONDITIONS

Yes, those were the "good old days." Charlie and Agnes worked as a team with some 45 years of experience between them, and other conditions helped cover their errors, oversights, and the liberal inventory investment Charlie's SWAG generated to ensure great customer service.

Inflation was a way of life. Every year costs went up 10 to 15 percent, but since that had been going on for a long time, distributors learned to live with it. The increased costs were passed on to customers, and hey . . . it wasn't all bad! Any inventory was *worth 15 percent more* the next year! Just like money in the bank or a great land investment in those days, inventory inflation generated its own profit. In fact, for some wheeler-dealer, "buy-the-business" distributors, inventory inflation developed the only profit they really had.

Gross margins were healthy (compared to today) . . . and because times were good, a distributor could expect a 15–20 percent increase in volume from year to year if he just kept the doors open. True, in many cases it wasn't real growth—just inflation at work—but who cared?

Especially for distributors in fast-developing industries, competition was less of a factor. One electronics distributor told me that in 1980 he had only eight competitors. Today, he has 80!

The old days sound like utopia, don't they? Runaway inflation, solid gross margins, consistently-increasing sales, and limited competition! Who needed a fancy computer in times like that? A manual inventory control system was adequate. Who cared that the inventory was too large? . . . or that too much dead stock was accumulating? . . . or that buying the truckload every time couldn't be justified? No great level of intelligence was required to buy. Any dumbo could do it! Charlie's SWAG seemed to do the job quite nicely.

Most distributors were sales *dominated,* consumed with just one driving objective: Take care of the customers, and do it at any cost! What computer systems there were in those days recognized all this quite clearly. "Take the customer's order smoothly. Fill & ship it efficiently. Handle any backorders without a foulup. Get invoices out quickly. Process any payments correctly. Do all the accounting work accurately!" If a system did all that, very little more was expected . . . or desired. The systems designers listened well. Their systems offered little, if any, inventory management help. "Give ol' Charlie a stock status report. He'll take it from there!" . . . and they did.

THE BIG TURN-AROUND

Distributors should have been *sales oriented,* of course, not *sales dominated,* and somewhere around 1978 this mis-emphasis or misalignment of

MUST YOU HAVE A COMPUTER TO CONTROL INVENTORIES? 3

priorities came home to roost. All the helpful conditions reversed in a short time span. To slow the runaway inflation, the government raised the prime interest rate all the way up to 21 percent. It hadn't been over 7 percent since World War II. Where before it had been Harvard-Business-School cool to have a highly-leveraged inventory, now it was a calamity. One distributor told me then that every time the prime went up a point, it cost him $50,000 off the bottom line because he had borrowed so heavily to finance inventories.

The high cost of money began to control inflation, but it also caused a severe slowdown in the economy. We went into a recession . . . a severe one in some parts of the country. Now, a distributor couldn't sell 15–20 percent more the next year. Likely it was 20 to 40 percent less! The sales pie was smaller in total, so to try to keep his share of the smaller pie, a distributor had to cut prices. Down came his margins. The squeeze was on. The old volumes and margins had covered a lot of sins.

This problem reached the manufacturers. They, too, began to reduce prices, and now the oversized distributor inventories were a big liability. It had been fun to watch the inventory increase in value 15 percent from year to year, but it wasn't fun at all to see it *go down* 10–15 percent! People that had converted to LIFO wished they hadn't.

LAST-IN FIRST-OUT

THE EFFECT OF THE TURN-AROUND

Great! High cost of money; less sales; lower margins; material costs coming down; and a huge deflating inventory . . . hmmmm, all things that are dangerous to corporate health! There should have been warning labels on the packages or something. But there were none, and we all know distributors who didn't survive. They bellied-up or sold out. The turn-around brought a new business climate and a definite need for improved efficiencies. The old business rules didn't work. You'd hear Papa say: "Son, I don't understand what's happening. We're doing everything just the way we have since I started this business in 1948, but we're losing a bundle. I'm tired. I want out!"

A COMPUTER IS NEEDED FOR TODAY'S INVENTORY MANAGEMENT!

This chapter's main question can now be answered: Yes, you *do* need a computer to handle the new business climate! You do need an improved skill level in Purchasing and Inventory Control. You need better-paid, more-dedicated, better-motivated people spending your money . . . but supported by software (computer programs) that removes their grunt work, handles the mountains of clerical transactions, performs revealing analyses, makes consistently accurate calculations, prints well-planned exception reports that promote profitable stock replenishment action, and returns information through inquiry that was lost when the old kardex disappeared.

HOW ABOUT SALES FEATURES?

In another area, you need a computer to make your inside telephone salesmen sound brilliant to the customers: Able to track down an order or a special price in seconds, or to offer an interchangable item when the customer requests some weird brand. You need a computer to permit customers to inquire and place orders into your system from terminals in their locations, using *their own part numbers!* We'll talk more about these sales-enhancement capabilities in a later chapter, but computer-fast information and value-added sales features are no longer optional. As Dr. Mike Workman of Texas A&M tells it: "Having such capabilities today isn't considered a great plus by your customers . . . but *not* having them is a definite minus!"

THE COMPUTER TOUCHES EVERYTHING YOU DO!

The computer assists every person, every department, every function in a distributor's operation. This book emphasizes Inventory Management, and I think you'll agree before you finish it that the emphasis is timely. Most computerized systems today are tardy offering useful help for this function, but make no mistake about this: In the 1990s and beyond, a computer will be an integral part of everything you're doing! Regular sales, telemarketing, systems selling, quoting, pricing, ship-complete's, tag & hold, warehouse pickups, cores & warranties, serial number tracking, credit screening, order processing, data gathering & manipulation, ordering-control calculations, lead time capturing, exception reporting, expediting, receiving, warehousing, bar coding, picking, assemblies, repairs, material processing, routing, shipping, delivery, returns, billing, sales commissions, accounting, rebates, cycle counting, physical inventories, dead stock identification . . . you finish the list . . . *everything* will be touched by the computer!

AVOID THE TRAPS!

Yes . . . you must have a computer today . . . but there are pitfalls to watch for! Hopefully, this book will help you design or select an effective system and avoid most of the headaches and upset stomachs others have suffered. The first traps lurking in wait are the hundreds of "Me, Too" packages on the market for durable goods distributors. Some have been around for years; some are very expensive; most were developed for specific vertical markets (electrical or plumbing and heating, for example) and have definite appeal for distributors in those industries. Their unique industry bells and whistles make such systems appear a perfect match, but in reality the features are just fluff. In the system elements you must have in the 1990s . . . the ones that really count, your *asset management* controls, they are vintage 1970.

That's why they're called "Me, Too" systems. We'll talk more about them in the next chapter, but each one performs about like the next. Developed for sales-dominated users, they handle the Sales and Accounting functions well, but Inventory Management . . . well, there's not much help. Good ol' Charlie's SWAG is accommodated smoothly. "Just tell us how you want to order, and we'll program the system accordingly. You can use a Min/Max system, Order Points, Order-Up-To, or anything you want!" . . . or maybe the system tries to forecast and calculate a bit, but the logic is too complex and the calculations are developed through very exotic math. Nobody understands where the answers come from, but what does that matter?

This book is to help you avoid both horns of this dilemma. Let's replace pure SWAG in your ordering controls, but let's do it with easy-to-understand, simple logic and very simple mathematics that anyone can duplicate with a hand calculator.

AVOID THE "FIELD/TENT" SYNDROME!

It's vital to sidestep another very common trap: The "Field/Tent" mentality. Think of it this way:

> Some poor guy is down on his luck. He lives out in a field. It's cold and wet out there, and the wind really bites. He knows he's miserable, but it's the best he can do right now. One day a salesman comes by and sells the poor fellow a tent.
>
> Boy, the tent is much better than the field. It's drier. It breaks the cold wind. Compared to where he was, the tent is quite an improvement. . . . problem is, the guy never bothers to look further. Down the road is a cottage with floors, windows, and heating. For the same money, he could have had the cottage. . . . or for very little more, move up to it from his tent.
>
> He's just so thrilled with the improvement provided by the tent, he never looks beyond it. If the supplier brings a prospect by to ask this guy how he

CHAPTER 1

likes his tent, wow, he loves it. What a glowing report he gives . . . a truly satisfied tent-user! And another tent is sold.

Do you see the analogy between this story and many of the computer packages offered to distributors today? There are hundreds of "tents" out there, and many have impressive user lists. The systems *have helped* the users . . . no argument about that. Unfortunately, the level of help isn't even close to what it should have been, considering the price paid. Often the cost of the tent system is just as high as a cottage.

In the years ahead, *you must extract from your computerized system* the maximum it can provide in Inventory Management and Purchasing assistance. Hopefully, in these pages you'll find the guidance to help you design or select a system that's a cottage or condo . . . not just a tent!

THE BASS-ACKWARD SYSTEM-SELECTION SEQUENCE

It may be too late for you to avoid this next trap. Many distributors have both legs locked tightly in its jaws already: The mistake of picking the hardware first and *THEN* trying to develop or find software that does an effective job. It's like buying a two-seat sports car and then marrying a woman with seven children. The next trip to California will be a bit cramped. Better that we see who will ride in the car and how far we're going . . . *before* picking the vehicle!

That's the purpose of this book and specifically of the next chapter: To show what a solid system does in a number of areas; To answer the age-old questions of "When?" and "How much?" to order; To demonstrate state-of-the-art features you'll want your system to have in years to come. When you've digested these concepts and filtered them all through your company's mesh of functions, organization, and objectives, . . . *then* you'll know what you want your system to do! When you know that, you're in position to plan or find software that does it. Finally, you're ready to pick the computer on which to run it.

That's the right sequence: Know what you want to do; plan the software (or find it on the market); decide which computer hardware to employ. If you reverse this sequence, you may limit severely what your system will be capable of doing . . . or worse, be forced to settle for second-rate, definitely "Me, Too" features.

Get a fresh cup of coffee, turn down the music, and let's get under way. You will soon discover that there's much more to effective Inventory Management today than you had expected. Stay alert, keep an open mind, and every time this thought pops in your mind: "Hold on . . . that's not the way we've always done it!" . . . be glad! You just learned something new that might give you an edge on competition or make you more money.

2

SYSTEM PLANNING: WHAT DOES A GOOD SYSTEM DO TODAY?

One of the more alarming statistics to surface recently is that the most profitable distributors of durable goods are those *without a computer at work in their businesses!* That's right! The distributors doing the best job are those on *manual* systems! Kinda scary isn't it? I carry on in Chapter 1 at length to convince you of the need for a computer, and the very next chapter starts like this. Confusing, isn't it?

Well, I still believe in computers. I still say you'll need one to remain competitive in the years ahead . . . so what's the problem today? You've already heard the answer. It's those two big traps at the end of Chapter 1: Picking a system "Bass-Ackwards" . . . with the reverse sequence of decisions (hardware first, then software, etc.), and then the most common trap of all: The "Field/Tent Syndrome" . . . never looking beyond the "tent" system to see the latest developments available.

ONE MORE LOOK AT THE TWO TRAPS

Backing into a system can be blamed on the hardware manufacturers if you're good at rationalizing. IBM, for example, makes excellent computers . . . as do Hewlett-Packard, Data General, Digital Equipment, NCR, Unisys, Honeywell, and a host of newcomers. If your past experience with one of these was good, from a service and capability standpoint, why not stay with the same brand when it's time to upgrade? The computer salesmen aren't dummies either. They always talk more about what the hardware will do than precisely how it will solve *your* problems . . . those of a distributor.

Or maybe you're unhappy with what you've had, so the logical move seems to be a switch to the hardware with the best reputation or one that's been (apparently) successful for a buddy in the same industry. It may have happened like this: The distributor executive receives a demo of some computer manufacturer's equipment at an association convention, and then visits another distributor's location to see it in operation. It looks good, so he places an order for the same computer.

NOW . . . he starts looking around for software (programs to run on his new equipment). Nothing currently available works very well, so he hires an outside firm to write all-new programs for his business or to modify what is available. This usually means that he merely transfers over to the computerized system all the "SWAG" (Scientific, Wild-Ass Guessing), all the weaknesses, all the sloppy paperwork, all the undisciplined steps of his old system. The new computer does accomplish one thing: It provides the same lousy results as before, but it does it faster!

What's the Right Sequence?

How should this executive have gone about the system selection steps?

1. Find out what a *good system* does. Learn the new disciplines, the new controls, the correct ways for material and paper to flow. Learn the proven stock replenishment controls that replace SWAG in the ordering process. In other words, find out where his current system is weak and determine that the new computerized system will correct the shortcomings. That's the objective of this book.
2. Find software that most closely achieves the objectives set out in Step 1.
3. Find hardware (computer equipment) that runs that software.
4. Determine if the package is affordable. If not, return to Step 1 and downgrade the requirements a bit until an affordable combination of software/hardware is developed.

The Second Trap: The "Field/Tent" Syndrome!

The "Field/Tent" attitude is a psychological phenomenon that's present in the human race: If we find an improvement to a very troubling situation, or a solution to long-standing headaches . . . then buddy, you just *TRY* to move us to something else! Only an earthquake would shake us loose. Where do you have your hair cut, your cleaning done, your car serviced? The outfit may not be the best around for the price, but if they perform to your satisfaction . . . and without the grief you had earlier until you found them . . . then you'll keep going back.

SYSTEM PLANNING: WHAT DOES A GOOD SYSTEM DO TODAY?   11

Many computerized systems today are in place because of this phenomenon. The system may be archaic, slow as Christmas, equivalent to driving a Model T on the L.A. Freeway . . . but it's better than walking . . . so the company just muddles along with it, never looking outside their "Tent" to see if anything better is available for the same money. The system provided big improvements eight years ago when it was installed. New reports, better information, more efficient people . . . so it's still their system.

Amazingly, other distributors also buy the same system today, even though it's badly outmoded. The systems company simply brings a prospect by to talk to the "Tent-User." As the old customer tells his story, the new guy (still out in the "Field," perhaps) thinks this is the finest system since indoor plumbing.

Who's to Blame?

With careful rationalizing, we can sidestep any responsibility for either of these two traps: The system selected by an improper sequence of decisions, or the Field/Tent syndrome. Both were *somebody else's fault!* The hardware manufacturers make such good equipment that they trap us with it. We already have our "car" before we know how far we need to go or how many people need to ride. . . . or we have psychological hang-ups (that *couldn't* be our fault!) to cause us to act in a strange, unprofitable manner for our company.

Silly logic, isn't it? We're all big boys and girls, and we must accept the responsibility for our decisions. This book was written to help you avoid winding up with a "Me, Too" system by falling victim to one of the traps. Today, there are several terrific systems available to durable goods distributors . . . not a vast host, but several. There *IS* a vast host of "Me, too" systems. Prices for the good systems are much less than a few years back, and the features much-improved, particularly in the area of true Inventory Management.

WHAT'S A "ME, TOO" SYSTEM?

A "Me, too" system tracks inventory by processing all sales, transfers, receipts, returns, etc., but then asks for your company SWAG to set the ordering rules . . . or worse, it tries to employ mathematics of such complexity (exponential smoothing, etc.) that no one in the place understands how the computer arrived at the figures. . . . so they follow them blindly. In other areas, a "Me, Too" system lags far behind state-of-the-art capabilities that you should have . . . perhaps even *must have* in the years ahead.

Today, you don't have to settle for a "Me, too" system. You shouldn't design and build one, nor should you purchase one. In this chapter, you'll find several major checkpoints . . . the features a good system has today. The rest of the book will show you the details, the specifics of what these features do and the advantages. Use this chapter as a quick "pulse-check" of your current system, the one for which you're in the planning stages now, or the package now under consideration for purchase.

Hopefully, you'll be on your way to completing Step 1 mentioned above (finding out what good systems do), so that you may design these features into your own system . . . or know the questions to ask as you see a demo of some package offered to you. This chapter and this book should cause you to look at *all* the real estate available before you move. Don't just move into one of the many "tents" now offered . . . or stay in a tent when better housing is available. Now, the checklist:

1. DOES THE SYSTEM MAKE A TEAM OUT OF THE COMPUTER AND YOUR PEOPLE?

This question pinpoints a problem mentioned earlier, where some systems attempt very sophisticated mathematics to manipulate the sales history data on stock items . . . all in an effort to come up with replenishment ordering controls. Human judgment or intervention isn't needed, supposedly. The systems designers (most of whom haven't worked in distribution) assume that the machine should be able to handle any condition that might occur with a stock item. Hmmm . . . but what would our machine do when an item's sales history looks like this?

June	July	Aug	Sep	Oct	Nov	Dec
14	24	3	31	9	185	?

What would it forecast as the usage to expect for December and beyond? Use any math at your disposal and come up with a figure . . . one you'd stake some of the company's money on with an inventory investment. There's an obvious problem, isn't there? What happened in November? How did we happen to sell 185? Can we expect that kind of activity to continue or not? Until we have some answers to these questions, there is no mathematical way to project a reliable figure for December.

What Should the System Do with This?

The better systems today make no attempt to project a usage rate when such a condition is found in history. The usage rate is an integral part of

SYSTEM PLANNING: WHAT DOES A GOOD SYSTEM DO TODAY?

all replenishment ordering formulas, and to insert a bad one would surely lead to a stockout or serious inventory excess. When the "big sale" shows up in history, the computer flags the item and then makes no attempt to reset the current ordering controls (as it would on all other stock items each month). Instead, a report prints for the buyer. It lists the item, shows the history, and also prints a list of all outgoing transactions on that item last month . . . so the unusually large one can be identified.

The computer asks the buyer, in effect: "Hey human, is that unusual sale going to recur? If so, you need to make some adjustments to my controls. If not, tell me so I won't consider that sale as I forecast what will happen on this item. Until you give me your input, human, I can do nothing further with this stock item!" . . . and the human finds out what he or she can, inserts that input into the computer files, and the "team" (computer/human) has performed properly . . . each team member carrying out the task for which it is the most capable.

Three other conditions can pop up in a stock item's history where, in similar fashion, the computer should attempt no forecast of usage nor a change in the replenishment controls. Chapter 6 will show you how to deal with each one. These three conditions, added to the unusual sale situation, account for 98 percent of the headaches you'll encounter with a stock item, but are present at any one time in only 15–20 percent of your stock items.

A good system uses very simple math to forecast usage and re-set replenishment controls on the other 80–85 percent every month . . . but brings out these four conditions on exception reports, asking for human research and then human guidance for the machine. Your system should function like this. Chapter 6 will help you design a new one that does, correct the one you have, or find a package on the market that uses this logic.

2. IS THE SYSTEM ON-LINE?

"On-Line" means that when transactions are keyed into the computer, the appropriate files change at once. A sale reduces the available-for-sale stock balance. A purchase order increases the quantity shown as on-order instantly . . . not tonight in a "batch" mode of operation, where batches of transactions process all at one time, and the files wait for this mass-processing step before they reflect the new totals or balances. Today, you need up-to-the-minute facts for two very important reasons:

1. To redistribute surplus stocks. One branch inquires the status of a needed item, finds excess material in a sister branch, and transfers

it in to fill the need. Making surplus inventory visible and accessible is one of the last "quick fixes" left in inventory control these days. I've seen multi-branch distributors improve their turns as much as 2 per year, by finding and repositioning excess stocks scattered around the company.

But . . . attempts to do this break down when the stocking information is old and out of date. If I ask for your surplus to fill an important customer's order, and you let me down with the excuse that "Shoot, we sold that stuff three weeks ago," I won't bother asking you again. An on-line system allows me to see the condition of all your stock as of the last transaction entered. With a batch system, the information may be three or four days old . . . dangerous to rely on.

2. For effective Cycle Counting. The key to success in inventory management is accuracy of the warehouse-shelf vs. computer-record stock balances. Are they in agreement? The only way to keep them in agreement is to Cycle Count a portion of your inventory some 200 nights a year . . . but Cycle Counting has a prerequisite: Computer records that change instantly when transactions are keyed-in. Cycle Counting is discussed in Chapter 14.

Don't settle for an old-fashioned, batch-mode system. On-line systems are not nearly as expensive today as they once were, and there are options (distributed processing, etc.) that do not require dedicated telephone lines between your locations, but still achieve at least a close-of-business-day status good enough for both requirements above.

3. CAN YOU EXPECT INVENTORY "TRACKING" OR INVENTORY MANAGEMENT?

Many distributors' home-grown systems, and far too many on the market, offer almost no help at all to the buyer as he or she answers the "When To Order?" and "How Much To Order?" questions . . . critical to service levels and turnover. The systems merely "track" the inventory. They record all transactions, changing the stock balances up or down, and keep track of the sales either year-to-date or month-by-month. They may even "accommodate" controls to help answer the two important questions, but no attempt is made to calculate them.

The Buyer determines how he or she wants to order each item and then puts this SWAG into the computer files. From then on, the computer triggers replenishment accordingly. Of course when conditions

SYSTEM PLANNING: WHAT DOES A GOOD SYSTEM DO TODAY?

change, the Buyer must come up with new figures and again get them into the computer records. If he or she watches over 10,000 stock items, you can guess how frequently new calculations are made . . . only when an item has a stockout. The system captures no lead times. You provide them. It figures no ordering quantities. You decide what they're to be and key them in, and you change them when they're wrong. If your SWAG is experienced and you know the products, and if you have lots of time to re-set and re-key controls, you may get along reasonably well. If you're new to the business or short on time, allowing controls to be based on old information, then good luck! The comfortable way to live with a system like this? . . . *LOTS* of inventory!

Let the Computer Work for You . . . at What It Does Best!

A good system today captures new information continually and then uses that data to re-set the important replenishment controls (Order Points, Line Points, EOQ's, etc.) every month where unusual conditions are not present in the sales histories. Buyers are guided to the right action for an item's condition, or to meet a supplier's total-order requirement, all under the restraint of service and turnover goals. The controls mentioned above and the right ways to develop them are discussed in Chapters 7–10.

Remember, you're in an entirely different business climate from the 60s or 70s. You need to make use of the latest concepts to control this major asset . . . Inventory. You don't dare depend on SWAG across the board on all items anymore. That would be like allowing your six-year-old to play with a water pistol, a BB gun, or a loaded 45. If he picks up the wrong "toy," he could blow himself away. Systems that accommodate anything the buyers want to do, rather than guiding them to the proper action, can blow away your profits. Use Chapters 7–10 to put solid controls in place.

4. ARE THERE SAFEGUARDS ON HOW BRANCH TRANSFERS ARE HANDLED?

If you have branches, this question is more important than you may have realized. If you don't have any yet, wait a week or so. You'll merge with someone, buy out another distributor, be bought out yourself, or perhaps just open your second company location. Branches offer many opportunities, positive and negative, but one of the negatives that often lurks inside a computer is the mishandling of branch transfers.

How so? What could be so dangerous about material simply moving from one company location to another? The answer: Non-recurring transfers that are recorded in the shipping branch's history. Branch 1 sees that Branch 2 has some surplus stock of an item he needs. The transfer is processed, and the activity recorded in Branch 2's history for that item. What might the computer do the next time it forecasts the usage to expect in Branch 2? You guessed it. Up goes the usage rate. Up goes the Order Point. The computer's logic: "Boy, this item is really beginning to move. I should raise the inventory level here at Branch 2!"

What *Do* You Do with Transfers Then?

Only *recurring* transfers are *ever* posted in a branch's history on a stock item! The central warehouse of a distributor may have sales of its own and responsibility to supply several outlying branches. Transfers from that warehouse to the branches are recurring. The branches depend on the warehouse resupplying them, so transfers out of the warehouse are posted in the warehouse histories. The computer helps build the warehouse stocks accordingly.

When a branch sends material over to a buddy, because it's surplus or to help him out with a customer, that's likely a one-time occurrence. His buddy may never want that item from him again. It's non-recurring activity and *should not* be posted in the shipping branch's history! Chapter 16 shows how to protect for this and several other branch-related pitfalls in a computerized system . . . like this one:

Robbing Stock for Customers' Orders

Stock in another location shouldn't be "fair game," meaning anyone else can have it, unless it's surplus. Many distributors live under executive edicts that say: "If you have an item sold, you may pull stock from any other branch that has it!" Bad Rule! Just because one branch has it sold is not—repeat *NOT*—justification to take his buddy's stock! Sure it's an old practice . . . been around for years, and for years it has caused big trouble.

Let's say I've been watching my inventory carefully as a branch manager, and I'm low on an item . . . not out, but running low. Another manager hasn't been so diligent. His inventory control is sloppy and he runs out of important items all the time. On my low item, he's out (as usual). A customer over at the other branch orders the critical item. The manager does an inquiry through the computer system and sees that I still have some stock . . . enough to fill his customer order if he takes

SYSTEM PLANNING: WHAT DOES A GOOD SYSTEM DO TODAY?

all I have. He processes a transfer and I have to (by executive edict) send him my stock. After all, he has it sold!

What do I tell *my* customers now? . . . and what do you suppose I'll do from here on when I replenish that item? Of course, I'll bring in a lifetime supply! It's the only way I can assure that I'll have stock for my customers, since the company allows anyone to get my stock if they have it sold. The overall result: Inventory "Backlash." Stock levels at all branches climb higher and higher as the managers lash back at the system . . . a system that won't let them protect any of their stock at all. Each manager must carry big excesses of all items. He never knows when somebody will pull away all the stock of a critical item. Chapter 16 explains how to build computerized safeguards to avoid this scene.

Had you thought about all this? Hmmm . . . it's good that you're reading this book now rather than after your new system is in place! Oh, you're not! The system is already installed. Well, that's why Excedrin is popular . . . or antacids, stomach pumps, and valium. One or the other can help you forget. Seriously, though, it's never too late. You can *still* make changes to offset the problems we're talking about in this chapter. It's just always better to *prevent* than to *correct*. Maybe now you understand why some distributors with computers are not among the most profitable.

5. DOES THE SYSTEM PROVIDE EXCEPTION REPORTS FOR BUYING?

Many older systems in use today prepare stock status reports on an entire product line, or all the products assigned to a buyer, or worst of all . . . every item in stock. Buyers are expected to scan through the thick report looking for items that need replenishment action. Two bad things can result:

1. A buyer will purchase something he or she shouldn't, or . . .
2. He or she will overlook items that should be bought.

The items to receive special attention may be marked with an asterisk (*), but the basic error is in giving the buyer an opportunity to purchase or not purchase items in the product line based on his or her SWAG evaluation of the information displayed. It often goes something like this:

Let's say there are 500 stock items in the supplier's line, it's late in the afternoon, I'm tired, I need to pick up my little boy at the daycare center by 6 PM, and yet I want to get this purchase order called-in today. How do you suppose I'll put together the P. O.? Easy. I'll fill out whatever quantity, weight, or dollars required by the supplier with the fastest-moving, most-popular items we stock! Never mind that most are nowhere near the point of needing replenishment. Never mind that I don't take the time to review all those less-popular items on the last 38 pages of the report.

Of course, all we have to say to a customer who orders one of the less-popular items is: "That item isn't very important to us. We're not careful about replenishing it in a timely fashion. . . . but heck, if you'll just order item 237X, it's one of our fastest-moving. We always have plenty of those!" Can you imagine the customer's answer? Can't even print it here.

Exception Reports on Planned Review Cycles

A good system prepares "Recommended Replenishment Action Reports," or something similar, which list *ONLY* the items in a product line close enough to order point to be candidates for purchasing . . . and list every one, fast or slow-moving, if you've told the customers that you carry it in stock. Reports like this are illustrated in Chapter 12.

If you'll employ carefully-calculated product line Review Cycles and Line Points, you'll place the purchase orders on a frequency in accord with how often you can justify the "Buy" . . . and you'll be sure to have enough weight, units, or dollars on each order to secure the total-order savings offered by the supplier. You've never heard about things like Review Cycles and Line Points? Maybe that explains why you could be one of the distributors with a computer that isn't helping your profit all that much. Chapter 9 may turn out to be one of your favorites.

6. ARE NON-STOCK ITEMS CONTROLLED FROM ORDERING TO SHIPMENT?

Non-stock items are important to almost every distributor. Surveys show that between 25–50 percent of all orders taken by distributors are for non-stock items. They account for a sizable chunk of your sales, gross profit, and hopefully, net profit, but old-fashioned order entry and processing systems dribble away profit through the inefficient, extra-work steps required to deliver a non-stock item.

You want an example? Some systems require that a "dummy" part number be assigned to a non-stock item (99999, etc.) before the sales

SYSTEM PLANNING: WHAT DOES A GOOD SYSTEM DO TODAY?   19

order can be accepted into the computer files. You must "fool" the computer, in effect, by making it think it's dealing with a stock item . . . because frankly, the system can't process a non-record (non-stock) item. A dummy inventory file must be established, with a complete history record, even though the item may never be bought again by the customer (odds are: only 2 of 10 non-stock items *are* reordered!).

Then, someone must make notations on the purchase order or receiving paperwork to tell the warehouse what to do when the item arrives: "Call Joe when this item shows up!," or "For ABC Industries order 245039," etc. Lots of extra work, unnecessary steps, and computer file space tied up because of an outmoded system.

There are several ways to accomplish routine but effective control over non-stock items, assuring that each will be handled smoothly at order entry and correctly when received. Chapter 3 gives the details. Be sure your programmer reads it and follows the guidelines.

7. HOW ABOUT DEAD STOCK? DOES THE SYSTEM HELP YOU FIND IT?

Anytime a list is compiled for material you intend to get rid of, some salesman will say: "Wait a minute! Don't get rid of that stuff. I think I can sell it!" . . . or, "The customers will think we're going out of business if we don't have *that* in stock!" Hmmm . . . really? If that's true, why do the records show no sales in over 18 months?

Most computerized systems in use today are far too liberal in identifying non-productive stock. . . . and here's a fact you'll find hard to believe until you make the study discussed in Chapter 15: Most distributors carry 30 to 40 percent more items & dollars in inventory than they need! The second condition feeds off the first. If your system doesn't pinpoint stock that does little or nothing for you, you'll probably keep sitting on it.

Chapter 15 offers an inventory analysis that's easy to program, or is offered in the better software on the market. The study will shock you. It will terrify your Management . . . but before you say "Our situation isn't that bad!" (as in the example), run the analysis. Talk about stomach pumps! You'll need 'em by the dozen. Since I've suggested this method of finding the non-productive portion of distributors' inventories, only very rarely will someone find that it takes more than 60–70 percent of the investment to account for 95 percent of the sales. 40 percent of *your* inventory may reflect poor stewardship of dollars also. Run the analysis and find out . . . and then be sure this capability is a regular part of your computerized system.

8. WILL YOUR SALESMEN BE CRIPPLED BY A MENU-DRIVEN SYSTEM?

When a customer calls to expedite an order or asks about stock status in the middle of one, the telephone salesman should answer within 20 seconds or so. This requires very quick screen-to-screen changes. The better systems today make seven screens accessible to a salesman . . . and changing from any one of them to any other requires only one or two keystrokes and no longer than five seconds:

1. Stock Item Inquiry
2. Sales Order Entry
3. Sales Order Inquiry
4. Purchase Order Entry (For Non-Stock Items)
5. Purchase Order Inquiry
6. Branch Transfer Entry
7. Branch Transfer Inquiry

Other departments don't need such speed, but Telephone Sales does! The old-fashioned systems are still "menu-driven." To go from one of the programs above to another may mean signing off, signing onto another program, waiting for a new menu of screen options, selecting the new screen, and waiting for it to appear. This can use up 30 or 40 seconds sometimes . . . all the time with a customer waiting impatiently for a reply.

Program your system to permit a salesman to key "SOI," for example, at the bottom of any screen and have the Sales Order Inquiry screen appear in five seconds . . . or "POI" and Purchase Order Inquiry is there, ready to advise the status of any item or order keyed. If the salesman enters the Sales Order & Line Number after "SOI," then the system has no delay whatsoever. The desired item information is there in five seconds—not just a screen to be filled in! If only the customer's PO Number is keyed, then all items appear in sequence.

Imagine the customer's reaction when he has an answer in 5 or 10 seconds rather than 45 or more. Menu-driven systems are still popular, partially because the systems designers & programmers don't know how to do anything else . . . but they're as archaic as push mowers. They still get the job done, but you work harder and it takes longer. Look for a system that moves a salesman from screen to important screen very quickly.

SYSTEM PLANNING: WHAT DOES A GOOD SYSTEM DO TODAY?

9. DOES THE SYSTEM OFFER UP-TO-DATE "IQ" CAPABILITY?

Finally, make certain that your new automated system allows management to employ the niftiest tool developed in many years: The "query" feature, or sometimes called "IQ" (for inquiry) or "report generator" . . . the ability to ask the computer to pull out some of its information, rearrange it, get totals or sub-totals, and pop out a special report in a few minutes. No need to wait three weeks for a programmer to do it, pay $600, and get the information too late to use it as you'd hoped.

Before you say: "Heck, we've had all that for years!," bear in mind that most of the older report generator systems have four major limitations:

1. You must know special "buzzwords" to make use of the system . . . learn to be a mini-programmer of sorts.

2. The computer files open to this kind of one-time fooling-around are very limited. The Boss is allowed to use only a few files.

3. The information that is made available can be pulled out for a report only as it is . . . no multiplying one figure by another or any of that foolishness, etc.

4. The programs to extract the data, prepare the report, and print it are ponderous, not well thought through, and as a result are "core-hogs" . . . meaning that they take all the computer's capability to run them, which in turn means that they can be run only at night.

Today, several newer systems have overcome these handicaps . . . and how! The Boss doesn't have to be a programmer. He can key in plain old English words to ask for the report he wants. A multitude of files are made available to him. He can ask for inventory information, sales data, accounts receivable facts, purchasing statistics, and more . . . *AND* often he can ask for percentages, totals, screening, or analysis before the computer presents the final report. The systems are beautifully programmed, with years of effort invested in the final product, so that they run very efficiently. Response times do not slow down when the President needs a special study in 15 minutes. He can ask for it at any time during the day.

Yes, report generators have been around for years. The good ones have been available only a short time, so be sure to ask the system salesman how his product performs on this feature. If you're the President, you'll lose an extremely valuable management tool unless you check this out. Just like air-conditioning is today, compared to 1947, . . . once you get used to it, it's hard to imagine life without it. The same is true of an effective query system. Don't try to program your own. Just look for one on the market. There's a pretty good query package today for almost any hardware.

SUMMARY

There you have 'em . . . nine tough, to-the-point questions to ask your programmer or the computer system salesman. Before you finish the book, you'll have many more. You don't have to settle for a "Me, Too" system. No one wants to lay out the kind of cash computer systems cost only to wind up with a system designed in 1974 that's behind the times on several vital functions. You must have dependable guidance for your buyers as they answer the "When?" and "How Much?" replenishment questions. Seek out or program a system that guards against inventory creep in the branches by restricting what managers can do without approval. Program or buy a system to find your dead stock, the stuff that drains off your cash and profit.

You'll find the details as you move through the chapters of this book, along with many other concepts or ideas for special situations. In nearly every section, I'll keep pressing home this point: *There's a lot more to effective Inventory Management, accomplished with the aid of a computer, than you thought!*

3

HOW A COMPUTER MAKES YOUR SALESMEN LOOK GOOD!

... And Eases Their Minds While Keeping Inventories Down!

Right off, I've infuriated all the female salespeople with the title of this chapter, but please . . . "salesman" is a generic term. In my mind, it covers anyone, male or female, who performs the function. Ladies, please don't get turned off by semantics and miss the message.

What message? That computers must facilitate the selling function for a distributor today and certainly in the 1990s! Another of the changes since the 50s and 60s is a deterioration of loyalties between distributors and customers. In those "good old days," customers often bought because a personal friendship had been established and nurtured over many years by the distributor's salesman. A salesman tended to work longer for a distributor, and it was common to see one receive a 20-year or a 30-year-pin. Today it's a different story.

THE GOOD OLD DAYS ARE GONE

Customers tend to buy on price alone, and salesmen have become much more "transient" than in years past. They bounce around from distributor to distributor. Rarely today do you find a 20-year distributor salesman calling on his old buddy, a 25-year purchasing agent for the customer. As a distributor executive, you must marshal every tool, every "weapon," every piece of information to help the selling function if you're to avoid competing on a price-only basis. The computer is one of your most effective tools, and there are several ways it can help the sales task. Bring its guns to bear (a lot of military talk . . . !) in that important moment when a customer calls with an inquiry or an order.

BUT WHAT DOES THIS HAVE TO DO WITH INVENTORY MANAGEMENT?

"Agreed," you reply, "and Graham, you can write all about this in your next book. Why are you telling us these things *here* in a book about Inventory Management?" For several reasons. First, there are a great number of computer system packages offered to distributors which do very little to enhance the inside telephone sales function . . . that is, very little beyond what forty-leven other systems do. It's important to look at this area carefully, just as with the Inventory Management functions, or you'll pay out big money and get a "Me, Too" inquiry, quoting, and order-entry system.

Secondly, as important as order entry is, the inquiry phase can hamstring your efforts to get the order at all. Getting the order is critical. That's why the inventory waits out in the warehouse. . . . but I've seen too many systems lose the order because insufficient information was made available to the telephone salesman or it was too hard to find it. The sale didn't happen; the inventory didn't move; and surprisingly it was *the system's fault!*

You'd like an example? The customer calls and asks for Brand X, item number 27J. Our salesman is fairly new. She's been with the company a year and on the phones only three months. One day, she'll be a wizard at item interchanges (in say, five to ten years), but right now she has no idea how to find an equivalent product for that 27J. . . . but the fact is, you carry Brand A's 49J in stock. You can see the turn this could take. Either the sale is lost or, at minimum, the customer inconvenienced by a long delay in fumbling through interchange manuals. The computer should have helped. In a few minutes, we'll see how it can provide "artificial intelligence" to make the new employee appear as smart as a 15-year veteran.

OTHER REASONS: SURPRISE STOCK, LOST CUSTOMERS, PROTECTED STOCK

Inventory Management is impacted by poor inquiry and ordering systems in other, much more subtle, ways. For example, a system that handles non-stock items sloppily or tediously leads to material winding up on warehouse shelves that shouldn't have been there . . . little surprises at year-end when the physical inventory is taken. You'll see how this happens later in the chapter when we discuss the proper way to process non-stock items.

A poor quotation system can lose orders or mis-price an order developed from a quote, and that drives away customers who would have bought part of the inventory. Inventory objectives and sales efforts are intertwined. Inventory Management works better when the sales

HOW A COMPUTER MAKES YOUR SALESMEN LOOK GOOD!

function is efficient. *That's why* we're talking about what the computer does for Sales!

A salesman who mistrusts the computerized inventory management system, particularly where the stock balances showing on his screen are inaccurate, can resort to his own private insurance measure: Protected Stock. He simply tells his customer:

> We're all fouled up around here ever since we put in this new computerized system. Why don't you give me a letter that says we *must* set aside certain stock items just for you if we want your business. My management would never do that unless you make it an official provision for you to buy from us.

It's a salesman-initiated deal. The customer didn't think of it. The salesman dreamed up the special-stock arrangement to make sure he could provide the stock items at a high service level. He doesn't trust the new system of ordering . . . but more to the point, he knows that the balances on the computer are very inaccurate. Special, protected stock almost *always* moves out at a low turnover rate. Do you see how a poor system can impact the inventory levels you'll carry? The "system" must support and enhance the sales effort; it must be accurate; it must build confidence by using proven principles that yield predictable results.

WHY SO MUCH EMPHASIS ON TELEPHONE SALES?

Before getting into the details of what a good system does for telephone sales, I'd better explain why this function should receive priority. When is the most critical time in the relationship between a customer and the distributor? Is it when as outside salesman first calls to introduce himself and the company? Is it during later visits when new products are discussed or the customer's technical question is answered? Is it during your last open house? On the big company fishing trip?

No . . . as important as those times or functions are, the *most crucial* moment is when the customer calls with an inquiry about your products or (more critical) with an order! Now the customer is testing your company, your information system, your knowledge, your inventory, your pricing, and all that stuff your outside salesman keeps saying you can do. If there's *ever* a time to look good, now's the time! The computer, therefore, must make your telephone salesman come off so effectively that the customer hangs up thinking:

> Wow, that's the sharpest outfit I deal with. That guy knew everything I asked in a flash, had obscure prices in his head, took my new order quickly, told me the status of my old one, and reminded me of stuff I'd forgotten to ask about! It sure makes my job easier to deal with people like

this. Their prices aren't always the lowest in town, but the absence of aggrivation makes up the difference!

What the customer doesn't know is that the salesman is quite new, very inexperienced, and knows very little of products or prices. The reason he or she performed so smoothly and had so much quick information was largely due to the computer's capabilities. Oh sure . . . what happens from here on with the order is important also. You'd better have the stock you promised; the merchandise must be delivered on time; it had better be the right stuff; the invoice must show the prices you quoted; you sure want to process the customer's payment correctly and quickly. That's all vital.

But none of that even gets the chance to take place if you irritate the customer (often enough) on the phone and don't get the order or drive him to the competition. The moment of telephone contact, in my opinion, is *THE* time when you want the computer to provide its maximum benefit to the sales function! Let's see now what it should do.

INTERCHANGES, SUPERSEDED PARTS, AND CUSTOMER PART NUMBERS

In many industries, several manufacturers make the same item and it can require years to become familiar enough with the various part numbers to interchange them in your head when a customer provides some number you don't stock. With bearings, for example, it's possible to find ten or more brands of the same exact bearing out in the market . . . some with identical part numbers but most being different. The problem then compounds as the manufacturers have to change item numbers for one reason or another, superseding one more than once perhaps in a five-year period. A telephone salesman may get hit with any of 10–15 part numbers, old or current, and all the same item as the one he stocks. The interchange must be made very quickly.

The Item Interchange File

A good computerized system includes an "open-ended" file of part numbers, that reference all interchangable part numbers to the one(s) you stock. As your system is installed, the file contains very little. As the years go by, however, you add more and more numbers until the file develops into one of your greatest selling assets. It's a slow process. Part numbers from other brands must be researched and approved by one or more people in your company with *the most product knowledge!* . . . necessary because the items listed must be 100 percent interchangable, not suggested upgrades. 100 percent means that one would work for the other in 100 percent of the customer applications.

Interchanges and Upgrades . . . What's the Difference?

True, you might also have information in the computer records on suggested upgrades where, for a higher price, you could offer a customer the 5,000 PSI valve when he asks about the 3,000 PSI. . . . but not in the interchange file. It includes 100 percent *either-way* substitutes only! With upgrades, you couldn't do the reverse: Sell a 3,000 PSI valve for a 5,000 PSI application. With interchanges, you could. That's the difference.

The Interchange File is "Open-Ended," meaning that an unlimited number of interchangable or superseded part numbers may be listed for any one item stocked. Most systems on the market today permit one or two substitutes per item but that's it. Distributors often find such systems to be extremely restrictive. It's true that some items have no interchanges. Others may have only one other competitor . . . but many have several, as with the bearings. After five years of use and revision, your file could very well contain an average of five interchange and superseded part numbers for each of your stocked items. A good system brings up the item(s) you stock for the telephone salesman when *any one* of the five (or ten, or twenty) interchanges is keyed-in.

Customer Part Numbers

The file should be open-ended for another reason. A fast-moving current trend allows customers to inquire and place orders directly into the distributor's computer using *their own part numbers!* The interchange file is a natural storage facility for 10 or 200 different customers' part numbers for a stock item. Just as with interchanges and supercedes, an inquiry keyed with one of these numbers returns a screen display showing stock status, pricing, and perhaps even backorder status of the brand and part number you stock. When special prices have been quoted to the customer, only his prices appear. If the customer has protected stock, only his stock's status is displayed.

An order entered by the customer, via his terminal or for him at your location, may be keyed with his part numbers. The picking ticket shows both your part numbers and his (following the description perhaps). Yours . . . to enable your warehouse crew to pick the order, and his numbers to avoid confusion at the customer's receiving dock when your packing list arrives. The invoice shows only the customer's part numbers.

Now, There's Real Added Value!

In distribution, we talk a lot about "Value Added" . . . the worth of a distributor's services to his customers . . . how much those services add to the value of the products purchased from him. This capability to let the customer inquire or order with his own part numbers is but one of many Value-Added features we'll discuss in this book.

"Remember-to-Ask-About" Product Information

Some products are rarely sold alone. Hose sells with fittings; A safety hat (in Winter) needs a liner; Certain units need installation kits, etc. Sales can be lost if your telephone salesman doesn't know these relationships and neither does the customer's buyer (or both get in a hurry and forget). It never hurts to ask: "Hey Joe, aren't you going to need some adhesive to go with those floor tiles?"

A good computerized system reminds the salesman. If complementary products (means they go together, not that they're free) should be mentioned, the system brings them up on the screen during either inquiry or entry of an order. Your experienced salesmen know to ask about the "completing" items, but the new people don't. Sales are lost and the inventory just sits. Be sure your system provides this capability, because you'll have more new employees to train quickly in the 1990s. You won't have the luxury of giving each one five years to learn about related items, interchanges, supercedes and upgrades.

NON-STOCK ITEM PROCESSING AND CONTROL

As stated earlier, non-stock items are very important to most durable goods distributors. Depending on the technology of the products, as high as 50 percent of all sales can be for items that must be special-ordered, "bought-out," or direct-shipped . . . meaning that shelf stock was not used to take care of the customers. The products had to be purchased (or transferred-in perhaps) after the customer placed his order.

There are four potential hazards involving non-stock items:

1. Once entered into the system, they're hard to track on the computer. To find the status, a salesman may have to expend a lot of legwork, contact Purchasing, etc.

2. When they arrive in Receiving, there can be confusion as to who they're for, what to do with the material.

3. It's all too easy for non-stock material to become stock . . . but stock that you don't want!

4. It can be difficult to see repetitive non-stock sales so as to make a decision to stock the material.

HOW A COMPUTER MAKES YOUR SALESMEN LOOK GOOD! 29

A good system solves all four headaches. Non-stock items are processed into and through the system with the same ease as stock items. Controls are present to assure proper handling at receipt and that unauthorized stock doesn't turn up during the next physical inventory. Here's how:

The Sales Order and Line Number Becomes the Part Number

A non-stock item must be identified at order-entry (an "N" or something similar keyed as part of the sales order line information). From then on, the computer considers the sales order number and line number (239400/002, for example) as the item's part number. The number is unique. Obviously, there will not be two sales orders numbered 239400, so there will be only one 239400, line item 002.

When the purchase order or transfer is keyed to secure the item, the actual part number (ordered by the customer) is not entered. Instead, 239400/002 is keyed as the part number. The computer thinks:

> What the heck is that? Oh, I know. Here on the P.O., I'm to enter the part number and description I find on sales order 239400, line item 002!

Whatever was entered on the sales order . . . part number, six lines of description, unit, etc. . . . is copied directly over to the purchase order or transfer line that will bring in the material. If the product is quite complex, requiring an extensive description with several dimensions or voltage/pressure/tolerance limits, the purchase order reflects the exact entry on the sales order. Purchasing can't omit an important data element or transpose digits, etc. This means, of course, that Sales *must write the sales order correctly and completely!* Purchasing will not clean up any mistakes or omissions.

Tracking the Non-Stock Item in the System

Later, the customer calls to ask the status of Apex part number 27J ordered last week. If the customer provides his P.O. number, the salesman locates the sales order at once by inquiry. He finds the 27J on line item 002. Tied to the sales order line (sales order 239400, line item 002 for example) is the fact that this material will arrive on purchase order 10340, line item 001 . . . and that P.O. is due May 1st.

Even without the customer's P.O. number, the item can be located quickly if he knows approximately when the order was placed. Without either P.O. number or date, the item can still be located but the salesman must scan all open sales orders for the customer . . . possibly a lengthy process if the customer orders frequently. If, however, the non-stock item was entered on the order under the same part numbering scheme as for stock items (a concept we'll discuss in a moment), a direct inquiry by part number finds the first open sales order.

Backorder Control at Receiving

When the purchase order arrives bringing in the non-stock material, the receiving clerk checks it in against the open P.O. information. He finds the 27J to be line item 001 on P.O. 10340. The full quantity of 100 is here. That's what gets keyed on the Receiving screen:

Purchase Order	Line Number	Quantity
10340	001	100

Nothing else is needed. The computer knows the date. It knows which P.O. and line number to post this receipt against . . . and it knows also which open sales backorder (239400, line item 002) to print for shipment. The sales backorder has been tied all along to this one line on this one P.O.

No one from Sales has to trot back to Receiving and write little notes on the open P.O. backorder explaining what to do when the material shows up. Receiving personnel don't waste time trying to figure out who should get some odd-ball item that just came in. If you choose, you may print the open backorder picking ticket just as soon as the receipt is keyed . . . and then take the merchandise straight to Shipping, rather than into the warehouse where there's no official place for it. Easy to lose it there.

Transfers that bring in non-stock material (here) from some other company location that does stock it can be processed exactly the same way. When the transfer is keyed, the sales order and line number are entered. The computer prints the actual item on the transfer. When the transfer and line number are received, the customer's backorder prints for shipment. The sales order line is tied to one line on one incoming transfer.

Controls to Keep Non-Stock Items from Becoming Unauthorized Stock

The sales order/line number tie in to the purchase order/line number permits another important control:

> A non-stock item may be purchased or transferred-in *ONLY* if the entire quantity has first been sold! Part numbers cannot be keyed for

HOW A COMPUTER MAKES YOUR SALESMEN LOOK GOOD! 31

non-stocks on P.O.'s or transfers. The computer rejects them. If the item is shown to be non-stock in your location, you must first enter a sales order for the full amount or you cannot enter a P.O. or transfer for the merchandise. If later, you attempt to cancel the sales order or reduce the quantity, the computer warns that an open P.O. must be dealt with first.

Salesmen usually see such restraints as too restrictive: "Shoot, this doggone computer is getting in the way! It won't let us sell!" No. That's not the objective. This restraint is to keep you from finding all those "write-in's" at next year's physical inventory . . . like the one where a salesman had only 6 pieces sold but bought 24 to get a good cost, and then had the other 18 put (somewhere) out in the warehouse.

There are only two kinds of items sold: Stock and Non-Stock. There should be tight controls and limited personnel involved in decisions to add new items to stock (see the chapter on "Dead Stock"). If a salesman thinks that an item should be stocked, there's a way to get that done . . . approval by the Sales Manager or Branch Manager, part number assigned, start-up information entered into the system, etc. You *do not want* stock established by the whim of each salesman. That's how you got a lot of the junk out in the warehouse right now. Non-Stock items, to be purchased and brought in, must first be sold. That's a rule I would *never violate*, Mr. Distributor President. If you do, you'll lose control. You'll also be a favorite of the distressed-merchandise and scrap dealers.

The Nasty Problem of Identifying Non-Stock Repeaters

One of the toughest problems for a distributor: How to spot the non-stock item that begins to sell repetitively and should be put on the shelf! To try to solve this, many systems designers require some kind of dummy part number (99999, etc.) on every non-stock item ordered, create a full-fledged inventory record for it, and then track the sales. Hopefully, the item description will be written consistently so that additional sales can be recorded in the same sales history.

Of course, the descriptions are not consistent, many of the items sell only once, and the computer files very soon contain thousands of "trash" records (several hundred bytes long) that have only one entry. Periodically these must be purged after printout or simply on a timed basis. If they're not, the data processing manager one day requests another disk drive . . . wasted money, because this approach rarely helps much to identify the repeating non-stock item sales.

The Same Part Number Scheme for Stock and Non-Stock

A better concept is to apply some discipline in how non-stock items are entered on the sales orders. For example, if stock items are written with a three-letter manufacturer prefix, followed by the manufacturer's official part number . . . then non-stock items are keyed the same way. You stock ABC manufacturing's 27J. The part number for the computer is ABC 27J. You don't stock ABC's 584X. If you sell one, enter the part number as ABC 584X. This is done consistently, across all suppliers and products. Salesmen are trained to look up these numbers and be sure they're entered on the sales orders in the part number field, rather than just the regular product description. Generic products, where brand is unimportant, get generic manufacturer prefixes (XXX, etc.) followed by part numbers that may be developed from the description: XXX 1/4 COP EL for a 1/4 inch copper elbow.

Periodic Listings of Non-Stock Sales

If you followed the earlier advice to code each non-stock item sales order line with an "N," the computer can find every non-stock sale in the morass of sales order detail records . . . back as far as you've stored them. If you also applied discipline in keying non-stock item numbers on the orders, it's a simple "Find & Sort" job for the computer to print out all non-stock sales for the last six months, sorted by manufacturer (or generic category) and part number. The incidence of sale on any one item is clear. You can see how many times it sold, the quantities, and the customers involved . . . all important considerations in a decision to stock it.

The Product Manager or Sales Manager reviews the printout and selects the repeaters for conversion to stock items. No permanent inventory files are involved. None have to be purged. File space hasn't been wasted. The exercise is repeated as often as you have time to make the analysis, going as far back into the sales detail as you specify each time.

Let's Review the Benefits of Tight Non-Stock Item Control

A system with such features allows these breakthroughs:

1. Non-stock items do not require dummy part numbers and do not take up the sizable file space in the computer that a regular stock item would need (13 months' history, etc.)

HOW A COMPUTER MAKES YOUR SALESMEN LOOK GOOD!

2. Purchase orders duplicate the information written on a sales order . . . very important with complex products where a buyer might inadvertently leave out a critical dimension or transpose a digit, etc.

3. Non-stock items are purchased *only* when they've first been sold (the entire quantity). No longer can a salesman buy 24 to get a good cost, sell 6, and put the other 18 on the warehouse shelf . . . to be found at the next annual physical inventory!

4. When non-stock material arrives, Receiving personnel know precisely who it's for. No more double handling by taking it first to the warehouse, or that costly scrambling to find the customer or branch for whom it was ordered. No chance that another sales order or a counterman might take the merchandise.

5. There's no longer a need for Tom, Dick, Harry and Mary Lou to dig into Receiving files, or Purchasing's files, to find what P.O. placed the item on order, or to write little notes as to what to do with it when it comes in. All such information and instructions are automatic, and can be seen any time through inquiries. In fact, there might be no paperwork at all filed in Receiving.

6. With order-entry discipline, it's easy to identify the non-stock repeaters without wasting voluminous file space in the computer.

Make sure that your system handles non-stock items routinely, effecting this kind of total control, rather than by the old-fashioned methods still offered by some distributor packages today.

AN OCCASIONAL NEED TO HANDLE STOCK ITEMS LIKE NON-STOCK

Once in a while, some customer needs a very large quantity of a stock item. As the order is discussed with him, the customer readily admits that he didn't expect you to have such a huge quantity on the shelf. When you tell him that you now have only 20 in stock, he replies: "Well, keep the 20, but go ahead and order my 500 pieces special. Deliver it just as soon as you receive it from your supplier!" You want to accomplish several things when you enter this sales order into the computer:

1. Key much less information than is needed for a non-stock item, get the sales history posted, but otherwise process the order in a non-stock mode.

2. Avoid shipping the 20 and backordering 480. The customer just told you *not* to do that! A regular stock item entry would attempt to ship the 20.

3. Place this stock item on order with your supplier, tied to this one customer's order. Usually, stock purchases are open to fill any waiting customer backorders for the item. Not this time.

4. Be sure all 500 go only to this customer. If other backorders develop before this stock arrives, they must wait for the next regular stock replenishment arrival. *This* 500 is for this one customer. It's possible that the price quoted to him was based on the 500 purchase. You don't want any of the material given to some other customer.

Another special line-item code at sales order entry does the trick. An "N" may have identified non-stock items, but now an "X," or whatever you choose, identifies a stock item *to be handled like a non-stock!* The sales order and line number go on the purchase order. This one line is now tied to one line on the P.O. This 500, when received, can be used to fill this one sales order only.

You might even be ordering the same stock item elsewhere on the P.O. for regular replenishment . . . and there you *did* enter the actual part number on the P.O. Other customer backorders are filled from that line on the P.O., but not from the special block of 500. That goes only to the one customer for whom it was purchased. The different line item code tells the computer:

> You are dealing here with a stock item that I want handled as if it were non-stock. However, I will not be providing a description, category code, unit (and perhaps not even the price) because you know all those. Also, because it's a stock item, I want you to record this sale in the item's history. Yes, it's exceptional, but I'll handle that later.

SHIP-COMPLETE AND TAG & HOLD ORDERS

These two special sales order types are very similar. A Ship-Complete order carries instructions from the customer to get together everything ordered . . . accumulate it, whether it's stock or non-stock . . . and then ship it all at one time. Tag & Hold instructions are the same, except that the distributor is not free to ship the merchandise when all items have been collected. Instead, the customer is to be notified or the material simply held until the customer provides shipping instructions. Both order types can be quite troublesome in four ways:

1. You may incur the wrath of the customer by shipping part of the order inadvertently.

2. Some item you thought was available, isn't when all other merchandise has been collected. It's been "robbed" and sold to another customer.

3. When everything is finally accumulated, the customer delays shipment indefinitely.

4. You can finally ship but when contacted the customer says: "Oh yeah, I got tired of waiting and bought the material somewhere else. I meant to call you and cancel this order!"

You oldtimers have been through these scenes many times. You know the damage that occurs when any one of the four take place. All are very expensive. How can the computerized system help out? Since the primary emphasis of this chapter is on telephone salesmen, how can the "system" ease the minds of those who take the orders, promise the customers that they'll be handled properly, and will have to explain if they aren't? How can the computer process these orders in a way that almost guarantees no foulups in shipping? What procedures and disciplines are needed in the warehouse for control? How can you sell this way with minimum detrimental impact on inventories?

A Special Picking Ticket

Control of Ship-Complete and Tag & Hold orders begins by identifying each at order entry through a special code in the "header" screen and record. The "header" includes all the general information about the order, as compared to line item information (facts pertaining to one item alone). As soon as the computer is told: "This is a Ship-Complete Order," an alternate picking ticket routine takes effect.

If there are stock items on the order, a picking ticket goes to the warehouse with instructions to fill these items and "stage" the material in an area set aside just for this purpose . . . to accumulate material, keeping it apart from all other stock. The picking ticket appears entirely different from one for a regular order. Only the customer's name, order number, date, items and quantities now available, and a very clear: *SHIP-COMPLETE ORDER* shows on the picking ticket. No one could ship the order. There's not enough information provided . . . no customer ship-to address, etc.

The Staging Area

The material is filled and moved to an order-staging area. There should be different types of space allotted . . . marked-off floor sections for big items, shelves or bins for smaller stuff, but each area is numbered: A–4, 123, Row 12/Section 20, etc., whatever suits your situation. The warehouse writes on the picking ticket the staging area number where this order is being accumulated, and that information is keyed into the computer to be tied to this sales order's record.

"Whoa!" you say. "We don't have room in our warehouse for that. We just leave the material where it is until the non-available material shows up. Then we pick the stock and ship the order." . . . hmmm, and I'll bet there've been times in the past when that led to trouble. Items available when the order first was accepted . . . aren't when you go back to get them later. My experience is that orders like this are much more easily controlled, and ship without major foulups, if they're staged from Day 1. Maybe you need to rearrange the warehouse a bit to establish the necessary staging areas.

The Order Accumulation Steps

Now, additional material starts to arrive for the staged order. As Receiving records the receipt and it's keyed-in, a backorder picking ticket prints. This one, too, is different. Only minimal information shows, and the only item listed is the one that just came in. The picking ticket says clearly: "This is part of Ship-Complete Order 239400. Take this material to Staging Area A–6!" . . . and that's what happens. There's no danger that this single item might ship inadvertently. There isn't enough information provided to send it out.

Finally, the last item arrives. When it's receipt is keyed, *NOW* an official picking ticket for shipping prints on the entire order. Every item is listed. The newly-received one is first, but for all others (those that have been accumulating), the storage location for picking is the staging area number, A–6 or whatever.

Of course, if the order is the "Tag & Hold" category, the final item gets a minimal-information picking ticket only and the material is placed with the rest of the order. Sales receives a report saying: "Order 239400 for ABC Industries is now all here. Call the customer for possible shipping instructions!"

The 60-Day Reminder for Sales

Another money-saving step to program for sales orders coded Ship-Complete or Tag & Hold is the 60-Day Reminder for Sales. After material accumulation has been going on for 60 days, and some items are still not in, the computer alerts Sales to check with the customer about this order. You may get approval to ship what's available. He may just tell you to keep after the missing items. He *may* want to cancel the whole deal . . . but better that you learn that now than three weeks from now when you try to ship the complete order and it's refused. You may prefer a 30-day reminder, or 90 days. Your industry and your customers' expectations will dictate which time limit is best.

Do you see the inventory implications in all this? When these special order types are mishandled, or just left to the memories and experience of the warehouse crew, bad things happen . . . and very often you'll wind up with merchandise you didn't want and can't return or sell, or too much stock of something you can. That's why "Inventory Management" and the people responsible for it must have the support of a computerized system and warehousing procedures that both control such orders and handle them with special care.

FUTURE ORDERS

Here's another order-type with negative inventory impact if its special problems aren't recognized. The customer calls in a large order with instructions to ship October 15th but not before. Today is May 1. Every item on the order is in stock right now. "OK Graham," you ask, "Do you want us to stage *this one* too?" No. Certainly not today. In fact, you shouldn't even allocate the stock (commit it) in the computer's records.

Premature Stock Replenishment Leads to Overstock

You'll learn later that the "Available-For-Sale" stock balance (the uncommitted stock) drives the inventory management system. Replenishment is triggered when the uncommitted stock on hand (plus what's on order already with suppliers) gets low. Normally, customers' orders for stock reduce the available-for-sale balance as soon as they're keyed-in. But not with future orders. If here on May 1 we reduce the AFS balance, that might trigger replenishment far too early on some of the stock items involved. The material won't actually ship until October 15th, and the longest lead time for resupply on any of the items is one month.

Missing the Ship-Date Has Dire Consequences

There is one objective, however, that must be met. On October 15th, we must ship this order complete. Having given us the order five and one-half months ahead of time, the customer just might not be too understanding if we don't perform. Obviously, October 15th is critical. We've been given this long advance notice because the customer *must have* delivery on that date. If you mess up orders like this, you'll need quick career counseling and a resume up to date. You could even wind up a consultant.

Reference-Order Status

When a future order is received, it too is coded in order entry to designate the special nature of the order. As far as the computer is concerned, it is classified as a "reference" order. That means it has been recorded. The customer could call back ten minutes later to discuss it, add an item, or change something and the salesman could instantly recall the order to his screen. If non-stock items are involved, Purchasing will be alerted to them on tomorrow morning's report . . . with the ship-date of the order of course . . . to let them set a time to buy the merchandise. *But no inventory is allocated!*

Determining the Date to Change the Order's Status

At some point in the future prior to October 15th, the reference order must be turned into a regular sales order, the stock allocated, the order staged, etc., because at that time it becomes a "Ship-Complete" order with a specified shipping date. When should the change take place? Far enough ahead of October 15th to recover if any of the stock items are not available. Earlier, I said that the longest lead time for any of the stock items ordered was one month. The computer knows that. Program it to change the order status from "Reference" to "Regular" two weeks plus the longest lead time ahead of the ship date. In our example, that's September 1.

At order entry, the computer scans the stock items to find the longest average lead time. It then backs off the requested ship-date by this lead time plus two weeks and sets that date for status-change. In our example, on September 1 the order becomes official. Stock is committed; the available-for-sale balances reduced; and staging begun on the order. If reducing the balances triggers replenishment of some items, that's OK. The order is now the same as any other. Stock is committed to it.

Allow the option at order entry for a salesman to establish the status-change date, rather than having the computer calculate it. The order may contain non-stock items only, or the date is so far into the future that current lead times in the files may be risky to use. The items may be seasonal with the ship-date in the season while the order-entry date is not.

I've worked with distributors where 50 percent of the sales were future orders, and nearly everyone sees a few periodically. Don't blame the purchasing people if you try to handle futures like all other orders and the inventory balloons out of sight . . . or merchandise is "missing" when the ship-date finally dawns. Use the "Reference-Order" technique to gain control.

DIRECT-SHIP ORDERS

Sometimes called "Drop-Ship" orders, these sales orders involve non-stock merchandise or such large quantities of stock that it's efficient to have the supplier ship the material directly to the customer. The distributor acts a bit like a broker, merely handling all the paperwork but never touching the merchandise. The gross margins for such sales are usually lower, since the distributor doesn't have as much work to do. Direct-ships are very common, so how could a computer cause problems here?

In three areas. First, be careful not to permit the grouping on one sales order of a mixture . . . some items to be shipped direct and others to come out of your warehouse. Even if the customer enters it that way, you still should split it into two orders. The order processing steps for the two segments will be entirely different. Freight charges might be involved on the direct-ship segment and none of the stuff you'll deliver. Invoicing almost certainly will take place at different times and perhaps on a different basis.

Secondly, program an interim check-step between the receipt of your supplier's invoice and your invoice being mailed to the customer. I mention this, because I've seen systems that tied the two together. When the supplier's invoice was set up for payment, the invoice to the customer went out automatically, with all information shown just as the order was entered originally. Before issuing your invoice, you should check several things:

1. Did the supplier ship the quantity we expected? You ordered 450 feet; the supplier shipped 438.
2. Was it the right item or perhaps was it a substitute of some form?
3. How about the price? Are we paying about what we expected? . . . particularly vital in boom times when the suppliers are oversold and accept orders on the basis of "price in effect at time of shipment."
4. Are there other changes or unexpected charges that should be added to the customer invoice?

Finally, be sure to program a cross-check to guarantee that the customer *does get billed!* One distributor told me of a $50,000 year-end inventory shortage that he tracked to unbilled direct shipments. When the suppliers' invoices were paid, dollars went onto the inventory books. Since the customers weren't billed, the dollars just stayed there. At physical inventory time, he naturally couldn't find the $50,000 in his warehouse. The material was all out in customer locations. A costly oversight in the paperwork system that no one caught because his salesmen received no commissions on direct-ships. They didn't bother to check to see that the customers were being invoiced.

"PICK-UP-ON-THE-WAY-TO-THE-CUSTOMER" SALES

This final order situation is most frequently encountered by distributors in the larger metroplex areas: Chicago, New York, Los Angeles, Atlanta, Dallas, etc. where several of the suppliers have positioned a regional stocking warehouse. The distributors elect to reduce the scope and depth of on-shelf inventory in these product lines because, for a relatively small price differential, most items are available in the supplier's local warehouse.

When a customer orders a warehouse item (non-stock in the distributor's inventory) the salesman never blinks an eye: "Yes, sir, we'll have that over to you this afternoon!" He'll make only 15 percent on it, perhaps, but it's not one of the more popular items in the line and the company has no inventory investment. A company truck will simply stop by the warehouse, pick up the material, and deliver it to the customer. Several customer orders may be "purchased" like this in a single stop at the warehouse.

How Does This Involve Salesmen? Isn't This a Purchasing Problem?

For many distributors, the telephone salesman handles these transactions from start to finish. He enters the customers' order; calls the supplier's warehouse to verify that stock is available; places the P.O. (while on the phone with the supplier); and perhaps even keys-in the purchase order. It wastes time to involve Purchasing people. The salesman knows where to get the material and the price. He might as well complete the process. Salesmen can buy non-stock material when they have it sold. They just can't buy stock!

There are a few hangups, however. Non-stock items are involved, and the computer knows you can't ship these until you have them. Since

HOW A COMPUTER MAKES YOUR SALESMEN LOOK GOOD!

delivery to the customer will take place before the driver returns, he must leave with paperwork showing that these non-stock items may be shipped: Ordered 5, Shipped 5, Backordered 0. . . . not 5, 0, and 5.

Accounts Payable personnel follow strict rules. They pay your suppliers' invoices only when records exist of material receipts. In this situation, a normal receipt won't occur . . . at your Receiving Dock, as with all other items. It occurs on your truck on the way to the customer. There won't be a normal receipt of the purchase order.

Accumulative Purchase Orders

Unusual situations call for unusual computer programming. The need here is for a special purchase order type: An "accumulative" purchase order. It's called "accumulative" because the supplier often allows you to add items all day long, all week long perhaps, and when a certain dollar, weight, or unit total is reached, you're invoiced. You receive the 2,000 pound price on all items, even though you picked them up one at a time with the largest quantity only 150 pounds. Obviously, this takes some negotiating with the supplier and he may grant this advantage only if your total volume from him is substantial.

Automatic Receipt and Backorder-Fill

When one of these open-ended purchase orders is entered, to run for a set time period (all week, etc.) or until a total-order amount is reached, then all pick-up purchases initiated by any salesman are added to the P.O. It carries a special "header" code for the computer's benefit. As soon as an item is added to the purchase order, it's *automatically received* and the customer's backorder filled. The official receipt record exists for Accounts Payable and the driver leaves with valid shipping paperwork that can later be invoiced.

Sure, there's the chance that the full quantity may not be picked up by your driver or delivered as it should be. Those risks are always present, but for nearly every pickup purchase and delivery, the salesman called the supplier first to verify stock availability (and price, if the pickup was at a competitor or some other local buyout source). 98 percent of the time the transaction occurs without a flaw. If you're a distributor in a metroplex area, these special programming features allow a potentially time-consuming sales order to be handled smoothly, quickly, and with all records intact.

And why is "Inventory Management" interested? Shoot, every item you can buy like this for the customers is one less in inventory, a few less dollars to gather dust perhaps, and makes easier the task of controlling the ones that are stocked. Service is good; turnover is good; inventory carrying costs are reduced; the gross margin sacrifice is minimal; salesman and purchasing time-use is efficient. . . . all good things!

QUOTATIONS

Quotations must be mentioned in any discussion of good computerized systems, but I needn't harass you about them (as with the earlier conditions) since most systems handle them pretty well. Here are the principles to follow:

1. The quotation-entry screen looks like the one for regular sales order-entry, except that when completed a special code is keyed to let the computer know that this is a quotation only . . . not an official order (yet).
2. The quote should have an expiration date or code entered. The prices are valid for 30 days, until March 15th, etc., or are open-ended (no expiration date).
3. The computer assigns a transaction number to the entry, as it does with a regular order, but the number is prefaced by a "Q" or some other designator you select.
4. Special prices and expiration dates quoted to the customer on stock items are copied into the regular file of special prices. The customer might order later without mentioning the quote or through a different salesman. He still receives the quoted prices if within the time frame.
5. If the quote is accepted, the salesman calls up the quotation number, enters a code, and changes the quote at once into an official sales order. If the prices were "one-time" only quotes, the regular pricing file now has these prices removed. With open-ended quotes, the prices remain.
6. Reports may be produced monthly or quarterly showing all quotations (customers, items, quantities, prices) that did not result in sales orders. . . . better to quote the next time.

SUMMARY

Isn't it a bit overwhelming to realize how a good or bad computerized system, one that starts the sales process smoothly or doesn't, impacts how much inventory you'll carry? For many years, distributors have used the inventory to "buffer" themselves from poor systems, lack of discipline, inefficient or untrained people, and general sloppiness all through the order handling process. Poor asset management now causes more distributor bankruptcies than any other cause, so they *simply cannot* carry the outsized inventories any longer. Be sure your system incorporates the features of this chapter to make your salesmen smarter, faster, and to allow them to stay at their desk taking orders rather than running around making sure yesterday's orders are being handled correctly.

Remember too the "Value-Added" concept. To compete in the years ahead on something other than price, you *must offer* features that add value to the products you sell. Your computerized system must allow you to provide information and perform steps quicker and more efficiently than the guy down the street. It then becomes more profitable for the customer to do business with you than with your competitor even when your price is higher.

4

CONVERTING THE SYSTEM

Your appetite's now whetted for a better system. You're envisioning fantastic improvements . . . customers overwhelmed and begging you to accept their orders, salesmen ultra-productive, vast stores of information at everyone's fingertips, perfect warehouse stock that never misses an order and never becomes slow-moving, and profits so large you don't dare store all the cash in one bank.

Good. I have your attention! Now I have to temper your enthusiasm a bit. Regardless of what the hardware or systems salesmen tell you, the final results won't be that glorious. You *should* anticipate the system improvements and features discussed in the last chapter and all through this book. You *should* push for them, argue for them, insist on better programming and better information, and waive aside much of the old thinking that says: "But that's not the way it's always been done."

It's just that there are always limitations. The computer you have may not be capable of file structures or operating systems necessary to do all I've suggested. You may be a small distributor with very limited funds, and the cost of such a system is beyond your means right now. Your disciplines in paperflow and operations may be poor. People won't do what you tell them today, and it's premature to consider a new system that requires much tighter disciplines. Maybe your people just resist change of any kind.

WHAT ARE WE REALLY LIKE?

Those of us who've worked in distribution recognize some rather unpleasant characteristics about ourselves. We're informal; pretty much undisciplined; relaxed in our approach to business; maybe a little lazy at times; often *very* resistant to change; with a tendency to follow "what everyone else is doing" in our industry. Then there are our habits . . . not necessarily bad things . . . but how we like to operate: We prefer sport shirts and jeans in the office; relationships with customers based more on friendship than on performance; and suppliers who tell us we're doing a great job.

MECHANICS CHANGE . . . BUT SO DOES YOUR INVENTORY PHILOSOPHY!

What's the point? Our limitations, our habits, and our tendencies have a definite impact on any attempt to change an existing system. That's particularly true of the concepts in this book. I'll ask you to use different reports, different data-gathering techniques, and different calculations. Those are mechanics . . . comparable to switching from one brand of auto to another. But as the old country boy said: "Now he's quit preachin' and gone to meddlin'!" . . . I will *also* ask you to change your entire philosophy of how and when products are ordered. That's much tougher. It's like changing from walking to riding a bicycle: Many new things to learn, a new sense of balance to master, legs aren't used the same way, etc.

This chapter's purpose is to sound an early warning: These wonderful, idealistic concepts will not come to pass without some grief. Significantly more education and training is needed to make this inventory control system work *for you* than if you were installing a new set of banking or insurance company procedures. Those are established industries with relatively stable and consistent practices. Distribution Inventory Management is anything *but* stable and established! SWAG is our way of life. It's much tougher to unseat with proven principles and techniques. It's hard to break a horse that's " . . . never been rode!"

THE FOUR STAGES OF A SYSTEM CHANGE

There are four fairly distinct phases through which any major system changeover project must progress:

I.	"Oh, Boy!"	—Honeymoon
II.	"Oh, S____!"	—Recovery Room
III.	"Oh, Well!"	—Resolution
IV.	"Oh, Wow!"	—Satisfaction

CONVERTING THE SYSTEM 47

Stage I: The "Oh, Boy!" Phase

This phase is the honeymoon period. You've seen an eye-catching demonstration by the computer manufacturer, some software house, or for a packaged system offered for distributors in your industry. You may have attended a major computer show or one sponsored by your association. Perhaps you heard about the package from a buddy who owns a tobacco and candy distributorship. You saw an ad in the industry trade journal.

If your's is a home-grown system, this stage is that euphoric response from those who've seen a brief overview of the new system now on the drawing board: "Gosh, that's magnificent! That system does everything. It seems to solve almost every problem we have now with the old package. Can we be the first (branch manager talking) to come up on the new system, Boss?"

If it's a popular system on the market, you've seen a demo, asked a lot of questions, visited other users, furnished mountains of facts about your company, negotiated a good price . . . and signed the contract. You feel quite good about your decision. Then the systems installers arrive.

Stage II: The Recovery Room Phase

"Shoot Boss, I didn't know I'd have to do all this stuff! This stupid computer's getting in our way. We can't sell anymore. We're too busy trying to learn all these new procedures. This thing may sink us if you don't get somebody in here to fix it . . . or just jerk it out!" Hmmm . . . the

"You mean I have to do all that! I don't like this new system. I hope they take it out!"

boss hadn't expected this. The system cost a bundle, it had been studied carefully, no one had any major objections before, but now . . . maybe it *was* a mistake!

This stage can be compared to how you feel after major surgery when you wake up in the Recovery Room. You're nauseous, the room is spinning, nurses are hovering nearby, tubes are inserted in several unpleasant places, and you're pretty sure you're dying. Can you imagine your response if the doctor walked up right then and asked: "Hey there, how'd you like the operation?" . . . or tried to present his bill? His timing is poor, and your answer would be rather sharp. At that moment, you hate the doctor, the hospital, and all others that had anything to do with how you feel. The same question a few days later when you're feeling better would get a much more civil reply.

That's how it is with major system changes in a company. The company's "metabolism" has been shaken up and no one feels comfortable in the new procedures. You shouldn't ask for nor expect an objective view of the new system from personnel caught up in the confusion of the first few days. You're in the intensive care period where several sympathetic, attentive, encouraging, highly-skilled "nurses" are needed to hold the patients' hands and listen to your people say a lot of things they don't really mean.

What Should Be Your Attitude?

As the Boss, don't listen too closely to what's said in Stage II. Don't panic. Don't overreact and order extensive system changes. Don't begin a big "witch-hunt" for scapegoats . . . the people who *must have* fouled-up to cause all these negative comments!

A good rule to follow: Other than to correct obvious bugs, don't make major programming changes for 30 days. Have the people work with the new procedures for 30 days before they may suggest improvements. You'll be surprised how many crisis-correction suggestions of the first week are unnecessary after 30 days. Why? The people are comfortable in the old procedures . . . very uncomfortable in the new.

Rather than really learning how a new step works, an employee notices only how different it is from what he did before. He leaps to a conclusion: This won't work! It leaves something uncovered or undone. 30 days later, he sees that the new step is smoother, easier, less work, and omits nothing. The change he requested on Day 3 (to move his job back closer to what it was in the old system) isn't needed after all.

There's also a learning curve involved. At first when everything is so new, the natural reaction is battle the whole concept a bit. "Gosh, this new screen seems cumbersome or busy. Why don't you change it to . . . ?"

CONVERTING THE SYSTEM

The Computer Project Cycle

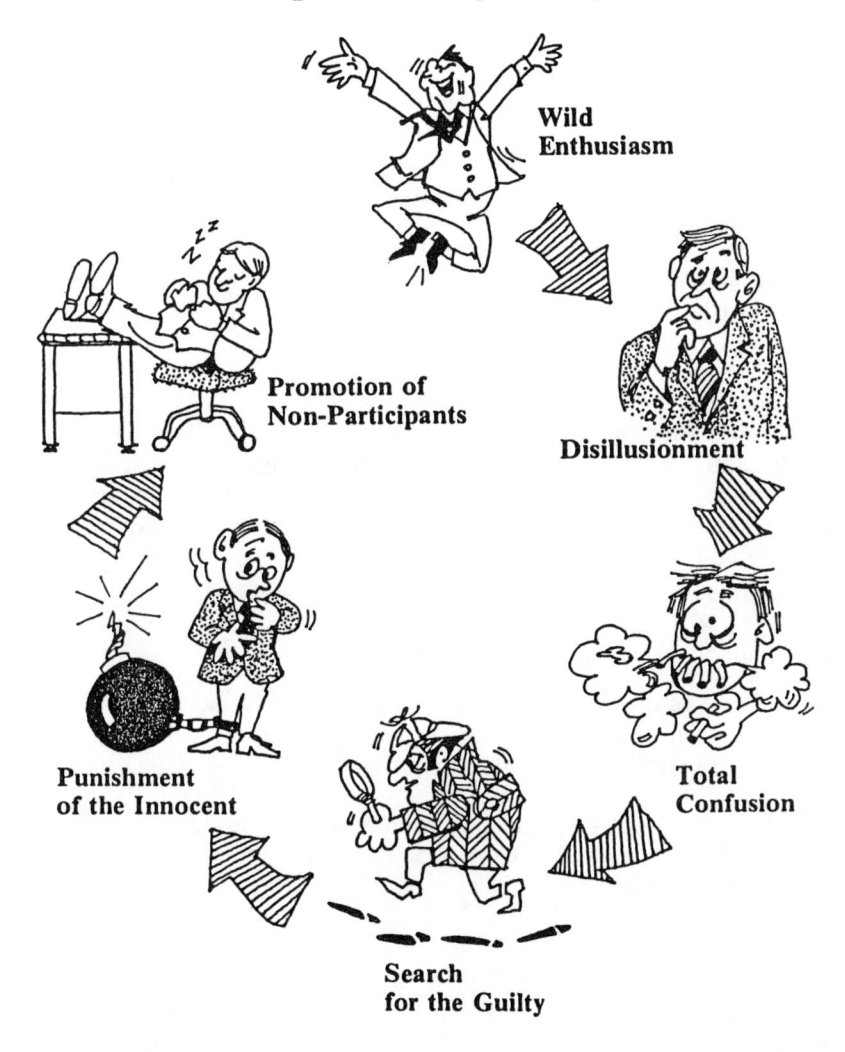

Wild Enthusiasm

Disillusionment

Total Confusion

Search for the Guilty

Punishment of the Innocent

Promotion of Non-Participants

After the learning period is over and the new screen has been used hundreds of times, it's now quite familiar. There's no longer a problem.

A Positive, Firm Stance

Instead of expecting everyone to give glowing reports as the new system gets underway, you should expect the opposite and then be ready with your response:

> We expected this. In fact, you were told over and over during our training sessions that it would be this way. The system will work. Our future rests on it, and all of us must make it work. If you do find a bug, tell us and we'll get it fixed quickly.

The firm, confident response soothes everyone's nerves. They're about to panic, but when they see that you don't . . . that all the confusion, all the mistakes, and all the new (and perhaps difficult) steps to learn haven't shaken *you* one bit, then they relax. It's the same feeling you have in the Recovery Room when the doctor comes by to say:

> Well, I know you feel terrible right now, but the operation was totally successful. Everybody feels this way when we cut on them like that. You will feel much better by Wednesday!

You still feel basically rotten, but the anxiety subsides and now you begin to concentrate on feeling better . . . *expecting it to happen,* rather than what you were expecting a minute ago: "All will go dark any second now and I'm a goner!" It's the same in a system change. Positive reassurances from the Boss when the crew is fighting tooth and nail to make a new system work is just as soothing. They begin to *expect* the system to smooth out, for things to get easier, and soon they do.

Watch for the "Hands-Off" Manager

Harold is a branch manager out in Branch 3. He liked the new system well enough in the early presentations, but when it's his turn to convert he tells the installation personnel:

> Somebody's got to keep the doors open around here while this new system is installed. I'll concentrate on sales. You people just train my employees in what they're to do!

. . . and the new system sort of slides in, around, and under ol' Harold, but he knows almost nothing about how it works. Harold takes a "hands-off" posture toward the whole thing. Then the installation staff leaves.

In the past, Harold's position of authority with his people was enhanced by the fact that he knew more than anyone about procedures and how things were to be done. He's been around for 18 years. Now . . . he knows zilch. Every time there's a question about the new system, the employee asks Harold but he doesn't know the answer. He looks bad. His position of authority has been eroded, so guess what his feelings are about the new system? . . . and guess how he'll answer when the Boss calls to find out how Harold likes it?

CONVERTING THE SYSTEM

Harold will give the system a D minus, but his reasons will have nothing to do with reality. Again, the Boss must come back with a very firm response:

> Harold, how much do you know about this new system? Nothing huh. Yes, I understand that somebody had to keep the doors open, someone had to keep the emphasis on sales. . . . but Harold, I want you to become the *resident expert* on this new system. I want you to know more about how it works and the procedures than anyone else in your branch. When you've done that, call me and we'll discuss how workable or unworkable this system is for your branch.

Stage III: The "Oh Well" Phase

Poor Harold. Now he must learn how the system functions. He has to read the manuals, allow his people to train him in some steps, talk regularly to the installation staff, and be able to perform each procedure himself. He's been pushed into the "Oh, Well" phase: "Oh well, I guess the Boss isn't going to junk this new system. I'd better learn how it works. Every time I do something wrong, somebody jumps me and asks why I haven't studied Section 3 or 8 or 18 of the Operations Manual."

Stage III is the Resolution phase: "Griping about the new system doesn't do much good. The Boss reacts negatively to that. He, and others, keep asking questions about the system that I can't answer. I guess I'd better resolve to give it a chance . . . to really learn how it works and what I'm supposed to do." Hallelujah! What a breakthrough! If the system is basically sound, you'll soon move right on into Stage IV. The compliance may be a bit half-hearted, but at least it's there. Now you'll see real progress as the people begin to accept the new system as their own.

The Disaster of a System Misfit

If the system is *not* basically sound, look out! If you've purchased or programmed a "Me, Too" system that really doesn't fit you very well and doesn't solve your headaches any better than the old system . . . in other words, if the patient will *STAY* in Intensive Care and never feel any better, you've got big trouble! The Boss can be as positive as he wants; as tough as leather on ol' Harold, and it won't help. How does the doctor explain to a patient in Recovery:

> Gosh, I realize that you feel bad but I have distressing news. We had a little problem with the oxygen unit in surgery and you have severe brain damage. You will never leave this intensive care unit.

If you do that to your company by inflicting a poor computerized system on them, then the changeover will be a nightmare. Stage II can last two years before you remove all the tubes and let the thing die. Stage II becomes the "Quicksand" stage. You step in, thrash around for a long time, and finally sink. You must throw out the new system, retrench and start all over. You can guess how receptive your people will be to your *next* attempt at a new system! "Here we go again!" they say (privately) to each other and Stage II this time is even tougher. When you're positive, they just reply: "Yeah, you told us all that same stuff *last time!*"

Stage IV: The "Wow" Phase

Once you've moved out of Stage II into III and employees are really trying to make the new system work, Stage IV arrives in a short time:

> Wow! This is the greatest thing we've ever done around here. How did we ever get along before we operated like this? The new system is a huge improvement over our old procedures and methods.

Newly-hired employees who were never exposed to the old system learn the new procedures and disciplines readily. They don't know that there was once another way to function. Just remember that system changeovers never progress from Stage I ("Oh, Boy!") to Stage IV ("Wow!") without going through Stage II . . . the Twilight Zone, "Quicksand," Recovery, Intensive Care, "Oh, S____!" or whatever name you've given it. Prepare for it. Train, train, train . . . beforehand to shorten Stage II's time and effect.

Don't let a hardware salesman, software peddler, package merchant, or programmer downplay Stage II. When he says: "We'll have you up-and-running in all locations in six months, no problems . . . just sign here!" back off a bit and ask more questions. If he says "Expect a tough changeover period!", then he's been there before. You can trust that guy.

SYSTEM DEGENERATION

Even when you pass successfully through the four stages of a systems change, there's another system crippler lurking in wait for you: System "Degeneration." It's a disease that often besets a newly-installed computerized system after everything has smoothed out and the Boss breathes a big sigh of relief. Degeneration is best illustrated by this little scene:

CONVERTING THE SYSTEM 53

Mary is a super employee whom you've assigned to be the new system data entry operator. She inputs all sales orders, transfers, purchase orders, receipts, . . . everything. She's well-trained and acts a bit like a traffic cop on paperwork and procedures. If someone fouls up, she's on 'em like a hawk to make out the order correctly, get the price right, code the transaction, etc., and she almost never makes an error in what she does.

But Mary's husband is transferred to California, and she gives her two-week notice. Donna, from Accounts Payable, is asked to take over Mary's job, and Mary proceeds to train her. Mary is great at her job but not very good at training. Some steps are forgotten, and others only mentioned sketchily. As Mary leaves, Donna knows perhaps 70 percent of what Mary did.

Donna is in the soup immediately. All kinds of things start to go wrong and Mary's long gone . . . no one to ask. She hates the new job. "Boss, can I have my old place back in Accounts Payable?" . . . and Sue is hired to take over. Guess who trains Sue? Donna, of course, and when Sue takes over, she knows about 30 percent of what Mary had down pat.

The system soon craters around your ears. All sorts of massive errors loom in nearly every phase. What had seemed a workable, productive system is now one huge headache. You're a victim of "degeneration."

The installation staff is on down the road at another branch scratching and clawing through the four stages . . . thinking all is well back in Branch 2 . . . but it isn't! Behind them, things are deteriorating.

"Mary is asked to train her replacement, Donna, in the two weeks before she leaves. Unfortunately Mary doesn't train others as well as she learns."

Another Form of Degeneration: Reverting!

As mentioned earlier, the Inventory Management concepts suggested in this book often represent a departure from long-standing practice for a distributor. "This isn't the way we've built our business!" . . . is a common argument from sales managers or buyers as they try to apply these new control techniques, new formulas, and particularly, new disciplines. Not only do the mechanics change with a new system, but also the *philosophy* of how to provide good service without an outsized inventory.

When the system is functioning, the four stages are in the past, and even with Mary still on the scene, you can encounter another trap: Reverting. A buyer studies a printout: "Boy, that looks screwy. It recommends that I buy just three weeks' supply on one of our best items. That's got to be wrong. I've always bought three months' supply in the past!" . . . and in goes a purchase order for 60 instead of 15.

The Boss liked the branch control rules of Chapter 16 when the system was being planned, but now . . . well, they're getting in the way of sales, or so he hears regularly. He orders the programmers to modify the system to remove some of the restrictions.

A salesman heard the instructions about paperwork being necessary before removing anything from the warehouse (Chapter 14), but he's in a big hurry this morning and an important customer needs a sample. "Shoot, we can't let that stupid computer run the company!" he reasons to himself, and he does again just what he's done for years.

From the top down, people are "reverting." They're falling back into old, comfortable habits, old SWAG, and pushing aside new guidelines or disciplines that seem restrictive. Oh sure, it all *sounded* good when they read the book, but this is the *real world!* Garbage! "Real World" is another of those indefinable cop-out phrases used by anyone who doesn't want to adapt to restrictions. The *real* "real world" today for distributors who keep on operating informally, sloppily, lazily, and with no disciplines in asset management is *BANKRUPTCY!*

INSPECTION . . . NOT EXPECTATION!

There's an old management proverb that says:

"People do what you *INSPECT* . . . not what you *EXPECT!*"

Reverting is a serious disease for a successful Inventory Management system, and we're discussing it here in the book for three reasons:

CONVERTING THE SYSTEM

1. As a distributor executive, you must develop an iron resolve *NOW* not to allow reverting to cripple your system after all the time, money, and effort you'll need to put it in place!
2. As you study the details of an effective system throughout the rest of the book, take note of the potential reverting hazards . . . those controls or disciplines that are most *unlike* what you do today. Where are people most likely to revert?
3. As part of your planning for installation staffing and timing, build in the preventative or corrective measures to handle reverting when (not "if") the symptoms start to appear.

The Preventative Measure

As a new system is installed, you should plan time for the installation team . . . those who train the employees . . . to return to each location on a regular basis: 3 months after everything is running smoothly; six months; and then 1 year, with annual visits thereafter. What for? To make sure that procedures are still being followed, that disciplines are in place, that SWAG hasn't crept back into the replenishment decisions, and that the system is being administered the way it was originally.

The second reason is to re-train any replacement personnel (Donna or Sue for Mary) at the same level, with the same intensity and detail, that the first crew received. Sure, you can cross-train extensively while Mary is still on the job and that's a good idea. Supplement that by spending the money to bring back the original trainers when key personnel are replaced.

Yes, this is expensive. Yes, it can slow down implementation of the new system in the other 11 branches. True, it is money you might be able to save. . . . but Reverting or Employee Turnover/Degeneration costs a lot more. The system will never deliver the promised benefits.

Don't Negotiate Re-Visits out of the Contract!

If you elect to purchase software or a package on the market, the price always seems high. Installation and Training are important elements in the cost, represented by some number of manhours, man-days, or even man-months of "hand-holding" to get your people up to speed on the new system. Distributors by nature are negotiators, so there's the normal inclination to hack away at the total price of the system.

A negotiable point, from the system supplier's side, is how much training time he offers as part of the package. Fight your natural urges!

Don't get so tough on price that the training and re-training time is cut in half or reduced drastically. You need it. The success of your system often depends on it. Remember our discussions about the Intensive Care Unit of a hospital. Patients in there have a lot of nurses hovering around to watch them closely. You wouldn't negotiate a lower price for the operation by reducing the nursing staff or time in ICU. Don't do it here either!

ASSIGN SOMEONE FULL-TIME TO "BIRD-DOG" YOUR INSTALLATION

If your's is a home-grown system, this section may be skipped. There's no danger that you'll try to install the new system in one location or a dozen branches without someone from your staff assigned full-time to plan, train, write manuals, coordinate, hold hands, followup, retrain, and be a liaison with Management until the system is fully operational. . . . and such systems usually go in pretty smoothly.

A strange phenomenon occurs, however, when a distributor contracts with an outside firm to write the software, provide existing programs, or perhaps provide a turnkey installation (hardware, software, and installation assistance). A little like ol' Harold, the hands-off branch manager discussed a few pages back, Management assumes a "you-guys-do-it" attitude. No one on the distributor's payroll is assigned to bird-dog, to coordinate the project. Oh sure, good old Sidney the Controller, is designated as the other firm's contact man . . . but it's purely a part-time assignment. Sidney is expected to carry on his regular duties right through the installation period. He just has to carve out whatever extra system time is needed.

Like Harold, you're headed for trouble. Most distributors make a major systems changeover only once every 10 years or so . . . and perhaps only *once in their corporate lifetime* does the Inventory Management "philosophy" change simultaneously with mechanics. You just can't treat this like it was a bunch of painters coming in to redo the office decor. You must make certain that your people—from top to bottom—become intimately involved and see the new concepts as "our system" . . . not "their system"! That requires a *full-time,* company-paid coordinator.

The Coordinator's Job

The Coordinator has nothing else to do but to see that the system goes in smoothly. He or she plans every step with the outside firm's staff; is

CONVERTING THE SYSTEM

the first to be trained on the new system; schedules and conducts much of the group training in each company location; helps set all schedules of timing or sequence; stays in daily touch with branch managers to assure that steps are being completed; prepares the "User's Guide" which translates into your company and industry language how the system functions, how screens are used, what reports mean; and keeps the President apprised continually of how things are going, where roadblocks have appeared, and where his special pressure is needed.

The Coordinator is sort of the company fuss-budget for the project . . . after which he or she may very well become the Management Information System Director. Be careful who is assigned to the job. It isn't for some dodo who's a relative of the Boss but must be retrained to drive to work every morning. This person should have future Vice President potential! Try to pick someone now employed, who knows the inner-workings of the company, rather than hiring an outsider who must then learn *both* the company idiosyncrasies and the new system.

SUMMARY

"Graham, when *are* you going to cut out all this preamble and get down to usage rates, Order Points, Safety Allowances, and all those neat controls we need on our computer? We didn't order this book to hear all this other stuff!" True, you probably didn't . . . and I haven't forgotten those either. Over the years, however, most of my gray hair was not caused by someone misunderstanding the Order Point formula or how to calculate an EOQ . . . but by system breakdowns in areas no one anticipated. Stage II once caught my Boss by surprise, and when he displayed a high degree of no-confidence in the new system, it was contagious. It took much longer than it should have to move through the stage. I've seen far too many installations stall and even crash when degeneration in one form or another took hold but no one knew how to deal with it. It wasn't *supposed* to happen, so there was no preparation for it. Remember something I've hammered on more than once in this chapter:

> If you adopt these control techniques and disciplines, you'll likely be asking your employees to change the principles . . . the philosophy of how they order and operate. That's much more involved, and requires much more training and re-training than when they change only screen types and report formats . . . mechanics.

That's why this chapter and those that preceded it are important to read *first!* Without the proper system foundation, the proper support for sales, and now here . . . an "eyes-wide-open" understanding of what's necessary to install a new philosophy wrapped up in new mechanics . . . you might be tempted to push changes through that will have no staying power and achieve nothing in the long run.

5

PLANNING FOR THE FUTURE: NEW ATTITUDES AND ORGANIZATION!

This chapter will be brief. There are long ones up ahead that deal with the meat of Inventory Management, so the points here need to be mentioned but not beaten into the ground. To a degree, the recommendations are common sense, but in distribution today, certainly *NOT* the norm! You may be uncomfortable hearing them . . . maybe even a bit angry, but hear out the logic before rejecting these ideas.

THE UNCERTAIN FUTURE

Inventory Management boils down to one huge, coordinated attempt to outguess the future. It's fraught with danger, pitfalls, missteps, profit-loss, career changes, and bankruptcy. Trying to figure out what items customers will buy, and how many, generated all the concepts, formulas, and procedures you'll learn in later chapters. That part of the future is always uncertain, but there are proven ways to handle it. We'll begin those discussions in the next chapter.

For other aspects of the future, there are no formulas. We're headed into the 1990s, followed by a real twilight zone: The 21st Century! What will conditions be like? How will distributors function? Where will our company fit in? What kind of system will be needed to keep us growing? The exhortation of this chapter is to look ahead. It's a strange phenomenon that well-laid plans for the future, made after careful study of what to expect, goals and objectives, and an inventory of resources available, have a way of becoming reality. Many things about the future you cannot predict or forestall, but some you *can!* Most challenges can be met if you see them coming.

What's Your Five-Year; Ten-Year Plan?

Now's the time to ask a lot of questions, *before* a computerized system is planned, programmed or purchased, and installed. What will your company look like, what will be your structure, what markets will you serve, how will you reach those markets . . . in five or ten years? If you have two locations now, with $5 million in sales, do you expect to be ten branches by 1998 with sales of $30 million? Are you considering a move to regional warehouses that resupply the satellite branch inventories? Are you mulling over changes in the way your products are marketed . . . more emphasis on telemarketing than on an outside sales force? Does bar coding have practical application in your warehouse?

WHY? WHAT DOES IT HAVE TO DO WITH INVENTORY CONTROL?

One of the most expensive blunders a distributor can stumble through is to spend thousands on computer hardware, software, and installation . . . only to find before the massive project is complete (or shortly thereafter) that the hardware isn't large enough, or that the software has been outstripped by company growth or restructuring . . . all of which was plainly visible early in the computer project planning stages. When a train heads toward you at night, the headlight is visible quite a while before the train is on top of you. The whistle sounds while it's still distant. You're pretty dumb if you get run over!
 . . . but for some unexplained reason, distributors will plan, program, or purchase and implement a new computerized system, while down the hall the top executives are talking mergers, new markets, changes from independent to regionalized branch operation, system contracts, bar coding, supplier-distributor hookups for ordering . . . and who knows what else . . . plans that never filter into the computer planning. Something like a husband who buys a two-seat sports car for family transportation, while for several weeks his wife has known she's pregnant with triplets . . . just hadn't gotten around to telling him!
 You can't afford slipups like this. A company changes computerized systems two or three times perhaps during the entire corporate existence. Each is very expensive and very traumatic. Consider some new attitudes, new responsibilities, even new organization as you plan your next system. Hmmm . . . here's where you may get upset.

THE PRESIDENT'S ROLE IN COMPUTER PLANNING

This advice could have been given in Chapter 4 as part of the system conversion discussion, but I felt it important enough to warrant special emphasis. It's easy to avoid communication mix-ups as a new system is planned and installed *and* to gain wonderful side-benefits for the future as well. How? The *PRESIDENT* heads up the computer planning team in your company! Oh boy, I can already hear your president screaming:

> Hold on! I don't know anything about computers, and I *don't want* to know very much! That's what I hired a CPA for . . . and Phyllis, the new Data Processing Manager. I've delegated this whole project to them. They're to study our needs, look at systems on the market, select one, and get it installed.

Sorry, Boss. That attitude was obsolete quite a while back. Today, the president *must* be knowledgable about computers! Earlier in the book, you heard that computers of the future will noodle into every company function. You, Mr. President, must not allow that . . . with all the accompanying hazards . . . without knowing quite a bit about what the machines do. By heading the team that plans, selects, and implements, you'll be forced to learn more about your company than you know now, and certainly more about computer hardware and software. In years to come, you'll be crippled as a manager without that knowledge.

A Tale of Two Distributors

Consider these two distributors who took different paths on this point. The first had a president who turned the entire computer operation and system over to a young data processing manager. When I visited, they were about to embark on a very expensive hardware upgrade. Even with limited computer knowledge, it was apparent to me that the upgrade wasn't needed. Their current equipment was being utilized to perhaps 50 percent of its capacity. Why were they upgrading? . . . because it wouldn't look good on the young data processing manager's resume to have worked with less than state-of-the-art hardware . . . and he planned to move on when he'd had some experience with the new equipment. The president was vulnerable. He knew totally zip about computers and depended entirely on what his specialist told him.

A Different Approach

The second company's president also knew very little about computers, but he determined to correct that when it was time for a new system. . . . and head the project, start to finish. It was painful. Many long hours of study, instruction, seminars, one-on-one discussions, site visits, and non-involvement in other company activities he enjoyed more. Today, that distributor has an excellent system, an effective blend of hardware, software, and personnel that will serve them for ten years or more. No one in the building knows more about what the computer can do, will do than the Boss. He can't program it; he can't turn it on and run it . . . but he's *the* most knowledgable computer-capability person in the building! I'd like stock in that company. It's a sure winner.

THE PLACE FOR DATA PROCESSING IN THE ORGANIZATION

You can guess what I'm about to say next. Yes, Data Processing or Management Information Services . . . whatever you call it . . . should report directly to the president! No one else in the company has a purely objective view. The computer assists all company functions. If it reported to one of them, the emphasis leans that way.

Sure, I know that most DP departments report to the Controller or Accounting. It was a logical choice in 1970 when the primary need was for a good recordkeeping system, and most computers were first brought in to improve the accounting function. Controllers picked the system, so they wound up supervising the function. Why do you need a computer today? How many company functions benefit when it performs as Chapters 2 and 3 suggested?

Computers Aren't Like Other Fixed Assets

Data Processing belongs under the president, directly. That, too, encourages him to find out how computers work, their capabilities, the costs, etc. In times past, distributor executives often viewed the computer much as they would a new heating unit for the building. The president calls the Operations Manager:

> Jack, it's cold around here. Our old heating unit is probably worn out. Shop around, find an inexpensive, energy-efficient unit and install it.

PLANNING FOR THE FUTURE   63

The president didn't have to become an expert on heating units. He just had to make a decision to spend some money. . . . and so he takes the same path when someone convinces him that a new computerized system is needed. The heating unit is maintained by Jack, the Operations Manager. The computer gets assigned to Doris, the Controller. She selected it. She runs it.

Recognize the Difference, Mr. President!

Computers are more like an airplane in which your entire company is about to fly. It will take you up, keep you all up there safely, keep you warm and dry in the process, arrive much more quickly at the destination than had you all walked, and go to the right place . . . or it will get up in the air, let you freeze and rain pour in, go off in the wrong direction, or perhaps even crash and burn. If *you* are to be the pilot, it makes sense to find out a lot about airplanes . . . not just delegate the job to someone else. Will it carry all our people? Will it have the right instruments; enough power to get off the ground? . . . and so on.

SUMMARY

Much of the future is uncertain, but too many distributors have to battle surprises that were plainly visible on the horizon . . . by somebody in the company, but their wee little voice wasn't heard. . . . or the right hand never found out, until it was too late, what the left hand was doing! Does your company have a five-year plan? Is it something more than: "We want to increase sales 15 percent each year!" Have you thought about new markets? How about some from which you should withdraw? How many branches will you have in ten years? Will you service them from regional warehouses?

All these are presidential-level questions. Meanwhile, a new computerized system is needed, and key personnel are involved up to their ears in that project. . . . and perhaps surprisingly to you, *THAT NEW COMPUTERIZED SYSTEM* is *also* a presidential-level project! He should step back from other responsibilities for a spell and head up the project team. It isn't nearly as much fun as a sales program (his old background). It's hard work; tedious; frustrating; and seems to go on forever. In years to come, however, nothing will pay back greater dividends to the company.

The president also has the computer operation reporting directly to him. It has such universal implications throughout the company, that no one else has a big-enough picture to handle it objectively. Plan for the future: The 1990s, the 21st Century . . . different days that will require new organizational structures, new managerial skills, new attitudes! The computer is here to stay. It can make or break your Inventory Management efforts. It will take top-level supervision to be sure it acts more like a "Superman" in your company . . . fighting the forces of evil (profit-loss and bankruptcy) than a "Frankenstein Monster" that gets out of control.

6

USAGE—THE MOST IMPORTANT ELEMENT OF INFORMATION!

It's time now to move into the material for which you bought this book in the first place: Inventory Control! Five chapters of preamble . . . that's a lot but certainly not too much. Inventory management efforts are enhanced or retarded significantly by all that stuff we talked about earlier. Horror stories abound in distribution where some poor company rushed into a computerized system, hoping to get a handle on runaway inventories, only to see things get worse. In Chapter 2, I mentioned a Texas A&M study revealing that, until recently, the most profitable distributors were *not* using a computer to control inventories. They weren't backward or stupid . . . just scared! They preferred to wait a while until Inventory Management on computers had been perfected a bit.

FORECASTING USAGE . . . ONE OF THE MORE HAZARDOUS TASKS!

One of the reasons some distributors postpone any serious computerized inventory control effort is the difficulty of forecasting usage on stock items. Future usage is the very heart of a control system, manual or computerized, but it's also the most slippery of the data elements needed. Just when you think you've got a pretty good handle on what to expect for a stock item . . . BAM . . . something screwy happens! A customer orders far more than anyone ever has; you run out of stock for an extended period and the history becomes misleading; one customer begins to dominate an item; or sales fall off for no apparent reason. Seasonality is involved; protected stock has to be set up; promotions muddy-up the picture . . . and on and on. This chapter begins the real "meat" of how to plan an effective inventory control system. Usage is the most important data element to be captured and analyzed. It's needed in nearly every technique or formula discussed throughout the rest of this book . . . but it's a wiggly critter!

OUTGUESSING THE FUTURE

Let's review some points I made in my first book. Inventory control is not an exact science. There's no chance at all of batting a thousand. Why? . . . because you're trying to outguess the future! The best anyone can expect is to increase the odds for success by applying proven techniques and systematic, time-tested logic—all drawing on the most complete, most accurate, most timely information you can develop.

What guesses about the future have to be made in inventory control? Well, there are the "quantity" guesses: Orders to expect from customers for specific stock items; replenishment needs for outlying branches; and how heavy to order when a supplier's price is about to go up. There are "time" estimates: How long will a manufacturer require to accept the order and deliver the goods? How frequently should a product line be reviewed and ordered? A few guesses just have a "Yes" or "No" answer: Will a new stock item sell as Sales thinks it will? Will customers live up to agreements under which special stock was ordered just for them? Does that outside salesman know what he's talking about when he asked for six new items to be put on the shelves?

Each answer lies in the future. No one knows what will happen, but the inventory control system has no choice. It must *predict* an answer for each question and then *proceed* full steam ahead on decisions (that have to be made now) in an effort to *prepare* the inventory to meet what occurs. Predict, Proceed, Prepare! That's what inventory control's all about! You can use SWAG to make the guesses or methods that predict a "range" of occurrences (with quantities and times). . . . much like the golfer who aims at a fairway 50 yards wide. He doesn't have to hit the very center—just land somewhere in the fairway and he's OK. Proven control methods shoot at a narrower fairway (less inventory protection). SWAG usually widens the target . . . but at a much greater inventory cost. A pro golfer has the ability to hit the narrow fairway. A solid inventory control system can too.

USAGE

The single most important prediction a distributor makes is how much of a stock item will be *used* in the future. *Used,* for inventory control

USAGE—THE MOST IMPORTANT ELEMENT OF INFORMATION! 67

purposes, means all withdrawals from stock at a specific company location (warehouse or branch) in sales to customers, replenishment of other branches on a regular basis, and internal company needs. For any stock item in any location, *usage* is a vital, dynamic, integral data element that must be estimated with reasonable accuracy if good service and a profitable turn rate is to result. The prediction of future usage has three requirements:

1. It must be developed for every stock item independently.
2. It must be expressed as a specific number of units—not dollars.
3. It must be related to a time period.

Assume that you stock a specific size of rubber rain boots. You have several other sizes and types, but now you must predict usage on just this one particular size and style in one particular branch. Your prediction is expressed as 38 pair per month. You'll see in a moment where the 38 number came from. The point here is that it's expressed per month and that it's a specific number of units. You may have expressed usage per day, per week, or year-to-date, etc. The formulas I'll show you in later chapters need the figure expressed per month. . . . and the estimate is very specific: 38 pair per month. You might sell 67, 15, or none. You predict 38 . . . one number around which you'll build inventory protection for a "range" of sales you can handle. The 38 relates to a specific product in a specific location, expressed as a specific quantity related to a specific time period. Is *that* specific enough?

Effective computerized records retain item detail like this. Inventory Control people are rarely interested in usage "lumps," like how many dollars of a product or product line were sold through all branches of the company. Oh sure, *somebody* is interested in such information, but not *you!* Lumps are valueless in the day-to-day control of a stock item. The person responsible for replenishment timing needs an estimate expressed as a definite rate of *unit* sale, per item, to anticipate in the period just ahead.

Remember that! Usage statistics others might need can be developed from your records if the item inventory files are structured as recommended in Chapter 7. Don't plan the records to accommodate the president's information needs. He can use a Query program for those (Chapter 13). I've seen too many poorly-performing systems where the computer file space allotted to usage was seriously inadequate. A buyer could see year-to-date "lumps" or perhaps what occurred in the last 30 days but could not see month-by-month figures at all . . . let alone back for a year, on line. You'll learn before the book is finished that usage information drives almost every decision relative to inventory. Don't skimp on the space set aside for it.

TYPES OF USAGE

There are three basic types of usage:

- Normal sales to customers (Regular Usage)
- Repetitive requirements of satellite branches from warehouse stocks (Transfer Usage)
- Material withdrawn for some other use (Repair parts, kit or assembly components, internal use, etc.)

The computer's recordkeeping system keeps track of all three for all stock items in all branches—item-by-item, month-by-month, back for one year. An item's history for October in Branch 2 might have just a single number recorded which represents the total of all three usage categories above . . . or if you have enough disc space, separate totals. As Chapter 7 will explain, the system generates additional year-to-date or month-to-date usage totals as well as for other types of inventory activity: Credit returns from customers, returns to suppliers, merchandise scrapped, etc., but these are just running totals—not individual monthly records.

Some Usage *Should Not* Be Recorded at All!

Repetitive usage only should be recorded in the monthly buckets for a stock item! Non-recurring transfers from one branch to another (to help out a buddy in trouble) are not posted. You'll learn more about that in Chapter 16. Returns to suppliers, surplus material that finally sells, stuff that is donated or sent to the dump, etc., are all *non-recurring* outgoing inventory activity. Certainly, you *do not want to protect* for this activity recurring, so the figures are not recorded at all in the regular monthly usage histories for stock items.

The individual item monthly records capture only those categories of usage that will recur and therefore provide a solid basis for estimating what to anticipate (and protect for) in the future. Regular sales and repetitive transfers, regular repair or kit usage . . . that's what you're after!

TRANSFER USAGE

Large distributors with central or regional warehouses that resupply smaller branches have an option, in designing the records in which to

USAGE—THE MOST IMPORTANT ELEMENT OF INFORMATION!

capture usage, that permits a lower warehouse inventory level with minimal service risk. The option has front-end expense . . . so much that it may be unacceptable to you, but consider the gains also.

History seems to show that anything costing money will be more expensive in years to come. Your inventory investment falls in that category. It makes sense, therefore, to control any asset as closely as you can. One way to carve a few bucks out of a multi-branch inventory control system is to treat transfers out of a central warehouse differently from sales, as the warehouse safety allowances are developed for service protection.

Separate Records of Sales and Transfers-Out

To do this, you must maintain *separate* history files for each stock item in the warehouse: One history file for regular sales and one for transfers out. "That requires a lot of disc space!" you say, and of course it does. But let's see how such segregated usage data can serve. Chapter 8 will detail how safety allowances are calculated . . . the "pad" in inventory that protects for a range of occurrences on an item. The safety allowance quantity is quite necessary to avoid stockouts, but it has the effect of a fixed asset. It does not turn over (on the average) across a year. Half the time you eat into it; half the time you don't need it. There has to be a saving when the safety allowance can be reduced without risking a stockout. One way to do that? Put *no safety at all* on branch usage out of a central warehouse!

Calculate a Safety Allowance Only on Warehouse Sales

For items in a central warehouse that experience heavy branch withdrawals, the safety allowance is calculated *only on the regular sales!* Branch transfer usage has no safety added at the warehouse level. All safety stock on the transfer usage is placed *at the branch level* (right next to the customer). In a network of many branches, served from regional warehouses offering thousands of items, this one adjustment doesn't harm the warehouse service level . . . but quite a few inventory investment dollars are saved.

The Information Helps Stock a New Regional Warehouse

If you can afford to keep similar records for branches who now buy on their own, a second benefit can accrue later. Let's say that several of your branches act independently but also transfer quite a bit of material between themselves. Management decides that they could be better served by a central warehouse. To make this change, it's vital to know the quantities each branch *sells to customers* apart from the units transferred to their buddies. Without separate records of sales and transfers, only guesswork picks the items and inventory levels to carry in the new warehouse that will supply the branches. Moves like this, to central or regional warehouses supporting clusters of branches, are becoming very popular today.

The discussion fits here to justify a need for two history files in a warehouse: One for sales, another for transfers-out. Make a note to review this section as you learn about Safety Allowances in Chapter 8.

HOW MUCH OF THE PAST IS IMPORTANT?

Now that you have a month-by-month history back for a year on both regular usage and transfers-out (if you can afford the space and you do feed branches from a warehouse), how much of that history should the computer be allowed to use in an attempt to forecast what will happen in the months ahead? What time period from the past is valid for predicting the future? Entire volumes have been written to answer these questions. There are as many differing opinions and complicated forecasting formulas as there are people who've wrestled with the problem. Everybody has his or her own technique.

The forecasting methods often carry exotic names, like exponential smoothing . . . a mathematical way to give more weight to the recent past, less weight the farther back in time you go, with an attempt to smooth out the wild fluctuations along the way. There are several "smoothing factors" from which to choose to vary how much weight is applied where . . . in other words, how the computer uses the history to develop a usage estimate for the future.

Many Still Depend on SWAG, but It's Expensive

Our old friend SWAG . . . guesswork still gets a lot of play in distribution circles. "Let's see now. We sold 36 so far this year. But this has been a bad year. Last year by this time we'd sold 60. Things are sure to pick up and besides, I just hired that new salesman. I think we'll sell 36 in the three months just ahead!" Sound familiar? You probably had buyers spend a bundle of your money in purchase orders just this morning with less of a thought-process than that . . . and *you're* snickering?

USAGE—THE MOST IMPORTANT ELEMENT OF INFORMATION! 71

Well, what's the answer? What should we use out of that expensive history file? To illustrate the principle behind the answer, here's a little story:

> Joe hates apples. He eats very few and then only in a pie. Joe's wife, Grace, knows that last month their family consumed just 10 apples. Joe ate zero. When Grace buys apples for next month, how many do you suppose she'll buy? With no company coming, she'll buy about 10 of course. That wasn't hard to figure out.
>
> Now Joe gets very sick. The doctor spells it out in plain language: "Joe, you've got Charvosis of the Gromp. You're a goner unless you start eating lots of apples! We don't know why, but the medical journals report a few cases where apples pulled a guy through."
>
> Next month, Joe eats 93 apples. The rest of the family, noting how much Joe enjoys them, increases their consumption to 15 apples, up from last month's 10. When Grace shops for the following month, she buys 108 apples.

The principle illustrated by Joe and his apples:

What will occur in the immediate future is most likely to be *what occurred in an equal time period from the immediate past.*

Please take note of the *most likely to be.* It is not "will be." If you had to pick one number as a usage estimate for the next six months, it will most likely be the amount used during the last six months. You used 73. Then 73 is your best guess for the six months immediately ahead. You may use 10 or 400, but 73 is the best estimate you can make today.

There Are Exceptions . . . But They're in the Minority

"Wait a minute!" you ask. "What about seasonal items, stockouts, large one-time sales, promotions, items that only one customer buys, and low-usage-per-year items? That magnificent principle up above wouldn't work when these conditions are present!" . . . and certainly you're right. Each condition will be discussed before this chapter ends, but for many, many items in your inventory (in fact, 80 percent or more), none of those conditions apply. For this 80 percent, without knowing anything more than the computer finds in history, your *best bet* for the period just ahead is the quantity used in the same amount of time from the immediate past. If you're trying to estimate usage for July through December, what was your usage from January through June? For most items, that's the best guess for the future.

USE THE LAST SIX MONTHS TO DEVELOP A USAGE RATE PER MONTH

How can this principle of using the past to predict the future be demonstrated in a specific procedure? A usage rate is needed for every stock item to be plugged into formulas you'll learn later on. The past is used to develop this anticipated usage rate.

The Usage "Rate"

You'll see this term "Usage Rate" many times throughout the book. As this chapter's title says, usage rates are the most important elements of information of the entire inventory management system. How many per month are expected to be withdrawn from stock of item 123A in the period just ahead? That's the *rate* of usage . . . and that's what the formulas need.

The Most Reliable Time Frame from the Past

For 80 percent of your stock items, the monthly usage rate is most accurately developed by selecting *the last six months of history,* totalling the figures, and dividing by six. "But Graham, wait a minute! We've captured 36 months of history on every item. Are you telling me that those other 30 months are worthless?" Well, not exactly worthless. They do help spot trends in items from year-to-year; perhaps identify an item on the decline that likely should be dropped from stock before you have no sales at all; or to pinpoint the seasonal usage patterns for an item . . . but for *most* of your items, that earlier 30 months is of almost no value at all.

Usage Patterns Are Dynamic . . . Always Changing!

The usage enjoyed on one of your better items three years ago doesn't reflect accurately what to expect next month . . . does it? A dynamic distributor adds or loses customers and business segments continually. Orders are captured or lost on a specific stock item for many reasons, but *recent conditions or occurrences* have much more impact as to why customers buy or don't buy than what happened two years or more back. Customers' needs change rapidly today because of economic recessions or booms, technology modifications, new products (or prices) in the market, or for something as simple as your salesman going to work for a competitor. When you're in the thick of competition, usage from the last

USAGE—THE MOST IMPORTANT ELEMENT OF INFORMATION!

six months is the best period for the computer to use as it develops a per-month estimate for the period just ahead.

Mar	Apr	May	Jun	Jul	Aug
29	17	37	15	20	20

Usage Rate = 23 per month

Don't Expect Perfection. Look for Consistency.

The last six months won't yield perfect estimates but will generate consistently better results than any other time period you might select from the past . . . *IF* you identify and handle correctly the other 20 percent of your stock items with the conditions you were worried about earlier. In my first book, I suggested a four-month period from the past. Additional experiences in other durable goods distribution industries proved (at least to me) that a six-month period was better. A wider range of items are covered by the concepts and techniques of this book. Just don't go too far back. Six months of the past provides an effective usage base.

SEASONAL ITEMS

For every principle, there are exceptions. The most obvious exception to the "Immediate Past" rule is the seasonal item. A plumbing and heating distributor about to enter the September-to-February period doesn't care how a critical item sold from March through August. On heating repair products, usage during the summer doesn't mean a thing. What he wants to know is how the item sold *last* September to February, and generally, how much business is up or down this year compared to last. Special programming is needed, first to identify the seasonal products (often a distributor has more than he thought), and second, to develop their anticipated usage rates from a different period of the past.

Definition of a Seasonal Item

An item is seasonal when 80 percent of the annual sales volume falls in six (or less) consecutive months. You could argue about these limits and no doubt many other items might be handled as seasonal even when the volume is a little less than 80 percent or the time frame is longer than six months . . . but those meeting the 80 percent/Six Month rule are *definitely* seasonal!

If you begin a new system with as much as 12 months' history recorded for stock items in the computer, then let the computer find the seasonal items. Program it to search for those meeting the 80 percent sales in six consecutive months criteria. A one-character field in the inventory record for each stocked item is either blank (non-seasonal) or has a code inserted to designate an item with a seasonal usage pattern.

The "Equivalent" Past Is Used for Seasonal Items

When the computer sees that code, it switches to a program that uses the *equivalent* six months from last season's history to calculate a usage rate. From last season's figures, it selects the six months just ahead of where you are now in the year. It's October 1. The history selected is October-November-December-January-February-March from last season's history. The usage figures from these months are totalled and divided by six for an average. A trend percentage is then applied, because some of the numbers are nearly a year old.

The Trend Percentage

The computer uses year-to-year totals by product line if such data is available to develop a percentage of business growth or decline to anticipate for the upcoming season. Is business in this product category up 15 percent this year compared to last, or down 10 percent? If you haven't been on the computer long enough to have year-to-year figures yet, someone should SWAG the trend percentage to use for each seasonal product line. That trend percentage is applied to the usage-rate-per-month estimate developed from last season's data to compute one to use for this season. On October 1 this year, here's how this looks in a sample problem:

Last Season's History						Trend
Oct	Nov	Dec	Jan	Feb	Mar	
6	18	47	56	38	21	Business is down this year 12% compared to last year.
Usage Rate from Last Season:			31 per month			To be reduced by 12%
Usage Rate to Enter This Year's Season:			27 per month			

The computer uses 27 per month as the initial usage rate for this item as you move into this year's season. That will be adjusted further along in the season, but 27 is a solid starting-point. It's too high for the early months and not high enough for mid-season, but it's a solid opening average to guide the inventory buildup decisions you must make *now!*

QUALIFYING THE HISTORY

Most of the exotic forecasting formulas include fantastic mathematical gymnastics in an attempt to "clean up" a stock item's history before using it to outguess the future. Huge, one-time customer orders; periods of promotional sales; stockouts that last too long; one customer who dominates the activity on an item; or service-type parts that must be stocked even with very low annual sales . . . all have misleading histories if used without modification to predict the future. The recorded sales and transfers are accurate in the sense that they show what happened. It's just that the history does not portray accurately what's *most likely* to occur in the immediate future. Some filtering or modification is needed. Everyone recognizes the problem and some great minds have searched for a solution. Today, you have three choices: A complex mathematical approach, a simple concept, or SWAG for the whole mess.

The High-Math Approach

The mathematicians have really gone after this problem. They employ tactics to manipulate an item's history information that would do justice to landing a spacecraft on the moon . . . all in an effort to get around the obvious problem (the history is misleading). One primary principle guided their work: The computer must not be subjected to the ultimate indignity: A human having to step in and apply human brainpower and logic! The formulas are staggering—totally incomprehensible to the average distributor employee. What's more . . . they still do a lousy job of handling the problem conditions mentioned above.

There Are Conditions That Have *NO* Mathematical Answer!

When you experience a huge, one-time customer order, the computer lacks the answer to a very important question. In fact, this question and answer hold the key as to what to do with the recorded history. The question? "Will the sale likely happen again, or was it a one-time shot?" Without the answer (which only a human can provide), the poor machine is up a creek no matter how exotic the math that's employed.

What's an alternative to the exotic math? How can you use the simple, six-month rolling-average usage rate I've suggested for most of your stock items . . . and yet avoid trouble when one of the unusual conditions pops up? *Qualify* an item's sales history before allowing the computer to use it! A qualified history can be used by the computer as is. A "disqualified" history cannot. A human must decide how (or if) a disqualified history may be used, develop a modified history, or set the item's ordering controls manually.

The Computer Does Most of the Disqualifying

Depending on the money you've budgeted for programming or the capabilities of your packaged system, the computer can identify and disqualify the history in two . . . perhaps more . . . of the conditions where it's misleading. Where it cannot, people are "programmed" to find the conditions.

CONDITIONS THAT SHOULD CAUSE HISTORY DISQUALIFICATION

There are four principal conditions that cause error when the history of a stock item is used without modification to predict the future:

1. Unusual sales or transfers in a month—including large one-time sales or withdrawals, promotional periods, etc.
2. Stockouts that last as long as two weeks during a month.
3. Items with only a single customer, or where one customer dominates the sales.
4. Items with very low sales per year (less than 1/2 unit per month).

These are the conditions either you or the computer must identify and handle apart from the regular, last-six-months, rolling-average usage rate calculation method. When these conditions are present, the last six months can be *very misleading* as a guide for what to expect in the future.

95 Percent of Your Headaches From Just a Few Items

These four conditions account for 95 percent of the headaches in inventory control of stocked items . . . but are found at any one time in only some 20 percent or less of the items in stock. If they're identified and handled correctly, the computer can use the six-month, rolling-average usage rate method *on all the other 80 percent!* No exotic math needed. Your employees understand how the computer made its computation because they can duplicate it on a desk calculator. Remember from earlier discussions, if they *don't* understand the math, they'll either follow

USAGE—THE MOST IMPORTANT ELEMENT OF INFORMATION! 77

all computer suggestions blindly like robots or ignore them totally and use SWAG every time. It's vital for your people to understand the mathematics. Your system should be simple enough that they can.

UNUSUAL SALES OR TRANSFERS

A customer comes in and buys 150 of an item at one time, when average sales per month have been running about 30. The history looks like this:

Jul	Aug	Sep	Oct	Nov	Dec
37	16	9	58	30	180

Now what? Should the computer weigh that 180 right in with the other months? Should you pull out the 150 sale, use only five months, throw out the high and low months, or what? Well, there's that big question ahead of these, isn't there? "Will this unusual sale recur or was it a one-time shot?" Until that's answered, you really don't know what to do (and *neither does the computer,* regardless of the math it's been programmed to use.) Selecting *any* option with this history, without knowing the chances of the big sale's recurrence, could lead to trouble.

Step 1: The Computer Inserts a Flag to Disqualify the History

The first thing to do, is to *prevent* the computer from using the history until it's reviewed, approved or modified *by a human!* The computer inserts a flag tied to the December history that says: "Don't make any changes on this item until a human tells you how to proceed!"

> **The Rule:** When the last month's posted history is equal to the total of the previous five months' figures, the last month showed at least five units sold, and the item unit cost is significant. . . . the computer inserts the disqualification flag.

Like this:

Jul	Aug	Sep	Oct	Nov	Dec
37	16	9	58	30	180
					* —Flag

The "five-units-sold" requirement prevents the computer from flagging this history picture:

Jul	Aug	Sep	Oct	Nov	Dec
0	0	1	0	0	1

December's only sale does equal the total sales from July through November, but would be silly to call out for buyer review. If, however, December had shown five units sold . . . yes, the item would be flagged. You should add a unit cost qualifier here, also. Some items cost so much ($500, $1,000, etc.) that even the history above deserves at least a quick review. Others cost so little (.008, .01, etc.) that the most current month would have to show 1,000 or more sold to trigger a flag. For most items, the 5-unit rule screens out unnecessary buyer reviews. Whatever the rule on this, the current month must equal the total usage of the previous five months to trigger the flag.

The Item's History Is Disqualified by the Flag

The history is now "hung up." As long as the asterisk appears with December, the computer cannot use any time period from the past that includes December to develop a new usage rate or new ordering controls for the item. The flag must be removed by a human. After what? After determining whether or not the 150 sale will recur . . . then adjusting the history, expected usage rate and controls, depending on the answer. From whom? From Sales! This project is about to become a team effort.

Inventory Control Is a Company Responsibility

First, the buyer is alerted to action. The system identifies quickly the unusual sales transaction(s) that caused the flag: Which order(s), what date(s), the customer(s), quantities, etc. All this formation was at a buyer's fingertips in the old manual systems. Today, the computer must make it visible just as quickly, perhaps through the "kardex" inquiry discussed in Chapter 7 or by showing the facts on a month-end report. The buyer relays the customer order facts to Sales: "Will this recur?"

The Sales Department now gets a chance to help out with inventory control. They may kick and scream about being asked to do it, but they're the only ones close enough to the customer to find out if the unusual sale will happen again. The details about the order are turned over to Sales. They get back to Purchasing after talking to the customer . . . but no changes are made in the item until they do.

No Answer . . . It's a *Non-Recurring* Sale!

If Sales doesn't want to bother, or the customer can't (or won't) provide information about future needs, the big sale is considered non-recurring!

USAGE—THE MOST IMPORTANT ELEMENT OF INFORMATION! 79

It will not be considered in building inventory protection for the future. You can't afford speculative inventory today. There's a good reason for this seemingly-harsh approach: 8 out of 10 times, a very unusual sale *IS* a one-time occurrence! Those are the odds. Without pretty good information from the customer, you must expect that you won't see that sale again. If it does recur (a 20 percent chance), you're in the soup . . . but remember, more distributors fail today because of mismanaged assets than for lack of sales. Speculative inventory costs the customer nothing . . . costs your salesman nothing . . . but could cost *you* your company!

I *Told* You Inventory Control Is Hard Work!

"Are you kidding? You expect a buyer and salesman to spend this much time and effort on a single stock item? . . . No way! Our people are overworked already." Well, you have an alternative . . . the one you've taken in the past: Load the warehouse on this item (and the other 10,000 stocked)! Inventory dollars provide a nice buffer against working smart or hard. If you want good service *and* good turnover, it takes effort. Also, reduce your stock item list by 40 percent (the stuff you don't need) and maybe your people can control the remaining good items in an effective manner without being overburdened.

"Duplicate" History Fields

In our example, the 150 sale is to be removed from consideration, but it's not wise to modify the records of what actually occurred in a stock item's history. That record has many other potential uses where the full picture is needed: Evaluating a product line's contribution to profit compared to the inventory investment; or preparing listings of all items and quantities sold for periodic review with important customers. The cold facts should be left intact . . . but on the other hand, the computer must not have access to misleading figures. So what's the answer? Duplicate or secondary histories.

When the activity recorded for an item at the end of a month is misleading, a duplicate history field is needed for that month. The modified usage figure is entered by the Inventory Analyst/Buyer. The computer uses *this field instead of* the regular data to develop the usage rate and ordering controls for this item. The history now looks like this:

Jul	Aug	Sep	Oct	Nov	Dec	
37	16	9	58	30	180	Usage rate for the future:
						30 per month
		Duplicate field—		Dec		(180 Jul-Dec usage ÷ 6)
				30		

December has two usage figures: What actually happened and the number the computer is to use for projecting future usage. As it selects this six-month history to develop a usage rate, it averages the 37-16-9-58-30-30. The 180 is ignored. It's misleading. When a duplicate field is present, it's the one used in the averaging. The duplicate field is created and data entered by a human. When the original history has been disqualified for automatic use by the computer, the human must decide if a modified history is needed . . . and insert the changes.

There are other programming methods to achieve the same result. A transaction can be flagged and then ignored by the computer when developing an average from the past. The trouble is . . . someone looking back at the monthly totals would see 37-16-9-58-30-180, for example, and wonder: "How did the stupid computer get an average of 30 per month out of *that?* It must be fouled up!" It's better to show *both* December histories on an inquiry screen or report. A buyer can see what was sold *and* the number being used to forecast future usage. You always want the buyer to be able to duplicate any calculations the computer has made.

What If the Sale *Will* Recur?

Sales checks with the customer and gets an answer: "Ol' Jack says that they intend to keep buying that item more heavily from us. You'd better expect the 150 to repeat pretty often!" Hmmm . . . now the 180 December history is valid, but simply weighing it in with the other five months won't yield a good average usage rate for the months ahead. A different modification is needed.

The buyer inserts an expected usage rate, sets the ordering controls for the computer to use, and *freezes* them . . . locks them in for a month or so to see what happens next. The order point, line point, and order quantity (discussed in later chapters) are increased and "frozen" . . . made off-limits to changes by the computer. More history is needed before the item can be turned over to the computer again. Any changes to this item are made by the buyer while the controls are frozen. We'll talk more about this in a few pages.

EXTENDED STOCKOUTS

An item's history is misleading also when you run out of stock and cannot be resupplied for two weeks or more in a given month. The history looks like this:

USAGE—THE MOST IMPORTANT ELEMENT OF INFORMATION!

Jul	Aug	Sep	Oct	Nov	Dec
47	20	68	61	30	9*

The problem: A stockout occurred December 2 and lasted until December 21. Sales were off . . . not because customers stopped trying to buy the item but because there was no stock to sell for 19 days. Again, the recorded history of material shipped in December is invalid for straight-averaging with the earlier five months to develop a usage rate for the future.

"Demand" Versus Actual Shipments Recorded as History

We have to pause here just a moment to discuss the merits of recording "demand" when it occurs, including "lost sales," etc., as opposed to posting invoiced shipments only in history. Some argue that when demand is recorded, there's no problem with extended stockouts. The history shows what customers wanted when they wanted it, rather than how the material was shipped. I prefer to record only shipments as the history.

My experience is that more headaches are introduced than solved when demand is used instead of shipments. If a customer returns an item, you must go back to the month in which it was ordered and correct the history figure. This means that a month is *never closed down!* The history numbers are always subject to adjustment. Today you look at last April and it shows a history of 20 sold on an item. Tomorrow, the figure might be 10 if a customer returns 10 bought in April. "Demand" in a current month always has a high degree of uncertainty . . . orders get cancelled, substitutes are made, quantities bounce around. The final numbers tend to be higher, but with some percentage of "fluff" built in . . . doubled-up figures, etc.

If shipments only are recorded in history, that never changes later. April is closed off when April is over. If the customer sends 10 back in July, the July usage history is lowered. You'll find this a much more workable method. Remember too, when you implement a solid system of controls, you *expect* most of the orders received from customers for stock items! They're not surprises. Most of the time, demand and shipment occur within hours of each other. The histories you've seen so far in this chapter are quantities shipped and invoiced in the months displayed!

The Computer Finds Extended Stockouts

Back to our stockout discussion. The computer records the date when stock available-for-sale on an item drops to zero—and then the date after that when material is again available. The number of days without available stock is "collected" by the computer as the month progresses. Then when all outgoing activity for the month is tallied-up and posted in an official history field, the computer checks the number of days with no stock available. If it was half the time (15 days), a flag is inserted in that item's history for this most recent month.

The flag serves just like the one for unusual sales: It stops the computer from doing anything with that history as it stands! The usage rate and all controls remain as they are until a human decides what modification to make in the item's history file. Of course, you could have the computer ignore the flagged month and develop the average from the other five, but a human has much more information at his or her disposal on which to base a modification decision than does the computer. It's better for a human to do it.

The duplicate history field is needed again. The actual withdrawal totals remain in the "official" history, but a duplicate field for the disqualified month contains the human's estimate of what would have sold if stock had been available for the entire month. The computer uses this duplicate field, instead of the actual history, next month and beyond when developing a usage rate on which to base future ordering controls for this item.

Stockouts Are Bad News . . . Someone Needs to Explain What Happened!

There's another reason for not allowing the computer to throw out the current month and try to guess what will happen by using the other numbers. An unintentional stockout is trouble. It represents a system breakdown somewhere. In Chapter 18, you'll see that I want an explanation from the buyer as to what happened and what adjustments have been made if any are needed. The steps recommended here, where an extended stockout forces the buyer to check out the item, helps keep the buyer on top of the situation.

SINGLE OR DOMINATE-CUSTOMER ITEM

A third condition that causes six-month history averaging to be invalid for future predictions is when only one customer buys an item or dominates the usage pattern. The history might look like this:

Jan	Feb	Mar	Apr	May	Jun
0	0	50	0	0	50

USAGE—THE MOST IMPORTANT ELEMENT OF INFORMATION! 83

Periodically, the customer buys 50 units. He's pretty regular, every three months or so, but not predictable. If the 100 sold in six months were averaged, the monthly rate comes out about 17 per month (100 divided by 6). That's silly! There's no "rate" involved. We sell 50 or none at all, not 17 per month! If we plug 17 into a normal order point formula, as you'll learn in Chapter 8, the answer might come out 25 or so, depending on the lead time. That's just not going to work. 30 pieces are on the shelf, safely above the order point, and the next order for 50 has part of it backordered. The customer is furious:

> What's the matter with you turkeys? I come in here every three months for 50 units; I have for a year or more; and now you can't take care of me! What's wrong with your system?

Of course, we have a perfect excuse: "Well you see sir, we just went on to this new computer system and it tells us when to order more stock and all that!" Somehow, I can't see the customer being very understanding.

How do you handle this usage pattern to prevent trouble? First, you or the computer must identify items where only one customer is buying (or dominates the sales pattern). The computer can isolate items with only one customer, but it might be a bit tougher for it to find the dominant . . . but not the only . . . customer. A human may have to identify these. Dominant-customer histories might look like this one:

Jan	Feb	Mar	Apr	May	Jun
2	53	0	2	51	1

Lock in Controls That Fit This Customer!

In either case, single or dominant customer, the buyer sets the replenishment order timing and quantity controls to meet the customer's buying habits and *locks them in* . . . freezes them! In our first example, the order point in a single customer situation might be set at zero; the order quantity set at 50. When you sell the 50 on the shelf, another 50 is ordered. In the dominant customer pattern, it might have to be 55 as the order point; 50 as the order quantity. When more than one customer buys, you still must be in position at all times to handle a 50-piece order. The order point must be much higher. Once set, the computer keeps its hands off. It does continue to record the actual transactions in history, but the history is not used to re-set the ordering controls. As long as the controls are in the "Frozen" status, only a human may make changes.

The Frozen Control Feature

What is this "Frozen Control" business? Several times in this chapter I've mentioned the need to lock-in controls to keep the computer from altering them. At the end of every month, the usage rates and all controls for non-frozen items are re-set by the computer . . . for all stocked items, in all company locations. When the computer or a human has inserted a code to "freeze" an item, then the computer just skips over it at month-end. This ability to freeze the controls is lacking today in many systems on the market. The systems suffer, because there are several times when a human should set the ordering parameters for an item and the computer shouldn't change them:

1. A brand new stock item, for which you have no history yet. You provide the opening order point and order quantity and want them to remain in effect until six months of history has been captured.

2. An item stocked for one customer and which will be sold *only* to that customer. The stock is reserved just for him, even if he doesn't buy regularly. The computer doesn't adjust the controls based on the sales history. They must remain as set until a human changes them.

3. Regular stock items that, unfortunately, only one customer is buying today . . . the condition just discussed where the historical usage pattern cannot be "averaged."

4. Items that have very low sales per year (to be discussed next).

5. Portions of stock that are part of a Systems Contract where a 100 percent service level is guaranteed . . . and you could suffer quite a penalty were you unable to deliver the contracted quantity, regardless of previous movement, if the customer released the stock.

6. A temporary freeze is needed to allow a little additional time to show what will happen on a questionable item. The item with an unusual sale is a good example. The controls are frozen to wait for another month or two of history to show whether or not the big sale will happen again.

There are likely other conditions you could add, but each time it's important for the ordering controls to remain unchanged as the computer performs its normal recalculation step for all other stock items at the end of the month.

USAGE—THE MOST IMPORTANT ELEMENT OF INFORMATION! 85

The Freeze Can Be Permanent or Temporary

Some items need an indefinite freeze. The computer is *never* to alter the controls on its own. Other items need only a temporary freeze of from one to six months, as an example. Both types are accomplished by a special field in each item's variable-information inventory record (you'll learn more about this in the next chapter). Usually the field is blank, because the item is not frozen. . . . but a human can insert a 1 through 12, telling the computer to skip one, two, six, or twelve monthly recalculation cycles for this item before reverting to using its history. The human could enter a 99 or XX code, for example, to order an indefinite freeze.

A Safety Measure: The Monthly List of Frozen Items

Some systems planners get all bent out of shape when I propose the freeze feature. They dislike locking out the computer on stock items. Why? They know that conditions change, and a buyer might forget that he has frozen the controls on an item. The computer is prevented from adjusting anything based on recent information . . . so WHAM . . . the item gets into trouble.

To protect against this, once a month the computer prints a list of all items with frozen controls . . . or any that have been locked-up by the computer itself but no one has yet made any modifications. Several things are shown:

- Buyer name
- Item number and description
- Why item was frozen
- Date of the freeze
- Date freeze will expire
- The last six months of actual usage history
- Details of unusually large sales/transfers

The buyer re-evaluates each item. "Do I still want these controls in place for this item, or has the picture changed?" If another buyer did the freezing but has quit, the new buyer gets a fresh look at each item. When unusual sales or extended stockout flags have caused the freeze . . . these inserted by the computer . . . the buyer determines if a duplicate history is needed, arbitrary controls should be set, or both. In some cases, all the buyer does is remove the flag. Nothing is wrong and the history should be used as it is. Until the flag is removed, however, the item appears on each monthly list of items frozen. The computer has done all it's permitted to do. The flag is the computer's way of saying: "Hey buyer, I've encountered a condition I'm not programmed to handle. Tell me what to do. Until you do, I'll make no changes!"

ITEMS WITH VERY LOW SALES

The fourth condition to spot in an item's history to keep the computer from charging ahead with an invalid usage prediction, is where less than half a unit sells per month . . . less frequently than one piece sold every other month. It could be a repair part, or expensive merchandise held for a special customer that you've agreed to keep on the shelf regardless of activity, or "support-type" products that bring in customers for other high-volume items. The history could look like this:

Jan	Feb	Mar	Apr	May	Jun
0	0	1	0	0	0

It doesn't take a mathematician to see clearly what "usage rate" per month the computer will generate if it's allowed to total the six months and divide by six. Even I can handle math like that. Zip per month! One-sixth of a unit per month rounds off nicely to zero. When that goose egg is plugged into an order point or order quantity formula, the system says: "You need no inventory at all—no controls—on this critter. You don't sell any!" The "system" proceeds to put you out of business on the item.

Maybe the Computer Knows Something!

Maybe you *should* be out of business on items like these. You'll learn in Chapter 15 that distributors often carry as much as 40 percent more inventory than they need. The single-customer item discussed earlier and this low-usage critter are examples of a generally unprofitable inventory investment. In both situations, someone in Management should ask: "Do we *have* to offer these as stock items?" Why not ask the customer who orders 50 every three months if he can give you two weeks' notice . . . enough time to bring in the material special for him. Look carefully at *every one* of the low-usage items. How much business would actually be lost if we offered this item on a special-order basis only?

Human-Set Controls Are Necessary If You Must Stock It

For now, let's assume that the Boss told you: "I don't care what you think about this item. We *will* keep it on the shelf! If you don't, you'll get a chance for a new career path!" Hmmm . . . with that incentive, we'd better figure out a way to control it. There is, of course, no economical way to do that. There are several options open, but all are expensive. Inventory that doesn't sell is a profit-drain. Still, the Boss weighed the costs and decided that the losses incurred on this item are offset by other benefits. Obviously the history cannot be used by the computer to set the ordering controls. This item must have arbitrary controls established by a human and then frozen indefinitely.

Set the order point at zero and the order quantity at one piece. Sell the one on the shelf and buy a replacement. If sales are slow but sporadic, the order point might have to be one and the order quantity one or two units. Whatever the buyer sets is *frozen!* The computer never uses the history to develop new controls. Each month, the item appears on a review list with all others in the frozen status, to give the buyer a chance to re-set the controls if that's advisable considering the most recent usage picture.

"Goodnight, Graham . . . this is one hellacious amount of time and effort expended on a stock item! Who has time for all this, and what is gained if we follow your hairbrained ideas?"

WHAT DOES ALL THIS ACCOMPLISH?

The computer identifies some of the problem conditions and humans must find the others. Computer-inserted flags or arbitrary, frozen controls keep the computer from using a disqualified history. It's a lot of trouble. It requires more time and human brainpower than other approaches or than you've applied to your inventory management thought-process in the past. . . . but the benefits are there.

First, that 20 percent of your stock with squirrelly conditions cause far fewer headaches. Your service level is better! You receive less irate phone calls from unhappy customers, salesmen, or worse . . . the Boss! Secondly, you operate year-round with much less inventory! You substitute a "hands on" control system, new skill levels by employees, and a new team approach to keeping inventories down . . . for all those "buffer" dollars that gathered dust on your warehouse shelves for years.

Next, the purchasing and inventory control personnel understand how the computer develops its answers. For 80 percent of the stocked items, it uses a simple, six-month rolling average of the history to get a usage rate. The process is not so mystical that only a math major can fathom the steps. When something looks wrong, your "money-spending" people are more likely to question the answer.

Purchasing personnel are not robots . . . buying blindly whatever the computer suggests. Nor do they view the computer as a "black box" which conjures up ridiculous suggestions, to be ignored totally in favor of their own judgment that has served so well (?) for years. They follow the suggestions if these mesh with logic they can duplicate from the same facts . . . but they challenge the recommendations when they can't. It's *vital* for your people to understand how the computer assists them—how to "drive" this vehicle, not just ride along to wherever it takes them. When the logic is too exotic for mortals to comprehend, most employees become passengers instead of pilots . . . most undesirable!

USAGE—THE VITAL DECISION

Several of the chapters ahead make repeated references to usage and monthly usage rates. When a building's foundation is laid in a faulty manner, the structure is in jeopardy . . . and so is your entire Inventory Management system when usage estimates are made carelessly or through incorrect logic. Every major ordering decision and most inventory investment or stock-positioning choices are made in accord with what you expect to sell or transfer. If the usage estimates are undependable, inconsistent, haphazardly developed, or otherwise unsound, how good can your decisions be? That's why this chapter deals with usage in such depth. Your inventory control system rests on a foundation of usage estimates.

"But why worry about usage at all? I don't plan to build my computerized system from scratch. I'm planning to adopt software that comes with the hardware our company has purchased . . . or select one of the packaged systems on the market!" Good luck!

"Wait a minute, Graham! Those guys have all this worked out . . . don't they? Can't I just plug in their system and have all this usage stuff take care of itself?" Hmmm . . . that's why I've written this book. Use the concepts outlined here to check out the system you'll be using. Does it invite (or even tolerate) human interjection of information, or does the computer handle all items the same way in every condition? Can you understand the math? Does it handle seasonality? How about separate records for sales and transfers? What happens with unusual sales or stockout periods or low-usage items? Can you modify the "usage" history but leave the "official" history alone? Can you freeze an item's controls?

Oh, the salesman told you not to worry about that kind of stuff, huh? Here's some new advice: *Worry!*

7

MORE INFORMATION REQUIRED FOR GOOD INVENTORY CONTROL

. . . And Efficient Use of People

Usage information and usage rates are critical for sure, but much more than usage is needed for solid inventory management . . . and even more facts must be gathered to round out a totally-integrated computer system. When your corporate survival, or least your profitability, depends on predicting the future accurately . . . it's smart to gather as much information as is practical to aid your estimates.

To maximize employee productivity, it's wise to use the computer for time-consuming, burdensome clerical functions. To process customer inquiries and orders quickly, multitudes of facts about your company, the customers, your merchandise, and your suppliers must be collected . . . and then retrieved easily for use by the machine or the people.

That's what this chapter is all about: The data gathering, data storage, and data use by a computer in a manner that efficiently assists the humans on your payroll. In years past, too much information needed regularly was scattered all over the company. A lot was in peoples' heads. . . . a measure of job security, since you had to keep them to get at all that stuff they alone knew. Facts were in briefcases in the trunks of salesmen's cars. Some were scribbled on the pull-out trays of secretaries' desks. There were 3 × 5 cards, kardex cards, supplier catalogs, letters in Accounts Receivables' files, notes pinned to the warehouse bulletin board . . . you name it . . . all with important facts about customers, suppliers, stock, and how to handle them.

HUMAN WORK-TIME IS VALUABLE . . . DON'T WASTE IT!

When employees were paid $3.00 per hour, it may have been cheaper to let them scurry around to find some fact or instruction than to gather it all into one central place. Today, you pay employees a lot more . . . $8, $10, $15, $20 per hour depending upon the job and their responsibility. If you waste *that kind* of time, you'll soon join the ranks of the non-profit (but not by design) organizations! Employees must use their hours doing what they're paid to do, using skills or knowledge that has value. You cannot afford for them to take 10 minutes in a task that should have required 30 seconds . . . looking for information, checking their memory, calling someone to ask, or worse . . . guessing because they don't have the time or inclination to search out the facts.

INFORMATION CLASSIFICATIONS

What information is needed? It falls into four broad classes:

1. Relatively fixed cost elements:
   - Cost of carrying inventory percentage
   - Cost of going through the replenishment cycle
2. Data that changes continually:
   - Usage rates (Discussed in Chapter 6)
   - Lead times from suppliers
   - Prices from suppliers
3. Combination of fixed and dynamic information about items, customers, suppliers:
   - Master inventory records
   - Customer records and special prices
   - Supplier records
4. Dynamic buying and selling facts:
   - Sales order records
   - Purchase order records

Obviously, there's much more needed in a total system, but these information elements are related directly or indirectly to Inventory Management. You'll see how as we move through the chapter.

THE COST OF CARRYING INVENTORY PERCENTAGE ("K" FACTOR)

It's no great revelation that there's a *cost* involved when merchandise is put out in the warehouse! Almost everyone in the company (except the salesmen) recognizes that. Money is invested; space is tied up; insurance premiums come due; tax levies are set by the state; material is stolen; other products become obsolete; people are hired to receive it, put it up, move it around, look for it, count it . . . all "hidden" costs to a degree. The money is spent, but for most of these categories no one ever sees a dollar amount listed separately on a financial operating statement or profit and loss report. The expenses are mixed-in with a bunch of others.

The Cost of Carrying Inventory is very important however. It can't be eliminated as long as a distributor carries inventory (his unique contribution to the business cycle), but it must be *considered* in nearly every inventory decision! Expressed as a percentage of each dollar carried on the average in inventory throughout a full year, the "K" Factor is used in several replenishment-decision calculations.

Think of It as Piranhas

If you need to cross a river in which the fierce piranhas of South America live, you'd do well not to wade or swim. You might become a refreshing treat for the bored little critters. The objective remains the same: To cross the river! How you'll do it, however, considers what's in the water. That's the way it is with the K Factor or Cost. You can't get rid of the costs. They're inherent in business, but *you'd better give consideration* to the fact that they're in your business waters! You must be alert also to how large the "fish" have become; how big a bite they can take out of your business hide. When the prime rate changes, so does K.

In the 50s, the K Cost was goldfish size: 15 percent. When the prime jumped to 21 percent in the early 80s, ol' K jumped too . . . to 45 percent! Great white shark class! Some distributors didn't notice the difference and kept right on wading and swimming just as they had before. They didn't change anything in the way they managed assets and you know what happened to them. As this book is prepared, K is down to something like piranhas. It's still dangerous to profits. Don't ignore it in your inventory decision-making.

What Does "K" Stand For?

"K" Factor is simply the name Inventory Management people have assigned to this cost for 30 years or more to give it a "mystic" character. Who could argue about it or question your vast store of inventory knowledge (or value to the company) when you banter about such an exotic term? "Yes Boss, my latest evaluation of why our inventory is so high indicates that perhaps we've used the wrong K Factor in our EOQ calculations!" It's during those kind of question and answer sessions that I *sure* don't want the boss to know what I'm talking about! . . . so we'll call this cost the K Cost at times during the rest of the book. Every profession needs some secrets. Take a look at the illustration for the K cost calculation.

The Material Handling expense total omits those activities that could be labeled "Sales-Generated" . . . the picking, packing, and shipping/delivery of a customer's order. It does include all people, functions and expense in bringing in material and putting it away, up to the point that the order-filling function starts. For most distributors, the expense segments to include are about 60 percent of the total warehouse and delivery expenses for a year.

Why omit the other activities? They're controlled more by customers than by the distributor. One customer ordering 100 pieces of a stock item is easier and cheaper to take care of than 100 customers wanting one piece each . . . same sales volume but a lot more effort required.

Remember . . . the costs to search out and use are total-company figures for an entire year. Theoretically, each branch or even a product could have a different K Cost but that isn't practical. Develop one K

MORE INFORMATION REQUIRED FOR GOOD INVENTORY CONTROL

CALCULATING THE COST OF CARRYING INVENTORY
ILLUSTRATION—ALL ANNUAL COSTS

Warehouse Space	$130,000
($10,850 per month rental for equivalent space as estimated by local real estate agent)	
Taxes	$ 65,000
(Taxes on Inventory only from Accounting's Records)	
Insurance	$ 40,000
(Premiums for protection of Inventory. Taxes and Insurance expenses for the warehouse are included in the Space costs.)	
Obsolescence and Shrinkage	$ 60,000
(How much was written off at year-end because you couldn't find it, or material was unsalable due to damage or obsolescence?)	
Material Handling	$ 64,800
(The cost of warehouse people and equipment used to receive, put away, move, and count merchandise. Do not include the expenses of order-filling, packing, shipping.)	
Cost of Money Invested	$200,000
(10% Prime Rate × $2,000,000 average inventory)	
TOTAL ANNUAL COSTS	$559,800

$$\frac{\text{Total Annual Costs} = \$559,800}{\text{Average Inventory Value} = \$2,000,000} = 28\% \text{ K Cost}$$

Note: This distributor spends 28¢ for every $1.00 carried in inventory on the average) for a year. The 28% rate becomes part of his calculations for stock replenishment and other special purchasing opportunities. The "K" Cost remains 28% until the calculation is made again the next year. The annual costs used should be total-company figures. The K percentage then applies anywhere in the company.

percentage figure to be used across the entire company and then refigure it just once a year.

The Shortcut Method for Developing Your K Cost Percentage

If this calculation seems too difficult or time-consuming to gather all the numbers, you may elect to use a shortcut method. Simply add 20 percent to the current prime rate for borrowing money and use that answer as your K percentage. You won't be too far off. If the prime rate is 10 percent, the K answer becomes 30 percent, etc. When the prime rate goes up or down by two points, you should alter the K percentage entered in the computer's records.

THE COST OF A REPLENISHMENT CYCLE ("R" COST)

Just as there's a cost to hold inventory in the warehouse, there's also money spent to go through the replenishment cycle on a stock item. First, you must pay for computer time to process all the transactions necessary to "track" an item's condition . . . all the sales, transfers, receipts, returns, cycle counts, etc., that tell you how much stock is available to sell. That stock balance is maintained primarily for two purposes:

1. To be able to commit material to a new customer order, and . . .
2. To start the stock replenishment steps early enough to maintain a continuity of supply . . . no unintentional stockouts.

Therefore, half of the total annual computer time expense needed to track all stock item balances belongs in the Cost of Replenishment. There's Purchasing effort used; Expediting work needed at times; Receiving steps involved; and even Accounts Payable work generated *each time* a buyer decides to go through the replenishment cycle on a stock item. Look at the illustration for the "R" Cost calculation.

How Is the R Cost Used?

In the example the R Cost is $5.00, which means $5.00 of cost spent per item per purchase order. If a P.O. listed 20 stock items, the Replenishment Cycle cost in total is $100.00. The R Cost is an integral part of the

MORE INFORMATION REQUIRED FOR GOOD INVENTORY CONTROL 95

CALCULATING THE COST OF A REPLENISHMENT CYCLE (R COST)

Illustration

One-half the total annual expense of the computer's time needed to maintain accurate balances of merchandise available for sale on all stock items	$ 59,000
The portion of Purchasing Department's annual expense spent looking at reports, making buying decisions, entering purchase orders or transfers. For most distributors, this is between 50% and 75% of the department's total annual budget, since stock purchases account for those percentages of total effort. Be sure to include the cost of office space, telephones, etc.	$120,000
The Annual expense of expediting stock items	$ 6,000
That portion of Account Payable's annual budget (including office space, telephones, etc.) that represents how much of their total time is expended in clearing, processing, writing/calling suppliers about invoices for stock merchandise. Could be 50% of their expense	$194,000
The *Fixed* portion of Receiving's annual expenses devoted to filing paperwork, keying P.O. receipt information, etc. Receiving must perform some steps with every P.O. regardless of the number of items or quantities involved	$ 21,000
Total Annual Costs	$400,000

1. Number of purchase orders created per year for stock   = 10,000
2. Average number of different stock items per order   =   8

Total number of times stock items were ordered (1 × 2) = 80,000

$$\frac{\text{Total Annual Costs}}{\text{Total Times Stock Items Were Ordered}} = \frac{\$400,000}{80,000} = \$5.00 \text{ R Cost}$$

Note: This distributor has spent or will spend a total of $5.00 each time a buyer decides to replenish a stock item. The $5.00 is used in calculations to determine how many to buy at a time (Chapter 10). Like K, the R Cost is a constant applied company-wide.

Economic Order Quantity calculation to be discussed in Chapter 10. It sets a value on the time and trouble necessary to buy an item and bring it in.

The logic for doing this becomes clear when you consider how many items you now have in stock that sell no more than $5.00 to $15.00 at cost during an entire year! If it costs $5.00 to go through a buying cycle, how many times a year does it make sense to do that on such items? 10 times? . . . or 4 times to be sure to get four turns on them? That would be pretty dumb wouldn't it? Better not grin too much until you check how you're ordering stuff like this today. Most Buyers are pressured by factors other than "R." The *president,* however, wants time used productively in Purchasing, Expediting, Receiving, and Accounts Payable. That's what the R Cost expresses. It's designed to help you allocate these efforts and expenses annually across the stock items in a cost-effective manner.

A Shortcut to Arrive at Your R Cost

An accurate R Cost is very difficult to calculate. The cost elements are sort of "gray" in nature . . . hard to search out. Often a distributor omits some portion of the cost or includes something incorrectly, and I've seen R Costs between $.28 and $76.00 . . . both way off! One extreme places almost no value on the cost of a replenishment cycle, while the other places way too much. If you did the job properly, you should wind up in the $4.00 to $6.00 range today. Because of that, I'd suggest that you assign $5.00 as your R Cost and not attempt the difficult calculation. Like "K," "R" is recorded in the computer files for company-wide application.

SUPPLIER LEAD TIMES

A very important data element in Inventory Management is the time required to resupply a stock item when it runs low. Here's the definition:

> Lead Time is the *total amount of time* between the date you recognize the need to reorder an item and the date replenishment merchandise is on the shelf, recorded in the computer and available for sale.

Lead time is *NOT* what the supplier says it is! The number of days or weeks he tells you covers only a portion of the total time represented in the definition above. To the manufacturer, lead time is from " . . . the date we receive your order until the day we ship." Let's say that the supplier tells you his lead time is six weeks, but this is what happens:

MORE INFORMATION REQUIRED FOR GOOD INVENTORY CONTROL 97

- 3 days: elapse from the time that an item's stock condition gets low enough to reorder and the time Purchasing is notified by a computer report.
- 7 days: are required for Purchasing to accumulate enough other items needing replenishment in the product line to meet the supplier's total-order discount.
- 1 day: is used to prepare, check and mail the P.O.
- 4 days: are required in the U.S. mails to get the order to the supplier.
- 42 days: are used by the manufacturer before he can ship the order, but he met his estimate: 6 weeks.
- 10 days: go by while the order is in-transit by rail.
- 1 day: is needed for Receiving paperwork procedures.
- 2 days: are needed for stock put-away and computer file update.

   70 days: total lead time.

70 days—ten full weeks—is the lead time to protect for . . . not six weeks as quoted by the supplier!

The Computer's Calculation of Lead Time

Now having made the big point above, let's revise the lead time definition for programming purposes. Here are the time frames the computer should capture and then use to record lead times:

From the date of purchase order entry to the date of the *first receipt* of material on an item.

Admittedly, this doesn't include those first two time segments above in the complete lead time picture . . . the time delays before the P.O. is actually placed. Don't worry about that. Those delays are covered by other factors in the Inventory Management system offered in this book.

We also must play the odds on receipts . . . that the first one on any stock item will include enough material to stay out of trouble until the balance shows up. You order 100 pieces and 65 come in on the first shipment. The lead time calculation cuts off right then on that item, that purchase order.

The Lead Time Records

A separate lead time is developed for each item on the purchase order. The computer has space for three lead time figures for each stock item:

The last delivery performance; the next-to-last; and then an average of these two. Most of the time, the average lead time is used in the Order Point calculation discussed in the next chapter. Lead time may be recorded in days, weeks, or months . . . it doesn't matter, but when used in the Order Point formula, it must be expressed in months:

```
1 week:  = .25 months    4 weeks: = 1.0  months
2 weeks: = .5  months    5 weeks: = 1.25 months    etc.
3 weeks: = .75 months    6 weeks: = 1.5  months
```

The usage rate in the formula is in months; the lead time must also be expressed in months, for the answer to be correct. Assume a 4-week month, rather than the actual 4.333 weeks. This has the effect of building a small amount of extra safety into the system.

Exceptions to the Use of an Average Lead Time

Like usage, there are exceptional situations that can occur with lead times. They bounce around so much and are so difficult to predict with accuracy that many systems make no attempt at all to calculate them. The system designers simply instruct the buyers: "You people tell us what lead times to use on all items; we'll plug those into the computer; and then use your estimates in any calculations!"

You can guess how that works. The poor buyer isn't about to list 543 different lead times just because the company stocks 543 items in a supplier's product line. He replies: "Just use 30 days on everything!" But that's too long on some items, too short on others. The supplier has more trouble on some items than others, and soon the distributor does too.

But when the computer tries to develop individual item lead times, it can run into strange occurrences and introduce serious "trash" into the replenishment control calculations you'll see in the next chapter. Here are the times when an average lead time is *NOT* developed from the last two delivery performances on an item:

1. When the next-to-last recorded lead time is over six months old. That's too far into the past to provide much help in anticipating what will occur in the time period just ahead. Use the last recorded lead time only (no average) in the order point formula.
2. When the new average (developed with the first-receipt of each new P.O. for this item) turns out to be 50 percent shorter or longer than the previous average. The newest delivery performance on the item is so bizarre, compared to what occurred before, that it caused a 50 percent change in the average lead time used earlier.

MORE INFORMATION REQUIRED FOR GOOD INVENTORY CONTROL

When condition 2 occurs, the computer inserts a flag in the file and makes no attempt to recompute the lead time or any of the other replenishment controls for this item. At month-end, the item is listed on an exception report for the buyer's review. The computer says in effect:

> Hey human, I don't know what to do with this item's lead time. Something very unusual seems to have happened the last time we got some in. Take a look at what occurred and tell me what lead time to use. Until then, I'll make no changes to the item's ordering controls.

Tell the Computer Upfront: "Ignore Lead Time!"

One small programming enhancement can prevent lead time trash right at the outset of a new purchase order. Add a field to the purchase order header screen labeled: "Ignore Lead Time." When the buyer is bringing in material by an unusual path (air freight, UPS, buying from a local warehouse or competitor, etc.), he inserts a code in this field to instruct the computer:

> Do not attempt to capture a lead time on this purchase order. I'm getting the material this time by an unusual method or from an unusual source. The lead time will be very short (or very long . . . overseas purchase). I do not want this lead time considered in the average calculation for this stock item.

"Goodnight . . . what a lot of trouble!" you say? Well, you can always do what distributors have done for years to avoid this kind of effort: Carry a warehouse jammed with inventory! Lead times are important. The computer (with your help once in a while) can capture and use them to guide replenishment action that achieves good service without loading the warehouse.

MASTER INVENTORY RECORDS

Some of you are old enough to remember the old kardex files, those handposted records that contained a wealth of information about your stock items. When the computer arrived, the manual cards became obsolete, but the data they held, and the function they served, is still very important. The computer needs a file to collect "everything you need to know about a stock item anywhere in the company you find it." Well, what do you need to know? Two different types of information: Fixed and Variable.

Fixed Information about a Stock Item

Some information about an item is the same no matter which branch stocks it:

- Part number
- Unit of measure (EA, LBS, etc.)
- Standard package
- Product category (Accounting code)
- Price break quantities for customers
- Supplier's quantity breaks and prices
- Description
- Supplier's part number
- Master carton quantity
- Package weight or cube
- Selling price (list)
- Date record established

You could argue reasonably about some of them, but basically these facts remain the same no matter where an item is located. It carries the same part number, description, unit, etc., everywhere. It weighs the same, has the same standard package quantity, and is in the same selling category.

There may be other information in your company or industry that qualifies as "fixed" for stock items, but whatever the list, the key objective is to store this data *just one time* in the computer files! If 10 branches stock an item, the fixed data is stored once. There are 10 additional files with the "variable" information to be discussed next. I sometimes catch flak from data processing types when I make this point. They argue: "Shoot, Graham, computer file space is cheap today. You don't have to be so careful about repeating the fixed data with each branch record!" True, file space is cheaper than in the past, but why waste it through lousy systems design or lazy programming?

Let's say that you stock 50,000 items, with a different mix in each of seven branches. The total SKUs (stockkeeping units . . . items times places you stock them) are 140,000. The average branch carries 20,000 items. How much file space would be needed to repeat 200 characters (or bytes) of data 140,000 times instead of just 50,000? The fixed information should be recorded for each of the 50,000 items *once!* Each of the seven branches that stock one specific item have a separate record of "variable" data about the item, tied to the one fixed data file. Clear? . . . probably not, unless you're a programmer or data processing manager.

Think of it this way: It's more economical to have one engine pull a long train of freight cars than for each freight car to have it's own engine. That's not the greatest example, but it illustrates the point. Valuable computer space is wasted when the fixed data is repeated in each branch record. If you have only a single location, it's not a problem (yet). If you stock 50,000 in seven branches, it's a doozie!

MORE INFORMATION REQUIRED FOR GOOD INVENTORY CONTROL 101

Variable Information

What qualifies as "variable" information? The facts about a stock item that vary from one branch to another:

- Quantity on hand
- Quantity committed to orders
- The available-for-sale balance
- Quantity on order with suppliers
- Quantity backordered to customers
- Usage history by month
- Usage rate per month
- Seasonal item identifier
- Product line review cycle
- Line point
- Date record established
- Date last out of stock
- Number of stockouts, last 12 mos.
- Total sales, year-to-date
- Total sales, year-to-date last year
- Warehouse storage location(s)
- Unit cost
- LIFO cost
- Next cost to be paid
- Inventory movement class
- Order point or minimum
- Order quantity or maximum
- Lead time average
- Lead time—last delivery
- Lead time—prior delivery
- Date of last cycle count
- Date of last sale
- Date of last receipt
- Number of picks, year-to-date
- Frozen control flag

Do you see the difference between this and the fixed information? These facts *do change* from one branch to the next! Each company location has a different usage rate for the same item, a different usage history, different replenishment controls, etc. This is a much longer record, with many more characters of storage space, than is needed for the fixed data file.

Variable Length Records and Versatile Operating Systems

The list above is by no means exhaustive. You may think of several other data elements for your variable record design. The better systems work with "variable-length" records or operating systems that permit additional facts to be captured and retained later. It's nearly impossible to think of everything you'll need in these files or the ones discussed next.

Systems that use "fixed-length" records permit no additions if you run out of space, requiring a deletion if something is added that was overlooked earlier, or waste space by reserving lots of room *in every record* for the facts everyone knows will be thought of later. "Space is cheap!" is the battle-cry of poor systems designers. If you forget that, you'll wind up with a system costing much more than it should.

Replace the Kardex Transaction Detail with an Inquiry

Before leaving the discussion of the Master Inventory Records, let's touch on one of my pet peeves: The lack of visibility with a computer of all that wonderful detail available in the old manual kardex-type systems. You could walk over to the kardex, flip open a record, and there was a super playback of who was buying the item, how often, the quantities, dates, when the last purchase order was placed, when the stuff came in, the last cost paid, and the buyer's birthday if you wanted it . . . a wealth of information captured by computers but much tougher (in most systems) to see on demand.

Your buyers *used* that detail often. They needed it then. They need it now! A myriad of questions can be answered about a stock item quickly when the track record detail is visible. Without it, having to get along with just a "snapshot" look at the file (the current controls, cost, history totals, etc.), the buyers fly a bit blind. The oldtimers still scream: "Give us the kardex back!" . . . and you can. A few systems already have.

Program an Inquiry Screen that brings up for display the last 30, 60, or whatever, transactions on a stock item. You'll see the receipts, the outgoing sales or transfers, the balances . . . back for 30 transactions, just as you could with the kardex. Show the detail: Customer name, sales order number, quantity, date, etc. It's probably wise to base it on a certain number of transactions, rather than the past 30 days, because some items might sell hundreds of times in 30 days; others not at all.

In Chapter 6's discussion of Usage calculations, you'll recall that there's often a need to find out which customer made an unusually large purchase, or to find items where one customer dominates the usage patterns. The "kardex" inquiry gives back to buyers, salesmen, or managers a valuable information source that they lost when computers took over.

MANUFACTURER-SUPPLIER (VENDOR) RECORDS

This file, in the same fashion as for stock, carries all the facts about a supplier: "Everything you will ever need to know about the manufacturer!" . . . and you know where a lot of this information has been up until now. In catalogs, filing cabinets, on price list sheets, in Accounts Payable, and Purchasing's desks. For example:

- Supplier account number
- Address for payables
- Address(es) for purchase orders
- Name
- Payment terms
- Expediting contact name

MORE INFORMATION REQUIRED FOR GOOD INVENTORY CONTROL 103

- Telephone number: Home office
- Local salesman's name
- Salesman's address and phone number
- Total-order discount schedule
- Rules on restocking charges
- Purchases: Year-to-date
- Purchases: Year-to-date, last year
- Percent of total purchases, this year
- Percent of total purchases, last year
- Stock item class breakdown
    (How many class 1, 2, 4, 10, etc?)
- Percent of inventory investment
    in dead/slow moving class
- Number of P.O. First shipments
    arriving past due date
- Percent: Late shipments to
    total shipments
- Computer tape or disc available for
    pricing update? (Yes/No)
- Next prices to be paid: Stock items

- Expediting phone number
- Minimum acceptable order
- Freight-paid order reqmt.
- Annual return provisions
- Product line review cycle
- Number of items stocked
- Inventory investment ($)

% TO TOTAL INVENTORY INVESTMENT

The list could go on. In your company or industry, you may need information not listed above. Just be sure that with this file too, you permit expansion or keep some space reserved for data you'll want to add after the system has been in place for a while.

CUSTOMER RECORDS

Just as for suppliers, there's a wealth of information needed about your customers. The computer offers a central storage method for accumulation of facts needed to guide sales planning, order processing, invoicing, payment processing or collection, and management decisions:

- Customer's account number
- Billing address
- Tax code(s)
- SIC code(s)
- Primary servicing branch(es)
- Contact name: Purchase orders
- P.O. contact telephone number
- Contact name: Receivables
- Receivable contact phone number

- Name
- Shipping address(es)
- Credit limit
- Permits backorders? (Yes/No)
- Current receivable total ($)
- Past-due amount ($)
- Your assigned outside salesman
- Your assigned inside salesman
- Date of last purchase

- Sales ($), year-to-date
- Sales ($), YTD, last year
- Returns ($), year-to-date
- Returns ($), YTD, last year
- Average dollar sale per order
- Overall customer rank: Purchase $
- Customer rank: Margin $
- Date file first established
- Requires job number controls? (Yes/No)
- Customer quoted special prices? (Yes/No)
- Requires P.O. numbers on invoices? (Yes/No)
- Special routing/shipping/delivery instructions
- Margin ($), year-to-date
- Margin ($), YTD, last year
- Margin %, year-to-date
- Margin %, YTD, last year
- Average margin $ per order
- Special inventory $ invested
- Special inventory turn rate

Programmers sometimes argue that it isn't necessary to carry all the year-to-date figures as running totals. They can be tabulated by a query program, for example, when you need them . . . and that's true, but the morass of detail the computer would have to find and sort is mountainous. A query request for some of these facts requires more computer power and time than you'd want to expend. Better that you tabulate them as you go, month by month, and have them ready for a much simpler (and faster) query effort.

Again, the list above isn't exhaustive. You may need other facts about your customers, so leave room in the file for these additions.

CUSTOMERS' SPECIAL PRICES FILE

Special prices quoted to customers by category, individually, or in accord with quantities ordered can do more harm than good if administered poorly. When some item is mis-priced a couple of times in a row, the customer narrows who he'll talk to when he calls: "Let me have Jack. He's the only one of you guys who gets my prices right!"

The computer should solve this problem, but this is another of those topics that I won't harp on long. Several of the better packaged systems have addressed the pricing function very successfully. Through "matrix" pricing or some other technique, prices may be quoted many different ways. Here are the main principles to follow in your system:

1. If a customer has been quoted special prices, permanently or with expiration dates, these prices must be recorded in the computer. Anyone can take the order. The computer will price the items correctly. No longer can a salesman make "informal" quotations. If you quote it, then the item, price, and conditions *must* be recorded!

2. The special prices file may contain quotations on other than stock items. If a non-stock item is quoted, record the item, price, and conditions. It's usually wise to add an expiration date and be sure the customer understands the limited-time nature of the quote.
3. Always try to quote individual items (outside of an already established pricing category) by coming down a percentage from the manufacturer's suggested list price or up a percentage from your cost. Enter the quote as the percentage into the computer.
4. Program the computer to use these percentages to calculate the stand-alone item special prices. Supplier's often provide computer-to-computer tapes or discs with their latest cost structure or suggested list prices. Where they don't, you still have a cost recorded for each stocked item. When the supplier changes prices, the computer can change not only your regular pricing structure but all special-quote prices also.

SALES ORDER RECORDS

"Everything you might need to know about a customer's order . . . from the time it's entered until he finally pays for all merchandise!" That's a summary of what's needed in the record established in the computer for every sales order. You want to pull from the Customer Record or ask for a lot of information when the order is received and keyed-in. You want the ability to retrieve quickly and display the order or any portion of it when there's a question, or when the customer expedites, or to add/change/delete something.

There Are Some Basics, But Everybody Needs a Few Unique Fields

With sales order records, I recognize that it's impossible to list precisely every field or data element you'll want to capture. Plumbing and heating distributors will need a few facts, perhaps, that a building materials guy doesn't need. Electronic distributors, selling to original equipment manufacturers, might require information that's useless to a mill supply house.

Those fields listed below are the basics. Nearly everybody needs these or most of them for an order. There could well be over 100 other optional data elements required by one distributor or another in bearings, paper, safety, electric supply, welding supply, industrial, steel service, power transmission, fluid power, office supplies, truck parts, specialty tools, fasteners, auto parts, floor coverings, material handling equipment, construction equipment, florist supply, air conditioning and refrigeration, pipe/valves/fittings, wheel and rim, shoe service, rubber products, plastics, wall coverings, beauty and barber supply, liquor wholesalers, or one of the other durable goods industries. Don't be too critical of my file structure below. Sales orders can require unique features in a particular industry.

Sales Order Heading Information

Some information about an order pertains to the whole thing, while other facts relate to one item only. The Sales Order Heading record has the data that applies to the order in total:

- Sales order number
- Date received from customer
- Customer's account number
- Customer's name
- Billing address
- Shipping address
- Customer's P.O. number
- Job number or name
- Taxable/Non-taxable
- Date material is required
- Routing/Shipping instructions
- Special instructions: This order only
- Backorders permitted this order? (Yes/No)

- Person placing the order
- Payment terms
- Freight terms (Outbound)
- Freight terms (Inbound)
- Order-handling code:
  - Regular order
  - Direct-ship
  - Ship-complete
  - Tag and hold
  - Future date
  - Will-call

The better systems allow you to enter this information or override data displayed from the customer's record on *one single screen* for an order. Old-fashioned systems may require two, three, or more screens just to record the heading. Speed of entry is vital. The cursor (bright dot on a screen that positions the next letter or number keyed) should not stop at a field, asking for information, if the computer *already knows the answer!* Example: The customer's tax status. If it's different for some reason on this order, the operator may go back and correct the entry, but the computer pulls the code from the customer's file and inserts it. The cursor stops only where information is needed that the computer does not know.

Transfers from branch to branch have "heading" information also, but the data needed is considerably less than for sales orders. With intracompany activity, the computer knows nearly everything necessary except

MORE INFORMATION REQUIRED FOR GOOD INVENTORY CONTROL

the shipping branch; the receiving location; any freight (bus, etc.) or other handling charges.

Line Item Detail Information

This segment of a sales order's record contains the data unique to a single item:

- Item number
- Description
- Unit of measure
- Customer's part number
- Quantity ordered
- Selling price
- Unit cost
- Accounting or sales category
- Special instructions—This item only
- Shipping history (quantities, dates, invoice numbers, etc.)
- Customer's payment history

- Code to dictate handling:
  - Stock—Substitute OK
  - Stock—No substitute
  - Non-stock item
  - Stock—Handle as non-stock
  - Surplus—No history posting
  - "Found" item

As with heading information, the computer *knows* much of this information on the stock items. Once an item number is entered, many of the other facts are filled-in automatically. The order-taker may override them if something is different (selling price, etc.). For non-stocks the computer knows nothing, and all required fields must be keyed.

The Line Item Handling Codes

One element may be new to you: The handling code inserted by the computer or keyed for each separate line on the order. Most of the time, the computer simply inserts the code based on the item ordered and instructions from this customer's file. If a customer doesn't allow substitutes, then the appropriate code is tied to any stock items that customer orders. . . . but once in a while an item may be so critical that the customer sets aside his restriction: "I've got to have this item or one that will work! Ship anything you have that will do the job!" The order-taker can override the usual non-sub code with the code that says "subs OK," . . . or it could work the reverse way: Most of the time subs are permitted, but not on this item for this one order.

The surplus stock code is inserted by the computer when an item sells that was categorized previously as dead or slow-moving, or the order-taker can insert it. The objective? To avoid posting the activity in the item's sales history, or at least causing the computer to ignore the sale when a future usage rate is calculated. How many times have you seen a dog item finally sell, only to have some dodo buy it back because the history showed new activity?

"Found" Items Should Be Handled . . . But Be Careful!

A "Found" item is a non-stock that just turns up in inventory and you can sell it on a one-time basis. Ol' Harry (a salesman) comes back to the office one day after wandering around the warehouse:

> Where in the world did we get that old ABC Industries Motor 486X? A customer asked me about one of those just the other day. Shoot, I didn't think we could get that motor anymore. I'll call that guy and see if he still wants it!

That's a "found" item. It's non-stock; there's no computer file on the thing; nobody knows (or will confess to) where it came from; and yet you can *sell it!* It's a one-time deal. You certainly don't want to go to all the trouble of setting up a formal computer record, but with non-stock items the computer thinks you have to buy or transfer them in before they can be sold. Not this time. The "Found" code tells the computer:

> This is a non-stock item for which we have inventory. Go ahead and indicate that I may ship the quantity I will enter as 'ordered.' I must also provide all the other information (description, unit, price, cost) since you know nothing about this product.

Found items are a bit dangerous. If they pop up frequently, it indicates very sloppy disciplines or someone trying to sidestep one of the most important system controls . . . not permitting the purchase of a non-stock item unless it's first been sold. You need the capability to process one within the system, but a lot of questions should be answered when one turns up.

PURCHASE ORDER RECORDS

Records are needed for purchase orders to suppliers just as for sales orders from customers. The purchase orders, too, have two segments to each file established in the computer: Heading and Line Item Detail. . . . and here again, the list that follows doesn't have every data

MORE INFORMATION REQUIRED FOR GOOD INVENTORY CONTROL

element needed by distributors in all the various durable goods industries. They're the basics.

Purchase Order Heading Information

- Purchase order number
- Date P.O. is entered
- Purchasing branch
- Ship-to branch or address
- Supplier number
- Supplier name
- Supplier address
- Payment terms
- Freight terms
- Requested ship-date
- Routing instructions
- Special instructions that apply to the entire order

- Order-handling code:
  - Regular P.O.
  - Direct-shipment
  - Split-delivery
  - Blanket order
  - Accumulative P.O.
  - Special purchase
- Confirming P.O.? (Yes/No)
- Person accepting order

The Order-Handling Codes

Some of the order-handling codes may be for P.O. types with which you're not familiar or perhaps call by some other name. Direct-Shipment may be "Drop-Ship" to you. Those and Accumulative P.O.'s were discussed in Chapter 3. A Split-Delivery P.O. is accepted in one piece by the supplier, but he agrees to ship portions to different branches. Internally, you'd do well to assign P.O. number suffixes to each separate ship-to segment. The basic P.O. is Number 20460; Branch 1's portion is 20460A; Branch 2's is 20460B, etc., . . . and negotiate with the supplier to invoice it that way! A multitude of paperwork problems are solved if he will. I've seen distributors who were forced to bring in all material to one location for redistribution, because the entire order was invoiced as a unit and they couldn't straighten out all the receipt vs. invoice steps when the stuff went direct.

Blanket Orders are similar in that the basic P.O. goes in as one big unit. Portions are to be shipped on different dates rather than to different destinations. Again, each "release" (items and quantities scheduled to ship together) should be assigned P.O. Number suffixes: P.O. Number 10570 is the blanket order; Release 1 for May 20 Ship-date is 10570-01; Release 2 for June 20 is 10570-02, etc.

Special Purchases: Pre-Season, Dating, Promotions

Special purchases are those made under pre-season, dating, or promotional pricing/payment terms and the supplier either has requested that the

P.O. be entered separately . . . or you wish to do so to alert him to the special pricing or payment provisions. Often these orders cannot be "priced-out" by the computer as it might for regular purchases. The code in the heading tells the computer not to try . . . that prices will be entered for each item.

Many distributors today do not actually mail a copy of the P.O. to the supplier. Orders are telephoned-in or entered via a computer-to-computer hookup, which saves time, reduces the overall lead time (sometimes significantly), and may even reduce errors. The computer-to-computer entry systems ("EDX" for electrical distributors, "REDINET" for NIDA/SIDA, etc.) also permit stock availability and price checks as orders are entered. The Confirming Order (Yes/No) field may become obsolete before too long.

Purchase Order Line Item Detail

- Part number
- Supplier's part number if different
- Sales order and line number for non-stock item
- Description
- Unit of measure (the inventory units *you* use)
- Quantity ordered (expressed in your units)
- Price per unit that you expect to pay
- Supplier's ordering unit (if different from yours)
- Quantity ordered (expressed in supplier's units)
- Price per supplier's unit
- Special instructions, this item only
- Expected receipt date for this item (due date)
- Supplier's shipment history (quantities, dates, invoice no.s)
- Your payment history

Carrying both your part number and the supplier's in the computer record for this item allows an inquiry by either number. Note also that the part number and description for a non-stock item are recorded in this file. They are *not keyed in entry,* however. The sales order and line number on which the item is sold is entered. The computer then copies to this P.O. line item file the identical part number and description found on that sales order and line number.

The two different units of measure are necessary when you stock a product under one unit but are required to order it by another. Example: You stock and sell files as each's, but the supplier requires that they be ordered as dozens. The P.O. line reads 12 *dozen* priced by the dozen,

MORE INFORMATION REQUIRED FOR GOOD INVENTORY CONTROL 111

and the supplier is satisfied. However, when the merchandise arrives, you want to receive 144 into inventory, costed as each's. The P.O. appears one way; the Receiving paperwork has your units shown.

Each line item on the P.O. has (at least potentially) a different expected receipt date from the supplier. The entire order very well may all arrive at one time, but remember . . . each stock item has its own individually calculated lead time developed from past performances. The projected due date is often different for each item on the order. This is transparent to the supplier. He is expected to ship everything as soon as he can or in accord with instructions, but for stockout control each item has a different anticipated lead time.

Let the Computer Do Most of the Work!

Let's repeat a vital point: All the information listed in the records for sales orders and purchase orders is not keyed at order entry! Any fact available from one of the permanent files is retrieved by the computer and inserted. Customer or supplier names and addresses, item descriptions, units for stock items, selling prices, or costs, accounting categories, standing instructions from customers . . . all are examples of data that wastes time and invites error if re-entered with each new order.

SUMMARY

Does your system capture all this information? Can you see how such facts are needed to answer customers' questions or take their orders quickly? Are your Sales, Purchasing, and Operational people more productive because of the system's help? Can they stay at their desks and get needed information or do they chase around the building looking first in this file drawer, next running over to talk to that person? Do they make better decisions? Faster decisions?

Or do you have to carry a big inventory in the warehouse as a "buffer," because you have incomplete data that's difficult to retrieve? Do your buyers rely on oversized stock levels to compensate for a computerized system that makes their jobs more difficult than before (kardex gone but SWAG still required, etc.)? Had you thought of the various order-handling codes and programming needed? Or the different ways a sales order line item may have to be processed? Or do your people regularly "go around the system" to handle an order because the system can't?

As we move on now into the guts of an effective Inventory Management system, the replenishment timing and quantity controls, remember this:

1. It won't matter which formula is applied, or what principle is adopted in the calculations . . . if the data used is incomplete, too old, mostly SWAG, or generated by a system designed in 1970. The answers will be lousy.

2. If people must work in an unproductive manner, performing steps the computer should have performed, then their time is wasted.
They *still* must make inventory decisions and they will! The decisions will be hastily made, important checks offered in the next chapters will be omitted, and the potential benefits will not be realized. The workday contains just so many hours. People shouldn't spend them in "grunt" work. That's the computer's job.

That's why this chapter is important. The information gathering steps are fundamental to what lies ahead.

8

YOUR SERVICE CONTROL: WHEN TO ORDER!

Inventory control, for distributors, boils down to how five important questions are answered:

1. What causes a new item to be stocked?
2. When should replenishment stock for an item be ordered?
3. How much of an item should be ordered at a time?
4. When is it smart to save freight or buy the truckload?
5. When should an item cease to be carried in stock?

Each question must be answered before you complete this book. Each is very important. This chapter's goal is Question 2: "When should I order?"

THE MOST MISUNDERSTOOD ASPECT OF INVENTORY MANAGEMENT

Remember the two objectives of a solid inventory control system: To provide the best possible customer service within the restraint of the lowest practical inventory costs. These are worthy goals, but unfortunately many distributors do not understand how the answers to Questions 2 and 3 affect the two targets. Good service is primarily the result of *ordering at the right time!* How many you purchase has some effect on service, but not nearly as much as *when* you order! The "How Many?" answer primarily impacts turnover. True . . . there's some impact by each answer on the opposite objective, but it's minor. Eighty percent of the service impact results from purchase order timing; 80 percent of the turnover impact results from quantities purchased.

You would be dismayed at how few distributor executives understand this. When the company has a service problem, the president walks into Purchasing and says:

> The salesmen are complaining that we keep running out of the important items. I want you people to increase the order quantities. Buy *more* of the good stuff! That ought to help.

What will this accomplish? Very little, from a service standpoint. Oh, temporarily, things will look a bit better when the larger quantities show up. Ultimately, you'll still run out because stockouts are the result of improper order *timing* . . . not improper quantities. The larger orders will do one thing, however: Balloon the inventories in total!

Proper Replenishment Timing

So let's talk about replenishment timing on a stock item. Keep in mind that inventory *control* is exercised when an item is ordered. If that activity is poorly done, everything done later falls in the category of inventory *correction!* . . . like having to dispose of dead or slow-moving stock. True "control" occurs right at the beginning when carefully-timed replenishment triggers incoming quantities that develop the lowest practical outgoing costs (as you'll see in Chapter 10). If the "When?" and "How Much?" questions are answered effectively, there isn't as much need later for massive dead stock programs, repositioning exercises that move material to other company locations, substitutions, conversions, and all the other expensive corrective steps distributors employ regularly.

The Foundation Must Be There . . . Complete Information And Accuracy!

The information elements discussed in Chapters 6 and 7, and the accuracy encouraged in Chapter 14, are developed or calculated to help you make the two primary ordering decisions with the best odds for success. Usage expected in months ahead, anticipated lead times, unit costs, costs for holding inventory and for "getting" it . . . all play a role. You'll see this information feed into simple (but effective) formulas to guide the replenishment decisions. "Why go to so much trouble?" you ask. Because these vital decisions must no longer be left to SWAG (Scientific, Wild-Ass Guessing) if both service and inventory turns are to improve.

   As stated earlier, each decision (When or How Much) has a different objective. Service improves when material is ordered *at the right time*. You don't run out of stock. Customers find that you nearly always have the merchandise when they order one of your stock items. They gain confidence in your company and increase your share of their business. Conversely, *how many* you order from the supplier impacts inventory size primarily. This is important. I'm not through repeating it.

How the Decisions Work Together

Here's an illustration. You stock an item that sells 100 per month and requires one month for resupply from the manufacturer. An opening order point (discussed in a moment) is 150 . . . the usage rate of 100 times the lead time of 1 month plus a safety factor. If this item can be purchased in a stand-alone manner, you wait until the total of stock on hand and on order drops to 150 . . . and then place a new purchase order. You can bring in 10 pieces at a time and not run out of stock, *IF* you keep placing a new order for 10 each time the combination of on-hand plus on-order reaches 150.

On the other hand, you can bring in 1,000 at a time, but if you've waited too long to order, the 1,000 arrives too late. You'll run out of stock and have stock that lasts about 10 months. Do you see the relationship? The two decisions achieve different goals: Order-Timing determines the service level; Order-Quantities impact turnover.

Customers Are Very Single-Minded!

The customers don't care how many you buy of an item. They care whether or not you have it when they order! Proper replenishment *timing* provides this protection! If you fall victim to the classic misunderstanding of which ordering decision affects service and which one affects costs, you'll make serious mistakes trying to manage inventories. It's "timing" that controls service.

THE ORDER POINT

Because distributors are primarily "selling" companies, customer service on stock items assumes a vital degree of importance. Every distributor should be sales *oriented* . . . but there's a thin line between that and being sales *dominated!* Always keep in mind the *twin* objectives: Good service with profitable turnover! We're now going to zero-in on service-improvement techniques, but they are always tempered by turnover requirements.

Still, if you *had* to favor one objective over the other, most distributors would agree that service gets the nod. Solid replenishment timing, based on properly developed order points, is the place to apply proven control techniques first. It's better to get the wrong quantity in when you need it than the right quantity after it's too late! The customers' needs (service) get the edge over turnover objectives (costs) as the place to begin a new system of controls. Then, we'll work on order quantities.

The Basis for Replenishment Timing

Order points and line points (discussed in the next chapter) are the service controls. They maintain a continuity of stock. Ask any of your salespeople how important that is to them. "Would you get more upset if we had too much of item 643C (their biggest customer's favorite item) or if we run out?" They'd think you were nuts for even asking such a dumb question.

What Exactly Is an Order Point?

An order point is the basis for replenishment timing on most stocked items in a distributor's inventory when he replenishes stock from sources outside the company. Notice, I said *the basis!* Some form of order point is needed on all items, either set arbitrarily or calculated. Many items require an additional higher control to help put "line buys" (freight-free orders, etc.) together, but that higher control is *based* on the order point. We'll talk about Line Points in Chapter 9.

An order point is a reference point. That is very important. It's an amount of material below which you should not go—on hand plus on order already with the supplier—without starting the replenishment process. It's a reference point, not necessarily a quantity of stock on hand. It's a point of reference against which the combined total of stock on hand *plus* material already on order with the supplier is compared, to decide whether or not more stock must be ordered.

Don't Be Confused on This

Order points often cause confusion for distributors. They get them mixed up with "minimums." The purchasing manager sees an order point of 50 on an expensive item with a long lead time and concludes: "That's ridiculous. We've never carried a minimum of more than 10 on that item. We'd *never* keep 50 on the shelf when it costs that much!" . . . and he's right. He's *wrong* as to how an order point works. The 50 is a reference point, against which the total of on-hand stock *plus* all open purchase orders (and there could be several staggered out weeks apart)

YOUR SERVICE CONTROL: WHEN TO ORDER!

for the item is compared. True, 50 pieces would never be on the shelf . . . but the correct order point might very definitely be 50.

Do you see the difference? In a "Min/Max" system (which often suits branch resupply from a central warehouse), the on-hand stock is generally all that's compared to the minimum to trigger replenishment. It isn't necessary to consider material "on order" because there usually isn't any. The internal company warehouse sends replenishment stock to the branch very quickly . . . in a day or two, each week, etc. An order point, however, is designed to serve locations who buy direct from the manufacturers. Those sources outside the company aren't so dependable and the lead times are longer. There can be outstanding quantities still undelivered when it's time to trigger still another purchase. The order point is compared to the *total* of what's on hand and on-order . . . not just on-hand.

It's an Important Point . . . Especially if You Have Branches

Lest you think I'm making too much of this difference, I've seen a number of systems develop far more inventory than was needed or run out of stock repeatedly, because the people or the computer overlooked the on-order quantities when triggering replenishment . . . or applied order points in the branches resupplied from regional warehouses. You'll read more in Chapter 16 about the proper application of controls for branches. It's often the little mistakes that cause a system to misfire or fail, and a systems designer could overlook a small detail like this unless he or she was quite familiar with inventory management.

Dependent versus Independent Demand

About now, a few inventory control "purists" are thinking: "Graham is really behind the times. Order points are old-fashioned. There are much better tools available today . . . like DRP (Distribution Requirements Planning)." Hmmm . . . well, there *is* a place for DRP, but it's not for the average distributor. DRP is an adaptation of MRP (Material Requirements Planning) used by manufacturers. Manufacturers enjoy a benefit in planning production known as "dependent" demand. If they start 100 assemblies down a production line today, they know precisely when every component is needed in assembly and in what quantity. The demand for components is *dependent* on when assembly begins and how many units are planned. MRP is a computerized technique that schedules each component to arrive at the proper point on the production line "just in time" (Japanese Kanban system).

"Physical Distribution" Is Not Necessarily Wholesale Distribution

DRP was born in "physical distribution" where some elements of dependent demand are present. "Physical Distribution" is defined as a manufacturer getting his products to the market, using his own warehouses, etc. Often, warehouse demand on the manufacturer has dependent characteristics forced into the situation. The warehouse must forecast their needs and can order only within specified limits around this forecast; they may order only once a week or twice a month; or they have limitations on how they may order a particular item. These restrictions allow the manufacturer to use a form of MRP to plan inventories to supply his warehouses' needs. That's DRP . . . but it doesn't fit "wholesale distribution" . . . those who must prepare for *independent* demand. They cannot dictate to their customers when, what, or how many they order. Imagine telling one of your customers:

> Sorry, Edgar . . . this isn't your day to order! . . . or no, you can't have 100 of that item. You forecasted a need for only 50 in this period. You can have 50!

Wholesale distributors must prepare for uncontrollable (but not entirely unpredictable) demand the customers place on their inventories. DRP breaks down if applied here, because it *must* have some restrictions or limits on usage if it's to perform well. Order points are designed to handle independent demand.

Please . . . No More Adaptations from Other Businesses!

This long-winded explanation was necessary. For years, distributors suffered through computerized systems that were nothing more than warmed-over manufacturing adaptations. It seemed to take forever for the major system suppliers to recognize the need for systems that solved the pure distributor's headaches . . . and here we are in danger of that same old thinking: "Hey, you dumb distributors. DRP works for us here in manufacturing as we distribute our products to our warehouses (official industry name for this: Physical Distribution). What's the matter with you? Why can't you use it?"

Sorry, but you don't really understand the wholesale distribution industry. It's not physical distribution. It's just plain *distribution* . . . and there's a whopping difference! Order points have been

YOUR SERVICE CONTROL: WHEN TO ORDER! 119

around for a while, but there's a good reason: They're still the most-effective controls for the distributor who must accommodate independent demand. Be sure to check out the credentials of anyone suggesting something else. Has that person ever worked in *wholesale* distribution . . . or are you being offered warmed-over stuff from some other business environment?

THE ORDER POINT FORMULA

All solid order point formulas include three basic elements:

Order point = (Usage rate × Lead time) + Safety allowance

Let's convert that to everyday language:

The order point consists of enough material (usage rate) to take care of customers during the time required to get more stock (lead time), plus a measured amount of "pad" (safety allowance).

There's not much argument about this basic formula, but there's all measure of disagreement about how each of the elements should be computed. Back in Chapter 6, you encountered the usage rate calculation, so you know that there are as many usage forecasting techniques (exponential smoothing, etc.) as forecasters. In Chapter 7, you learned that figuring anticipated lead times accurately is often difficult . . . but usage and lead time are the "prime movers" of the order point formula. As tough as they are, you *do* know how to compute each one, if you digested the discussions in Chapters 6 and 7.

The Safety Allowance Is Very Important

Notice, however, that usage and lead time are not alone in the formula. If they were, and no safety allowance were added, your service level would be about 50 percent! Why? . . . because both usage rate and lead time are developed as averages: Using six history months and the last two delivery performances. Averages are derived from highs and lows. What happens the next time you replenish an item and encounter a high-usage month *or* a longer delivery? With no safety . . . stockout! Of course, you might hit a low-usage month or short delivery. Funny thing about the safety allowance . . . half the time you need it and half the time you don't! But who knows which half it'll be the next time you reorder? Here's an illustration:

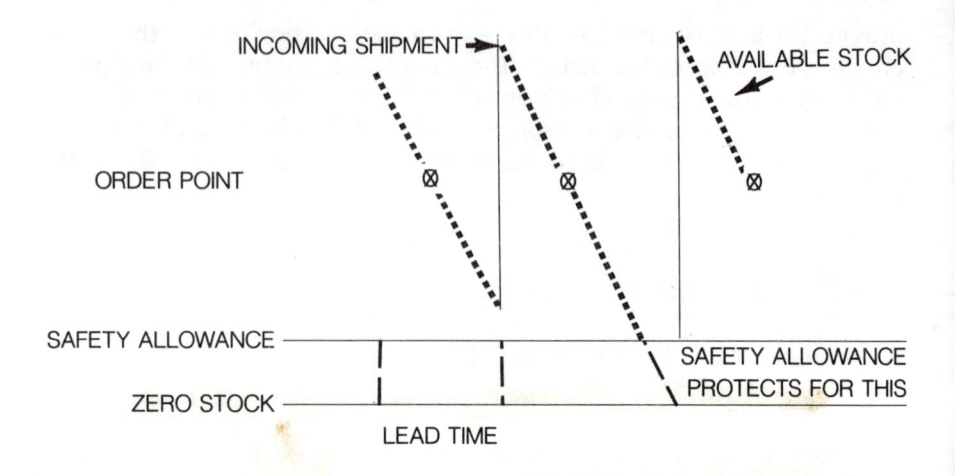

```
                    INCOMING SHIPMENT →         AVAILABLE STOCK
                                                      ←
ORDER POINT              ⊗         ⊗          ⊗

SAFETY ALLOWANCE ─────┬─────┬─────────┬──────────────
                      │     │         \  SAFETY ALLOWANCE
ZERO STOCK    ────────┴─────┴──────────\ PROTECTS FOR THIS
                    LEAD TIME
```

The S.A. Turns Zero Times

The safety allowance forms a "pad" of material to take care of reasonable variations in usage or lead time from the averages anticipated. It must be included. Make no mistake about that! . . . but because half the time you use some of it and half the time you don't, *on the average, it's always on the shelf!* The safety allowance, whatever the quantity, becomes a fixed asset! It turns zero times! Therefore, don't add more safety than is necessary. In other words, you *must not* "hedge" when figuring each element of the OP formula, like this:

> Hmmm . . . that 100 per month was developed from a history that includes one month of 165. I'd better make the usage rate 125!" or "That lead time of 1.0 was figured from two performances by the vendor, but one was six weeks. I'd better edge that up to 1.25 months!

. . . and then you *also* add a full safety allowance on top of that! There's safety in the usage rate, safety in the lead time, and now more pad in the regular safety allowance. Do that on 6,000 items in five locations and watch what happens to your inventory! Remember, all that safety turns zero times!

THE SAFETY ALLOWANCE COMPUTATION

Some of the toughest mathematics in inventory management are encountered in attempts to set the safety allowance, or "safety stock" as it's sometimes called. There are systems on the market that offer up to

YOUR SERVICE CONTROL: WHEN TO ORDER!

nine formula options in computing safety. Experience shows, however, that most of the high math is downright ridiculous in the degree to which it tries to reduce outguessing the future to an exact science. I've seen mathematical gyrations applied here that rival those necessary to put a spacecraft in orbit . . . only to run out of stock on the item. The reason? The future is not precisely predictable. A good system, therefore, does all that is *reasonable* to predict what will occur, prepare for this, and protect for a "range" of occurrences around the prediction. *Predict, Prepare, Protect!* Sounds very similar to something you heard earlier, doesn't it?

The "Kiss" Principle *Really* Applies Here!

Just as with the usage rate calculation, it's very important to keep the safety allowance calculation as simple as possible. My version of "KISS" is "Keep It Super Simple!" Your people must understand how the computer arrives at the answers! If you employ mathematical wizardry beyond what they can understand, you run the risk that they'll become robots in following the computer's suggestions or they'll revert to SWAG . . . both bad! Safety stock is another calculation to keep as simple as possible while still affording good protection against a reasonable range of variances in usage and lead time. Surprisingly, this is easy to do.

The Exotic S.A. Formulas Yield Similar Answers

Consider this: No matter which of some 15 involved safety allowance formulas you could select, 95 percent of the time the safety added is between 25 percent and 75 percent of the basic order point formula (usage rate × lead time). With sales of 100 per month and an expected lead time of 1 month, the high-math formulas add between 25 and 75 to the basic calculation (100 × 1.0) to set the order point between 125 and 175 . . . and that percentage range results on 95 percent of the items in stock for most distributors.

A Simplified Approach: Use a 50 Percent Safety Factor

Since that's true, why not forget the high math and set the opening safety allowances right in the middle of this range? In other words, start your new control system with this order point formula on all items:

> Order Point = (Usage rate × Lead time) + 50% Safety
> Example OP = (100 × 1) + 50
> OP = 150

First, multiply the usage rate by the lead time, expressed in months. 100 per month times 1 month LT equals 100. *Then,* add 50 percent of the answer to complete the order point. Half of the 100 answer is 50. That's the safety allowance. 50 added to 100 makes the order point 150. I make this point because a common error with this formula is to add 50 percent only to the usage rate . . . not the usage rate times lead time answer.

For nearly all your stock items, 50 percent added to the basic calculation generates a service level of 90 percent without putting too much money in the fixed-asset category. That would be easy to program, wouldn't it? . . . and easy for an inventory buyer/analyst to duplicate in his or her head or on a small calculator. 90 percent service, the way it's measured in Chapter 18, is excellent. It's almost certainly better than how you're performing today, with all the data manipulation most distributors employ to make the service level figures look better . . . 95 percent, 98 percent, etc. Your salespeople know better!

When 50 Percent Isn't Enough

What about the other items . . . those where the 50 percent isn't enough or might be too much? How can such items be identified? A few will show up the hard way, of course. You'll run out of stock. Anytime you do run out of stock on an item that's not in the "DNR" (Do Not Reorder) category, or one that has something other than zero as the order point, the control system failed to control. Something's wrong. In Chapter 18, you'll see that the buyer should review the controls, the history, frozen status, etc., to find out what happened.

Usually, the safety allowance isn't the culprit. You didn't run out because of insufficient safety stock. It's more likely an incorrectly-computed usage rate . . . one where the history wasn't flagged properly; a lead time average developed from bad figures; or an order point set months ago and never recalculated. The system failed because misleading history information found its way into the OP calculation—that type of problem—rather than the 50 percent safety being inadequate.

Three Conditions That Need Additional Safety

But there are three conditions where more than 50 percent should be added to the basic calculation:

1. An item with an extremely erratic usage pattern
2. An item with a totally unpredictable lead time
3. An item for which you must provide 100 percent service (protected stock, systems contract item, etc.)

YOUR SERVICE CONTROL: WHEN TO ORDER!

A stock item shows this six-month usage history:

2865   41   18   9761   5609   36

Or the supplier delivers the item in two weeks or five months, and you have no way of knowing which it will be next time. 100 percent safety, perhaps more, is required on items like this to provide good service. They have such erratic tendencies that much more safety is needed to handle the extreme range of (what for them is) normal occurrences. You're probably thinking: "All my items are like that!" . . . but they're really not. You probably have very few with highly erratic characteristics. *All items* are erratic to some degree. More safety is necessary only on the *real* roller-coasters.

You Must Buffer Your Customer from Unreliable Suppliers

Let's say that one of your product lines comes from a very unreliable supplier in terms of delivery. A purchase order arrives in a week one time, four weeks the next. A standard 50 percent safety factor is inadequate for the stock items in this line. If you tried to get by with that, there would be lots of stockouts on critical items. Of course, you could always tell a customer:

> Gosh, I'm sorry we're out of those items you need so badly, but we have a very unreliable supplier!

The customer's reply: "*I do, too!*" Disaster. You cannot afford to let customers get that impression about *you!* You must buffer your customers (with inventory) from the unreliability of your suppliers. That's what the safety allowance does . . . and it has to be high enough to provide the buffer, regardless of conditions. That's "value added!" That added value causes your customers to buy from you rather than directly from the manufacturer.

A Negotiating Point with Suppliers

Yes, you must add the extra safety when a supplier's delivery is erratic, but it does give you a negotiating point later. The supplier's sales representative is making his biweekly call. He starts your visit off the usual way: "What can I do for you this time?" He's thinking Dallas Cowboy tickets . . . but this time you have a different reply:

> Jack, do you realize that your company delivers so poorly that we have to double our safety allowances on every item of your's that we stock? Take a

look at this printout. All 326 of your items are shown. The normal safety allowance is shown for each . . . and the quantity we had to add as extra safety.

All safety stock turns zero times per year, but all that extra pad we carry on your products amounts to $34,000 additional no-turn merchandise . . . necessary just because you guys deliver so erratically. We have to carry the extra stock to protect our customers.

That $34,000 reduces our profits by $9,520 per year ($34,000 × .28 annual cost of carrying inventory) . . . and we must get that *back from you* in the form of an additional discount . . . or we're going to find another source!

The supplier's representative will turn green, maybe begin to shake a little, but he'll go back and relay what you said to his boss. The sales people can't improve the factory delivery performance, of course, but what *CAN* they do? Sure, they can cut the price when you give them an economic justification (that they can show their management) to do so. If the supplier dominates his market, and you must have his products . . . no real options . . . well, this exercise is a waste of time. But with many suppliers, you can use this situation to improve your costs. If they don't budge, and you do have options, begin the search for a new product line.

How to Check Your Safety Stock's Effectiveness

Do you recall why the safety stock turns zero times? It's because half the time you need it when a replenishment shipment arrives from the supplier and half the time you don't. This peculiarity provides a good way, then, to check how well a safety allowance is set. If for an item, you sell *exactly* the expected usage rate during the lead time and experience *precisely* the average lead time anticipated, then *exactly the safety stock quantity* will be waiting on the shelf when the new purchase order shows up . . . provided that you did indeed order right at the order point. This set of conditions very rarely happens, but can you see how to measure whether or not the safety allowance is set correctly?

Half the time, when a replenishment shipment arrives on an item, more than the safety allowance is waiting on the shelf. Half the time, there's less. What if you check an item's last three receipts of new PO's and find, every time, that less than the safety allowance was on hand? Not enough safety! What if you find that three out of four times, more than the safety amount is on hand when the new shipment comes in? You likely could reduce the safety percentage without harm . . . but first check the usage rate and lead time history figures. It is possible that the item enjoys very steady usage, has a very reliable supplier, or both.

Establish a Universal Service Level on All Stock Items!

I must digress here just a moment to sound a warning. There's a popular school of thought circulating through distribution today that is dangerous. The logic sounds plausible but is unsound. The concept:

> Some items are more important to us than others. Some sell very well; others quite slowly. It's much more critical to provide excellent levels of service on the good items than on the little chaff. Be satisfied with 70 percent or 80 percent service on low-class items, but shoot for 90 percent on the top items!

The safety allowance percentage is reduced on the slower-moving products. There's more about this in Chapter 18 in the discussions on measuring service levels but for now . . . *DON'T FALL VICTIM TO THIS LOGIC!* How would a customer react if you told him:

> Yes, Harry, we're out of this item you need . . . but heck, it's a real slow-mover for us. We strive for a 70 percent service level on it. Now, if you'll buy one of *THESE,* they sell real well and we keep plenty on hand!

What category is the item the customer wanted . . . to *HIM?* Boy, it's Class 1, "A" Class, always! It's the most important item on his mind right now, and you said you stocked it. He depended on you and you've let him down. If an item isn't important enough to justify a 50 percent safety allowance . . . striving for the 90 percent service level which it will generate, then *DON'T STOCK IT!* Don't put it on the shelf, tell customers to get it from you, and then lower the safety percentage. That's a self-fulfilling prophecy: You'll do a lousy job of service on the item because you *intend* to! Good items get better because you set them up to perform well; bad items do worse because you've crippled them from the start.

THE EXCEPTIONS

I've suggested a very simple order point formula to begin new controls on all your stock items:

Order point = (Usage rate × Lead time) + 50%

For the vast majority, this will do a significantly better job of preventing stockouts than what you're doing now, and it won't overload the inventory. One by one, the others are identified that have truly erratic tendencies and more than 50 percent can be added. There are other conditions, however, where the formula should not be used:

1. Items resupplied from within the company, as when a branch gets all items from a central or regional warehouse. The lead times are very short and the "supplier" is controllable, thereby quite reliable. Chapter 16 shows how to set branch stock replenishment controls.

2. Items with one customer only, or one customer who dominates the sales picture. Assign arbitrarily—and freeze—the order point in accord with the customer's buying pattern.

3. Items with low sales per year. Again, set the order point at zero or one piece, perhaps, and lock it in. The computer does not refigure the order point each month as for most other stock items.

4. Brand new items where no usage history exists or less than six months is available. Assign an opening order point (after conferring with Sales) and freeze it for six months.

5. Protected stock that may be sold to one customer only. A permanent, "untouchable" order point includes 100 percent or more in safety to guarantee better than a 90 percent service level. Systems Contract items often require frozen controls. (Stock like this should be isolated in the warehouse in a controlled area, away from the regular stock of the same items.)

Eliminate Safety Stock on Branch Usage out of a Central Warehouse

In Chapter 6, there was a brief discussion of a way to reduce inventories in a central warehouse that resupplies branches. You'll recall that safety stock is placed only on warehouse sales to their customers but none on the branch withdrawals. Here's the way a warehouse order point is constructed for an item that the warehouse both sells and supplies to other branches:

Warehouse sales to customers	= 100 per month
Branch withdrawals	= 100 per month
Lead time for resupply	= 1 Month

YOUR SERVICE CONTROL: WHEN TO ORDER! 127

```
(Warehouse sales × Lead time) + 50% Safety allowance
    (100         ×     1)    +  50                      = 150
                    Added to
(Branch usage   × Lead time) + No safety stock
    (100         ×     1)    +  0                       = 100
                              Full order point          = 250
```

No safety allowance is built into the warehouse order point for branch usage. The safety is put at branch level, right next to the customers. This does mean, however, that when the warehouse stock gets down to the safety allowance (in the example, 50 units) . . . no more shipments are made to branches until a replenishment order arrives from the manufacturer.

SUMMARY

Replenishment order timing . . . the most important facet of an inventory system in developing good customer service. Order points serve well to maintain a continuity of supply on stock items where a distributor buys from sources outside the company. Order points handle the problem of independent demand . . . customers who can buy what they want, in whatever quantity, whenever they please . . . as opposed to dependent demand, where manufacturers have some control over the way their own warehouses may order.

Safety allowances are necessary because the other order point elements are developed from averages, but the SA's do become fixed assets. Avoid putting safety on safety on safety by hedging with the usage and lead time. Develop those two properly and place *all* the safety stock in the one element which allows it to be predicted and measured. You'll know exactly how much safety stock you need and how much you have.

"Outsiders" Drive the Order Points

The order points are "driven," controlled, set as they are, by outsiders . . . people outside your company. Customers control the usage rates. Suppliers dictate lead times. Since none of these poeple are *you,* then you shouldn't play games with the service controls: The Order Point, with it's protective safety allowance, nor the Line Point . . . to be discussed in the next chapter. Allow these replenishment-timing controls to find their proper levels in accord with the proven formulas. It's OK to provide more protection on super-critical items through a service level higher than 90 percent, but *never* (by design) set out to provide less than the 90 percent service objective on any item! Better that you drop it from stock and offer it only on a special-order basis.

9

SOLVING THE "LINE BUYING" PROBLEM

Line Buying is one of the toughest problems a distributor's purchasing people face. The term may be new to you, but the headache isn't: "Which stock items in this supplier's line should be purchased so that the total order meets the freight-free requirement? . . . or gets an extra 10 percent? . . . or qualifies for the carload discount that Sales says they must have to sell the products competitively?" Now do you recognize the problem?

Answering these questions is another facet of the order "timing" decision, introduced in the last chapter. Regardless of how the array of items is selected to go on the purchase order, your decisions cause each one to be ordered *now* from the supplier! Remember that order timing affects Service primarily, so the Line Buying decisions impact Service too. In a lesser but important way, the decisions also affect costs, positively, by lowering how much you pay the manufacturer . . . and negatively, by requiring you to carry more inventory in the product line.

Yes, Line Buying offers a way to reduce incoming costs on your purchases, but it also places a definite restraint on your ability to replenish stock properly. A single item in a supplier's line reaches its order point. No other items are at order point yet, but you simply cannot buy the one item all by itself. You'd pay an outrageous price, because the purchase order total wouldn't be anywhere near the amount that supplier requires for a freight-paid shipment (or perhaps his minimum) . . . so you look around for other items to add to the P.O. You don't really need anything else right now, but that's beside the point. You *must* have that discount!

Today, your poor buyers will tell you that this ordering requirement pins them in a corner and causes (what later turn out to be) expensive purchasing decisions more often than any other facet of their job. Sometimes the Sales Department sets their selling prices to customers presuming that *they will always get* that extra 5 or 10 percent. The buyers are up against the wall. They *must* get the extra discount on every purchase or costs will go up, and then they'd have to endure the wrath of salesmen whose gross margin and commission have been reduced and also feel that they can no longer sell the products competitively . . . but the Boss repeatedly tells them that their inventory is too high, climbing too fast!

The buyers feel pinched. If they delay in ordering the one item at order point (waiting for others to get low enough to order), they risk a stockout . . . but they can't buy just the single item without driving its cost out of sight. That means buying a lot of stuff now that they don't need now . . . an inventory excess! The buyer will likely catch some flak either way, but guess which course he or she picks most of the time? Sure, *OVERORDER!* The buyer would rather answer once a year why the inventory is so high, than have a salesman corner him every day about a stockout.

THE WAY IT'S ALWAYS BEEN DONE

You know, of course, how the Line Buying problem has traditionally been solved over the years. One item hits order point and needs to be replenished. The buyer flips through the Kardex trays, or scans a computer printout of all items in that manufacturer's line, and soon he finds one of the fast-movers. "Shoot, this item always sells well. I'll just put 200 on the purchase order. There can't be any harm in that! I know we'll sell 'em!" In a minute, another "good" item is added; then another; and zappo, the P.O. is ready to call in. The total-order requirement is met. Never mind that none of these hot items were anywhere near the point where they should be replenished. Never mind that many other items in the product line were not considered, because the order was filled only halfway through the trays or list. Sound familiar?

You can't make more mistakes than that in Line Buying if you sat up all night trying! It's easy to fill up a purchase order with fast-movers in most product lines, but what happens when you do? Your inventory investment in the product line becomes badly imbalanced. The fast-movers, which should be turning over quickly and thereby offsetting the low turn of lower-class items (see Chapter 10), instead turn over slowly themselves. The problem compounds. The supplier's requirement is more difficult to reach on the next purchase; on the next, a little tougher yet. Many other items in the line sell moderately, but as they reach their order points they can't be purchased. There's such a glut in the fast-movers that future stock purchases from this supplier must be postponed to sell off some inventory. The inventory investment is high, but more stockouts occur every day . . . and the Boss wants to know why!

SOLVING THE "LINE BUYING" PROBLEM 131

The Need for an "Upper Limit" Control: Line Points

For those product lines where a Line Buying target is desirable, all stock items need an additional control . . . one set higher than the regular order point, to help the buyer select the *right* array of items for the next purchase order. Obviously, the objective is to include only those items at or close to their order points. The question is: "How close?" Line Points provide the answer. The guesswork (SWAG) is removed from the decision-making process, as the Line Points tell you to include some items in the purchase order and leave others out. They set upper limits on how close stock items must be to their order points for inclusion on the next P.O.

A Brief Review of the Order-Timing Decision

In the last chapter we discussed Order Points, the order-timing triggers for stock items. When the stock available-for sale plus the amount on order with the supplier, totaled together, drops down to the order point, the replenishment process *must* begin on a stock item . . . or you'll risk a stockout! All stock items need some form of order point. It might be called a "Minimum" out in a branch, but when the order point or minimum is reached, replenishment must be initiated if the safety allowance is to protect you for variances in expected usage or lead time. If you intentionally go below the order point without reordering, you're using up the safety. It can't be used-up before the order is placed and still offer protection at the other end . . . when the material arrives from the supplier.

Stock Items That "Stand Alone"

Some items need only an order point. All alone, they meet whatever requirement the supplier has set. Perhaps he requires only a $25 minimum order and offers no further discounts in any form for more than a $25 order. You have no trouble buying $25 of any item you stock in that line, so an order point is the only replenishment-timing control needed on the items in that product line. When the on-hand + on-order total for an item drops to its order point, bingo . . . the computer tells the buyer: "It's time to place a purchase order. Don't wait to accumulate more units, dollars, or weight. You've got enough with this one item. Order it now!"

A Higher Control: The Line Point

For the other items, those that *don't* meet the supplier's requirement on a stand-alone basis (likely the majority of your stock items), a higher control is needed. Here's the Line Point formula:

> Line point = Order point + Usage during the Review Cycle

I'm sure that little formula cleared all this up for you, right? There's no need for further discussion is there? Of course there is. Obviously, I must explain that term "Review Cycle" and how line points help to select items for the next truckload purchase.

Review Cycles

The Review Cycle for a product line is how frequently it's scanned to determine whether or not a P.O. should be placed with the supplier. When vendors offer discounts for large total-orders, distributors don't try to buy every line every day. That just wouldn't work. Some lines are bought weekly; some suppliers get a purchase order every other week; some lines are ordered every three weeks; a few are bought monthly; and some lines get ordered even less frequently than that. These are the "cycles" on which the lines are reviewed for possible replenishment.

Often, these cycles are established by SWAG. Sometimes, they're forced. A Buyer is told: "Lucille, you must always get the truckload discount on this product line if our salesmen are to work from competitive costs . . . *and* you should place a P.O. on this line weekly!" Poor Lucille. She can follow these executive edicts, OK, but if ordering weekly is the wrong cycle for this product line, the only way to do it will be to overorder each time and carry a huge, outsized inventory *all the time!*

The Review Cycle Formula

There is, of course, a non-SWAG way to develop the right Review Cycle for each supplier's product line. How often can Lucille order that truckload to assure low material costs but not balloon the inventory in the process? Is there a "right" frequency in which this product line should be scanned in an effort to build a truckload order? Yes! Here's the way to establish the correct ordering frequency for a non-seasonal product line:

$$\text{Review Cycle} = \frac{\text{Total Annual Purchases (\$) Stock + Non-stock}}{\text{Total-Order Purchasing Target (\$)}}$$

Your *total* purchases (less any direct-ships) of qualifying items for a year are divided by the targeted buying objective (the truckload, for example). For now, let's not debate whether or not it's smart to buy a truckload. We'll assume that you feel you must to develop competitive product costs. Here, then, is how a Review Cycle calculation might turn out:

SOLVING THE "LINE BUYING" PROBLEM

$350,000 purchased in the last 12 months (Stock + Non-stock)
$7,000 order (the truckload) gets the freight paid

$$\frac{\$350,000}{\$7,000} = 50 \text{ Times per year}$$

A freight-paid purchase can be accumulated 50 times a year, based on the total purchases of qualifying products, stock and non-stock, during the last 12 months. Non-stock purchases (other than direct-ship's) are included, because they usually help you make the weight or dollars needed. Well, how often is 50 times a year? Just about once a week. With *this* annual purchasing history and *this* ordering requirement from the supplier, the correct review cycle is weekly! But here's a different set of conditions:

80,000 pounds purchased last year
20,000 pounds for a truckload

$$\frac{80,000}{20,000} = 4 \text{ Times per year}$$

How often can this distributor expect to buy a truckload? Four times a year, or every three months. The review cycle for this product line is three months . . . *not* every month or twice a month! The only way to buy a truckload monthly would be to overload the inventory. The proper review cycle is often an eye-opener to the Boss. He begins to understand the impossible requirements he's placed on his buyers in the past: "Always buy the truckload . . . *and* get a satisfactory inventory turn on the product line . . . *and* don't wait more than a month between orders!" With the situation above, the poor buyer hasn't a chance of accomplishing all three! He or she will buy monthly truckloads, overstock the line, and pray!

Note that the annual purchases are expressed in the same terms (dollars, weight, or units) in which the supplier specified the P.O. requirement . . . or you must convert the buying requirement to dollars. The 20,000 pound truckload may represent an average purchase of $7,000. The 1,000 units required for an extra 10 percent off results in an average purchase of $2,800 . . . based on a review of the last few P.O.s. *Dollars* of annual purchases must be divided by *dollars* required, pounds by pounds, or units by units, to get a proper review frequency and cycle.

Review Cycles for Seasonal Product Lines

Now let's complicate matters a bit. What about product lines with seasonal usage patterns? Let's consider the following conditions:

$$\frac{\text{Annual Purchases: } \$200{,}000}{\text{Vendor Requirement: } \$20{,}000} = 10$$

We'll add one more fact: 80 percent of the sales, and 80 percent of the $200,000 in purchases takes place in a six-month period. The products are seasonal. The "10" annual ordering frequency is really 8 during the six-month season and 2 outside the season. The $20,000 is ordered 8 times in the six-month season and only twice the rest of the year. In the season, the Review Cycle is about every three weeks (8 times in 6 months). The rest of the year, the Review Cycle is every three months (2 times in 6 months). The computer is programmed to change the Review Cycle for this product line for different periods of the year . . . and change the Line Points also, as we'll see in a bit. For seasonal product lines, you must tell the computer the dates of the season so it knows when to make the switch. Generally, a line is seasonal if 80 percent of the annual sales are condensed into a six-month period.

Product Lines with Sub-Divided Offers from the Supplier

Suppliers often like to complicate life by breaking out a portion of their product line for some special purchasing opportunity. A total order of $2,000 across all products gets a freight-paid shipment, but if you'll buy 50 total from a special list of tools, there's an extra 25 percent off just on the tool group. Now you have two Line Buying problems . . . one sort of wrapped up inside the other. The tool list Review Cycle may turn out considerably different than the overall line's cycle. Only the tool purchases last year are divided by the 50-unit average order value. You may be able to put together a freight-paid order every week, but a 50-unit tool order only once a month. Good thing you have a computer to assist your buyers through such a maze!

Calculating Line Points

Now . . . that the various product lines' Review Cycles have been set properly, you're ready to establish Line Points for the stock items involved. Remember the formula of a few pages back:

Line point = Order point + Usage during the review cycle

To each item's order point, add the amount of usage you'd expect during the Review Cycle. If the line's cycle is weekly, add one week's worth of usage (the usage rate $\times$ .25) to each item's order point. If the cycle is monthly, add a full month's worth of usage (usage rate $\times$ 1.0) to each order point. If the cycle is every other week, then two weeks' usage is added to all order points of products in that line. Look at these examples:

SOLVING THE "LINE BUYING" PROBLEM

Usage rate = 100   Lead time = 1.0   Review Cycle = 2 Weeks
Order point = (100 × 1.0) + 50 = 150
Line point = 150 + 50 (2 Weeks' worth of usage) = 200

Usage rate = 20   Lead time = .5   Review cycle = Monthly
Order point = (20 × .5) + 5 = 15
Line point = 15 + 20 (1 Month's usage) = 35

For the first item's product line, the Review Cycle is every two weeks. Two weeks' worth of usage is added to every item's order point to set the Line Point. The other item's product line is reviewed monthly. A full month's worth of usage is added to the order point of each item in the product line to set the Line Point.

How Often Should New Line Points and Review Cycles Be Set?

Just as with order points back in Chapter 8, the Line Points are recalculated each month for every stock item that has not been flagged due to an unusual condition in the usage history or frozen for some period of time by the buyer. Review Cycles can be recalculated less frequently ... once a quarter is adequate, unless a series of purchases in a line indicates repetitively that the cycle is too long or short (you always have too many or too few items as the targeted buy is attempted.)

What the Line Point Accomplishes

OK. The Review Cycles have been set properly and they, together with each item's order point, establish effective Line Points. Now what? How do the new Line Points function? How do they guide a buyer's selection of some items to include on the next purchase order and cause others to be omitted? Take a look at this cross-sectional view of a group of products in a line that might be candidates for ordering at the time the computer scans the line (Review Cycle date):

```
                    X
        X       X
    ————————X——————————————— Line Points
     X              X
        X               X
     X              X
    ————————————————————X——— Order Points
           X        X

    ————————————————————————— Safety Allowances

    ————————————————————————— Zero Stock
```

Line Points set the *OUTSIDE LIMIT* for including an item on the next P.O. from the supplier. Any items where the on hand + on order total is at or below the Line Point should be ordered. Any above Line Point are excluded . . . left for the *next* purchase order! Don't be confused by the little picture above. All order points and all line points are not exactly the same. Each is calculated individually based on an item's usage rate, lead time, and then the line's Review Cycle. The picture shows simply how items might be positioned, relative to the controls, at the time of the computer's review.

There are ten items at or below Line Point and three (that we can see here) above Line Point. The ten are ordered. The three are not, *regardless of how fast they sell* . . . *how popular they are!* Only the items below Line Point are ordered. Hmmm, "That's nice," you say, " . . . but how can I be confident that the ten items below Line Point will total enough weight, units, or dollars to meet the supplier's requirement?" By the method that established the Review Cycle for this line, which in turn set the individual item Line Points. Remember . . . you determined how frequently your historical purchases from this supplier during the past year justified the truckload (or whatever) he requires. You're trying to buy on that cycle. On the average, you should have enough stock items below Line Point (and non-stock items waiting for the next P.O., where customers agreed to the delay) to meet the requirement on *this buying frequency!*

Well, What If the Items below Line Point *Don't* Provide Enough Weight?

Since the Review Cycle approximates the average time between purchase orders in the past, there'll be times when an insufficient number of items are below Line Point to satisfy the supplier's requirement. We haven't talked yet about the quantities of each item to be purchased. That's the subject of Chapter 10. Each item below Line Point has an individually-calculated order quantity, just as it has an individual order point and Line Point. Generally, the Review Cycle considers how you've purchased individual items in the past and projects about the same quantities in the future. But what happens when the Line Point items' quantities just won't get the job done? Do you reach up and pull in a fast-mover to add on to the P.O.? *NO!* Don't do it! Instead, program the computer to increase the quantity of each Line Point item proportionately by the percent the total order is now short of the supplier's requirement. If, for example, you had 4,500 pounds in items below Line Point but need to order 5,000 pounds, that's 500 pounds (10 percent) short. Increase each item's quantity by 10 percent and round off to standard pack.

If you include items above Line Point, you'll destroy the heart of the *next* purchase order. The situation will likely be even more critical next

SOLVING THE "LINE BUYING" PROBLEM

time . . . *and* you'll ruin the turnover you must achieve on fast-moving, high-dollar items (as you learn in the next chapter). Don't make the order requirement that way. Instead, increase the order quantity of only those items now below Line Point. If you have to do this on two or three purchases in a row, it's a solid indication that the Review Cycle is too short. You're not enjoying the sales you did in the past and the buying frequency should be lengthened.

Why Buy All Items below Line Point if They Aren't Needed to Make Weight?

All items below Line Point are ordered now, on this purchase order being accumulated, because they'll be below order point by the time the next Review Cycle date rolls around . . . and it's *never* your intention to let an item get below order point without starting the replenishment process. It will happen, of course, but it's never done *intentionally!* When you go below order point and delay ordering, you're eating into the safety allowance before you start, and it was designed to help protect you at the receiving end of the replenishment process. If, however, time after time you find more items below Line Point than you need, it's a good indication that the Review Cycle needs to be changed. It's too long. Perhaps sales on the line have increased dramatically, purchases have followed the pattern, and the cycle should be shortened.

DANGEROUS PRODUCT LINES

When the previous purchasing history for a product line develops a Review Cycle longer than one month . . . *it's a dangerous product line!* Management should take a very close, very intense look at the line to determine if you should continue to stock it or to buy it as you have. Why? The extra, zero-turn inventory you must carry (at 25–35 percent per year cost) on all items in the line to be able to purchase truckloads, or whatever, likely far outweighs the savings made through the large orders. Here is another picture to be studied:

When you must Line-Buy a product line, we said earlier that you cannot allow an item to drop down to its order point before starting the "accumulation" of other items to go with it on the P.O. If you did, you'd be using up that item's safety allowance while the accumulation process took place. Instead, it's necessary to trigger replenishment on an item when its somewhere between the line point and order point. If things go as you plan, you're always *at or above* the order point when an item is purchased. Where—exactly—will an item be on the average, then, when you put it on a purchase order? Halfway between line point and order point.

Half the time, the item will be lower than that. Half the time, it will be up closer to the line point. On the average, it will be halfway between the line point and order point. What do you suppose the amount of material represented by this position becomes? You guessed it . . . more zero-turn inventory! More safety allowance, in effect. Half the time, you're below this amount of stock when the item is ordered; half the time you're above. On the average, *it's always out there!* You may recall that when lead times were calculated, it was from the date of the P.O. to the date of first receipt of material. The accumulation time for the purchase order was ignored. This extra safety allowance, this amount of stock represented by half the distance between line point and order point, is your accumulation-time protection!

How Much Accumulation-Time Protection Can You Afford?

When the Review Cycle on a product line is one month, you add one full month's worth of usage to each item's order point to set the line points. That means, also, that two weeks' worth of usage has been added as accumulation-time protection stock on every item . . . and this protection-stock turns over zero times a year! For *my* company, that's the outside limit of the extra stock I'll finance to get the big-order savings, unless those savings are truly fantastic. Two weeks' worth of every item in a product line sitting out in the warehouse (*in addition to* the normal safety allowance), turning zero times, costs me the full carrying cost percentage on this money (25–35 percent) per year. For most suppliers' "wonderful" buying offers with which I'm familiar, that's all the cost I can stand. That's all the savings will support. I'll bet it's the same for most of your suppliers' big-order discounts too.

Now . . . what if, in order to make the truckload buy and save $500 freight, you have to set a Review Cycle of 2 months on this line? Two months' worth of usage is added to every item's order point to set the line points. Now how much zero-turn stock will you have all the time on every item? *One full month's usage!* Can you imagine what that costs at 30 percent per year, for example? You may be saving $500 freight and incurring $1,000 in holding cost *every month* on the zero-turn stock you carry to make the savings. Smart, isn't it? Heck no, it's downright stupid, and if you keep it up you'll become a non-profit organization!

Savings versus Cost Can Be Calculated

Obviously, the smarter approach would be to determine how much zero-turn stock the potential savings will offset . . . and then permit a Review Cycle that generates only that much inventory (half the line point minus order point). Even at that, you'd just break even! Most discount offers from suppliers can't offset the inventory carrying costs for more than two weeks' worth of accumulation-protection stock . . . a 1-Month Review Cycle maximum.

Another Aspect: The Review Cycle Dictates Minimum Order Quantities!

You'll hear more about this in the next chapter, but for the fastest-moving, high-dollar items in a product line the turnover objective can be destroyed by a Review Cycle longer than a month. When a substantial amount of money moves through the inventory each month on an item, you *must* turn the inventory frequently. There are control techniques to achieve this (EOQ, etc.), and they often develop ordering quantities of no more than two weeks' stock or 1 month's stock.

The Review Cycle can muddle this up. How could you buy only one month's stock of an item if the computer scans the product line only every two months? You'd *have to buy at least* two months' worth of every item! That would be OK on some, but not on the fast-movers. Their turnover would be wrecked . . . and with them, the entire line's! It's another reason to restrict all Review Cycles to a maximum of one month.

What Can Management Do about Dangerous Product Lines?

If a product line seems to require longer than a 1 Month Review Cycle, what options does the president have? . . . and it is the *president* who should make these decisions! No one else has the objectivity to decide between the competitive and economic issues. Here are the president's options:

1. Continue as you are . . . losing your shirt through inventory carrying costs on each purchase order to derive a low "incoming" cost.

This makes it easier, of course, for the salesmen to sell the products, and underlies their continued pressure to "Get the freight paid!"

2. Continue as you are . . . for a specified period that has a definite time limit. The president tells Sales, in effect: "Ladies & Gentlemen, I'm going to permit this losing proposition to continue only until January 1st. If by that time you haven't built up the sales on this line enough to justify a 1-Month Review Cycle, we will move to one of the following options!"

3. Forget this level of volume-purchase savings and either drop to a lower-discount buying target . . . or work only with order points, purchasing one item at a time. The freight savings or "extra 5 percent" are bypassed in favor of reasonable inventory carrying costs on the products.

4. Raise all selling prices for products in the line to generate additional gross margin sufficient to offset the excessive inventory carrying costs.

5. Drop the product line from stock and offer it to customers only on a special-order basis . . . an option that likely will cause the supplier to drop you as an authorized distributor, but better than losing money on each purchase.

Do you see the point? For many years, distribution management received steady input from the sales force on the necessity of "buying right." Suppliers provided some input too. During his annual sales call, the vice president of Marketing tells your president: "Harry, do you realize that only 71 percent of your purchases from us last year were at the best price? Do you know what that cost you?" Even consultants put in their two cents. The Boss attends a seminar or convention-workshop where the leader proves convincingly that a penny saved in product cost drops straight to the bottom line. Hmmm . . . trouble is, as the old song says, "It ain't necessarily so!" Inventory carrying costs *do* have their impact! That average extra stock of $20 carried on 100 items, carried in all ten branches, isn't free! . . . and if it's $50, or $200? Well you can see clearly that the truckload savings *had better* offset the carrying cost of the extra stock you'll have, or it's *not* a good deal . . . regardless of what the sales force, your suppliers, or the consultants say!

It's time that distributor owners and presidents considered the economic impact of "buying in the last column" as well as the competitive advantages. *Then* . . . make a decision on what to do. Remember this: If your company does go bankrupt, that salesman who pushed so hard for the lowest cost from the supplier will have another job (with your

SOLVING THE "LINE BUYING" PROBLEM

competitor) in about 23 minutes. That supplier who kept encouraging the big-volume purchases will find another distributor in your area for his products in less than 24 hours. It'll be the owners, the stockholders, the officers who will suffer serious loss. That's why you must develop or find a computerized system that shows the president the economic impact of major-dollar purchasing decisions to be weighed against all the competitive input he gets today . . . and that's why he should make the final decision when product lines appear to be profit-drains the way you're buying them.

INTERRUPTING THE NORMAL REVIEW CYCLE

There will always be times when a product line's Review Cycle . . . the date when the computer scans the line to find purchase order candidates . . . is still a ways off and something happens that says: "Hey, forget the cycle. Buy *Now!*" There are two basic conditions that should force a "Demand Buy," so to speak:

1. Non-stock orders from customers for items in the product line have been accumulating (waiting for the next official P.O.), to the point that now you have half the total order required by the supplier. He requires 5,000 pounds, and there are 2,500 pounds worth of non-stock items waiting.
    The computer is programmed to scan the product line right now. "Forget the cycle. Tell me right now how many stock items you find below line point!" There's an excellent chance you can place the purchase order at once, without overextending the inventory.

2. One item in the product line has its stock on hand drop to the order point . . . and nothing is on order for this item with the supplier. Again the computer is told (through programming): "Forget the cycle. List all items below line point right now!"
    Obviously, this is a surprise. Perhaps a customer bought a large quantity of some item that has sold very little in the past. When this occurs, the odds are good that you *will not* be able to put together the regular truckload without seriously imbalancing the inventory. Still, you want to take a quick look to find out.
    If all the items below line point would permit a P.O. of less than half what's required, don't place the normal order. Instead, try to buy the one item in trouble from a competitor at whatever price you must . . . or simply place an order for the one item alone from the supplier.

Sure it runs the cost out of sight on the item, but what would the carrying costs be on all that extra stock of unneeded items you'd have to bring in to keep the one item's cost at $1.40 instead of $1.90?

SUMMARY

Line Buying is a difficult compromise. The obvious competitive and apparent economic advantages can often be offset by confining purchasing requirements and hidden inventory carrying costs, thus making the problem one of the most difficult a distributor must solve. Too often in the past, pressurized SWAG settled the whole issue. The pressure was applied by Sales: "Be sure to get the freight paid or we can't be competitive!", so Purchasing people yielded and bought at the lowest cost from the supplier, the last column, etc. The result: Good item costs but huge, expensive inventories!

Properly-determined Review Cycles, and the corresponding line points, offer a predictable, consistent, profitable approach that removes the SWAG and assures that Line Buying savings aren't eaten away by excessive inventory carrying costs. The buyers are off the hook. They know when to buy the product line. They know which items to include in the P.O. and which to leave for the next time. Also, the president no longer must rely only on competitive "feel" to evaluate a product line's true profit contribution. There are new economic measurements afforded.

Order timing . . . so critical for good service! But also an area where most distributors become overprotective with stock and press for the lowest costs from suppliers. These last two chapters can help you on both counts, but now it's time to move on to the ordering decisions that have the greatest impact on inventory carrying costs: The "How Much to Buy" decisions.

10

YOUR TURNOVER CONTROL: HOW MUCH TO BUY?

Do you remember the discussion at the beginning of Chapter 8 about the most misunderstood aspect of inventory control . . . that "When" replenishment is triggered has the greatest impact on service, and "How Many" you order at a time of an item largely controls turnover? Fine. Chapters 8 and 9 dealt with order timing. This chapter considers internal cost objectives. Let's talk now about the *quantity* of a stock item to bring in, when the controls of those earlier chapters say it's time to do so.

BE AWARE OF PAST CONFUSION

For years, distributors' buyers tended to "mush together" the two basic ordering decisions (when and how much) into one confused mess. They couldn't grasp an important fact: The two decisions solve problems that are basically independent, although they do have some cross-impact! Does a customer care, for example, the turns you achieve on an item when he or she orders it and you're out of stock? If your company goes bankrupt because you can no longer finance huge, oversized inventories, do your salesmen really suffer all that much? . . . those guys who pressed you to always "buy the truckload so we'll have a competitive cost!"

Let's emphasize one more time (are you sick of it yet?) the *BALANCE* to be maintained between service and turnover objectives . . . a difficult tightrope to walk, I'll admit, but so necessary these days when costs are much higher than in the 60s and 70s. Some distributors have been sales *dominated* outfits since they began the business, where they should have been sales *oriented*. Today, sales dominated companies are failing right and left.

Another Confusing Point: The Total-Order Required by the Supplier

For now, try to put into the back of your mind the realities of Line Buying. Yes, I know that most of the time you can't buy just one item all by itself . . . but for each item you *do* include on the purchase order, some quantity has to be selected. That's the subject of this chapter: How much of each individual item to purchase? In Chapter 11, we'll then expand Chapter 9's discussion of line buying to show how to select the best of several total-order options offered by a supplier.

THE OUTGOING COST CONCEPT

First, let's mention a cost which is rarely considered as a distributor decides how much of an item to buy: The "Outgoing" Cost. Simply, it's the *total amount of cost* an average unit of stock carries with it as it goes out the warehouse door to your customer. It isn't calculated. You can't find it on a profit and loss statement or even a budget. . . . but it's very real! If it becomes too high, the distributor becomes a non-profit organization. Here are the cost elements that make it up:

Incoming Cost   That's easy enough. It's what you paid the manufacturer per unit for the item, including freight if that was a significant percentage of the cost paid.

The "K" Cost   In inventory control language, that's the Cost of Carrying Inventory . . . calculated as the amount the average unit accumulated during the time you had it on the shelf.

The "R" Cost   The cost of going through the replenishment cycle in your company, again, figured down to an incremental unit basis.

You know these costs. The incoming cost is simply the unit cost paid to the supplier. Both "K" and "R" were discussed back in Chapter 7. You'll recall that back there we expressed "K" as a percentage: 28 percent per year (for example) on the average dollar carried in stock. In this chapter, we'll see it worked out to a specific figure developed from how much you paid for the item and how long it stays in stock before being sold.

The same is true of "R," the Cost of Going Through a Replenishment Cycle. In Chapter 7, it came out $5.00 per item each time it was purchased, regardless of how many of the product was ordered. For

YOUR TURNOVER CONTROL: HOW MUCH TO BUY?

Outgoing Cost, we'll divide the $5.00 by the quantity to get an incremental cost per piece. You'll never have to do this on either K or R. A formula will do it for you, but the Outgoing Cost exercise illustrates a very important concept.

The Outgoing Cost Calculation

Let's see how a typical outgoing cost calculation might turn out:

Incoming Cost	$1.00
"K" Cost	.17
"R" Cost	.05
Outgoing Cost	$1.22
Selling Price	1.22
Gross Profit	.22
Commission to Salesman	.02

Gross Profit computed on difference between Incoming Cost and Selling Price.

The $1.00 is what we paid the supplier. To get that $1.00 cost, we had to be sure to get the freight paid. That meant a large purchase of all items, and since this item is a popular-seller, we went extra heavy on it. The average unit, therefore, was out in the warehouse long enough to accumulate .17 worth of inventory carrying cost ("K"). We bought 100 units, so the $5.00 "R" cost spread over the 100 is .05 per piece.

Competition is tough on this item. Sales managed to get only $1.22 per unit when it sold (average, during the time we had it in stock). We paid a 10 percent commission on the gross profit of .22 each or about .02. . . . but the total outgoing cost was $1.22! Are you beginning to see a problem? When all costs were considered, we just broke even on the item, *and then* we paid out a sales commission beyond that!

ACHIEVING THE LOWEST OUTGOING COST

This outgoing cost is important. The fact that most distributors didn't consider it in the past makes it no less important today. Today—*in this economic climate*—if you ignore it, you'll wish you hadn't! The following illustration shows how the lowest possible outgoing cost is developed.

The outgoing cost is actually the sum of the two costs ("K" and "R") that work on an item as you bring it in and then hold it in stock . . . added to what you paid the supplier. The chart below shows how the two costs accumulate as you buy more and more of a stock item. The "K"

FINDING THE LOWEST TOTAL COST

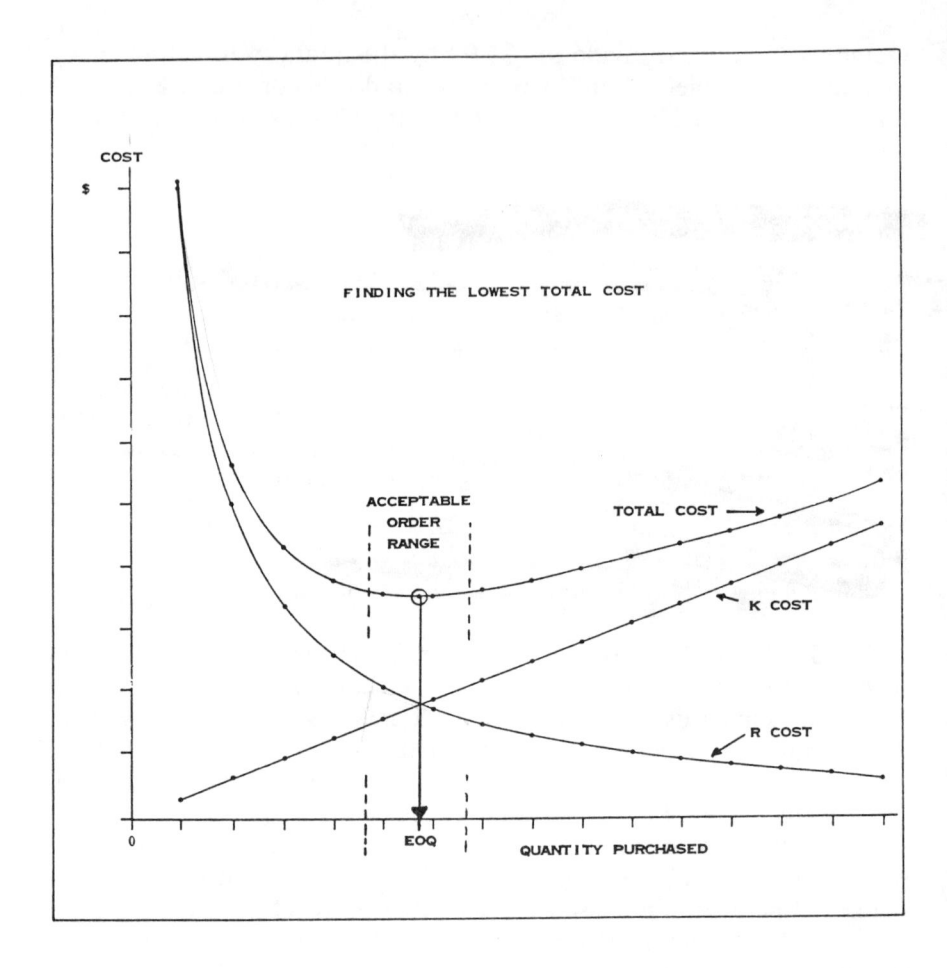

cost has a direct relationship. The more you buy, the longer the stock sits before it is sold, so the more "K" cost you'll incur. The "R" cost isn't like that. All $5.00 would have to be assigned to a single unit in stock if you were to buy just that one piece. When you purchase 100 of the item for example, then the $5.00 is spread over the 100 units. As you go from 1 unit bought on up, the total of these two costs starts high, dips to a low point, and then climbs again.

The lowest outgoing cost results when you purchase a quantity that balances exactly the incremental unit carrying cost (K) against the incremental cost of going through the replenishment cycle (R). Any purchased quantity lower or higher than this ideal results in a higher total cost when the average piece of stock leaves your warehouse. That ideal buying target for the item is called an Economic Order Quantity (EOQ).

YOUR TURNOVER CONTROL: HOW MUCH TO BUY?   147

How neat! All you have to do is to graph this little problem on all 10,000 of your stock items . . . and you'll know just how many to buy at a time for each one. Whoever did it would also be in the funny farm by the time they finished. Fortunately, there's a better way.

THE ECONOMIC ORDER QUANTITY (EOQ) CALCULATION

The formula below solves the problem just discussed. It finds a quantity to purchase that will develop the lowest outgoing cost for the item:

$$EOQ = \sqrt{\frac{24 \times \text{Cost of Ordering (``R'')} \times \text{Usage Rate}}{\text{Cost of Carrying Inventory (``K'')} \times \text{Unit Cost}}}$$

Everything we've discussed is considered by the formula. The Incoming Cost is what you paid the supplier: the unit cost. "R" is there. "K" is there, and a constant: 24 . . . and then the bad news: It's all under a square-root sign! The formula has been around in basic form for a long time. Originally, it called for annual usage rather than a monthly rate of usage as above. The constant was a 2 . . . but that had to be multiplied by 12 when annual usage was modified to monthly usage, which is much more reflective of how an item's sales change. Don't worry about the 24. It helps to solve mathematically the problem that was graphed earlier. Here's a typical EOQ calculation:

Usage Rate = 20 per month   Unit Cost = $7.00
"R"   = $5.00   "K"   = .30

$$EOQ = \sqrt{\frac{24 \times 5.00 \times 20}{.30 \times 7.00}}$$

$$EOQ = \sqrt{\frac{120 \times 20}{2.1}}$$

$$EOQ = \sqrt{\frac{2400}{2.1}}$$

$$EOQ = \sqrt{1142.86}$$

EOQ = 34 (Rounded off to even units)

For this item, the most profitable quantity to buy as long as the cost remains $7.00 from the supplier and the usage rate remains at 20 per month is exactly 34 units . . . about 1 and ¾ months' supply. The "R" and "K" can also change, of course, but they do much less frequently than unit costs and usage. "R" and "K" may be considered fixed for several months at a time.

What turnover would we achieve on this item if we buy 34 at a time? Well, just on the inventory level impacted by the order quantity, we'd get about eight turns a year. We'd buy it every six weeks, approximately, or about eight times a year. Great! "Eight turns . . . fine!" says the distributor owner. Actual turns would be somewhat less, because we must carry some zero-turn merchandise in the order-timing safety allowance, as you learned in an earlier chapter, and more perhaps in P.O. accumulation-time stock if you can't buy this item all by itself. Still, six or seven turns isn't bad, when the gross margin is in a normal range for hardgoods distributors: 20 to 30 percent. Let's now try the same calculation on a cheaper item:

$$\text{Usage Rate} = 20 \quad \text{Unit Cost} = .10$$
$$\text{"R"} = \$5.00 \quad \text{"K"} = .30$$

$$\text{EOQ} = \sqrt{\frac{24 \times 5.00 \times 20}{.30 \times .10}}$$

$$\text{EOQ} = \sqrt{\frac{2400}{.03}}$$

$$\text{EOQ} = \sqrt{80000}$$

$$\text{EOQ} = 283 \text{ (Nearest even units)}$$

With this little cheapie, costing a dime and selling only 20 per month, the ideal purchasing quantity would be 283. 14 month's supply! . . . and the turns on it would be less than 1 per year. "Now I know this Graham is crazy!", you scream. "I can't afford turnover like that!"

Really? How much money would you have to invest in inventory to buy, let's say, a year's supply of this little turkey? $20 \times 12 \times .10 = \$2.40$. Wow! $2.40! . . . and all at one time, too. How about that first item? What would a year's supply of it cost? $20 \times 12 \times 7.00 = \$1,680$. Hmmm . . . that's a different story, isn't it. We're not about to spend $1,680 on this one item and get only one turn per year.

Are you beginning to see how the EOQ formula works? It recommends a quantity to buy related to how much money moves through your inventory on the item each month or each year. Lots of money . . . a low quantity in terms of months' supply and high turnover per year. Not much money . . . a higher months' supply, lower turns.

WHERE AND WHEN TO USE EOQ . . . AND WHEN NOT TO!

As long as EOQ's been around, there've been those who didn't like it. "EOQ often gives squirrely answers!", they argue. They laugh and point to examples when the EOQ approach recommended a 10-minute supply or perhaps a five-year supply. "You see? . . . that's what happens when you use EOQ!" "You're really behind the times to use such an outdated method!"

Is EOQ really that hazardous or old-fashioned? Not on your life! Those that say such things display clearly that they've misapplied the EOQ concept and that they do not understand where and when it's to be used . . . and how the answers must be adjusted. Like any tool, there's a right application and a wrong one. Would you toss your hammer in the trash, vowing never to use it again, if you tried to use it where a screwdriver was called for? Of course not. The hammer is right for some jobs . . . the screwdriver for others, and the value of one can't be measured properly if it's used incorrectly. That's just how it is with EOQ. There's a right and a wrong time to use it. Here are the conditions for a stock item that should be present for EOQ to be effective:

1. The price paid to the supplier does not vary when you buy more of this one item. You may have a "total-order" economic advantage for buying more, but the price quoted by the manufacturer for this item doesn't improve when you purchase more of this single item. No price-breaks.

2. The usage rate of the item is higher than $1/2$ unit per month. You move at least one piece every other month.

3. The supplier's lowest permissible purchasing quantity on the item is reasonable for you to attain . . . it does not represent three or four times the calculated EOQ amount.

Later in this chapter, we'll address the way you pick the right quantity to buy when the supplier offers several quantity-breaks on a single item . . . but EOQ is out of its element there. Secondly, there's a range of usage for an item when formulas work. Very high or very low usage rates throw *any* formula for a loop, and less than $1/2$ unit sold per month is too low for formulized help. You should set arbitrary ordering controls on items like this. "When we get down to one piece, we'll order two!" . . . something like that. Don't attempt to apply *any* formula for the order point or order quantity.

20 to 25 Percent of the Stock Items Need Human-Set Controls!

Most durable goods distributors have as many as 25 percent of their stock items in this category! Shocking? You don't believe it? Look at your own stock item list and the usages . . . then argue! Some computerized systems yield lousy results because they attempt to handle all stock items under the same rules and formulas. Don't make that mistake. Recognize that up to a fourth of your stock items likely require you SWAG to set (and lock in) the controls.

Finally, you'll find a few items where the supplier packs them in very large quantities (at least, for you). The EOQ might come out six, but you can buy the item only in boxes of 24. In nearly every case, you should consider discontinuing the item as stock. You simply don't have enough usage to buy the thing economically. If you must stock it, try to get it down the street from a competitor six at a time and pay whatever you must. If you must buy it from the supplier . . . well, you're stuck. Buy 24 and forget the EOQ.

Adjusting the EOQ Answers

In our earlier examples, the EOQ answers came out 34 and 283. "But what if the items come packed 10?" you ask. Obviously, sending in purchase orders for 34 or 283 would make us look pretty dumb and might incur a broken-package charge to boot. We should round off the answer to standard pack . . . but there are other "rounding" requirements too. Let's list all four:

1. Round the EOQ answer off to the nearest standard package. Go up if the calculated quantity is more than halfway to the next multiple . . . down if it isn't. If it's less than $1/2$ of a single standard carton, the computer should not round up automatically . . . but show the pack size to the buyer. He or she then decides what to do.

2. Round the EOQ answer up to at least two weeks' supply if it's lower than that. For a few expensive items that sell very well, the EOQ concept recommends a very high turnover achieved by buying maybe only three or four days' supply. Don't do it. 20 or more

YOUR TURNOVER CONTROL: HOW MUCH TO BUY?   151

turns per year is good enough on anything. You don't want to fool with any item any more frequently than once every two weeks, unless there's a severe space limitation in storing the item.

3. Round the EOQ answer back to a limit of one year's supply if it calculates out higher than that. The risk of damage, obsolescence, shrinkage, and theft increases when material sits in a warehouse longer than a year . . . increases dramatically! EOQ assumes a fixed inventory carrying cost and it is relatively fixed, until you go out beyond a year's supply. Then it begins to climb exponentially.

4. Check the EOQ against the product line's Review Cycle times the monthly usage rate of the item:

   Review Cycle: 1 month   Usage Rate per Month: 100

   Calculation: 1 × 100 = 100

EOQ must be raised to 100 if it calculated out less.

If a product line is ordered just once a month, then you can order no less than 1 month's supply of each item when it's replenished.

Considering these rules, the earlier EOQ answers would be adjusted to 30 and 240. The first, to standard packages of 10; the second, back to a year's supply (20 per month × 12) and to standard pack. Program these round-off rules into your system to avoid odd-ball EOQ answers!

Don't Be Afraid of Economic Order Quantities

OK, I admit that the square root sign makes an EOQ calculation a bit tough to do by hand. After all, it's high-school math, and most of us forgot that the day after we finished the course . . . but a computer handles it easily. EOQ affords very cost-effective ordering quantities *and* will cause some 65 percent of your stock items (that sell) to come up for reordering only once or twice per year. You'd buy six months' to a year's supply of over half your stock items.

"You're kidding!" you scream. "We'll go broke! We can't afford to buy six months' to a year's supply of over half our items!" Oh yes you can, if you restrict it to the proper half as EOQ does. The *other 35 percent* will turn much faster than before . . . and that's where most of the dollars move through your inventory. You achieve much higher turns on those dollars, far more than off-setting what happens on the 65 percent that move poorly (and represent small change moving through the inventory). If you gut it up and deal with your dead stock, the subject of another chapter, you should get between five and six turns per year on your total inventory investment . . . much better than most distributors achieve today!

Review and Replenish Most Items Less Frequently!

Another great benefit accrues also: Your buyers see the majority of items only once or twice per year. They have more time to handle the others, the big-money-through-the-inventory items. More time to check out unusual orders with Sales; more time to look into squirrely lead times. More time to be thinkers/planners/analyzers, rather than clerks.

AN ALTERNATE APPROACH: BUYING BY INVENTORY CLASS!

Yes, EOQs do a good job, but they also violate one of Graham's rules: If a calculation is too tough for an average person to duplicate on a hand calculator, it may lead to trouble. EOQs, with the square root, can be a mystery to ol' Harry who's been buying your merchandise for 25 years. Since Harry can't understand it, he may follow it blindly (the "robot" syndrome), or he may override it every time with his more-comfortable judgment ("SWAG").

You may have some "Harrys" in your company. If you do, and you think that the EOQ approach would throw them for a loop, then consider an alternate method of developing order quantities . . . a less complicated method that still derives most of the EOQ benefits. You could use this "Buying By Inventory Class" technique to begin your new control system, and then evolve slowly to EOQs as you see your purchasing personnel adapting to the new buying philosophy.

Classification: A Take-off from the Old "A-B-C" Control

Do you recall the old approach to classifying an inventory by the way items sold? "A" items were those with lots of money moving through the inventory in a year; "Bs" were the next group with less money involved; "Cs" were numerous but collectively accounted for very few dollars moving through the inventory . . . and "Ds" were the dogs . . . defunct . . . dead stock items. The first step to be able to purchase by inventory class is to classify your stock items in a similar way. However, instead of just four classes, you must identify 13. New classes 1 and 2 sub-divide the old A group. Classes 3 and 4 are finer breakdowns of the old Bs, while

YOUR TURNOVER CONTROL: HOW MUCH TO BUY?

Classes 5 through 12 establish eight levels within the group that used to be lumped together as Cs. Class 13 hasn't changed much. It's still the dogs, the old "D" designation.

The Classification Procedure

With a computer and a complete, accurate history of sales on stock items, the classification step is a breeze. Refer to the illustration.

CLASSIFICATION STEPS

1. Separately for all stock items in each branch, multiply the annual usage in units by unit cost to determine the annual dollar amount moving through the inventory for each item.

    100 units sold in a year × 4.20 cost = $420

2. Sequence all items according to the dollar-movement answers. The best items with most dollars moving through the inventory are at the top of the list. Zero's are all at the bottom.

3. Decide where the "Dead" item breakpoint is to be. Suggestion: Any item that sells less than $10 at cost for a whole year is considered "D" Class (Dead, Defunct, Dog, etc.)

4. Remove all D items from the classification exercise. They are now to be handled under the Disposition Program (chapter 15).

5. Assign each item remaining on the list (after the D's are removed from the bottom) an Inventory Class as follows:

Top	7 1/2% of the items	-	Class 1
Next	7 1/2%	-	Class 2
Next	10%	-	Class 3
Next	10%	-	Class 4
Next	8%	-	Class 5
	8%	-	Class 6
	8%	-	Class 7
	8%	-	Class 8
	8%	-	Class 9
	8%	-	Class 10
	8%	-	Class 11
Last	9%	-	Class 12
	100%		

    The percentages are of the total number of items on the list. If, for example, you had 5000 items remaining in the study after taking out the D's, Class 1 would have 7 1/2% of 5000 or 375 items. Class 2 would also have 375. Class 3 would have 500 items, etc.

Include *all stock items,* good or bad, in the exercise except the new ones for which you have less than six months of activity history. You've now assigned a class designation to every one of your stock items, dogs included, except those too new to be classified just yet. An item is Class 1, or Class 4, or Class 9, or maybe Class 13 (the dogs). The class of each is developed by relating the money for it that moves through the inventory in a year to the same figure for all other items. Class 1 and 2 represent lots of money moving through the inventory. Class 11 and 12 are at the other end: Not many dollars, relative to all the others. Be sure to do the classification exercise separately for each branch.

Buy the Months' Supply That Corresponds to an Item's Class!

Now the easiest step of all. When it's time to replenish a stock item, buy an amount of material according to this little formula:

CLASS × MONTHLY USAGE RATE

Class	Months Supply to Purchase	Turns per Year to Expect
1	1	12
2	2	6
3	3	4
4	4	3
5	5	2.4
6	6	2
7	7	1.7
8	8	1.5
9	9	1.3
10	10	1.2
11	11	1.1
12	12	1
13	Zero	0

Instead of computing an EOQ, the computer is programmed to determine item classes perhaps once a quarter. Order quantities are developed by multiplying usage rate times class for each item . . . and then rounding off that figure to the nearest standard package. Class 13 items, when they do appear on replenishment action reports, show no computer-recommended order quantity (unless the buyer previously locked-in a figure). If he *must* perpetuate a "dog" item, the buyer decides how many to buy. Hopefully in most cases, the decision will be to drop it from stock instead.

YOUR TURNOVER CONTROL: HOW MUCH TO BUY?

What Results from This Method?

When you review how items are sequenced as the classification step is completed, you'll note that Classes 1 and 2 have only 15 percent of your non-dog items . . . but account for 65 percent of the annual dollar-movement through inventory. Classes 3 and 4 add 20 percent more of the item total and 25 percent of the money movement. Consider that! Classes 1, 2, 3, and 4 account for 35 percent of all your good stock items . . . *BUT 90 PERCENT OF THE ANNUAL MOVEMENT OF DOLLARS THROUGH INVENTORY!* All the rest of the "good" stock items (65 percent of the total number) account for how much of the annual dollar movement? Wow! A whopping 10 percent! Who cares what turns you get on that 65 percent? Sure, it'll be low, but the high turnover on the first four classes . . . about 7 turns average across that group . . . more than offsets the zilch turnover on the 65 percent in classes 5 through 12.

Get Most . . . But Not All of EOQ's Benefits without the EOQ Math!

The Classification Method approximates the results you'd get with EOQ . . . not as precisely, mind you, but certainly within an order quantity's general range for any specific stock item. Classification is easier to understand, very easy to program, and easier to adapt to. A buyer might be mystified by EOQs math and yet have no trouble at all grasping how classification works.

Are there drawbacks? Well . . . yes. EOQ offers very precise turnover results on each item. It will recommend 1.3 months' supply, or three weeks' supply, or 4.8 months' supply . . . very precise! With Classification, you buy exactly 1 month's supply, 2 months' supply, six, 12, etc. . . . nothing in between. EOQ might suggest 24 turns on a very high money-movement-per-year item. Classification will direct you to only 12 turns a year, unless you identified a group of "Super Class 1" items.

EOQ Develops about One More Turn per Year Than the Class Method

EOQ also develops a better overall turn rate than you'll achieve with Classification . . . about one full turn per year. EOQ is a superior method. It's more complicated. It's tougher to understand and sometimes easy to misapply. Classification avoids the complication and rarely recommends a foolish order quantity unless you attempt to classify an item without sufficient history. EOQ gets better results when both methods are applied correctly. One thing is certain. ==For the 80 percent of your stock items with moderate or better sales, and no squirrely conditions in history, EOQ *or* Classification beats pure SWAG! Be sure to use one or the other!==

WHAT TO DO WHEN THE SUPPLIER OFFERS A PRICE BREAK BY THE ITEM

Let's talk now about that condition mentioned earlier where EOQ, or Classification, would be out of place if applied: When the supplier offers a direct savings per unit to encourage you to buy more of an individual item. Remember now, this is *not* a total-order discount! It's just a better base price for the item if you'll increase the order quantity on it alone. You may also get some form of economic advantage for buying 5,000 lbs., or whatever, when all items on the purchase order are totaled . . . but that's not the problem in view here.

EOQ or Classification can't help out, because they both assume no change in the base unit price with an increase in order quantity. When the unit price *does* change with a higher quantity ordered, new factors are introduced that are not part of the EOQ or Classification evaluation.

One fact hasn't changed: The more inventory you buy of an item, the longer it will take to sell it . . . and the longer it stays in your warehouse, the more inventory holding cost ("K") you'll incur. The new factor, of course, is that you now have a chance to save on the unit cost if you do purchase more of the item. Oversimplified, the problem comes down to finding how far you can go, how much you can buy, before the holding costs on the larger inventory outweighs the savings . . . to find the lowest *NET* unit cost . . . one that considers the K cost likely to be incurred if you bought each option. With EOQ, the incoming cost (what you pay the supplier) doesn't change if you buy more of this one item . . . but in this problem, it does. A new calculation is needed to find the lowest "outgoing" cost. It's a computer exercise.

The Average Inventory

Before proceeding, let's look at another inventory management principle:

> When a quantity of material goes on your shelf, the "average" inventory carried during the time it takes to sell the material is exactly one-half the amount purchased . . . no matter how much you bought or how long it takes to sell that quantity.

> *Illustration*: 100 pieces are delivered January 1st. The last one sells March 31st. The average inventory for the January-through-March period is 50.

That principle becomes very important in this problem. We must determine the average inventory we'd expect to carry during the time required to sell what we purchase, for *each* of the quantity breaks offered by the supplier. The new calculation then adds the K costs for this average dollar investment to the total cash outlay required . . . divides by the quantity of units being considered . . . and develops a "Net" unit cost for each quantity break. The most profitable buy is of course the level with the lowest net unit cost.

Obviously, both good and bad things can happen when you "load up" on one of your stock items. The good is easy to see. The incoming unit cost is lower and the salesmen sure like that. Their selling job is easier. They can sell at a lower price and still make a nice commission on an acceptable level of gross profit. Their advice: "*ALWAYS* go for the lowest incoming cost the supplier offers! Purchasing, buy in the last column! Don't worry about the inventory carrying costs. Get us a good cost or we can't be competitive in the marketplace!" Sound familiar?

Also when you go heavy on an item, the stock lasts longer. You don't have to replenish it as often and that does improve your chances of having material, even a large order, when customers call. That's why I said earlier that the order quantity does indeed have some impact on service . . . not as much as it does on turnover . . . but yes, service is affected by how many you buy of an item. Those are the good things: Lower unit cost, easier selling job, and likely a better service performance.

There's Always a Trade-off

What are the negatives when you load up? It's all too easy for the Inventory Carrying Cost (K) to eat up all the savings generated by purchasing the larger quantity . . . and remember, the salesmen really don't care! They want the lowest *INCOMING* cost possible. That makes their selling job easier. If the company becomes a non-profit organization because of all the excess stock laying around . . . well, that's not their problem. Most of them will have jobs with the competitors within the first week you're out of business. Am I being too tough on the poor salesmen? No . . . just realistic. I'd have that same attitude if I sold for you.

The Quantity Discount Evaluation

Let's determine how the computer can evaluate a series of price breaks to find one that offers the best chance for profit, considering the savings offered, the time an item will be on the shelf, and the holding cost. Remember: This is the supplier's pricing for *a single item,* apart from all others. It's not a "Line Buy" being considered. We're trying to decide how many of this one item to buy right now:

A Quantity	B Price	C Total Investment	D Holding Cost	E Investment + Holding Cost	E ÷ A Net Cost per Unit
1	$10.00	$ 10.00	-	$ 10.00	$10.00
10	9.00	90.00	1.31	91.31	9.13
25	8.50	212.50	7.75	220.25	8.81
50	7.50	375.00	27.35	402.35	8.05
100	6.50	650.00	94.79	744.79	7.45
200	6.25	1250.00	364.58	1614.58	8.07
Usage Rate = 10/Month			K = 35% per Year		

NOTE: Thanks to Dr. Dan Parris of National Welding Supply in Fort Worth, Texas for his assistance in developing this evaluation technique.

The holding cost at each level is calculated like this (using the 100 level as an example):

$$\frac{\text{Average inventory across the 10 months}}{\text{this material will be in stock}} = 50 \ (100 \div 2)$$

50 × $6.50 = $325   (Average inventory investment)

.35 of $325 = $113.75   (Total annual carrying cost)

10/12th's of $113.75 = $94.79   (Carrying cost for 10 months)

You can see that the 100-level purchase affords the lowest net unit cost of all the options. The supplier offers a little more up-front savings for buying 200, but the extra holding costs across the 20 months would eat away all the savings and more. The "net unit cost" is calculated by dividing the quantity being considered into the total of investment and holding cost for the average inventory while the material is in stock . . . and yes, it's assumed that we'll continue to sell 10 units per month. If we sell more, we're OK but if we sell less . . . heck, we're likely in trouble, but that's the nature of all inventory decisions: Trying to outguess the future . . . *always* dangerous! The answer might be different with a 30 or 40 percent K factor.

A Logistical Problem with This Solution

Anyway, that's how you can program your computer to evaluate the various quantity buying levels offered on an item and select the one that will provide the lowest net unit cost (holding cost considered) if you continue to sell the item at about the rate you have in the past. It's not very difficult to understand or program the logic . . . but there is a hangup.

YOUR TURNOVER CONTROL: HOW MUCH TO BUY?

Let's suppose you stock 5,000 items with pricing like this: 5,000 items with an average of six possible buying levels for each . . . 30,000 prices. You ask Agnes (a very dedicated employee who likes to work evenings, weekends, and holidays) to key in all 30,000 prices into your computer files. So she does. For the next six weeks, Agnes works night and day to get the prices entered so that your new programming logic can help Purchasing pick the proper levels to buy on the 5,000 items. Finally, exhausted, Agnes announces: "They're all in, Boss!" . . . and then what happens? You know. The suppliers send out all new price sheets. When you ask Agnes to do the job over, her comments are very unlady-like.

For you, then, this entire exercise of having the computer compute holding costs, add them to the investment for each buying level option, and develop the lowest "net" unit cost . . . may have to wait awhile. As nice as that would be, the logistics of maintaining thousands and thousands of prices in the computer records might be too ponderous. The cost of maintaining the prices could wind up more than the savings you'd gain by buying the proper quantities.

In some industries, however, this exercise is practical right now. These industries enjoy the benefit of suppliers who offer computer tapes when prices change . . . or there's an industry pricing service (usually a private concern) who offers computer-to-computer pricing data for nearly all suppliers. Poor ol' Agnes doesn't have to key-in new prices one item at a time, six levels each. Your computer processes the pricing data in the form provided by the suppliers or the pricing service. 30,000 prices can be changed in an hour. Be sure to find out where your industry stands on this feature . . . which manufacturers offer pricing tapes or discs; if there's a pricing service company available, etc. Then, *before* you design your system or purchase one, make certain it accommodates the computer-to-computer linkups available to you.

SUMMARY

The order quantity . . . a very important decision in an effective inventory management system! For too many years, distributors' buyers just took the easy way out on every purchase order and brought in " . . . what we ordered last time." Today, that's expensive SWAG. It's lazy. It leads to lots of slow-moving stock. It's done to get the lowest incoming cost possible to keep the sales force happy, but with no thought to the more important cost . . . the *out-going* cost!

There are solid control methods you can use to assure the right turnover on each stock item and the lowest outgoing cost. The EOQ or Purchasing By Inventory Class approach . . . either one . . . causes an item's inventory investment in dollars to turn over in accord with how much money is moving through the inventory each month. As we just discussed, there's a quick, easy way for the computer to develop the lowest "net" unit cost when a buyer must select one ordering quantity from several options.

"Gosh!" you say. "There's a lot more to effective inventory control than I ever thought . . . or than we've ever done in the past! This looks like a lot of work!" True. I warned you about that back in the early chapters. There *is* a lot more thought, planning and effort required to meet those twin goals of Good Service and Low Costs, than in the past when we just covered all our SWAG with lots of inventory. If you carry plenty of stock on all items, you don't have to worry about all this stuff we've talked about. You'll also go bankrupt.

11

SPECIAL ORDERING SITUATIONS

Distributors must solve three special buying problems that manufacturers see much less frequently:

1. How to select the most profitable option when a supplier offers several total-order discount levels.
2. How much to buy ahead of a price increase.
3. How much to buy of an item when the supplier offers some terrific (but temporary) promotional price.

Manufacturers do get a chance, once in a while, to buy in ahead of a price increase. Very often, however, their suppliers raise prices without warning or announce the increase on the next bid for their business. Manufacturers seldom see promotional pricing or the "line buying" problem discussed back in Chapter 9, but distributors wrestle with all these headaches daily.

These ordering situations, then, are not "special" because a distributor sees them infrequently, but because they're special to distributors. Each offers (what appears to be) an opportunity for extra profit. Guess what else they each offer? A chance to lose money if you get too greedy, listen to all that advice from your salesmen, or fail to weigh carefully the savings offered in relation to the *real* costs involved.

A TIME-TESTED INVENTORY PRINCIPLE TO REMEMBER

Before we discuss the three buying problems, there's another whiskered old inventory control adage that must not be overlooked:

You are justified in carrying some inventory of an item if you sell it regularly and the customers expect to find it on your shelves. The proper quantity you should have, however, is dictated by your normal ordering controls: the Order Point, Line Point, and Order Quantity. When you exceed this proper amount to gain some additional economic advantage, you've left the principles of inventory management. Now, you're "speculating" with the inventory dollars.

All three special buying situations offer the chance for *extra* profit, beyond what you'd make through normal inventory management of the items involved and sale of these products to customers at a normal markup. I won't argue that perhaps you *have* to do it for competitive reasons, but the facts are . . . you're speculating! You want an incoming unit cost lower than it would be normally, so that extra gross margin can be squeezed out when the item sells. You want to buy low and sell high. In the stock market, a land investment, or with inventory, that's speculation!

When you speculate, there's always a downside risk. You may buy low and wind up selling lower. You may buy low and not sell at all. You may buy low and get a chance a little later to buy even lower still. There are distributors working with the bankruptcy courts right now who were terrific speculators. They made some of the best buys you ever heard of. Now you can buy those distributors . . . cheap!

A "great" buy, obviously, is truly great only if the savings over the long haul . . . when the merchandise finally sells . . . outweigh the total costs incurred along the way. Just as in the last chapter on order quantities, it's the *outgoing cost,* the total cost, that matters. Only when that cost is compared to the tempting up-front unit cost savings can you tell if the buy was great or maybe not-so-great after all. Simply put, the savings *must be greater* than the total cost of the extra inventory you must buy! Otherwise, you've taken another step toward becoming a nonprofit organization.

Seems logical doesn't it? Quit grinning! You know you've bought lots of "deals" without a thought to what your inventory carrying costs would be before you could unload the material, and so have many other distributors. But that's how we'll evaluate these three buying opportunities.

Picking the Right Total-Order Level

The total-order discount evaluation is similar to the item quantity discount problem of Chapter 10. There is, however, one major difference. You must solve the problem (pick the buying level) using only those items below line point at the time you must place the purchase order.

SPECIAL ORDERING SITUATIONS

They are the only candidates for ordering right now. All other items in the product line are more than one review cycle away (in time) from their order points. The below-line-point group represents a certain number of dollars of monthly usage . . . and for *this* P.O., that's all you have to work with. Look at this problem:

DISCOUNT OFFERED FOR A TOTAL LINE-BUY ORDER

Buying Level (A)	Discount (B)	Investment (C)	Months' Supply (D)	Holding Cost (E)	Investment + Holding Cost (F)	Net Purchasing Dollar (F ÷ A)
$ 500	2%	$ 490	.33	$ 2.36	$ 492.36	$.98
1000	5%	950	.67	9.29	959.29	.96
2500	7%	2325	1.67	56.49	2381.49	.95
5000	10%	4500	3.33	218.75	4718.75	.94
10000	12%	8800	6.67	855.56	9655.56	.97

Usage of Items at OP or LP = $1500 per Month   K = 35% per Year

Holding Cost Calculations

$ 490 × ½ = $ 245 × .35 = $ 83.75 ÷ 36.4 = $ 2.36
  950   =   475   =   166.25 ÷ 17.9 =   9.29
 2325   = 1162   =   406.70 ÷ 7.2 =   56.49
 4500   = 2250   =   787.50 ÷ 3.6 =   218.75
 8800   = 4400   =   1540.00 ÷ 1.8 =   855.56

The candidates for the purchase order are only those items now at line point or order point. In this problem, that group amounts collectively to $1500 in usage per month (their usage rates × their unit costs).

With $1500 per month in usage to work with, the number of months' supply is shown for each buying level. That in turn permits a calculation of expected holding costs at each level.

The goal is to find out (considering the savings and holding cost at each level) where we achieve the most discount per purchasing dollar. At the $5000 level, the net discount is .06. For all other levels, either the lack of savings or the holding costs cause it to be less.

For each buying option, we've determined the total holding cost. Since there's $1,500 of usage per month in the items below line point, we can calculate how many months' supply (on the average) will arrive if we purchase $1,000, or $5,000, or $10,000 . . . and knowing the months' supply for each option allows a calculation of inventory holding costs. The calculation is shown.

The holding cost at each total-order level is added to that level's actual up-front inventory investment . . . what we actually lay out in cash. Column F shows the result for each purchasing option. Dividing *that total* at each level by the undiscounted dollars ($2,500, $5,000, $10,000, etc.) required by the supplier yields a *net purchasing dollar* . . . or in reverse, shows just how many cents off *each dollar* you will actually realize when the material finally moves out of the warehouse. Note that the $5,000 level develops a final discount on each dollar of .06. The net purchasing dollar for that buy would be .94. Obviously, the most profitable total order is the one that results in the lowest net purchasing dollar after the savings and inventory holding costs are melded together. All other total order options in the problem result in less "when-all-is-said-and-done" savings per-dollar.

Make a New Evaluation on Each Purchase Order

The next P.O. in this product line should receive a new evaluation by the computer. The next time, there likely will be an entirely different group of items below line point. Usually, the answer will come out the same . . . but it might not. A line's review cycle (Chapter 9) dictates the general frequency of purchase orders, which means that each P.O. *should* contain items of a similar usage mix. However, the next P.O. has a brand new array of items below line point, and sales are growing in these products perhaps. Who knows? Maybe the next bunch to be bought will justify a higher level. It's worth a fresh look by the computer.

The Total-Order Options Must Be Expressed in Dollars

If the supplier expresses the total-order options in units, pounds, volume, or anything other than dollars, convert it to dollars before making the evaluation. That's not as tough as it sounds. Look back at your old purchase orders to this supplier and figure out the average dollars per pound or per unit over the last several months. Use that to make the conversion.

Keep It Simple. Don't Try to Program Every Element into the Evaluation!

Recognize that countless other elements might cause an adjustment to the answer. You may not have the space or money; an item may be too bulky to buy just by economics; a shelf life might be involved; entering or leaving the "season" is a consideration; and then there's always competition that could force a less-than-the-most-profitable buy.

SPECIAL ORDERING SITUATIONS

You need a simplistic answer to guide the inexperienced buyer . . . the guy or gal who's been with you two months . . . not 20 years! The computer should be programmed to recommend answers that make sense when none of these other elements are present . . . and that's most of the time. The solution becomes too complicated if programming attempts to work in "everything" that could *ever* affect an answer.

The buyer needs guidance as to which total-order level to achieve this time, but he also needs management protection. He needs to know that if he follows the computer's recommendation, he's following the *company's official policy* on buying truckloads or LTL, etc! That's important. When an item's unit cost goes up after a purchase, the buyer must not be subjected to harassment from one or more salesmen: "Why didn't you get the truckload cost, dumbo?" If you adopt this total-order evaluation technique, make certain that Sales knows it . . . and stays off of Purchasing's back. You're after a profitable *outgoing cost,* and that may not be the lowest incoming cost where large total-orders are required by the supplier.

Buying Ahead of a Price Increase

The second purchasing situation a distributor's buyer faces often is what to do when a supplier announces an impending price increase . . . but allows a purchase right now at the old prices. "All prices are going up 10 percent effective tomorrow morning! Anything you order today, however, will be invoiced at the old prices." . . . and the supplier's salesman leaves to visit his other distributors to give them the news. You must call in your order by 4 PM this afternoon, and you stock 427 items in this product line. You *know* you should do something . . . buy some of the better items, but it's 2:30 now. How can you review 427 items and make a defendable buying decision on each one before the deadline? Well, if you're to do it without resorting totally to SWAG, you'll need help from the computer.

A Basic Assumption before We Begin

To evaluate this buying problem, we have to assume one thing:

> You *will* raise your selling prices immediately on the items in this product line! The savings made on the buying end will go into your company pocket . . . not simply be passed on to your customers.

Oh sure, I *know* you can't always do this. Many times, you cannot raise your prices until competition does. All or part of the savings will have to be passed on to your customers, at least for a while, because of competitive pressure in the same or similar product lines. . . . but a different evaluation is needed for these conditions, and we'll talk about that later. Right now, let's look at a way to evaluate the economics when you *can* raise prices tomorrow.

The Three Buying Options

When prices are going up, you have three (rather obvious) buying options:

1. Buy a popular, fast-moving item now and reap the savings in unit cost.
2. Forego the savings on the popular item. Pay the higher cost later.
3. On slow-moving items, forget any attempt at savings. Don't buy now.

No one has much of a problem with Option 3. We all know that it isn't very smart to buy more of a "dog" item for any reason. . . . but boy do we wrestle with Options 1 and 2! When is it wise to go ahead and buy? When should we hold off? Take a look at the problem on the next page. The supplier will raise his price from $10 to $11 on a very popular item. The usage rate is 1,000 per month. (That's $10,000 per month moving through the inventory—a Class 1 item for sure!) Note that the Order Point is 1,500; the Line Point is 2,000; the Normal Order Quantity is 500 (EOQ adjusted upward to two weeks' supply); and that there are 2,000 on hand and on order (at the $10 price) with the supplier. . . . and it's decision time. If we're to beat the price increase, a P.O. must go in *today!* How many, if any, should be ordered?

The lead time is one month. What we order today will arrive one month from today. No dating; no special payment terms. The savings . . . the *only* savings is the $1 per unit we get by placing a P.O. ahead of the price increase deadline. Something else to consider: How long will the 2,000 last that are already on hand and on order? Selling 1,000 per month, that stock will last two months. Whatever we purchase today will arrive in one month. In the problem, today is January 1. A new purchase arrives February 1, but we won't begin to sell any of it until March 1. Does that matter? Yes.

How K Cost Impacts the Average Inventory or the Full Purchase

The annual carrying cost percentage (K) as you can see is 36 percent . . . or 3 percent per month. Normally, the K is applied against

HOW MUCH TO BUY BEFORE THE PRICE GOES UP

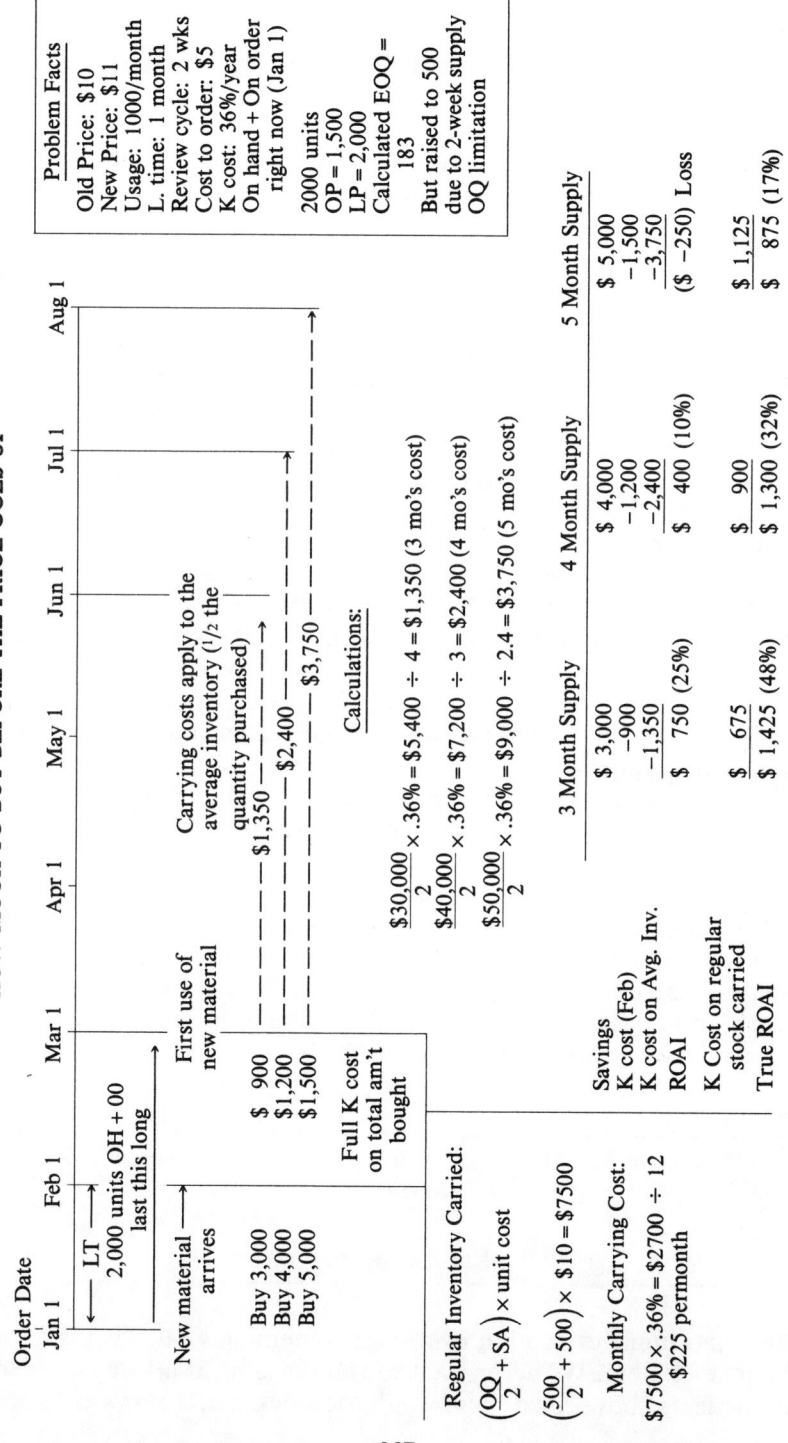

Order Date								
Jan 1	Feb 1	Mar 1	Apr 1	May 1	Jun 1	Jul 1	Aug 1	

← LT →
2,000 units OH + OO last this long

First use of new material ← New material arrives

Buy 3,000 $ 900
Buy 4,000 $1,200
Buy 5,000 $1,500

Full K cost on total am't bought

Carrying costs apply to the average inventory (1/2 the quantity purchased)

———— $1,350 ————→
———————— $2,400 ————————→
———————————————— $3,750 ————————————————→

Problem Facts
Old Price: $10
New Price: $11
Usage: 1000/month
L. time: 1 month
Review cycle: 2 wks
Cost to order: $5
K cost: 36%/year
On hand + On order right now (Jan 1)
2000 units
OP = 1,500
LP = 2,000
Calculated EOQ = 183
But raised to 500 due to 2-week supply OQ limitation

Calculations:

$\dfrac{\$30,000}{2} \times .36\% = \$5,400 \div 4 = \$1,350$ (3 mo's cost)

$\dfrac{\$40,000}{2} \times .36\% = \$7,200 \div 3 = \$2,400$ (4 mo's cost)

$\dfrac{\$50,000}{2} \times .36\% = \$9,000 \div 2.4 = \$3,750$ (5 mo's cost)

	3 Month Supply	4 Month Supply	5 Month Supply
Savings	$ 3,000	$ 4,000	$ 5,000
K cost (Feb)	−900	−1,200	−1,500
K cost on Avg. Inv.	−1,350	−2,400	−3,750
ROAI	$ 750 (25%)	$ 400 (10%)	($ −250) Loss
K Cost on regular stock carried	$ 675	$ 900	$ 1,125
True ROAI	$ 1,425 (48%)	$ 1,300 (32%)	$ 875 (17%)

Regular Inventory Carried:
$\left(\dfrac{OQ}{2} + SA\right) \times$ unit cost

$\left(\dfrac{500}{2} + 500\right) \times \$10 = \$7500$

Monthly Carrying Cost:
$\$7500 \times .36\% = \$2700 \div 12$
$\$225$ per month

167

the "average" inventory or one-half the quantity purchased for the portion of the year the material is in the warehouse. When you buy three months' supply of an item, you start with the full quantity on the shelf and sell it off over three months. At the end of the period, you have nothing left from this particular purchase. Across the three months, the average inventory is one-half what you bought.

That's the normal situation. Not so here. Whatever we buy will sit around for one full month before we begin to sell it, so the 3 percent per month K cost for that first month impacts the full purchased amount . . . not half. *Then,* the normal conditions apply and from that point on, the K cost works against the average inventory.

In the problem example, three quantity options are considered: Buy 3,000 of this item now, or 4,000, or 5,000. Please understand . . . this is just to demonstrate how to evaluate the economics. Obviously, there are countless other quantities that could have been included: Buy none; Buy 20,000, etc.

For these three, however, you can see the February holding costs of $900, $1,200, or $1,500. That's 3 percent ($1/12$th of a year's holding cost) on the full investment ($30,000, $40,000, or $50,000) for each buying option. Why? Remember, for the entire month of February, we won't sell any of the stock bought now to beat the price increase. On March 1, we will begin to sell it, and you can see the holding costs for the three, four, or five months while the stock is being sold off at 1,000 per month ($1,350, $2,400, or $3,750). When the new stock is selling, the 3 percent per month K cost now works against the average inventory we'd generate with each quantity option.

Another Complication

It would be nice if this problem ended here. We'd compare the savings for each option against the February K cost and the rest of the holding cost, and see where we would come out the best:

					ROI
Buy 3000	Save $3000	Less $ 900	Less $1350	=	$750 Profit
Buy 4000	$4000	$1200	$2400	=	$400 Profit
Buy 5000	$5000	$1500	$3750	=	$250 Loss
	ROI = Return on Investment				

But this simple evaluation overlooks something vital. This is an important stock item. We never want to run out of it. If all we considered were the facts above, then there would be stockouts. There's an average

SPECIAL ORDERING SITUATIONS

inventory size to expect on this item all the time . . . required to satisfy our service and normal turnover objectives. This inventory has *nothing to do* with the problem with which we're wrestling here . . . how to buy low and sell high. We'll have it regardless of whether we buy something extra now to beat the price increase, or whether we buy nothing at all. That average inventory in somewhat abbreviated form is calculated under "Regular Inventory Carried."

Yes, we'd have an average of $7,500 of this item on hand all the time under the controls now being used, and that $7,500 has a holding cost: $225 per month when the K is 36 percent per year. That holding cost must be considered in any economic evaluation of how much *more* stock, how much extra stock, we can afford in speculation. When the $225 per month is added back to the answer from the original evaluation, the true ROAI (Return on *ADDED* Investment) for the buy options considered is $1,425, $1,300, or $875.

So What? What's the Purpose of This Confusing Exercise?

When you decide to invest additional money, to risk funds beyond what's required for normal service and turnover goals, and you're doing it for speculative purposes . . . well, the factors are complex. There's much more to think about than most distributor purchasing people ever considered in the past. When suppliers announced price increases, the buyers simply reacted to pressure from Sales, or Management, and "loaded up," especially on popular items. Is it surprising then that today distributors rate "Poor Turnover" as their most serious problem . . . and that mismanaged assets is the Number 1 cause of distributor bankruptcy?

This exercise was to show you the complex factors . . . to demonstrate why it's so doggone easy to wind up losing money when, on the surface, the great buy looked so appealing. I hope you drew another conclusion: It would be hopeless to try to solve a problem like this on 427 items in a product line, evaluating the countless quantity-options for each, without a computer to do the work *and* a formula to find *the most profitable of all buying options* for each item.

The Pre-Price Increase Formula

Thanks to Mr. Alan Silver of Highland Park, New Jersey, there is a very workable formula to help evaluate the savings versus holding cost conditions when there's a chance to (as we say in Texas) "kill a fat hog" by buying low with intent to sell high:

$$\text{ROAI} = \frac{24 \times \text{Discount Percentage}}{\text{Extra Months' Supply to Purchase}} - \text{K Cost \%}$$

"Buddy" Silver's complete formula actually contains several more elements, but becomes rather difficult for the average distributor to employ effectively when all the other factors are included. This abbreviated version isn't perfect . . . but it does derive buying answers that I've found to be quite profitable (if perhaps conservatively so) for most pre-price-increase opportunities.

Let's plug the facts from our earlier problem into this formula and see how it comes out:

$$\text{ROAI} = \frac{24 \times .10}{\text{Extra Months' Stock to Purchase}} - .36$$

Hmmm . . . we still can't solve for an answer, because there are two unknowns in the formula: The ROAI and How Much To Purchase. If we were to arbitrarily assign a value to one of these unknowns, then there'd be only one—and we could get an answer. Let's assign 40 percent as the ROAI (Return on Added Investment). The other unknown . . . how much to buy . . . is what we want the formula to tell us.

Why 40 percent? Well, remember that this ROAI is the goal, the targeted *NET* bottom line return we want by adding this extra money into inventory. But what are we doing here? We're speculating! . . . with the company's money! What could happen? Lots of things, and some of them would be disasters. A competitive supplier introduces a superior product at a lower price just after you load up on this item. You lose most of the 1,000 per month sales to competition right after the carload arrives. You'd look like a hero, right? Heck no, it's buying decisions like this that will get you into the consulting business quicker than you planned.

So, if I speculate with company money, I want a *very substantial* net profit return goal . . . 40 percent! You can put whatever figure in there you'd be happy with. It's your targeted return on the extra money you're investing for speculative purposes. With 40 percent assigned as the ROAI, now the formula can be switched around a bit:

$$\text{Extra Months' Stock to Purchase} = \frac{24 \times \text{Discount Percentage}}{\text{ROAI} + \text{K \%}}$$

$$\text{Extra Months' Stock to Purchase} = \frac{24 \times .10}{.40 + .36} \quad \text{or} \quad \frac{2.4}{.76}$$

Extra Months' Stock to Purchase = 3.1

SPECIAL ORDERING SITUATIONS

What Kind of an Answer Is That?

What does that mean . . . 3.1? For all items in this product line where the conditions are the same, the distributor should order now—before the price goes up—enough material so as to have no more than 3.1 months of *EXTRA* stock, if he does indeed raise the selling prices immediately. Since we began by saying that all 427 items were going up 10 percent, then conditions are the same for all. There's nothing unique to the item, so far, in what the formula used to get the answer. The usage rate or unit cost hasn't been considered (yet). The answer says simply: You can afford to have 3.1 months of *EXTRA* stock of every item in the line where the price is about to go up 10 percent, and that's all of them. Common sense says: "Wait a minute. That would be stupid!" It would. There's one step left before you place the purchase order.

The Key to Using the Answer

Note that the answer is the *extra stock* you're allowed. "Extra" above what amount or condition? The rules to follow:

1. If stock on-hand + on-order for an item is now below Line Point, you will soon be buying the item . . . regardless of whether the price is going up or not. Follow the formula answer.

2. If the item is above Line Point (on-hand + on-order), the computer calculates how long in time it will be before the Line Point is reached . . . using the item's usage rate, etc. That time is subtracted from the formula's answer.

3. If the item will not be down to Line Point within the time of the formula's answer, nothing is purchased.

In this one special buying problem only, the Line Point defines what stock is considered "extra" and what isn't. When an item is below Line Point, the formula allows you to buy on beyond it. When an item is above Line Point already, then from this problem's perspective the distributor already has "extra" stock. The formula sets the limit on how much more, if any, can be purchased for speculative purposes.

The Effect: Your Purchase Is Restricted to Faster-Moving Items

Perhaps you're grasping something quite important in how this approach helps select the items to buy: Only your high-class items (1s, 2s, 3s, etc.) will be down close to Line Point most of the time. Most of the slower-moving items, where you might have bought routinely a six, seven, or ten-months' supply, will be way above Line Point. This speculative purchase to beat the price increase is limited by the formula to faster-moving items. The others will be too far above Line Point to be considered. If you are going to speculate, it's safer to invest the added money in those items that sell the best. You risk less. That's just common sense, of course, but this formula offers a consistent method . . . other than pure SWAG . . . to select the items.

Relax! You've Got a Great Computer System to Help You . . . Don't You?

As you review how we started this discussion about price increases, wouldn't it be nice if all you had to do was feed into the computer how much in percent the prices for the 427 items were going up? . . . and the computer takes off to find, first, the items where anything at all should be purchased now. Then, using the usage rates, modifies the quantities in accord with where each item is relative to its Line Point. Long before the 4 PM ordering deadline, you receive a report advising which items to buy and how many of each. . . . and you get a good night's sleep, assured that the company will generate a 40 percent (my ROAI minimum) bottom-line return on the money invested *IF* you do raise the selling prices right now.

Aren't you glad you have a computerized system that's programmed to do all this for you, to remove such burdensome decisions from your poor overworked buyers . . . to replace all that costly SWAG of the past? "WE DON'T HAVE A SYSTEM THAT DOES THIS!" you say. Hmmm . . . that's too bad. Well, aren't you glad then you're reading this book? Perhaps you can program this feature soon into your system or, with your next system, purchase one on the market that functions like this.

OK, What If You Can't Raise Selling Prices Right Now?

It isn't always possible to raise selling prices as soon as you know of an increase from your supplier to you. The products may be highly competitive, or most of your business for them generated through systems contracts that have specific time rules as to when prices may be adjusted. So how can you apply what you've learned in this chapter when Sales screams: "You're crazy! We can't raise our prices now on those items!"

You have to reply with a question: "Well, when *can* we raise our selling prices?" Sales must then try to estimate, based on their intimate knowledge of the market conditions, when the prices can go up on these

SPECIAL ORDERING SITUATIONS

products. Sure, it's guesswork, but who's better qualified than Sales to do it? They may come back with any one of several answers:

1. We can raise prices only after we receive from our suppliers stock for which we actually paid the higher costs. (Sales *could* say something like this, of course, but frankly such a requirement is not their's to lay down. This falls more in the realm of Finance or Top Management.)

2. We can raise prices after sufficient notice (30 days, for example) has been given to the major system contract customers, in accord with each contract's terms.

3. We can raise selling prices when competition does, and we estimate that this will occur about June 1, etc.

4. We can raise our prices slightly now . . . not the full amount of the increase to us . . . and ease them on up the rest of the way on June 1.

5. We don't want to raise prices at all . . . even though we must pay a higher price to our supplier. "Don't worry! We'll make it up with more volume. We'll be even more competitive than before in the marketplace!"

(Recommendation: *DON'T FALL FOR THIS ONE!*)

If prices can't go up right now, does the problem change? Certainly does!

Competitive Versus Speculative Economic Decisions

Up until now, the emphasis in all this talk about supplier cost increases has been on economics. How much can we buy of an item, intending to buy low and sell high, before the inventory carrying costs eat up all the savings? A simple question of economics: cost versus savings.

But when you can't raise the selling price, the problem changes. You may still want to lay in extra stock to beat the cost increase, but it won't be for economic reasons. It's a competitive decision. You'll buy enough stock to keep the salesmen competitive until they *can* raise selling prices . . . whenever that is, and *then* make an economic decision.

In the problem example used in this exercise, the "day of decision" is January 1. That's the day we must buy or pay a higher price. If Sales says they can't raise prices until June 1, how long will any stock bought now *for the purpose of selling at a higher price* sit in the warehouse before it sells? Four months (from February 1 receipt to June 1). Four months at a 3 percent per month carrying cost . . . and a savings of only 10 percent! Do you see how the problem changed? Buy enough stock, if you must, to keep Sales competitive until June 1 . . . but you can't justify any at all for economic reasons.

The formula can still be used as we discussed, but the stock you buy for competitive reasons (prior to *your* selling price raise) *must be added to* whatever you have now on hand and on order . . . to determine an item's position relative to Line Point . . . which in turn must be subtracted from the formula's answer if the position turns out to be above the Line Point. That will always reduce the number of items that qualify for an economic purchase, and lower the quantity of the ones that do qualify. If the selling price increase is delayed more than two months, most economic purchasing becomes too marginal to risk. You buy two months' supply of popular items for competitive reasons and forget any "buy low/sell high" inventory investment.

The Third Special Buying Situation: Promotions

If you've grasped the concepts of the last few pages, buying ahead of a promotion will be easy to understand. The reason? Promotional buying is an almost identical problem to the one just discussed, Buying Ahead of Price Increases From Suppliers. "How so?" you ask. "I see no connection between the two problems!" Ahhh, but there definitely is one.

When the supplier announces a price increase, he's saying simply that his prices are going up:

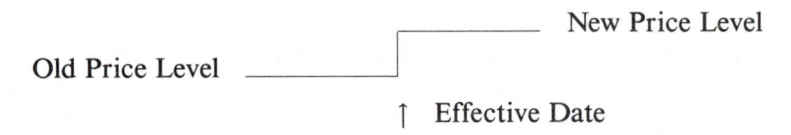

```
                                            ─────── New Price Level
   Old Price Level  ─────────┘
                             ↑ Effective Date
```

When the supplier announces a promotion, and a period of lower prices to support it, he says that prices are going down . . . but later will go back up.

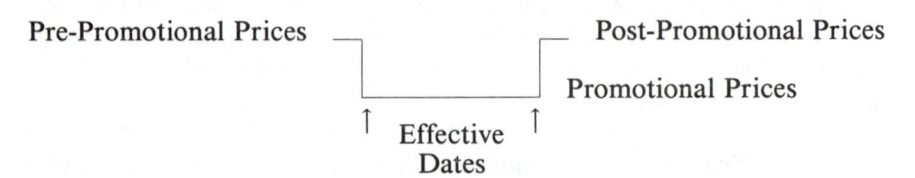

```
Pre-Promotional Prices  ─────┐         ┌─── Post-Promotional Prices
                             └─────────┘    Promotional Prices
                            ↑  Effective  ↑
                               Dates
```

Do you see the similarity in the two conditions? In one, prices are going up. In the next, prices are going down temporarily and then *back*

SPECIAL ORDERING SITUATIONS

up! The buying problem is also similar. For promotions, you buy enough stock to be competitive during the promotional period, and then right before the promotion ends, make an economic (buy low/sell high) buying decision. . . . or, if you must buy all promotionally-priced material before the promotion begins, then the problem is just like the one of the earlier section where selling prices couldn't be raised immediately. You buy two blocks of stock:

1. Stock to be sold at lower prices during the promotion. Nothing magic about this quantity. It's whatever the sales people say they can sell during the promotion at the reduced prices.
2. Stock to be sold at regular prices after the promotion. This is a bit tricky. You must be careful to consider several elements.

How much Number 2 stock? Work the formula. Add the Number 1 material to what you have now on hand at regular costs. Determine the position of each item relative to Line Point. If allowed, buy the difference (in month's supply) for each item, compared to the formula's answer.

But Don't Forget the Effects of a Promotion

Remember, as you attempt this exercise, that the usage rates on most promotional items will fall off when the promotion ends. Why? Well, there's no great mystery here. Most customers load up during the promotion. You won't sell as much after it ends as you did before it began. An item sells at 500 per month before the promotion; 2,000 per month during; and 230 per month afterward . . . for a while. Then the customers use up that low-priced material and start coming back.

Hopefully, the new usage rate when things settle down will be higher than pre-promotion days (650, for example). That's the objective of a promotion: Get more people using the product; the same customers using more of it; or both . . . but that won't happen immediately. Expect that temporary usage drop as you make the original buying decision on any post-promotion "buy low-sell high" inventory.

SUMMARY

Three special buying situations for distributors:

1. Picking the most profitable total-order discount
2. Buying profitably ahead of a supplier's price increase
3. Buying for a promotion

Each offers significant opportunity for terrific savings . . . or a real profit drain, and as you've learned, you need the computer's analytical ability and mass data manipulation to get the right answers when large supplier product lines are involved. Program your system to handle these three conditions correctly. Replace the SWAG that ruled all three until now. These three conditions have in the past been prime contributors to the poor inventory turnover rates with which many distributors suffered. Employ these improved techniques to be sure they don't hurt your company's turn rates next year.

12

REPLENISHMENT ACTION: WHEN "CONTROL" IS EXERCISED!

It's time now to see the fruits of the computer's labor. Usage Rates and Lead Times have been captured; Seasonal items identified; Order Points and Safety Allowances calculated; Review Cycles and Line Points set; EOQs or some other order quantity developed; and Total-Order Discounts evaluated. . . . a lot of work, but for what? When is it used and how?

Let's review one of the time-honored Inventory Control proverbs:

> Inventory *CONTROL* is exercised when you replenish material. If you do a poor job then, everything done afterward is Inventory *CORRECTION!*

We're about to put all that data-gathering, all those calculations, all the evaluations to work. They were done to give us the best chance possible to perform effectively *NOW* . . . when material replenishment is needed. In fact, the entire Inventory Management system has one specific aim: Spend the company's money wisely when it's time to do so! "Wisely," of course, means in a *timely fashion,* so as to assure a continuity of supply on items customers expect to find on our shelves. That's the job of Order Points and Safety Allowances.

"Wisely" means in amounts that assure the lowest Outgoing Cost and turns the dollar investment appropriately for each item. That's the assignment carried out by EOQs or Inventory Class Buying. "Wisely" includes buying product lines on economical frequencies . . . the job of Review Cycles, and putting the right items in the truckload . . . the task for Line Points.

REPORTS DESIGNED TO MAXIMIZE WHAT'S ALREADY BEEN DONE!

If all those control elements are programmed correctly; if the right data has been gathered for the right time frames; if it's been used regularly to re-set the controls; if humans have intervened when the computer identified conditions it couldn't handle; and if the people responsible for Purchasing cared enough to work a bit smarter . . . the "moment of truth" when replenishment decisions are made is productive. If not, the report format won't matter much. If so, the "action report" for ordering can be the most useful tool of your inventory control effort.

What's an "Action Report"?

As it's title implies, an Action Report is one where every entry requires some form of action. Pretty hard to argue with that, huh? . . . but that's in comparison to the kind of reports many computerized systems pump out in huge stacks: "Hmmm . . . that's nice to know!" Most of the information shown is in the "reference" category. It's there in case someone needs to see it, but no immediate action is called for. You find reference reports all over the building, stacked up neatly under or behind peoples' desks, on top of filing cabinets, etc. Some get occasional use, but many come out month after month without anybody looking at them. An Action Report is different. Every entry needs action now!

The Stock Status Report . . . Dangerous!

A typical "Hmmm . . . that's nice to know report" is Purchasing's old standby: The Stock Status. Periodically, every item in a product line (or perhaps in the branch) is listed for someone to study. A few items might be marked with asterisks to indicate they need attention, but there are pages of others that need nothing. A buyer scans the lengthy printout, selects the items to be replenished, and places an order. All too often, two bad things happen:

1. Items are put on the P.O. that shouldn't be there.
2. Others are omitted that should have been ordered.

Remember this little scene from Chapter 2:

> It's 5:30 PM, and I'm the buyer of a product line where we stock 267 items. I really need to get this P.O. called in to the supplier tonight, but I'm also supposed to pick up my little girl at the daycare center by 6:00 PM.

A 20-page printout is on my desk showing the status of all 267 items. How can I get a truckload order put together quickly without risk of a major foulup? Easy. Just pick out the fastest-moving items, order the same quantities as last time, and get on the phone. I'm out of here by 5:45. Oh sure, I didn't review a whole bunch of less-important items . . . but I'll get 'em next time.

No problem, right? . . . except what do you say to a customer who orders one of those "less-important" items? "Sorry, sir. The item you want isn't very important to us, and we aren't careful to maintain our stock in a consistent manner. Now if you'll order the 986XB, boy we have a *lot* of that one in stock!" Most customers would understand that, wouldn't they?

Then of course the overstock on faster-moving products destroys your turnover objectives, eats up your profit with excess carrying costs, and makes the *next* truckload even tougher to put together. But other than that, everything's fine. You have a regular arrangement with a local United Fund outlet where you can donate unneeded material later, and the buyer *did* get to the daycare center on time. How ridiculous, but perhaps you can see why it *is* dangerous to plop every item in front of a buyer. Better that you print out *only* those that need attention . . . and all of them!

Follow the Exception Principle

The exception principle should drive your "action" reports. The listings to guide replenishment action include only those items that have reached a pre-determined condition. If an item appears, something needs to be done. If an item isn't shown, then the buyer is *not authorized* to add it to the purchase order without management approval. In this chapter, we'll discuss two important Action Reports needed in a solid Inventory Control system:

1. Recommended Replenishment Action Report
2. Expedite Report

RECOMMENDED REPLENISHMENT ACTION REPORT

In my first book, I called this report the "Recommended Buy." The name had to change. When you give a Recommended *Buy* Report to a *Buyer,* what happens? Sure, a Purchase Order goes in to the supplier.

Fresh company dollars are spent on more merchandise . . . the *most expensive* replenishment option possible! The new name, hopefully, causes the Buyer, the Inventory Analyst, the Purchasing Manager, or whomever, to remember: "There are several other options to consider *AHEAD OF* just picking up the phone to place a new purchase!" We'll talk about those in a bit, but keep this in mind as you study the report.

There's an example of the Recommended Replenishment Action Report shown in this chapter, but it's much more important for you to follow the principles of the report than the format. You might want to argue about the arrangement in the example, or that something you'd want is omitted. If you do that, you may miss the more important points . . . what the report does and how best to use it. Here are the *principles* to follow:

1. Generally, the report for a product line prints on the established Review Cycle (Chapter 9). The cycle can be interrupted, of course, when conditions call for immediate replenishment action.

2. Each buyer (if you have more than one) receives a report with his or her items only . . . the product lines he or she buys apart from all others.

3. It's an exception report. Items appear only if they require some kind of action. All are below the Line Point or Order Point. The action may not be replenishment, but something needs to be done.

4. The balance shown as "On Hand" is actually the stock available-for-sale . . . what you still own less those quantities committed to customers, other branches, ship-complete orders, will-call, or other uninvoiced (but promised) commitments.

5. Surplus stock of an item in other company locations shows on the report. The quantities should be as of close-of-business the previous day . . . very current. Put the surplus *here* on this report. Don't make the buyer look at some other report or screen.

6. Show each item's Inventory Class (1, 2, 9, 13, etc.) to encourage non-replenishment . . . dropping from stock the slower-moving products with sales approval.

7. Show as much of the sales history, month-by-month, as you have room for. It's *now* at this critical moment of inventory control that a buyer needs to see the history that set the ordering controls as they are. If anything looks strange, *now's* the time to catch it!

RECOMMENDED REPLENISHMENT ACTION REPORT

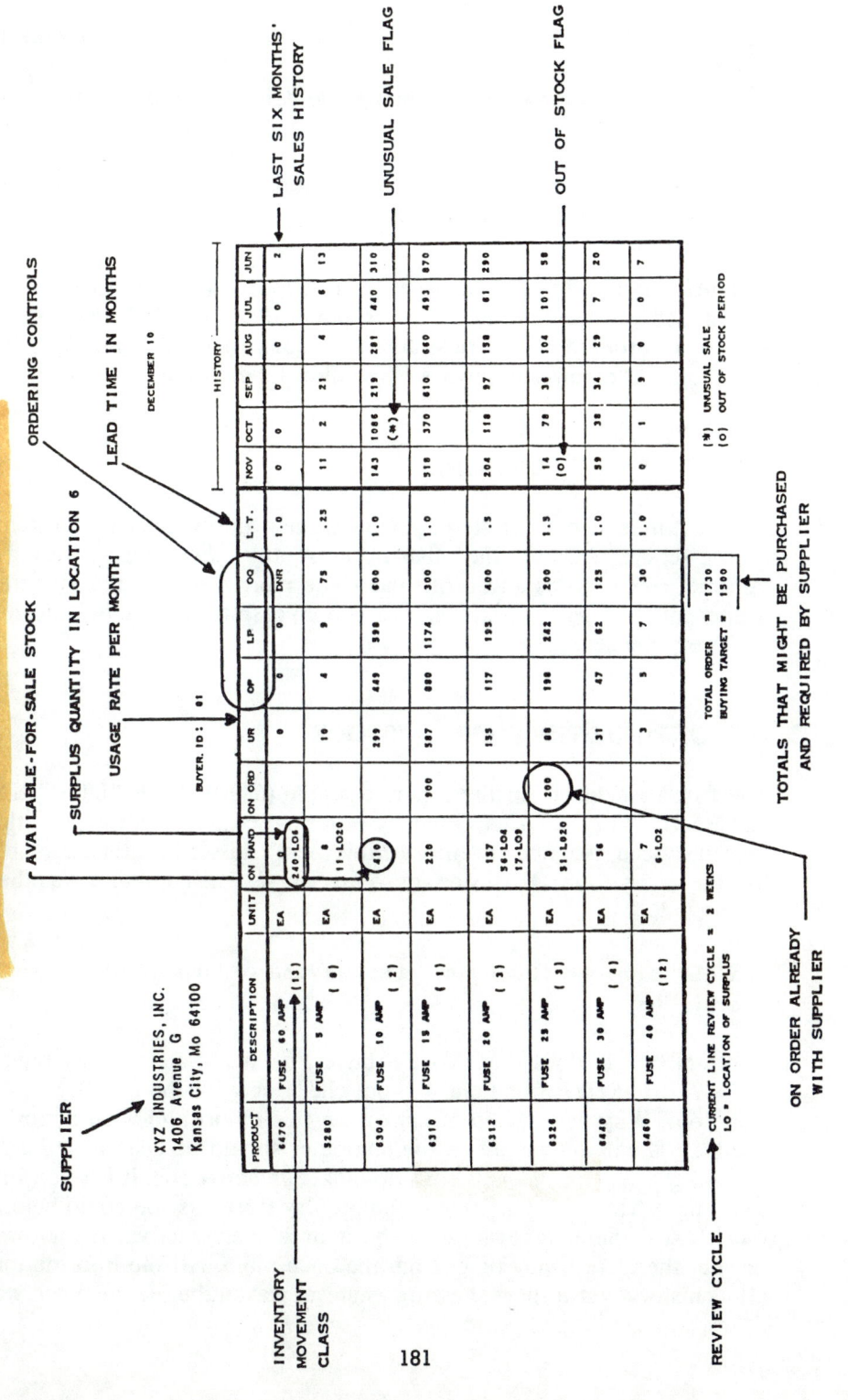

XYZ INDUSTRIES, INC.
1406 Avenue G
Kansas City, Mo 64100

BUYER ID: 01   DECEMBER 10

PRODUCT	DESCRIPTION	UNIT	ON HAND	ON ORD	UR	OP	LP	OQ	L.T.	NOV	OCT	SEP	AUG	JUL	JUN
6470	FUSE 60 AMP (13)	EA	240-LO6		0	0	0	DNR	1.0	0	0	0	0	0	2
5280	FUSE 5 AMP (8)	EA	8 11-LO20		10	4	9	75	.25	11	2	21	4	6	13
6304	FUSE 10 AMP (2)	EA	410		299	440	598	600	1.0	143	1086 (*)	219	281	440	310
6310	FUSE 15 AMP (1)	EA	220	900	597	880	1174	300	1.0	318	370	610	660	493	870
6312	FUSE 20 AMP (3)	EA	157 56-LO4 17-LO9		135	117	195	400	.5	204	118	97	158	61	290
6325	FUSE 25 AMP (3)	EA	0 51-LO20	200	88	198	242	200	1.5	14 (0)	78	36	104	101	58
6440	FUSE 30 AMP (4)	EA	56		31	47	62	125	1.0	59	38	34	29	7	20
6460	FUSE 40 AMP (12)	EA	7 6-LO2		3	5	7	30	1.0	0	1	9	0	0	7

TOTAL ORDER = 1730
BUYING TARGET = 1500

(*) UNUSUAL SALE
(0) OUT OF STOCK PERIOD

CURRENT LINE REVIEW CYCLE = 2 WEEKS
LO = LOCATION OF SURPLUS

8. If you stock directly interchangeable items in other brands, it can be advisable to show the status of these just below the item needing replenishment, or at least suggest that the buyer consider that stock. Again with sales approval, Brand B's overstock can be used to fill all customer demand for a while to avoid placing a new P.O. for Brand A.

9. At the bottom (or last page) of the report, show the totals: How much you have in units, dollars, pounds, or cube if all listed items were ordered in the recommended quantities . . . and what the supplier requires to receive his total-order discount.

REPLENISHMENT OPTIONS

Since the most expensive step is to place a new purchase order for items on the report, what are the other options? *Any other choice* offering a minimal risk to sales and profit has to be more desirable than digging deeper into company pockets for additional cash to finance inventories. Let's consider several.

DISCONTINUE THE ITEM AS "STOCK"

The first item listed on the report example (6470) shows "DNR" (Do Not Reorder) in the Order Quantity column. Sometime in the past, this item has been assigned Inventory Movement Class 13 (parenthesis, below the description). It's a slow-mover or worse. The computer was then instructed:

> When we run out of this turkey, let us know and we'll remove it from your active files.

The DNR code does that. To the buyer, it's a red-alert: "Hey buyer, *DON'T REORDER* this item without checking with the Boss!" So now we're out. Why does the item appear on this report and what action is needed? The item's record in the computer should be deactivated . . . not deleted . . *. deactivated!* It's no longer an active file. It isn't on-line any longer. You can't call it up on an inquiry screen as you could before, but it's still there somewhere. If the item is ever reactivated for some reason, the record may be put on-line once more. All the information, all its history is still there showing whatever was in the file the day it was deactivated.

REPLENISHMENT ACTION: WHEN "CONTROL" IS EXERCISED!

In the days of the old kardex records, the card wasn't thrown away when an item was dropped from stock. It was simply filed in another tray, a filing cabinet or a shoe box in the closet. If it was ever needed again (physical inventory at year end finds 15 more against the back wall), the card could be pulled, posted and reactivated. Do the same thing with the computer file for an item. Don't throw it away. Keep it off-line forever.

Nothing shows in history for item 6470 because the stock may have been transferred to another branch on a non-recurring basis (Chapter 16). Activity like that doesn't appear in history.

SURPLUS MATERIAL IN OTHER LOCATIONS

For several items on the report example, surplus quantities appear just below the on-hand figure. For example, there's no stock of item 6470 here in our branch, but Location 6 has 240 that are surplus. For item 6312, there's surplus in two other places: 56 at Branch 4, and 17 at Branch 9. . . . and a rather obvious replenishment option is presented: Use the other guy's surplus if it's practical to do so!

Information Accuracy Is Critical, and No "Game-Playing"!

The quantities shown must be accurate and current. The foundation of an effective system is record accuracy (Chapter 14), so the numbers must be correct and the status as of close-of-business last night. Otherwise, no one will bother to transfer surplus after one or two abortive attempts. Branch managers must not be permitted to play games either. If the computer shows that you have surplus stock, you'd damn well better *NOT* tell me: "Oh shoot, we sold that stuff three weeks ago!" . . . when you're actually squirreling it away because you want to hold on to the stuff. Management really has to crack down on that.

The Definition of "Surplus"

A distributor's central or regional warehouse supplying other branches, or a company that has only one location, should use this formula to calculate surplus stock on an item:

Surplus = Any quantity on hand in excess of Line Point + Order Quantity

Example: On hand = 150   LP = 50   OQ = 50

Surplus = 50

When you've followed the control suggestions of Chapters 8, 9, and 10—then the maximum allowable stock is the Line Point plus the regular replenishment quantity. The worst thing that could happen is that you've ordered when the item's condition is just barely at Line Point, and . . . horrors . . . not one piece sells before replenishment stock arrives. That happens *very* infrequently, but you shouldn't be penalized or considered to have surplus if it does occur. . . . but any amount *more* than LP + OQ would surely be surplus! It won't harm you at all and will definitely help the company if it can be moved elsewhere and sold.

In branches using Min-Max controls (Chapter 16), surplus is any amount on hand in excess of the Maximum.

Do You Really Want to Be Popular? Put *This* Rule into Effect!

The location with surplus stock has to pay the freight to move it to the location requesting it! There are incentives on both sides of that rule:

1. Don't override the system without excellent reasons. If you keep using your SWAG, and that results in surplus—as calculated by the computer—you'll have to pay the freight to move it to the other branch.

2. Use the other guy's surplus when you see it on a report. It costs you nothing in transportation cost to bring it in!

When It Isn't Practical to Transfer-in Surplus

Certainly there are conditions where it could be silly for anyone to spend company money to move material from one place to another:

- The surplus quantity is small in the other location, but the regular replenishment quantity now called for is large. Example: Our EOQ is 500; Surplus at the other branch: 6.
- The unit cost of the material is low, and transportation costs would be more than the value of the surplus stock. Example: Seal, with a cost of .12; Surplus quantity: 15. Value: $1.80.
- The distance is very great between the locations, and again, transportation costs (no matter who pays it) would be as much as 15 percent of the value of material being moved.

If you're a distributor with many branches, establish "zones" within

the computer files. Merchandise must meet rigid total-value rules to move between distant zones; less to adjacent zones; much less within a zone.
- Accepting the surplus would disrupt completely your ability to meet the supplier's total-order discount on the remaining items with no surplus available.

The key word here is "completely." Buyers often use this excuse when they don't want to transfer surplus from another branch. Some order quantities may have to be juggled, but with a little extra work the P.O. can usually be assembled. It's the "extra work" that makes using the surplus distasteful.
- The particular brand of material is not authorized for sale in the branch who needs resupply. Brand A is low; Branch 2 has a lifetime supply of the same product in Brand B . . . but if you bring it in, you could have big trouble with one or both suppliers.

One way of saving transportation costs but still moving surplus stock to more advantageous locations is to have one branch tell another:

> The next time you have a full-weight or freight-paid shipment headed our way, include these listed items.

It might be several weeks before the merchandise arrives, but eventually it is repositioned to a branch with better chances for a sale. Meanwhile, the requesting location doesn't count on the stock. They go ahead and order a full quantity from the supplier.

CONSIDER USING ALTERNATE BRANDS

When your company is authorized to sell more than one brand of a product in any locale, then using alternate brands to meet all customer demand for a brief period can save lots of cash. For example, there's a need to replenish Brand A, but there's plenty of Brand B stock (same item) either in your warehouse or elsewhere in the company. The easiest course is to conclude: "Oh we can't substitute B for A. The customers might not like it, and Sales would be up in arms!" But what if you could? What if Sales explained to the customers:

> For the next two months, any order for product 12345-A will be supplied in Brand B. We recognize that the normal price for B is higher than for Brand A, but during this two-month stock readjustment period, we'll drop B's price.

Most of the time, perhaps, that little exercise wouldn't fly. . . . but wherever it did, whatever percent of the time, it provides a wonderful opportunity to re-balance your stock. Isn't it worth the question? The buyer should ask the Sales Manager for a quick answer . . . quick, because if the answer is "No way!" then resupply of Brand A must be initiated now. Management must agree also, since there may have to be selling price and sales commission adjustments programmed into the computer, tied to Brand B.

Watch the Posting of Item Sales Histories

You have to be careful, too, how the usage history is posted during the two months. Which brand should show the usage? If these are actually to be Brand A sales, converted, then A's history is posted to assure that the computer develops accurate replenishment controls for the future. You wouldn't want A to show no activity for two months, B to show impressive new volume, and another big stock of B material to be reordered. Special programming may be needed to put the B activity in A records during the two month stock adjustment.

The exercise is not advertised to the two suppliers ahead of time. Neither will like the results very much. Brand A loses volume for a while, but B may *really* be reduced when the current stock is gone. If one or the other complains, remind them that this is *your* stock, *your* money, and *your* problem! Solving it is one of those management decisions required for business health and continuance. That's a nice way of saying: "It ain't none of your business!"

How Can the Replenishment Report Help Here?

The earlier report example has no entry like this, but when you do have one or more directly-substitutable brands available within the company, it can be good to show their status directly below the item needing resupply. OK, I *know* that violates my own prime rule . . . not to put "nice to know" information on the report. But there's an overriding objective: Make it as easy as possible, with all pertinent facts displayed, for a buyer to choose the most profitable inventory "control" option. Don't make him look elsewhere for data that should be considered.

If a new purchase order can be avoided by using existing stock, then the facts about that stock are an integral part of the decision-making process and . . . even though technically it's "reference" data (action not necessarily needed) . . . it should appear with the item about to be purchased.

Of course, if you're *never* permitted by Sales to sub one brand for another to clean up stock imbalances, then there's no reason to clutter up the report. It might be an area for top management to review. Sales' objections sometimes can be more preferential than real . . . meaning that they just don't want to be bothered by explaining *anything* unusual to the customers. . . . makes a golfing sales call uncomfortable.

EASE OF PURCHASING OR TRANSFERRING-IN MERCHANDISE . . . IMPORTANT!

The printed recommended replenishment action report acts as a working document for the buyer or Inventory Analyst. When all options have been considered and decisions made on each item, the report is marked-up accordingly. Now, the buyer or someone else turns to a computer screen to record the decisions and get things moving. An image or copy of the Report is retained in the computer files for 48 hours. The buyer calls up the report:

1. Line-by-line, each listed item must be approved, deleted, or modified. There is no one key that can be pressed to turn all a supplier's listed items into a purchase order! Why? That's *too* easy.

   The computer has merely recommended items and quantities. It's still the buyer's responsibility to make the final replenishment option decision . . . whether to buy, pull in surplus, substitute, drop the item from stock, etc. Since *this* is the critical moment when control is exercised, or lost, then a human must approve each item. A one-key code beside each line item does the job.

2. If the decision is to pull in surplus from some other location, the cursor is moved adjacent to that entry on the screen. When a special code is keyed, the transfer is set up automatically. It prints in the shipping location.

   This is an important feature. Buyers sometimes are reluctant to use surplus elsewhere simply because it's so much trouble to go through the system steps required. They might have to "sign off" the purchase order entry program, "sign on" a transfer program, key all item information in total . . . a lengthy process. It's quicker and easier just to buy the stuff from the supplier. This way, the surplus-transfer process is a by-product of P.O. entry and approval.

3. When the buyer elects not to transfer in available surplus, the computer warns: *"SURPLUS AVAILABLE"* perhaps by flashing it on the screen as he presses the key to set up the item for purchase. No problem. He or she can override that. It's the buyer's decision to

buy fresh or use surplus . . . but now a special report will print tomorrow for management's review. The Boss may ask why you bought 20 units of brand new stock when 135 were surplus just 30 miles away.

4. As each item is added to the purchase order, the computer displays a running total in units, dollars, pounds, or cubic feet—however the supplier has expressed the total-order requirement or discount offer. The buyer is aware of where he stands, how much more is needed, etc.

5. When all is complete, the buyer presses a key to end the purchase order. If, however, the desired total-order quantity or value hasn't yet been reached, the computer flashes a warning something like this:

    20,000 lbs. required. Order now totals 18,260.

6. The buyer can do one of three things:
    - Go back and increase selected quantities manually.
    - Override and place the order for 18,260, etc.
    - Press a key that causes the computer to proportionately increase all stock items on the order just enough to total 20,000 . . . but limiting lower-class items to 1 year's supply.

Don't Add Other Items to the Order!

You're probably wondering why one of your favorite options is missing: Adding additional items . . . those still above Line Point . . . onto the purchase order to fill out the requirement. "Gosh, we've been doing that for years" you say. True. Most distributors buy that way. It's a bad practice for two important reasons:

1. When you reach up to pull items into the purchase that are above Line Point, you are making the next cyclical buy even tougher. Those items could well be the nucleus of the order to be placed three weeks from now. Next time, you'll be even farther away from the total-order requirement, and the situation gets worse and worse.

2. The most likely candidates to help make more weight or dollars are the faster-moving products. There's little obsolescence risk in a larger stock of popular items, but their turnover is lowered if ordered early. Operating with a smaller stock on Class 1 and 2 items

REPLENISHMENT ACTION: WHEN "CONTROL" IS EXERCISED!

allows you to buy 6 months' worth on 65 percent of your inventory. . . . but all that is upset when you load up on the better products.

It's better to simply expand proportionately the order quantities of the stock items now below Line Point. If you're 10 percent short of the weight needed, for example, all quantities go up 10 percent . . . except where doing that would run beyond 1 year's supply (the absolute outside limit) on a Class 10, 11, or 12 item. Another little challenge to keep your programmers from boredom!

Review Cycle Check and Adjustment

When a product line's Review Cycle (scheduled buying frequency, Chapter 9) is set correctly, then half the time you'll need a slight increase in order quantities to meet the supplier requirement. Half the time, you'll have a little more than is needed. One order, you'll need $5,000 and have only $4,850. The next purchase cycle, you'll have $5,700.

However, if three orders in a row show more weight, units, or dollars than required—the Review Cycle is *too long!* Plan to buy the line more often. If three orders in a row must all be increased, then the Review Cycle is *too short!* Buy the product line less frequently.

That's the way to correct the problem of not having enough weight, etc. Don't fill out purchases with items nowhere near the point of needing replenishment just because they're fast-moving. Instead, lengthen the Review Cycle . . . and if *that* doesn't work (you'd have to buy less frequently than once a month), you should consider dropping the product line from stock or stop trying to buy the "truckload." You don't have the sales to justify it.

EXPEDITING AND THE EXPEDITE REPORT

Replenishment action has been initiated. The purchase order's been sent. Everything came off like clockwork . . . usage recorded and a rate figured; lead times captured and used; order point and line point calculated; report triggered right on time; and intelligent options selected by the buyer. The computer couldn't have been better programmed; information couldn't have been more accurate or timely; the humans couldn't have been more disciplined . . . but the merchandise hasn't arrived.

The Need for "Recovery" Capability

Expediting provides your "recovery" capability. When I play golf, I know exactly what to do up on the tee . . . the grip, stance, address, swing, the right club to use, the direction and distance desired. That's all my "system" of getting play underway on the hole. I may execute all those elements perfectly and *still* have the ball wind up in a fairway trap if something happens I hadn't counted on . . . a crosswind gusts just as I hit. If I mess up one of the basic system parts, the ball finds trouble for sure or doesn't go nearly as far as I'd hoped.

If I walk out to the fairway trap, step in there and then use the same club, same stance, same swing, touch the club to the sand . . . all perfectly fine back on the tee . . . bad things happen. I incur a penalty and the ball may go 15 feet or 150 yards. I need a different "system" to recover if my original system (for whatever reason) results in trouble. Expediting is like that. It provides a recovery system when what you did earlier in replenishment-timing hasn't worked. Trouble is either on you already or looming large just ahead.

I'm pretty lousy at getting out of sand traps. I hate them, I don't practice the shots required, and my results are usually bad. The pro golfers don't seem to mind the traps all that much. They generally don't want to hit into one but if they do, there's no real trauma involved. They walk up, pop the ball 178 yards onto the green and start thinking about lunch. What's the difference? They practice . . . I don't! They're good at sand shots, because each week they hit 150 practice shots out of all kinds of bunker conditions. Hitting out of the sand, they've learned, must be executed with just as much skill as was employed back on the tee. Sand shots have become a regular part of their golfing system.

When Most Distributors Expedite

Distributors often spend lots of time and money planning and programming their system to hit tee shots . . . to be sure replenishment action is begun sensibly and that the right quantities are ordered. As you read in earlier chapters, these efforts often "joust with minutia," as Bob VanDeMark was fond of saying. They strain at gnats. Exponential Smoothing and other exotic forecasting math is used; complicated "modeling" techniques are employed; Distribution Requirements Planning might be tried.

But when something goes wrong *after* the P.O. is placed . . . and no matter which concepts you adopt . . . something often does, there's little or no planned recovery capability provided. The buyers just scramble as best they can, waiting to do anything until customers and salesmen

REPLENISHMENT ACTION: WHEN "CONTROL" IS EXERCISED! 191

are screaming, and then expedite in a panic mode. Expediting is extra work. There's no time allotted to it as part of the job. Buyers figure that their job is to buy . . . and when they've done that, the real task is over. It isn't *their* fault if the stupid supplier can't perform!

Preventative Rather Than Corrective Medicine: Planned Expediting

Obviously, the time for pro golfers to learn how to play sand shots isn't during the U.S. Open. The time to take injections for smallpox isn't after you've already contracted the disease. The best time to expedite is *before* the customers and salesmen are screaming. Here are the four conditions that should cause the computer to generate an Expedite Report for material on open purchase orders with suppliers:

1. *Stock available-for-sale has dropped down to the Safety Allowance* for an item, and the item's usage is sufficient to develop a S.A. of at least five units.

    You'll recall from Chapter 8 that the Safety Allowance is a "pad" of inventory carried to compensate for a usage variance while material is being replenished or a variance in the lead time itself. When the S.A. is set correctly, half the time you'll have more on the shelf when a replenishment shipment arrives; half the time you'll have less. Stock is now at the safety allowance, so which half is occurring on this replenishment? That's right. The pad is being used this time.

    If usage and lead time had been as you expected, new stock should have arrived. Usage is higher or the lead time is longer than the average. It's a good time to determine the exact status of the replenishment order. Out pops an action report for expediting.

    The five-unit qualifier is necessary, because items with zero or one piece as the order point (very low usage items), have a zero safety allowance. It would be silly to order the item today and have the computer tell you to expedite tomorrow. When an item has enough usage to generate an SA of 5 units, it's effective to expedite when stock drops to that level.

2. *The purchase order is 10 days late.* On stock items, the computer knows the average lead time to expect. A projected due date can be established even when the supplier does not acknowledge the purchase order or advise a delivery date.

    The computer treats each stock item on the order independently since each has a separate delivery history, separate lead time calculation, and separate anticipated due date. When an item is 10 days overdue, it's time for more expediting action. You may have called the vendor earlier for Condition 1. Now you call him *again*.

3. *Stock has been at zero for 30 days.* No customer backorders yet exist; the salesmen aren't complaining; but no stock is available. "Why not just zero stock?" you ask. "Why wait so long with no stock?" Obviously, you can modify this time frame downward if you want, but as many as 10-15 percent of your stock items could have an order point of zero or 1 piece.

    Being out of stock is a *planned condition!* You intend to run out. You want to run out. Expected usage on the item is very low; replenishment may be based on: "Sell the one piece we have and then order a replacement!" Being out of stock isn't bad, but being out too long could be. A stockout on *any item* for 30 days could be serious, regardless of its anticipated usage. It's time to see where the replacement is.

4. *Zero stock and a customer backorder exists,* or a salesman has complained of a lost sale. This is the panic mode. Certainly, expediting action is needed. Usually, "lost orders" are too vague to require much action. Very rarely should the information cause correction of an item's usage rate, for example. . . . but here, well sure. A lost sale, real or imagined, should trigger serious expediting effort.

Report Timing

Generally, the four conditions above are more serious as you move from Condition 1 down to 4. The computer is programmed to pump out an Expedite Report when Condition 1 occurs . . . sort of an "early warning." It won't do that again on this item, this purchase order, this condition.

If the item drifts down into Condition 2, the expediter receives another report for this item, this P.O. A third might come out if Condition 3 occurs, and a fourth report for Condition 4. . . . or the first three might be skipped entirely and just one report generated, if an item degenerates rapidly from no-trouble to Condition 4. Rarely would an item progress through all four stages. Likely, you'd get a report for Conditions 1 and 4, or 1 and 2, etc.

THE EXPEDITE REPORT FORMAT

Appearance of the Expedite Report is even less important than for the Recommended Replenishment Action Report. A typical report example is shown in the illustration.

EXPEDITE REPORT EXAMPLE

SUPPLIER → XYZ Industries, Inc.
Kansas City, Mo.

Buyer: 01

AVAILABLE-FOR-SALE STOCK RIGHT NOW ON DATE OF REPORT

PROJECTED DUE DATE BASED ON LEAD TIME OR PROMISED DATE

NEW EXPECTED DATE PROMISED AFTER TODAY'S EXPEDITING

DATE OF REPORT — January 15

Item	Description	Unit	On Hand	Quantity Ordered	PO Date	P.O. Number	Date Expected	Ship History	B/O's Customers	New Date
6310	Fuse 15 AMP	ea	0	300	12/11	42830	1/11	100—1/12 50—1/15	30 ABC Indus. 50 DEF, Inc.	1/26
8550	Extension 50'	ea	0	750	12/18	42904	1/12	100—1/06	200 RAMCO 100 ABC Indus.	1/19
7820	Wiring Device	ea	5	25	12/18	42904	1/10			1/26

CONTACT NAME: Jack Harris (312)840-6000

THE PERSON TO CALL ABOUT THESE ORDERS NAME AND NUMBER

SHIPMENTS RECEIVED SO FAR ON THE ORDER AND DATES

CUSTOMERS WAITING FOR MATERIAL QUANTITIES FOR EACH

193

The objective is to provide something quite simple. The expediter should see at a glance what supplier to call, the person, the telephone number, the items to ask about, a history of what's happened so far, and current conditions. If customer backorders exist, who are the customers and how much material do we owe each one? How much stock is on hand right now? When was the P.O. placed? How much was ordered? How much has already come in? What's the expected delivery date?

You might want other information on your report: Item usage rate; Safety Allowance quantity; sales so far this month; lead time in days; the date of any customer backorders, etc. Put whatever you need on the report, but try to keep it simple. The expediter needs only enough facts to convey a proper sense of urgency to the supplier.

Who Should Expedite?

Distributors large enough to have three buyers for stock items are candidates for a full-time expediter. Smaller distributors assign the job to the buyer responsible for the product line or category . . . but allow time in the workday for expediting activity, recognizing it as a regular part of the job. Expediting is done *every day!* Regularly, systematically, under an obvious plan. The suppliers form an opinion about you:

> When ABC Supply calls, they mean business! They're organized. They don't ask me continually to get them out of a bind that they caused themselves by ordering late. Also, they expedite only when it's important. They don't waste my time by making routine followup inquiries on every order, whether they need the material or not. They anticipate trouble and call for my help before their customers are mad at both of us.

Expediting, like any skill, can be honed. Just as the pro golfer uses his skill to recover out of the sand and get the ball back into the fairway or onto the green . . . you use expediting to "recover" and maintain continuity of supply on an item when earlier system elements mis-fire or resupply is affected by unforeseen circumstances. What you *can't* afford is to say to a customer: "Boy I'm sorry that we're out of stock on the item you want, but we have an unreliable supplier!" . . . and have the customer reply: "Hmmm, *so do I!*"

An Ace in the Hole for Expediting

There is one sure-fire way to get material you need: Try to cancel the purchase order! That usually gets it moving toward you, dated retroactively. If that doesn't work, you can use the steps that follow. But be warned: If you abuse this approach . . . use it when one of the required conditions hasn't been met . . . then don't attribute it to me! I don't want anything to do with you. You're not being fair with the supplier. Here are the required conditions:

1. The item involved is very important. It's critical to several customers or it's for just one . . . but that customer is very important. This is not little chaff that's a nuisance but doing no real harm.
2. You ordered just as you should have, in accord with the supplier's stated requirements. He just hasn't performed. It's *NOT* a case of you pressuring him to correct your foul-up!
3. You've already tried all the normal expediting channels. You've talked to Customer Service, the Service Manager, the VP of Marketing . . . whomever is designated as the chain of command for expediting. Still no merchandise.

Now, here's the way to get the merchandise moving to you. First, gather all the facts about the order, whom you've talked to, what they said, etc. Walk into your president's office and say:

> Boss, I need your help. Would you call this telephone number tonight at 10:30 PM and expedite this critical purchase order for our best account, ABC Industries?

The Boss isn't very enthused about doing that, so he replies:

> What? Who's number is this? . . . and why can't I call him now, instead of 10:30 tonight?

Who's number indeed? It's the supplier *PRESIDENT'S* unlisted home phone number! (I'll tell you in a minute how to get it). . . . or the number of the Division General Manager, whomever, but the highest-ranking official in the organization that could help get the material on its way.

Tonight your Boss calls, wakes up the supplier president at home, and explains your critical need for the merchandise. Remember the conditions. You're lily-white in the deal. The entire fault for non-delivery belongs to the supplier, and it's important enough for *your president* to call the supplier's top man at home at 10:30 PM! Can you guess the supplier president's attitude when he walks into his customer service manager's office the next morning?

> Jack, I don't even want to know what went wrong on this order. Just get the guy his merchandise . . . but let me add one more thing: If he *EVER*

calls me at home again, some of you people down here may get a chance for new career paths!

Tomorrow, material will arrive on your dock that wasn't in our particular solar system yesterday. That customer service manager will find it somewhere. He may borrow from another customer, fly it in from the Seattle warehouse, or buy it on the market . . . but it'll arrive! For the next six weeks, your merchandise will flow in like magic. Of course, your name is bantered about in his department with disdain. Your ancestry is questioned . . . your mother's occupation is discussed . . . your sexual lifestyle debated.

Who cares! This isn't a popularity contest. It's a business relationship. Your company's health depends on the supplier performing as he should. You ordered properly; the need was critical; and you gave the regular personnel plenty of chances to avoid trouble. Just take care to use this extreme method very sparingly.

How to Get the Unlisted Number

The top executive's number may not be that tough to get. The supplier's switchboard operator can tell you who he is and maybe what suburb (in a big metroplex area) he lives in. The number may be listed. Call information in that area code and find out.

If it is unlisted, ask the supplier's local sales representative to get it for you. He'll ask: "What in the world do you want *that* for?" Your reply: "Don't ask. Just get it for me, and whatever we do with it, no one in your company will ever know where it came from." Be sure you do keep that confidence later on.

Of course, he or she won't do it. . . . but the next time the salesman calls, have your receptionist ask about the "special number" you need. You'll be too busy to see him . . . from now on . . . until you get the number. Also, you may have to study a restructuring of your purchases of his products. Translation: Your orders may go to his competition for a while . . . and how long depends on him. This moderate pressure usually gets what you want.

Obviously, this won't work for all distributors or all the time. How large you are, how much you buy from this supplier, whether or not you have options for resupply, how much this supplier dominates the market, how important you are to him . . . all dictate the degree to which a representative responds. Just get whatever number you can for as high-ranking an official as you can. Then use the "ace" very sparingly.

REPLENISHMENT ACTION: WHEN "CONTROL" IS EXERCISED! 197

SUMMARY

Replenishment action! There's no more important time or function in inventory management. The entire computerized data-gathering, screening, calculating, and reporting system is designed to support and enhance the effectiveness of those assigned the job of making the choices and taking the replenishment steps.

Ability, motivation, and dedication are expected of the people. No longer can distributors afford to have huge sums of money spent by buyers who are lazy, set-in-their-ways, just hanging on until retirement, obstinate about new ideas, while being overworked, underpaid, and supported by an out-of-date computerized system.

The reports of this chapter; the options presented; the conditions outlined . . . all require a higher-level of inventory management skill than most distributors thought was necessary in the past. Your "money-spenders" must be paid well, have enough time to do their work efficiently without a 70-hour week, receive training in the job, be supported by a system which has Management's full support and defense when followed, and then be assisted by action reports to maximize their time and skills as inventory dollars are committed.

Please keep a basic objective in mind with reports, just as for all other elements of the control system: The computer does all it can in the areas where it works best. The humans step in to do what they do best . . . evaluate, make choices, select options, and start the action. The computer/human team is most effective when the functions are divided and assigned properly. The system is ineffective if they're not.

13

REFERENCE INFORMATION AND THE QUERY FEATURE

Action reports based on the exception principle are the heart of any effective control system, as Chapter 12 said. Most of the time, action reports trigger replenishment, expediting, surplus stock transfer, and the other steps leading to good service and profitable use of the inventory investment. Still, there are other reports that come in handy on occasion. Situations arise that require information stored in the computer. Decisions must be made and, somewhere in the computer files, facts are recorded that make the options clear and point to the right one.

THE NEED FOR "BACKUP" REPORTS

Reference information—a dump of the facts a file contains—serves well as protection against an extended computer equipment failure. Those of you who've worked with an integrated system where all transactions are keyed into the computer and minute-to-minute information is retrieved by on-line inquiry know the trauma that results when the computer goes down for 20 minutes. Aren't you frustrated when an airline reservation clerk tells you: "I'm sorry. I can't confirm anything right now. Our computer is down!"? It's maddening. Nobody can function. All activities are at a standstill. There *must be* some way to operate when the computer can't do its thing!

The Stock Status Report

Periodically, the computer should print out on paper or microfiche the status of all stocked items in all locations. The quantities available to sell; usage rates; lead times; unit costs; ordering controls; quantities on order with suppliers; backorder totals; the sales history month-by-month as far back as you have room to show; surplus stock . . . as many facts as are practical to include. If the computer goes down, the microfiche is your standby system. Inside telephone salesmen can still answer questions; Purchasing people can still buy; the company isn't shut down.

True . . . the information gets stale quickly, but it's better than nothing! Print a full Stock Status Report onto microfiche twice weekly (Tuesday and Friday afternoons, for example), so that the information shown is rarely more than 48 hours old. A branch on Monday can see on microfiche what the main warehouse or another branch had in stock at close-of-business Friday afternoon. For most items listed, the data is still valid.

Is this expensive? Relatively . . . no. There is the expense of the microfiche process; mailing it twice a week to all locations; the readers at each branch . . . but compared to the chaos and lost business when the computer goes down for a day and a half . . . it's pretty cheap insurance.

Put Credit Information on the Microfiche

The Accounts Receivable files (what customers owe) should be on microfiche backup also, although you might elect to limit the data shown only to accounts with past-due bills, those past or nearing their credit limits, etc. Consider the retail stores who check out your credit card to see if it's stolen. Their lists don't have every card in existence . . . just the bad ones. Backup credit information should be the same in your system. The microfiche lists only problem or potentially-problem accounts and facts. If a customer doesn't appear, it's OK to accept his new order when the computer is down.

Reference Screens When the Computer Is Functioning

A second category of reference information has nothing to do with malfunction insurance. It's useful even when there's no need at the moment to replenish stock. You just need to know something *right now* about a stock item: How many of these have we sold this year? What's the unit cost? What's the lead time on this product? What's the review cycle, the order point, the safety allowance, the EOQ? Who buys this item? What's the due date of our next replenishment purchase order?

A Snapshot Look at the Inventory Master Record

Most of the questions can be answered when the system provides an inquiry into a stock item's inventory master record. A screen is

REFERENCE INFORMATION AND THE QUERY FEATURE

displayed with all the pertinent facts about the item in this location; a second screen shows the same facts in another branch, etc. It's the same information that was recorded on the heading of a kardex card in a manual system. Instead of walking over to the kardex trays and flipping open a record, today a buyer needs to "flip open" the computer records with an inquiry.

"Common sense!" you say? You'd be amazed at the systems I see—some still sold on the open market—that offer no such capability. Buyers can see the facts about an item on regular replenishment reports, or perhaps on a weekly stock status, but cannot get such data about an individual item on demand. They have to fly blind to a degree in between purchases. Follow this principle in your system:

> *Any* data element, any fact is visible on some inquiry screen in the system, and all are modifiable. Access is restricted by terminal identification codes or passwords . . . but *someone* can see and/or change every piece of information in the system!

The "Kardex" Inquiry

We discussed this special inquiry in Chapter 7, so I won't rehash it here, but this (new to most of you) inquiry screen displays the IN-OUT-BALANCE information on a stock item back for the last 50 transactions or so. You see exactly the same facts the kardex record yielded in years past: The date of a customer's order; the order number; his name; quantity shipped; and stock available-for-sale after the transaction. Similar information is shown for receipts. Be sure your system replaces this valuable feature that disappeared for far too many distributors when a computerized system took over the recordkeeping.

THE QUERY FEATURE . . . A NEW APPROACH TO REPORTS

Back in Chapter 2, there was a mention of "IQ," "Query," or "Report Writer." It's a feature given several names over the years . . . but is simply the ability to have the computer find an array of facts, screen out what isn't applicable, sort them, develop percentages and totals, and then print or display the results in a matter of seconds or minutes. The general idea has been around for a long time. Almost every system on the market today says that it offers such a capability.

The better systems, however, have overcome five big restrictions that have limited Report Writer programs in the past:

1. You had to use a special group of words and commands, in very limited sequences. An executive had to have semi-programming skills to make use of the feature.

2. Only a few files were available to Query.

3. If Query was using information from a file, no other program had access to the file until it was through. . . . no stock on-hand inquiry by sales, etc.

4. The information pulled from a file could be "dumped" pretty much as it was, but very little manipulation done with the information, or comparisons made to data from other files.

5. The program required a huge chunk of the computer's capacity, so it was practical to request special reports only in slow periods or to be printed the next day. Everything else slowed down way too much if someone tried to run a Query report during normal working hours.

These limitations had the effect of putting most Report Writer use on the back burner. It was too much trouble to learn to use it, and by the time a report was ready no one cared to see the information. Be sure your system enjoys the benefits of a well-programmed Query feature. Today, you need not be restricted by these five problems.

How Is Query Used?

I once heard a systems salesman make this comment as part of his sales pitch:

> Our system offers every report you will ever need. The report writer capability is limited, but with all our pre-programmed report options, you wouldn't use it much anyway!

A pretty magnificent claim . . . and impossible to back up! You'll recall from Chapter 7 that a wealth of information is captured by the computer in the course of day-to-day activity. There's an almost infinite number of ways the data might be arranged, screened, sorted, sequenced, analyzed, and displayed. Nobody is smart enough to work out ahead of time *all* the ways someone might need to use the information. When you hear statements like the one above, mark it down that the system is weak in it's Query capability, is old-fashioned, and someone is covering up.

REFERENCE INFORMATION AND THE QUERY FEATURE

Suppose you're the Sales Manager and it's time for a semi-annual review of ol' Jack's performance (one of your key salesmen). You turn to your terminal and key-in this request:

> Let me see all of Jack's customers where the gross margin dollars are up or down by 15 percent this year compared to last. Arrange them in descending order by total margin dollars generated. Show the GP percent for each customer, both years.

Fifteen minutes later, you have the report. If it isn't quite what you wanted, a slight modification in the instructions re-runs it with just the information needed. If you like the analysis, it's given a code so that the computer can regenerate it for some other salesman whenever you like. Each time you may alter the parameters.

You're the President of a small distributor. Today, the Vice President of Marketing for a key manufacturer is making his annual visit. Usually, it's more of a public relations call than anything, really sort of a time-waster. You decide to make the visit worthwhile:

> Computer, let me see all stock items in the ABC Manufacturing line where we've sold less than $10 at cost during the last year. Arrange the items in descending order by the inventory dollars invested in each one. Show the total dollars invested in all these items, and the percent this represents of all inventory dollars in that product line.

You're ready to negotiate a special material return with this big shot when he comes in. You have all the facts; they're current; the devastating impact to your profit picture is very clear. The computer provided specific facts for a one-time need, delivered only what was requested, and did it in a few minutes. Throw that same request this afternoon at your programmer or your outside systems people. You can guess the reply:

> Well we can do it, but it'll take about three days of programming effort and will cost about $2,000. . . . and we have so many projects ahead of this, we can't do it for six weeks!

Heck, in six weeks I won't care anymore. That would be too late . . . and who could have thought of all the possible ways anyone might ever need to see the inventory information so as to pre-program such a study?

An efficient Query capability is like air-conditioning in your car in Texas in July. In 1940, nobody had it, so no one felt deprived because they were hot driving around in Houston. It was just a way of life.

Ahhh . . . but today, *just try* to sell a non-air-conditioned car in Houston! There's such a difference arriving at your destination with dry pants that people *do* feel deprived without the A/C feature. It's the same with Query. Once you've used its magnificent abilities to provide quick information for management decisions, you'll feel deprived . . . restricted . . . hamstrung . . . without it!

Don't settle for mediocre Query capabilities. If you've programmed your own system, there are packages offered by the computer hardware manufacturers as separate modules. Some are much better than others, of course, and you may have to accept one that's less than fantastic simply because of the computer brand you're locked into. If you have the option of selecting a totally-integrated package on the market, be *sure* to check out the Query feature carefully! When the salesman says (and he will): "Oh sure, our system does all that!", ask for a demonstration. Otherwise, you may wind up with a car where the air conditioning is supplied by rolling down the windows.

SUMMARY

Reference information . . . the "that's nice to know" facts that are needed from time to time, but not all the time or in a form consistent enough for pre-programmed reports. Query offers the alternative to huge, voluminous printouts that gather dust most of the time. Managers select the data needed and receive it in a myriad of options within minutes. Inquiry screens permit "snapshot" looks at the sales history, controls, lead times, and the latest transactions . . . allowing buyers to "flip open" the computer just as they could in years past with manual recordkeeping systems.

Reference information . . . used as "insurance" so that the company continues to function when the computer goes down for a few hours. Microfiche serves well as a backup system when it's prepared on a regular schedule and distributed to all company locations. Inventory on hand; selling prices; credit information, etc., lend themselves to the microfiche concept. Customers never hear: "I'll have to call you back on this. Our computer is down and we don't know how we stand on anything!"

14

PHYSICAL CONTROL: THE FOUNDATION OF YOUR SYSTEM!

Most distributors identify with the following story:

> We've just installed a fantastic new computerized system with outstanding features and capabilities. It keeps track of what we have, how many are sold, estimates future usage, and guides our stock replenishment decisions. After some "getting-used-to" conditioning, most employees have now accepted the new system.
>
> One day, an important customer calls: "Do you have 18 of part number ABC42J?", he asks. "I need them today!" The inside salesman answers quickly: "Just a minute, sir. We've just installed a new computer. I'll check our stock." He keys in the part number and . . . pronto, back comes the answer on the screen on his desk. "Yes sir, we've got 'em! Come on over. They'll be waiting!"
>
> The order is keyed-in, a picking ticket prints in the warehouse, and all seems calm . . . for a few minutes. Then, in walks a warehouseman carrying the order, and guess what he says? You know too well, don't you? "I don't care what your stupid computer says. We don't have any of these! . . . and we never had these problems before we changed to this new system!"
>
> Now it's panic time. The customer is furious. He was told we had the 18 he wanted; he depended on us; and now when he shows up, we can't provide the merchandise. To salvage this customer, we promise some expensive scrambling . . . calling a competitor or perhaps flying in some stock to deliver tomorrow. Because he has no options, the customer allows us to do that, but in his opinion, both our service *and* our new system stink!
>
> Then, there's the sequel. Saturday morning, guess who walks (a little sheepishly) into the office? It's the warehouseman. What does he say this

time? "We found those ABC42Js over against the back wall, all covered up. I don't know how they got there. I guess ol' Joe put them there the day we fired him!"

This all-too-familiar story reveals a total system breakdown when our performance is measured against the twin objectives of good Inventory Control:

1. To provide the *best possible customer service* . . .

2. At the *lowest practical cost*!

On this customer's order, we blew both ends. We gave lousy service at an exorbitant cost. Not only that. Neither should have happened. We *had* the stock the customer wanted; we had it where and when he wanted it, but we couldn't lay our little hands on it! . . . the same as not having it! We had to wiggle out of the mess by the most expensive method possible, when all along there was stock available at a profitable cost. Does this story sound like we just walked through your warehouse?

PHYSICAL CONTROL

The problem is Physical Control . . . or the lack of it. The "system" functioned just as designed. Sales histories and lead times were captured and considered; purchase orders to the suppliers were entered on time; replenishment stock arrived at the right price (freight paid, etc.); and the computer's records were posted properly. "Physical Control" broke down however, so all our best efforts (and money spent on the computer system) went for naught when the chips were down . . . that day a customer tested our system by placing an order!

Let's define Physical Control: It's looking at a computer display or printout that says 18 pieces are out on the warehouse shelf available for sale, going out to the warehouse at the close of a business day and—miracle of miracles—*18* are there, right where they're supposed to be! . . . 98 percent of the time . . . on 98 percent of the stock items!

What Would We Find in *Your* Warehouse?

How's *your* physical control? If we wandered out there late this afternoon after all activity has ceased, counted 100 stock items at random, and then compared the counts to your records . . . what percent would be in exact agreement? 60 percent . . . 45 percent . . . 15 percent?

PHYSICAL CONTROL: THE FOUNDATION OF YOUR SYSTEM!

Would most of those that did agree be the slowmovers? Hmmmm . . . why don't you find out? You may get quite a shock!

WHAT UNDERGIRDS YOUR ORDERING DECISIONS?

Stripping away all fluff and getting down to basics, a distributor's inventory control "system" boils down to the answers to two questions:

1. When do I order?
2. How much at a time?

The answers determine the service levels to be provided, how much stock will be carried, and therefore develop also the stock-availability information that will be given to customers. This "system" of questions and answers rests on two vital foundations. If either is unstable, the system performs poorly. The foundations:

1. Accuracy of stock records — What do you have on the shelf?
2. Accuracy of sales history — Are all transactions recorded?

Too many distributors' systems rest on very unstable foundations. One or the other of the foundation blocks above are cracked . . . inaccurate, incomplete, untimely information. Data that's just plain wrong! And these distributors wonder why their inventory control efforts produce so many stockouts and so much dead stock! Their system is limping along at 65 percent or 45 percent or 15 percent efficiency rate. Two or more cylinders are misfiring in a six-cylinder engine, so how smooth a ride can they expect? This chapter deals only with the first foundation stone . . . accuracy of the stock records . . . but both are important!

DON'T CHASE THE CAUSES FIRST!

When a distributor executive realizes that the stock records are lousy, he or she may launch a major campaign to find and correct the causes. As reasonable as that sounds, *Don't Do It!* . . . at least, not as your first step . . . at least not all the causes. The records are bad for many reasons. There may be 15 or more problems contributing to the inaccuracies. If you chase down 15 rabbit trails at once, looking for the culprits who made the mistakes, you won't accomplish much. You'll get discouraged trying to fight 15 brush fires on all sides, and as some distributors have . . . give up the fight and be resigned to your fate, whatever that is, with inaccurate records.

What's the Cost of Lousy Stock Records?

If you do give up, be prepared to accept the expensive consequences: Twice the inventory you really need (your people will compensate for the undependable records) and more inside telephone salesmen than necessary (they must go or talk to the warehouse continually for stock checks). You don't believe that, huh? Consider this scene:

> A buyer is adjusting to your brand new computerized system with all its strange usage rate calculations, order points, line points, and EOQs. It's uncomfortable. The controls cause him to buy quite differently than when he used pure SWAG in the old system. . . . but you're the boss, so he goes along with all this new stuff.
>
> On a critical item, he waits to order until the stock drops to an order point of 20. "Boy, that's low!" he thinks. "I've always ordered before when we were down to 100." But what can he do? *You* instructed him to follow the new control system. Now his worst fears come true: He runs out of stock. There weren't 20 in the warehouse when he sent in the P.O. The records were wrong. Only 6 were there.
>
> The salesmen are very understanding, aren't they? They come in to console him: "That's OK, Jack. Everybody makes mistakes. You'll do better next time."
>
> If you really think that's what they'll say, welcome to distribution! You're obviously new to the business. No. Those salesmen will come on like this: "You jerk! How could you run out of that item? It's one of the best-selling we have. You're going to lose me a bundle of business. You're doing a lousy job here in purchasing. In fact, I think I'm going to go tell the president what a stinking job you're doing!"
>
> What do you think poor ol' Jack will do the next time he orders that item? You guessed it. He'll bring in twelve carloads and he'll order when he's down to 250. When you ask: "Hey Jack, why aren't you following the new control system?" how does he reply? "Are you kidding? I tried that stupid new system. It fouled me up. The records are terrible. You can't believe anything on the reports. I have to keep stock in here for our customers!"

That's why inaccurate records lead to excessive inventories. The people responsible for service must compensate. Who cares how inaccurate the computer stock balances are if there's a lifetime supply of all items in the warehouse?

PHYSICAL CONTROL: THE FOUNDATION OF YOUR SYSTEM!

CYCLE COUNTING: THE FIRST STEP!

Correction begins with an effective Cycle Count program . . . a physical inventory of a portion of the warehouse each evening, so that the computer's stock balances may be verified or modified. The objective? To effect a dramatic improvement in stock-record versus shelf-stock accuracy . . . in other words, to remove errors at the same rate they're being generated. THEN, attack the various causes!

Why? Some causes exist because of the lousy records. For example, too many unauthorized people wandering around the warehouse will result in record errors (filling their own orders, robbing complete units for parts, taking samples without paperwork, making substitutions without changing the sales order, etc.). Why are all these people going into the warehouse? They *have to*! . . . or think they do. An inside salesman says: "The computer records are terrible. No one believes them. I must always check the shelf before committing stock for sure to a customer!" He's right. You can't keep him out of the warehouse until the records are better. It's a "chicken/egg" situation. The records stink because too many people consider the warehouse "open house," but they go out there because the records stink. You can't keep them out until the records are more accurate. Cycle counting will do that!

THE GOAL: GET THE AVAILABLE-FOR-SALE BALANCE RIGHT!

Cycle Counting's goal is to keep the "Available-For-Sale" stock balance accurate. That's the *only* balance that matters a twit for *unit* inventory control. An inquiring customer is told that he can or cannot have stock based on the available balance. Stock is replenished when the available balance drops to the Order Point or Line Point. Oh sure, you must maintain an "on hand" (within the four walls) balance for financial figures, to be relieved when an invoice or transfer is processed. Most distributors keep a "committed" figure also. On hand minus committed = available-for-sale . . . but only the available balance triggers replenishment or promises stock to a new sales order.

The Toughest Balance to Keep Accurate

For most distributors, verifying available balance accuracy is almost impossible other than at year-end during the annual physical inventory. A check of the shelf finds 63. The computer shows 40 available. Which is right? If there's a lot of paperwork floating around or material all over the place, the numbers could *both* be right! As new orders are keyed-in, the available balance is reduced. . . . but if these orders haven't been filled, the shelf count could be correct. The only way to find out would be to "inventory" the paper float . . . a nasty prospect!

Where might customer orders be? In someone's desk waiting for pricing or credit approval, on a warehouse shelf partially filled, in a salesman's car glove compartment . . . and who knows where else? If orders and material are scattered all over the place . . . a lot of paper or material "float," you might count the "four-wall" stock but verifying the available balance is practically out of the question. That's too bad. It's the available balance that really matters as you attempt to maintain a continuity of stock but not overload the warehouse.

REMOVE THE PAPER FLOAT WITH "A-DAY'S-WORK-IN-A-DAY!"

The distributor who desires an accurate available-for-sale balance can have it . . . but in the words of an old country boy, "It ain't gonna come easy!" The paper and material "float" must be eliminated entirely. At the end of each business day, the *only* material still on a warehouse shelf or in a designated storage area is material available for sale. Everything else has been moved to staging or accumulation areas.

A customer calls at 4 PM with an order for tomorrow morning's deliveries. If you enter that order into the computer, the available-for-sale balances are reduced for all stock items on the order. The warehouse crew must fill that order . . . not ship it, just fill it . . . before they leave! You could have waited to key it in until tomorrow morning, of course. . . . but if you enter it tonight, the warehouse people must fill it tonight.

Special Programming Eases the Pressure to Enter Late-Arriving Orders

You may need special programming to permit acceptance of "Reference" sales orders. Late-afternoon orders may be keyed-in, but the computer considers them as "reference" orders until 7 AM tomorrow morning. The balances are unaffected until then. A customer could call back to add something, and there's no confusion. The order may be called up on a screen and changed. The purchasing process may be started for any non-stock items; but stock items need not be filled until tomorrow morning.

PHYSICAL CONTROL: THE FOUNDATION OF YOUR SYSTEM!

At 7 AM, the computer will change the order status to "regular" and then print it in the warehouse for filling.

Similar disciplines have to be applied in Receiving. A big truckload arrives at 3 PM. Likely you must get the material unloaded, sign the shipping paperwork and get the driver on his way . . . but you don't have to officially receive the shipment. *If you do key it in,* then it must all be put up in the correct locations before the warehouse crew leaves for the night. If you entered the receipt tomorrow morning, the shipment can be put up tomorrow. If only part of the truckload can be put up today, then *only those items* are posted as received today! You don't post the whole truck as received. You don't wait to post anything until a couple of days from now when all items have been put away. You post *today* what is put away *today*! . . . a day's-work-in-a-day!

A Tough Attitude about Paperwork and "Committed" Material

This disciplined attitude about filling orders and putting material away gives you a chance to maintain accurate available-for-sale stock balances. The regular warehouse shelves and storage areas contain only merchandise that's available to sell. If it's been "committed" in any fashion at all, the material is located elsewhere. Hmmm . . . that means a "Will-Call" order has been filled and moved over to the holding area; stock items on a "Ship-Complete" order have been filled and moved to an order "accumulation" or staging area; the stock going to Branch 14 on next Tuesday's truck has been pulled and moved to a transfer staging area. Then there's the paperwork side.

If the repair department pulled out parts today to repair a pump, it's recorded *today* . . . not next week when the job is finally billed to the customer! If a salesman takes out a sample, he must leave a copy of a sample withdrawal form. If merchandise comes back from a customer and a credit is processed, the stock must go back onto the shelves *today* (if it's salable) . . . not three weeks from now when you get around to cleaning out the returned goods rats' nest!

Why? What Does All This Accomplish?

Tonight, when a cycle counter or counters check an item's shelf stock against the computer's record of what's supposed to be there (the available-for-sale merchandise), it's possible to identify the records that should be corrected. There's no float of paperwork or material. If paperwork is everywhere; if material is partially put away or partially filled; if sales orders that have committed merchandise are on credit hold or on some salesman's desk waiting for prices; if delivery paperwork is in a salesman's glove compartment or briefcase (to be turned in before month-end when he gets paid) . . . well, cycle counting is a waste of time. If the computer says you're supposed to have 15 pieces available for sale, the counter finds 12, and all these conditions are present, which is right . . . 12 or 15? Who knows? No correction is possible. If you have cleaned up this mess, then 12 is right. The computer's balance may be dropped by 3. There's no paperwork or material floating around. Both are under control.

Already you're probably thinking of how difficult this would be to establish in your warehouse . . . and you're right! It's tough. Your people will throw 47 reasons at you as to why they can't do it. The difficulties have caused some distributors to give up. They just concede that they'll never have accurate records . . . but that concession carries a huge cost: Perhaps twice the inventory they really need and more people as well! The benefits of cycle counting are worth the effort, but the prerequisite to its success is "A-Day's-Work-In-A-Day." You must remove the paperwork and material "float."

CYCLE COUNT IN THE "GAP"

Cycle counting works best when performed in the "gap" . . . that period of time in your 24-hour program of business activity when nothing is moving. Material has stopped flowing. Paperwork has stopped too. Take a look at this picture:

```
              5 PM            7 AM
Paperwork →    |               | — Paperwork →
               |               |
Material  → |← | — — GAP — — →| — Material  →
               |               |
               └─ Cycle count in this time
                  frame for best results
```

In most distributors' operations, material stops flowing about 5 PM and begins about 7 AM the next morning. Paperwork follows a similar pattern. Orders and receipts cease in the late afternoon and start up again early the next day. This creates a natural "gap" . . . an effective cutoff which permits shelf counts to be compared to record balances and corrections made where they're needed, PROVIDED that there's no material or paperwork float!

PHYSICAL CONTROL: THE FOUNDATION OF YOUR SYSTEM!   213

The Computer-Prepared Cycle Count List

About 5:15 PM, a warehouseman receives a printed list from the computer showing the area he's to count this evening. The list contains 200 items, perhaps, and it also tells him *the computer's available-for-sale balance* on each listed item. Before you come unglued, I *know* you'd never do that with untrained counters during an annual physical inventory, but this cycle counter is a professional! He or she works with the material every day. Product variations won't cause confusion; the counter knows the difference between items packed 10 to a box or singly; he knows the correct units of measure; he's familiar with pallet patterns; he won't count coils instead of feet nor pounds as each. He's told how many are supposed to be on the shelf so that he'll know how to look for overflow stock or misplaced material, rather than just mark down a zero when 100 are shown as available. You *want* his or her knowledge of products, storage locations, and warehouse material flow applied to the task!

USE THE BLOCK METHOD

The printed list tells the counter to start at Bin 01 of Row 001, for example, and count every item on the shelves until he completes 200, or whatever number the list contains (I'll explain in a minute how to determine the number). The counter takes a *wall-to-wall* inventory of a small portion of the warehouse tonight . . . a "block" of space, counting everything he finds whether it's on the list or not. Hopefully, most items will be on the list if your warehouse item location maintenance is disciplined. The Block cycle count method will find anything that isn't.

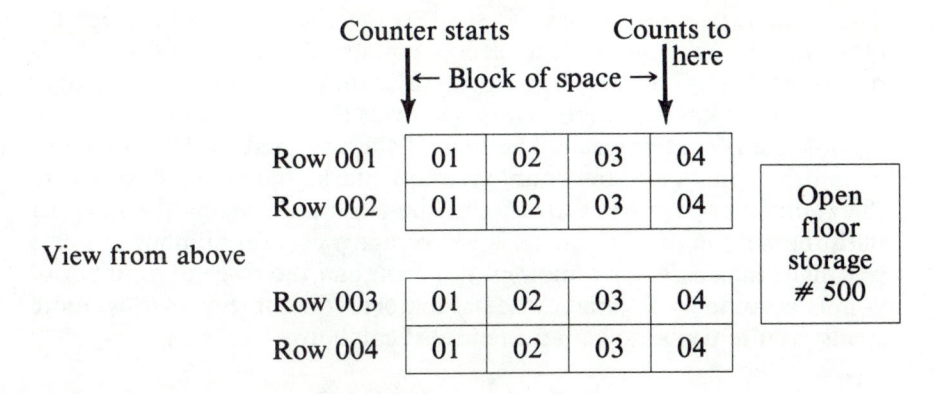

```
                    Counter starts        Counts to
                         |                  | here
                         | ← Block of space →|
                         ↓                   ↓
                   Row 001  | 01 | 02 | 03 | 04 |
                   Row 002  | 01 | 02 | 03 | 04 |    Open
View from above                                      floor
                                                    storage
                   Row 003  | 01 | 02 | 03 | 04 |    # 500
                   Row 004  | 01 | 02 | 03 | 04 |
```

The "Shelf-to-Sheet" Counting Technique

It's *very* important for the counter to work *FROM THE SHELF TO THE SHEET* and not the other way around! The goal is to find everything you have, recorded or not, find exactly where it's located, find all misplaced items, and verify the quantities. Here's how the counter works:

> Hmmm. What's that first item up there on the top shelf? Oh yeah, I know that one. It's a 4226JX switch, packed 10 to a box. We've got 4 boxes and 3 loose ones. That's 43. What does the list say? Yeah, here it is. The list says 44. We're one unit off. I have to enter 43 here in the correction column.
>
> Is the location correct on the list? Yes, that's OK. It says that the item is stored here in Row 001, Bin 01.
>
> What's that next item up there on the shelf? Shoot, that's a 4220JX. I didn't know we stocked that thing. How many are there? 14. I wonder where in the world we got those dogs? Yeah, just as I thought. The 4220JX isn't listed. I'll have to write it in here at the bottom of the sheet with the quantity and warehouse location, so we can get the critter into the computer records.
>
> Now, what's next on the shelf? Hey, that's an Ajax Manufacturing 4335LX! That's way out of place! Its proper location is way over on Aisle 26. I wonder who the devil put it here . . . stupid jerk! No wonder we couldn't find any the other day. I'm going to move it to aisle 26 right now!
>
> Let's see, what's next? The bin is empty but there's an overflow stock tag . . . says there's more on top of Bin 14 here in this row. We're supposed to have 100. I'll bet they're down at 14. I'll check and move the stock to this location!

That's the procedure: From the shelf to the sheet . . . and never the other way around! The warehouseman counts everything he finds. If it's on his list, fine. If it's not, he writes it in or moves the item to its proper location if he knows where that is. He takes a wall-to-wall inventory of the assigned locations each evening. If the assigned number of items cannot be completed, the counter simply marks the list to show where the counts ended. Tomorrow night, the computer begins the new list with the next item. The intent is to average a certain number of items per night (discussed in a moment). If less than the targeted number of counts is completed tonight, the list tomorrow night should show more items. You're trying to help the counters catch up.

Entering the Record Corrections

When a count shows the computer's balance for an item to be off, the correction is entered as a +6 or a −17, etc. Don't enter the correction by erasing what the computer shows and replacing it with the accurate count. Why? If you did, the correction would have to be keyed before 7 AM . . . or whenever paperwork and material begins flowing again. That could be difficult. Someone would have to be scheduled to come in at 6 AM, for example, to key all cycle count changes. Also, the computer must process them before inside salesmen begin making stock status inquiries or entering orders at 7:30.

When the correction is entered as a plus or minus adjustment, then it may be keyed at any time in the next 24 hours. The computer can insert the correction at any point into the "stream" of transactions being processed and the proper adjustment will be made. No matter what available-for-sale balance is shown at the time the correction is applied, it will be adjusted by plus 6 or minus 17, etc., . . . and the figure is correct from that point on.

Avoid That Annual Physical Inventory!

What does this accomplish, as opposed to other methods of cycle counting? The other methods (Inventory Class, Reorder, Receiver, etc.) send a counter to the warehouse with a list of items, selected by how frequently they move, by the fact that they should be replenished, or some similar criteria. The objective is to count faster-moving items often and slower items less frequently. However, when the counter finds the listed item and counts them, he's through. He doesn't look for items not on the list. All the junk, all the "strangers" that somehow find their way onto your warehouse shelves, all the items out of place . . . he doesn't count at all.

When it's time for your annual physical inventory, you cannot satisfy the auditors' desire for accuracy by simply "dumping" out the counts from your computer records. The auditors might accept as accurate the computer balances for items you can list . . . but what about all that other stuff in your warehouse that you don't even know you have or is misplaced? The "Block" cycle count method generates four *wall-to-wall* inventories per year. The other methods fail to take even one.

With the Block approach, you can dump out your computer's balances as the "official" counts for warehouse stock—the available stock—and have to count only the committed material during the annual physical. That's much more accurate than sending the army of "volunteers" into the warehouse at year-end (the office girls, outside salesmen, vendor salesmen . . . who just love being out there and who know they won't have to straighten out any mistakes they make). You'll satisfy the auditors, who won't be able to find items without a record. No item is further away than 3 months from a record/count verification, and the average item is but a month and a half away from its last count.

HOW MANY ITEMS PER NIGHT?

Now to the question of how many items to count each evening. As stated above, every stocked item should be counted four times a year. Record accuracy remains very good because all items are relatively close to the time (1½ months average) when the available-for-sale balance was last verified.

You should expect to count only some 200 evenings per year: 50 weeks (with a vacation for the counter), holidays considered, and count activity planned just four nights each week. It's not wise to schedule counting on Friday nights. With 200 nights to count, and each item counted four times during the year, it's not difficult to determine the average number of items to count each evening. Let's say you have 10,000 items in stock:

$$10{,}000 \text{ items} \times 4 \text{ counts each} = 40{,}000 \text{ counts for the year}$$

$$\frac{40{,}000 \text{ counts per year}}{200 \text{ nights to count}} = 200 \text{ items per night}$$

Put your number of stocked items in the calculation. You may find that you must count only 100 per night, or 50, or perhaps 400. Whatever the answer, the counter (or counters) should average that many items per evening. With small, easy-to-count items, he may do better. With larger, bulkier, difficult-to-count material, he may get fewer on a particular night . . . but the goal is to average the 200 per evening (in our example). The counter reports each night where he stopped on the list. Program the computer to begin the next night's list right at that point. As stated earlier, if the schedule falls behind, the next night's list shows 215 items, in an effort to catch up.

Once cycle counting begins, it has to become a way of life in your company. You simply cannot accept the multitude of reasons why "I couldn't finish, Boss!" . . . or, "We just couldn't get to it last night!" You *must* get to it! You have to finish! Cycle counting, too, is part of a "Day's-Work-In-A-Day."

Who Counts and When Do They Work?

The counter's hours might have to be staggered, where he or she reports to work at 10 AM and gets off around 7 PM, for example. He must be the kind of employee you trust to work alone, unsupervised, with a key to the building perhaps . . . a professional warehouseman who really knows the material, who takes pride in a clean, well-organized warehouse and in his or her job. You say you don't have anybody like that? Hmmmm . . . sounds like you've got problems bigger than how to cycle count! You'd better upgrade the caliber of your warehouse personnel before attempting anything as disciplined as cycle counting. Cycle counting can't be successful when the warehousemen don't give a rip about anything . . . and are paid so low you can't find better ones! Start by paying a premium for the cycle count work. That should at least attract the best of your crew to the task.

What If You Have a Round-The-Clock Operation?

Some distributors don't have a "gap" in which they can count. A new shift arrives about 4 PM, works until midnight, and another group comes in then to work until morning. Order filling, receiving, putting stock away, staging material, loading trucks . . . it all goes on all night. Now what? Do they have to forget cycle counting? Do they have to live with lousy records, the excess inventories, with no hope of ever having accuracy? No, they can cycle count, but the headaches are more intense.

Find the Time When Warehouse Activity Is Slowest

It's necessary to identify that period in the 24-hour work cycle when activity is at its lowest ebb. Maybe it's between 3 and 4 AM. Maybe it's just as the shifts change at midnight. Each night, a specific portion of the warehouse is targeted for cycle counting . . . a row, or section of bins, etc., just as with normal cycle counting procedures . . . a block of space. The counters work that area in the low-ebb period.

Two additional aids are needed. First, the computer is programmed to "cut off" release of new orders to be filled, or receipts to be put away, for *just* items in the count area . . . early enough each evening to permit completion of the work before the counting time. Available-for-sale balances are computed for these items as of the 3 AM cutoff time, for example.

Secondly, the count area is off-limits during the counting period. No one goes in there to fill an order or to put material away. Orders and receipts for affected items wait until after counting is completed. The computer goes ahead and issues them, but items in the count area are specially-marked to say in effect: "Warehousemen, you may fill these items or put this material away only after 4:30 AM! . . . not before!" Earlier orders were marked just the reverse: "You must complete this order or receipt by 3 AM!"

Is this difficult to pull off? Of course! It's very tough. It requires a high degree of programming sophistication and warehousing discipline. But it's worth the effort and learning curve (sometimes called "trial and error") frustration you'll experience before it works effectively.

"Sounds Like This Will Cost a Bundle!"

Is all this expensive? You'd better believe it! . . . but what does it cost to operate year-round with far more inventory (and more inside salespeople) than necessary? Cycle counting's expense is paid back many times over every year through the benefits of accurate records that all employees *trust*, rather than records so lousy that everyone in the place compensates with extra stock.

Distributors, today, that have achieved the 98 percent accuracy level would *never go back* to the old ways, where "negative" balances were a way of life and the computer records were just a joke. The effort required to reach the accurate status was so monumental . . . and the benefits so substantial . . . that nothing (or no one) will be permitted to cause such error again. It's something like a young lady weighing 260 pounds whose doctor tells her she must get down to 125. It's one of the toughest things she's ever done to lose the weight. . . . but wow, it's nice to hear the whistles when she wears her new bikini at the beach. The combination of effort required and benefits derived, makes her dedicate herself to never weigh 260 again! It's just like that with stock record accuracy.

What About the Causes of the Errors?

Ok . . . *NOW* that you've established an improved level of stock record accuracy by cycle counting, you can attack the other causes of record error. Now, you'll have some success! Almost certainly, you eliminated one of the major culprits when the paper and material "float" was removed through the "Day's-Work-In-A-Day" disciplines. When that's the normal environment, many of the record discrepancies disappear almost miraculously. Isn't *that* funny? . . . but what else can mess up the records? Where else should the search for problem

PHYSICAL CONTROL: THE FOUNDATION OF YOUR SYSTEM! 219

conditions or people be concentrated? Here's my "Lucky 13" problem group to find and correct:

1. *Lack of a warehouse locator system* . . . aisle, row, rack, bin, floor storage, yard numbers that designate all areas where material can be stored. The logic: "We're too small for such discipline. Our people know where the material is stored!" Oh yeah? You should go out there one day and watch a new warehouseman trying to fill an order. Talk about lost motion!

2. *Failure to designate a primary storage area for each item* . . . and recording this location assignment in the computer records. Some distributors still store their material in order by suppliers' part numbers, with employees expected to remember all part locations. This almost always leads to misplaced items.

3. *Poor discipline in handling overflow stock* . . . material that won't fit in the primary storage location and has to be placed elsewhere. Overflow "tags" should be used to indicate where any excess has been placed. A tag is placed at the primary location to tell where more stock of this item can be found (not how many are there . . . just *where* more stock is stored). Additional tags on the overflow material say, in effect, "This is overflow for stuff you keep regularly in Row 01, Bin 046."

   The cycle counter includes any overflow quantities in the total count for an item when working the primary storage location. When working the overflow area, he simply marks the item (with a sticker or pen) to show he didn't overlook it . . . but does not count it. He'll count that material when he counts its primary location.

4. *Training new warehouse personnel by assigning them first to Receiving* . . . the worst possible place to turn loose an untrained employee. Errors made in Receiving are like a virus. Once in your "system," they cause multiplied problems until they're found and corrected.

   Put your very best warehouse person or people in Receiving. It's the highest paid warehousing job you have, and therefore the top hands want to work there. Start brand new employees filling customer orders . . . checked by someone experienced before the material goes out the door. The quantities are smaller going out than coming in. Generally, a Receiving error is far more damaging than one made on a customer's order. "Heresy!" you say? Well, would it hurt worse if your bank misapplied one of your deposits or one of your checks?

5. *"Open House" in the warehouse* . . . in terms of security. Anybody and everybody wanders around back there as they please. No one can be held accountable, therefore, for what goes on, the necessary operational disciplines, etc. Take Note: This is *not* the first area to correct. You must make the records so good through cycle counting that no one needs to go in the warehouse. *Then,* you can start a long-range program to restrict access!

Eventually (maybe after 3 to 4 years of preparation), begin to close off the warehouse to all but authorized employees. Outside salesmen, inside salesmen, supplier salesmen and reps, office personnel, incoming truck drivers, customers (unless accompanied) . . . all stay out of the warehouse. If a mistake occurs out there, you can hold someone accountable. Generally, the counter salesmen are considered "authorized."

6. *Poor control over who has the authority to add an item to stock for the first time.* Inside salesmen, outside salesmen, buyers, countermen . . . anybody can buy material for stock that's never been stocked before. The system should require that a non-stock item be sold before permitting it on a purchase order to your supplier! . . . and this is a restriction the computer should enforce. Require the sales order to be keyed. *Then* a purchase order for that item and quantity may be entered!

You must stop the unauthorized person who decides to buy 24 (to get a good cost), sells only 6, and has the rest put in the warehouse . . . somewhere, usually with no official record. You know all too well when most items like this are discovered, don't you? At the next annual physical or cycle count! Crippling to profits.

7. *Poor backorder disciplines when new material comes in from a supplier.* Old backorders are overlooked, some are filled out of sequence, or filled after everything has been taken to the warehouse shelves. Non-stock items are often missed and inadvertently put in stock, with a good chance to be lost.

It might require some rearrangement to create more staging room in Receiving, but the most effective procedure is to fill all stock and non-stock customer backorders *right there* in Receiving. Don't let "committed" material be taken on into the warehouse to be handled (again) later. When material leaves, it's either to Shipping, to an order-staging area, and only if available-for-sale, to the warehouse.

8. *Sloppy, ponderous handling of customer returns* . . . items are slow being returned to the shelves, paperwork processed, etc. No

PHYSICAL CONTROL: THE FOUNDATION OF YOUR SYSTEM! 221

one assigned officially to clean out the returned goods area on a schedule monitored by management.

Most distributors' returned goods areas are "rats' nests". They get around to cleaning them up (or out) when there's no longer room for anything more. Credits have long since been processed . . . increasing the stock balances at times, and the material is still in the holding area. Another cause of inaccurate computer records!

9. *No official system (or perhaps no enforcement) for ordering replacements quickly when components are "robbed" from complete units in stock to satisfy customer emergencies.*

There are times when a part must be removed from a complete assembly or product to take care of a customer, but you must establish very tight discipline to assure that a replacement is put on order at once . . . *and* the warehouse knows what to do with it when it comes in. This may require a special little paperflow system just to handle the problem.

10. *A Poor system of paperwork when salesmen remove "samples" to take along on a sales call* . . . or when they fill their own orders, but wait until month-end to turn in the paperwork.

Frankly, you have to adopt a tough posture on this. Salesmen must be told: "Effective Monday, if you are seen leaving the building with material but without the right paperwork made out by the right people, it will be considered theft!"

Can you imagine a bank employee entering the vault and removing some of the "inventory" kept in there, without the right paperwork to authorize the action? "But we don't have money in our warehouse!" you say. Hmmm . . . guess again.

11. *Repair work that takes several days or weeks* . . . using material off the shelves, but not reported as withdrawn until the job is completed and billed.

If you allow employees to withdraw regular stock to be used in repair work (as opposed to having a separate inventory), then *each day* they must report the items and quantities pulled. You can't afford to wait several days or weeks to reflect that these quantities have been "committed."

12. *Unit of measure conversion errors* . . . where the sale is entered as 1 "coil" at $450, when the proper quantity should have been 500 "feet" at .90, etc.

Effective screens can be programmed to help with this headache. Fields for each stock item give the range of acceptable selling prices. If a price outside this range is entered, the computer alerts the entry operator that either the wrong item number or an incorrect unit is present. The item can sell between .01 and 1.00 per foot. A $250 price signals an incorrect unit or the wrong item number.

13. *Attempting to keep "protected" stock (guaranteed under a systems contract, etc.) and regular stock in the same warehouse location.* It's too easy for someone to "borrow" the protected inventory. For control, it should be in a caged-off area of the warehouse.

Boy, do I get some screaming at times when I recommend this to a client! . . . but my experience has been that if the customer is so important that you've agreed to protected merchandise just for him . . . then *you'd better protect it*! Too many bad things can happen if it's left right in with the regular material. One warehouseman is assigned to put away material and fill all orders. No one else touches the caged-off stock.

Now remember . . . *Don't* try to ferret out and clean up all these problems as a first step! "Day's-Work-in-a-Day" comes first to remove the paperwork and material float, thereby creating an environment in which cycle counting will do some good. Cycle counting is next. That improves the record accuracy even with all the problem conditions introducing their error. Cycle counting takes out errors at the same rate all the other problems are feeding them in. THEN, you can start your campaign to find any or all of the 13 (and others of your own that I didn't mention) and fix the conditions.

As stated earlier, cycle counting once begun, becomes a way of life! You'll need it from now on . . . perhaps not as intensively when you've established very accurate records, but always in some form. Plan and begin your program soon. Find answers for each of the 47 reasons your employees will give as to why " . . . we can't do that, Boss!" Decide now to stop putting up with those lousy records. As they say in the TV commercials, "You'll be glad you did!" (when you look at your profits).

Physical control . . . a lightly-treated, often-overlooked, rarely-discussed topic when the system salesman comes to call. If it's weak in your company, you have a very unstable foundation on which to set the new computerized concepts. It won't make much difference which system you buy, or how much care is devoted to the programming. It never will produce great results.

15

DEAD STOCK: THE PROFIT AND CONTROL SYSTEM CRIPPLER!

Most durable goods distributors carry about 40 percent more items in stock than they really need! Does *that* get your attention? Yes, it's true. Before this chapter ends, I'll show you how to find your 40 percent but the situation is very common. Now before you have a coronary, let me add this: Many of the 40 percent do sell . . . a little. They're not completely dead. The trickle of sales they produce, however, doesn't generate anywhere near enough profit to justify the dollars invested in inventory. That's the problem.

WHEN INVENTORY "CONTROL" IS EXERCISED

Let's assume that my wild statement above is true . . . that most distributors' productive-to-nonproductive stock profiles look like this:

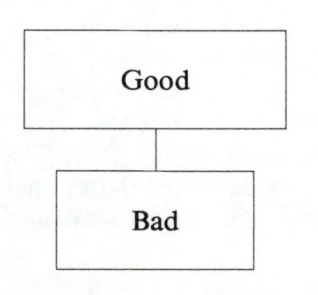

Good ← The controls of earlier chapters (order points, line points, EOQ's, etc.) work up here. . . . impacting these good items and causing their total inventory dollars to turn about 5 to 6 times a year.

Bad ← The controls have little or no impact with this group. They are not replenished. Turns are less than 1 per year.

All of which illustrates our important Inventory Management principle:

> Inventory *CONTROL* is exercised when you bring in stock . . . either for the first time or in replenishment. Everything you do after that point must be classed as Inventory *CORRECTION!*

The turns for both groups above, combined, likely will be about 1.9 to 2.3 per year. Why? . . . because the inventory controls impact only the good stuff. That's the material being reordered. The bad stuff just sits. The replenishment controls have no effect. It isn't reordered.

The Wrong Way to Correct the Problem

In an effort to stop inventory build-up and correct a lousy overall turn rate, a distributor president might issue this sweeping executive edict:

> We've got way too much inventory around here! Listen you people in Purchasing, quit buying so much of our stocked material . . . and wait longer to order it! Let our stock run lower before you place the P.O.'s!

What's *that* going to accomplish if Purchasing follows this directive? You've learned well! Yes, the service levels for good material will go to pot if you drop the Line Points and Order Points arbitrarily. *They are what they are* because *outsiders* (customers and suppliers) set them through performance and their offers of purchasing discounts. Buying smaller quantities of the better items will improve the turn rate slightly, but of course you'll work everyone too hard . . . spend too much control money to keep the items resupplied. And the overall turn rate? . . . well, it won't change much, maybe up to 2.5.

The real source of the turnover problem is the dead and slow-moving stock. *That's* where the action is needed! The president tried to apply correction in the easiest place: What Purchasing is doing today, tomorrow, and the next day. He's hoping for a quick fix. Unfortunately, for this problem, there isn't one. It's going to require a planned, administered, monitored program to identify and rid the company of the dead material . . . a program that the president must take part in, if the turns are to improve. With the profile you saw above (40 percent of the stock non-productive), you'd have to turn the good stuff 20 times a year to get 6 overall. You wouldn't want to try that. The expense and strain on your people would be prohibitive. Better that you attack the real problem . . . the excessive amount of slow and dead stock.

The President's Five Major Priorities

A little later, you'll see a Four-Part Dead Stock Prevention, Identification and Disposition Program to help rid your company of the "millstone" that's dragging down the turns and tying up your cash. But a major decision has to be made first. Your president has to add one more priority to the four he has already:

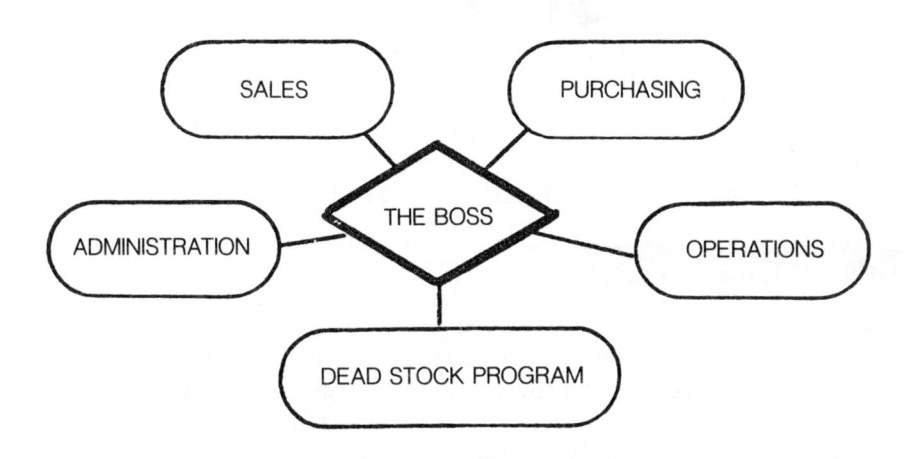

```
          SALES           PURCHASING

ADMINISTRATION   THE BOSS    OPERATIONS

           DEAD STOCK PROGRAM
```

The president must be *very* interested in the dead stock program. It must be one of his five major priorities, or not much will happen. It's a business phenomenon that other people take an active interest in those activities in which the Boss is directly involved. If he or she is following up, asking lots of questions about progress, etc., *things happen!*

Don't misunderstand. The president isn't to get rid of the nonproductive stuff personally. That would be an expensive waste of his time. . . . but the program to get rid of it is one of his five major priorities! He's as involved on a day-to-day basis in this program as in what's going on in Sales, in Purchasing, in Administration (Accounting, Data Processing, Keeping "Score"), and in Operations (Warehouse, Trucks, Delivery). You'll see clearly as the Dead Stock Program is explained how the president is involved . . . but his involvement is a prerequisite to success. He provides the power to drive the program.

THE FOUR-PART DEAD STOCK PROGRAM

An effective effort to move out the deadwood from inventory has four distinct phases:

1. Prevention
2. Identification
3. Coordination
4. Disposition Steps

Each is important. Each has its impact. Resist that urge to bypass the first three parts and jump immediately to the fourth. It's a bit like painting your house. Preparation is perhaps more important than the final steps when you see the clean, new surfaces. In your program, allow each of the four steps to effect the benefit it alone can introduce.

Phase 1: Prevention

The first phase, Prevention, requires some new thinking. You need an entirely new attitude about putting items in stock for the first time. Frankly, you should adopt a tough, "up-front" posture as new items are considered for inventory. Why? . . . because most dead items didn't evolve to that status. They were not once great sellers, only to gradually lose steam and wind up dogs. They were dogs from Day 1! They *never did* sell worth a hoot.

The odds are these: If you add 10 new stock items today, under the same logic distributors have used for years, only 2 will be good movers after a year. The other 8 will range all the way from "Ugh" (you'd like to throw up) to marginal at best. Obviously, we need a change in logic if we're to have even a 50/50 chance of new items becoming winners.

Three Groups That Influence a Stocking Decision

Three different groups of people exert pressure on a distributor to add new items to stock: Customers, the distributor's own Salesmen, and Suppliers. Let's see how the new up-front, decision-making toughness applies to each of these groups.

Customers: Old Joe over at ABC Industries calls your salesman with a request:

DEAD STOCK: THE PROFIT AND CONTROL SYSTEM CRIPPLER!

> Harry, I'd like your company to start carrying these six items in stock for me. If you will, I'll buy about ten each per month from you. . . . and don't worry about the inventory. Whatever I haven't taken by December 31, you may ship and bill! Oh, and this will give you a golden opportunity to get a lot of new business from us. We favor distributors who support us with special stocks.

In the past, the phone wasn't even cool before the special stock of six new items was arriving at your dock. . . . but what about today? What should you ask for *today* that would have been out of the question in 1975? That's right, a *COMMITMENT*, and in writing! You should ask the customer to give you something in writing that expresses his commitment to you to buy the new stock.

Quit snickering! I *know* you likely cannot enforce it. I realize that if you tried, you'd probably lose the customer. The written commitment is for psychological reasons. Customers have a nasty habit of making the same special stock arrangements with more than one distributor (I know you're shocked and disappointed, but alas, it's true). They want to be covered no matter how scarce the products might become. The customer knows he hasn't enough business for all three distributors next year. . . . so guess who gets most (or all) of his orders if you have a written commitment in almost any form, and two other distributors have only verbal deals? Sure, you get 'em! The customer isn't too sure what legal grounds you have with a written agreement, but he *knows* what the other two guys can do . . . zippo! You get the orders. They get apologies.

It doesn't have to be fancy. A blanket order with release dates; A blanket order with no release dates; A signed letter on the customer's stationery; A napkin he signed at lunch . . . anything. Just be sure it's in writing!

Your Own Salesmen: Harry (your salesman) walks into your office with this complaint:

> Boss, you recall that Joe over at ABC Industries wants us to add those six new stock items just for him, and you told me to get something in writing from him. Well he won't do that! Joe says he never puts such gentlemanly arrangements in writing for anyone. Boss, if we want this business, we'll have to do it without a formal commitment from him!

Now what? You can't get a written commitment from ABC Industries, but who *can* you get one from? Ol' Harry, your salesman! Out of your desk comes a form letter with blanks to be filled in. Your reply to Harry goes like this:

> Harry, we definitely want that new business from ABC, and we certainly want to support your dedicated sales effort. Just fill in here on this letter the six new items you want us to add, and *how many you commit to sell to ABC Industries per month,* sign the letter, and we'll add the inventory. Oh, please note that last paragraph. If any of the original stock, of the first batch we bring in, still remains on the shelves after six months, *YOU* and the company will share the 30 percent per year carrying cost!

Harry will likely fall over onto the floor with apoplexy (the sudden loss of bodily function). "Are you crazy?", he screams. "I'm not going to sign any such letter!" Well, now the decision is simple. No commitment, no new inventory! *SOMEBODY* has to commit to buy or sell this stuff! If they won't, then why take the risk? Isn't that how you got most of the deadwood that's out on your shelves right now?

Harry wants the company to take a big investment risk, based on his word and ability to sell. If he *really* thinks the customer will buy these six items, the letter presents no hazard for him. If you replenish any of the items before the six months are up, Harry's off the hook on them. He's committing only to sell the *original* inventory! Perhaps he'll downgrade his request from six items to four, and the commitment on sales from ten a month to five. Harry will list only what he's sure he can sell. Great! Until that day arrives when you close off the warehouse to Harry (Chapter 14), he may see some dusty material out there as he wanders around.

> Goodnight, look at all that dusty stuff up there! . . . and the Boss has a signed letter of commitment where I said I'd sell it all by October. Boy, I'm going to call Joe over at ABC Industries as soon as I walk back into the office!

That's exactly what we want him to do. "Don't forget why that inventory is here! YOU said you'd sell it!" You may elect not to have Harry pay directly half the carrying cost on dusty material that can't be returned, but the letter is still a good idea. Commitment . . . that's the concept!

Suppliers: How about the manufacturers? They, too, often exert pressure to add new stock items, and you can be sure there's very little "commitment" involved. For those suppliers you've had for years, where you *must* (or feel you must) have their product lines, there's not a lot to be done now. You made your bed years ago with these folks, and now you have to sleep in it. When you signed the Supplier/Distributor Agreement, your ability to negotiate pretty much ended right there.

In the years to come, however, many other suppliers will court you in hopes that you'll take on their products. With these, you have significant

DEAD STOCK: THE PROFIT AND CONTROL SYSTEM CRIPPLER! 229

negotiating possibilities. With these, you need not wake up three years from now to find most of the original stock still around. Here's the scene as the potential supplier's salesman tries to seal the bargain:

> Well, Mr. Harris . . . we're *so* glad that you've agreed to be our distributor in this area! All I need now from you is a purchase order for our standard array of products as your initial stock . . . every distributor starts this way. It requires a $10,000 purchase, but don't worry about a thing. Whatever doesn't sell after a year, we'll take back with no restocking charge. Of course, you will have to pay the freight, our low inspection charge, and agree to purchase an equal value of products that do sell for the stuff you return.

With this statement, the salesman pulls a very official-looking document from his briefcase . . . it's the "Supplier/Distributor Agreement," that sets out the terms he just outlined. This baby is impressive. It's printed; has an eagle at the top; a scroll down the side, a huge seal at the bottom; and is signed by some high dignitary. It looks like a will. Who in the world would dare to question such a document?

Your Own Version of the Agreement

YOU would! From your middle desk drawer comes an even *more* impressive document. It's printed in gold; a double-eagle at the top; gold scrolling, two seals, signed by someone in Washington. This is *your company's* Distributor/Supplier agreement! It sets out your provisions for taking on a new product line:

1. You must see a Classification of the supplier's products just as you did for your own items back in Chapter 10. . . . best to worst! The items that have sold well in your industry, geographic area, or nationally (whichever would be more revealing) are listed first; the "dogs" down at the bottom.

2. You will take the list, sit down with your Marketing or Sales staff and let them review it. Whatever they commit to sell will be ordered. You reserve the right to "cherry pick" the product line. It might turn out to be a $2,800 purchase order . . . not $10,000!

3. Whatever doesn't sell goes back to the supplier after six months; he pays the freight; no restocking or inspection charges; and no exchange requirements!

Rather than signing the supplier's document, slide your version across the desk to him. Watch him turn red. . . . and then leave in a huff. "If we did this for you," he sobs, "we'd have to do it for any new distributor!" Let him go. Thank him for his time, and be sure he has your business card. "Call me when you're ready to discuss this!" you reply.

In a few days, the salesman's boss will call: "Let's get together and discuss how we can get you on board as our distributor!" Great! Now you can negotiate the provisions of the agreement. . . . and every single provision *IS* negotiable! The supplier simply used one of the oldest techniques in the book on you. It's called "Authenticity." If you lay an authentic-enough document in front of most people . . . one that's printed and obviously is never to be tampered with, most people will sign without a murmur. Don't fall for it. Give him an even more impressive dose of the same technique.

Likely, you'll wind up with an agreement somewhere between what he specified and what your gold document set forth. That's OK. It's all part of your game to get the line with better terms up front . . . better initial stock requirements and not-so-one-sided return provisions. Distributors, today, are negotiating much better arrangements than in the 60s, 70s, and even the 80s. They can't afford the slow-moving and dead inventories that resulted from taking on new product lines when the supplier laid down all the terms.

Prevention! That's Phase 1 in your Dead Stock Program. It's a new attitude that, once adopted, becomes permanent. You have to be tougher up front with customers, your own salesmen, and new suppliers to prevent new stock items from becoming deadwood in a year or two. Your Prevention efforts won't be 100 percent successful, of course. In spite of the tougher up-front screening, items will still slip through and become dogs. . . . but you'll net a bunch of em' that otherwise would have wound up on your shelves.

Phase 2: Identification

On the junk you already have, it's a bit late for "Prevention." The prevent defense failed to work. Someone made a judgment call on this stock back in the past, and it has turned out to be an expensive decision. Inventory "Control" misfired. All that's left now is Inventory "Correction."

How many times, though, has a list been prepared in your company of items for disposition, only to have someone scream: "Oh, no! Don't get rid of *that!* I know we'll sell it sooner or later, and even if we don't, the customers would think we're going out of business if we don't have it on the shelf!" Hmmm . . . are you saying you must carry the stock for "show"? Are you in "Show Business" or the "Profit-Making" business?

Frankly, you can afford very little "show" stock. The only justification for having an item on the shelf is that customers buy it. If they've

DEAD STOCK: THE PROFIT AND CONTROL SYSTEM CRIPPLER! 231

proven that they don't want it *from you,* then why keep incurring the 30 percent per year (or whatever) carrying cost? Couldn't you find a better use for the cash? You need a method to identify non-productive inventory that cuts into the junk and cuts out the arguing.

The Inventory Analysis Report

This analysis begins just like the Inventory Classification back in Chapter 10, except that this exercise is done on a company-wide basis. All activity in all branches for a stock item is lumped together. After calculating how much was sold at cost for each stock item over the last twelve months, the items are then sequenced by the answer. In the illustration, the best item sold $120,710 total at cost; the next-best item totaled $105,119 for the year. Column C provides the cumulative percent of *all* stock sales represented by the first item, then the first and second together, then the first, second and third, etc. If your sales histories are complete and accurate, eventually this analysis will account for 100 percent of the stock sales over the last twelve months.

The right-hand section gives the inventory picture. The current inventory investment for each item is shown in units and dollars, while Column E develops the cumulative percent of all inventory dollars as you move down the list. In the example, when 100 percent of sales is reached in Column C, only 61 percent of the inventory dollars are accounted for in Column E. Let's say that another way: It required only 61 percent of the inventory investment to generate 100 percent of the stock sales! . . . which means that the other 39 percent of the inventory dollars generated how many sales? Zero!

The items below the 100 percent sales line generated nothing, and if the company disposed of them, what would be risked? Let's go farther, though. If we moved back up the listing to the 99 percent sales point, what kind of items will be found in that last 1 percent of sales? You guessed it . . . the dogs! Stuff that for the entire last year sold $2.16 worth, or maybe $9.67, or even $0.59 worth. But how much of the inventory might be sitting there to develop that last 1 percent of sales? In many companies, it's as much as 10 percent! In the illustration, that would mean 99 percent of the sales are generated by 51 percent of the inventory dollars! 49 percent of the inventory provided 1 percent of sales!

Of course you're thinking: "Our inventory isn't like that! 99 percent of our sales would require a much higher percent of the total inventory investment!" Want to bet? Why not run this analysis and find out. You may just get the shock of your life. One distributor president heard all this in a training session and was certain his situation was nothing like

Inventory analysis report

	(Section 1) Sold over the past year				(Section 2) Still in stock		
	A	B	C	D		E	
Item No.	Units sold in past year	Cost per unit	Extension (A × B)	Cumulative % of all sales	Units now in stock	Units × unit cost (B × D)	Cumulative % of total inventory
12346	1247	$96.80	$120,710	0.008%	196	$18,973	0.020%
45678	15,436	$6.81	$105,119	0.015%	3214	$21,887	0.043%
34629	18	$2456.10	$44,210	0.020%	3	$7,368	0.050%

(This list continues until the figures under Cumulative % of all sales (Column C) totals 100%.)

| etc. | etc. | etc. | etc. | etc. | etc. | etc. | etc. |
| 327345 | 1 | $0.18 | — | 100% | 516 | $93 | 61% |

(The significant figure is 61% in Column E. This indicates that (100% − 61% = 39%) 39% of the inventory didn't sell.)

Rationale:

- The report shows an entry for every stocked item in this branch. The first item listed is the one that enjoyed the highest sales (units × unit cost) during the previous 12 months. The second item listed is the second best selling item in terms of total value moved through the inventory. The listing continues through many pages until all sales of all stock items are accounted for. Many items at the end of the list will show no sales activity at all.

- The right-hand section of the report shows the current inventory investment for each item listed and a running cumulative percent as the list progresses of how much of the total inventory investment has been accounted for to this point.

- The astute reader may have already guessed what this analysis will reveal. When 99%, for example, of the sales at cost for the year (through stock) has been reached on the list, what percent of the total inventory investment will have been accounted for? 60%? . . . or 53%? . . . or hopefully, 90%?

- The analysis identifies all stock items that are contributing less than 1%, or 5%, or whatever level you select of the sales. You could get rid of all those items and risk losing only 1% of the sales you experienced during the last 12 months. A branch manager might really want to argue this statement. "We have to keep that stock of item 908762 to assure that we'll get the good stuff XXX Mfg. buys from us!" No problem. Keep it. Keep every one of the items someone can give a specific reason for retaining. But get rid of all the rest. The fact is: They are contributing nothing!

- In too many distributors' inventories, as much as 30% or 40% of the total investment may be below the 100% sales line. Zero turns per year. No sales activity at all. Obviously, these are the candidates for disposition. Realistically, you should cut more deeply. Items below the 98% sales line ought to be dropped from stock as a general rule.

- Often, a distributor will keep a stock item active if one unit sells in a year's time. More than likely, he could have supplied the item on a special order to the manufacturer and his customer would not have complained. But because one piece sold, the item stays on the shelf for another year.

DEAD STOCK: THE PROFIT AND CONTROL SYSTEM CRIPPLER!

the one above. He was right. After running the analysis, he called me from the Coronary Unit. 88 percent of his sales came out of only 17 percent of the inventory. It was far worse than my example. You'd better run *your company* analysis before you decide: "Ours couldn't be that bad!"

Now What? What's Done with the Items Below 99 Percent of Sales?

The next step is to list all items below the 99 percent sales line. Send the list to Sales with these instructions:

> Ladies and gentlemen, our company plans to dispose of all inventory on this list (one way or another) unless you people provide *very specific* reasons, on an item-by-item basis, why some should be kept in stock.

Certainly, there *are* good reasons why selected items should be kept:

1. The item is new. It really shouldn't have been included in the study because there's not yet 12 months of sales history on it.
2. An item "supports" other products sold previously. Repair parts often fall in this category. A designated parts list is maintained in stock, under either a legal or moral obligation to the customers who bought primary units . . . whether the parts sell or not. The obligation usually has a time limit, however.
3. An item on the shelf . . . even though non-moving . . . causes major customers to buy many other profitable items. This logic (for continuing to stock a dog) will be overused by Sales. Require specifics: Which customers buy what other items just because the dog is also available from stock?
4. The item is "protected" stock for a major customer. It's been set aside for just that one account, to be maintained in stock whether he ever buys any or not . . . or until the agreement expires. Systems Contract inventory can be of this type.

A good reason is *not:* "Boy, we sure *used to* sell those!" That's not news! In fact, it's the *problem* . . . not a valid reason for keeping the item! Neither is: "That customer has shut down production of the products that use these stock items. If they start up again, they'll expect us to have them!" How long are you going to sit on the non-moving items waiting? A year? . . . two years? At 30 percent holding cost per year! Better that you rid yourself of the stock now, and add it back if the customer ever does need the items in the future.

How Much of the List Can Sales Justify Keeping?

If you now have 10,000 items in stock, the stuff below the 99 percent sales line could well total 4,000 items. Of these, Sales will likely have valid and acceptable reasons why 10 percent of the list (400 or so) should be kept. Fine, keep 'em all! Keep every stock item that Sales feels, with reasonable logic, that shelf stock must be maintained. The intent of the Dead Stock Program is not to cripple the company. It's to get rid of the non-productive inventory investment with a minimum of risk to sales.

The Other Foundation Stone: Accurate Sales Histories

In the discussion of Physical Control in Chapter 14, you learned of a critical foundation stone to support a successful system . . . accurate records of what's on the shelf. That foundation is important here also, but the other one is even more important in a Dead Stock Identification exercise. Can you imagine how silly you'd feel to list a bunch of items, telling Sales "these don't move," and that you intend to get rid of them . . . only to have some salesman hand you a bunch of sales order copies with the items shown? "Hey, look here!" the salesman says. "I told you we sell these! Your stupid computer has always been fouled up. It doesn't show these sales at all!"

If your sales and transfer histories on stock items are incomplete; if stock items get coded as non-stock because someone didn't want to look up the part numbers; if paperwork is often processed around the computer; well . . . you can throw your Inventory Analysis Report in the trash. You'd be laughed out of the building when you showed it to Sales. The second foundation stone—accurate, complete, timely sales histories for all stocked items—is vital to the success of your dead stock identification phase.

Phase 3: Coordination

Most distributors' efforts to rid themselves of dead and slow stock are "hit-or-miss" affairs. The efforts are fragmented. The president may even assign a committee of Sales, Purchasing and Operational executives to get rid of the junk, or at least to develop a suggested program for his approval. Nobody *wants* to work on dead stock, of course. It's a nuisance, frustrating, and very time-consuming. Most of the activity, related to dead stock, is a concentrated effort by all employees to avoid being assigned to work on it. No one can get fired over dead stock. So what's the answer?

DEAD STOCK: THE PROFIT AND CONTROL SYSTEM CRIPPLER!

The Dead Stock Coordinator

Someone must be put in charge who *CAN* get fired over dead stock! Every distributor needs a Dead Stock Coordinator who, for this responsibility, reports directly to the president. If you have as much as $5 million total invested in inventory, the job should be full-time, because there's a good chance 40 percent of the $5 million is non-productive. 30 percent per year carrying cost on $2 million is $600,000 . . . and that would pay for a bunch of coordinators, wouldn't it?

If you have less than $5 million invested, you could start with a part-time position. Either way, the Coordinator reports to the Boss for all dead stock responsibilities. He or she is to function as the president's eyes, ears, and nose for this program . . . making sure that the Boss stays well informed, since the program involves one of the president's five major priorities. But let's clarify something very quickly: The Coordinator is *not* responsible to get rid of the deadwood. His or her job is to administer a management-approved program that will dispose of the non-productive inventory. Failure to administer the program as instructed could get the person fired.

The Team

Working with the Coordinator is a team of people appointed by the president. By the nature of their jobs, certain executives definitely should be included: The Sales Manager, Purchasing Manager, Operations Manager, and perhaps others in your particular company. The Coordinator's job, like the entire program, is permanent. You'll always generate some dead stock. You'll always need the function. You don't want your dead stock efforts to be hot for a while and then cool off. Now, to understand how the Coordinator works, let's discuss the last phase of the Dead Stock Program.

Phase 4: Disposition Steps

No activity begins until the President, the Coordinator, and all President-appointed team members sit down in a meeting or series of meetings to work out the steps of the disposition plan. They start by asking a basic question: "What's the best thing possible that could happen to a block of dead stock around here?" The answer . . . which becomes Step 1 in the plan: Sell it, at full price, right where it sits. Don't move it somewhere else! Give that a try. Sales gets the job. Allow about two weeks to see what happens, and then move to Step 2.

==Step 2 should be: Sell it, right where it is, at cost or above!== For whatever doesn't move in Step 1, you'll now accept any amount down to cost. Sales gets this step also. Step 3 might be: Move it to another company location where you feel there's a chance to sell it at cost or better! Why not try that earlier? Well, when you move the dead stuff, you must invest additional money in pick/pack/ship expenses and freight costs perhaps. It's cheaper to sell it where it is at cost. Step 3 might be assigned to Purchasing, the Corporate Operations Manager (if you have one), or to the Coordinator.

Step 7 or 8 might be to send material back to the supplier if you can. Purchasing gets the job with 30 days to arrange the return. Why is this step so far down the list? By the time you pay the freight, restocking charges, inspection charges, etc., what will you get back . . . 50 cents on the dollar? Better to try other ideas first. Step 16, ten months into the program perhaps, is to donate the material. Step 17 (or whatever)? Call the scrap dealer.

That's the concept. The President, Coordinator, and Team work out the step sequence, the assignments, the time allowances. *NOW,* the Coordinator can go to work. Now the Coordinator has a management-approved package, a progression of stock-disposition alternatives, a definite plan to administer, and others in the company (assigned by the Boss) to help execute the plan. For most steps, the Coordinator is the administrator . . . the other team members are responsible for execution.

The Plan Gets Underway

First, the Coordinator divides all the material for disposition into several blocks or lists. The first blocks have the most money. The obvious goal of the entire program is to return as much cash out of the deadwood as possible, so common sense says: Start with items representing the most money in inventory! The original list for disposition is now subdivided into perhaps ten or twelve smaller lists. It's time to begin the program. The Coordinator walks into the sales manager's office:

> Jack, here's the first group of dead items for our new program. It's time for Step 1. You remember . . . you were in on the meetings where we worked out the series of steps. I'll be back in two weeks to see what's been sold.

Let's pretend that the Sales Manager's interest has really cooled since the meetings a few weeks back. He's having a bad day; had a fight with his wife this morning; lost a key salesman; and is in no mood to fool around with dead stock. He replies:

> Get the heck out of here! I haven't got time or people to devote to this junk! I can't work on it right now.

DEAD STOCK: THE PROFIT AND CONTROL SYSTEM CRIPPLER!

The Coordinator couldn't care less. He also has a reply:

> Fine with me. Just sign here on this form that you're taking no action on Block No. 1. It might be a good idea to put down your reasons, but if not, it's OK by me.

The Sales Manager signs. Where do you suppose the Coordinator trots off to next? Sure, the President's office. Now the President makes a call:

> Jack, get in here! What's this stuff about 'No Action' on the first list of dead items? You sat in the meetings where we all worked out the plan; you heard me tell you how vital it is to recover our cash from this trash that *YOU* pleaded with me to stock; and that getting rid of it is one of my five major priorities from now on! Well buster, it's one of *YOUR* major priorities also. I expect you to follow the plan. I expect you to devote some effort to the program each week, and I do *not* want to see any more 'No Action' reports from you!

Do you get the picture? The power to drive the program comes from the President . . . not the Coordinator. The Coordinator is in trouble if he or she fails to administer the program: Get the lists to the proper people; follow up after the allowable time; mark up a master list to remove what's been sold; get the revised list to the person responsible for the next step; report to the President each week how much has been sold, in what steps, who's cooperating and who isn't. Only the Boss can see that people perform, but the Coordinator keeps him well-informed. It's a very important job . . . maybe not all that popular, but important.

Find Your "Agnes"!

In my training sessions, I tell the attendees: "One of the great advantages of attending this session is that you can avoid this job! Already, you're plotting who's the 'bulldog' in your company that would be perfect as the Coordinator." Maybe that's true here also. The advantage in reading this book is that you can avoid the job. In a sense, the Coordinator is sort of the company "rat fink," who causes the Boss to get on someone's case if they fail to work on the program as they should. Every week, they'd *better* spend some time on the step assigned to them, because ol' Agnes will be checking up on Friday and reporting both good and bad results to the Boss.

Revising the Program

Nothing about the program is set in concrete. Periodically, the President, Coordinator, and Team get back together to assess the program's success.

238   CHAPTER 15

The sequence of steps might be rearranged; new steps tried; other steps deleted if they've proven ineffective; the time allowances are altered; responsibilities are reassigned. The program works because the company *works it* and because they *work on it!*

Success results from this as well as one other important aspect: The light is never off the problem! The heat (provided by the Boss with help from the Coordinator) is always on! As tedious as it is to put effort into dead stock; as much as everyone involved would rather work on (what they consider to be) more productive pursuits; as slow as results are in coming . . . all involved *must* spend some time each week on the program. That's why it works. That's why it returns to service lots of cash that had been "trapped" (as Bruce Merrifield says).

The Steps to Try . . . Your Disposition Alternatives!

Now to the secrets you've been waiting for since this chapter began: My guaranteed, mystical, beautifully-developed methods for getting rid of dead and slow-moving merchandise:

              1.   4.
              2.   5.
              3.   6.

Six ought to be enough. Does it surprise you that there *are no* brilliant, "hidden-until-now" techniques to turn dead stock into cash overnight? How long did it require your company to accumulate all your deadwood? In the same way, you won't rid yourself of it in a few weeks unless you're willing to accept 10 cents on the dollar.

That's why the term "disposition" must be qualified. Anybody can dispose of material one way or another. The intent of the dead stock program recommended in this chapter is to recover the maximum investment percentage (even a profit if possible) through a downward progression of alternatives. You'll recover the most if you can move the stock in Step 1; less in Step 2; while Step 15 may get nothing back but scrap value.

Each distributor finds some steps more effective than others. The sequence, or timing, or responsibility-assignments vary from industry to industry, from one geographic area to another, from one set of competitive conditions to another. *YOU* must work out *YOUR OWN* company's program! . . . but to assist a bit, let's now review the time-tested, "good ol' standby" methods for disposing of non-productive merchandise. Notice that there are no numbers assigned to these ideas . . . on purpose! They're provided as food for thought, not as the sequence you should adopt:

DEAD STOCK: THE PROFIT AND CONTROL SYSTEM CRIPPLER! 239

- *Sales "Push" Campaigns* which place a planned, coordinated, measured emphasis on the dead and slow stuff, but with prices at normal levels. Incentives offered to all salesmen.

- *"Close-Out" Sales Efforts* which offer merchandise to customers at discounted prices . . . down to actual cost. Don't get greedy here! If you'll be satisfied with cost, let the salesmen have anything they get above cost.

- *Transfers* of material to other company locations with a history of activity on the items. A branch might become overloaded on an item, but it's better for *all* the stock to be there with a chance to sell at cost or above, than for any of it to be elsewhere.

- *One-Time Sale To Specific Customer.* Occasionally, a large block of stock can be sold to one account (especially when you tell him that it will no longer be available locally), where "piece-meal" sales efforts might recover more but require a lot more selling time.

- *Sales To Competitors* at cost, or at cost + 10 percent.

- *Sales To Anybody* at 80 to 90 percent of cost.

- *Returns To The Suppliers* while absorbing the restocking charges and freight, or perhaps only the freight if the vendor agrees to an offsetting purchase order.

- *Lists Supplied To Vendors,* enlisting their direct help in moving stock to distributors in other areas.

- *Trade Association "Clearance" Newsletters,* where you're permitted to list a limited or unlimited number of items. The trade association circulates the lists to all members as one of their services.

- *Substituting* slow-moving, expensive material when customers order less-expensive products. A customer doesn't care which hammer he receives, so you ship higher-priced (but non-selling) Brand 2 when he orders Brand 1. The customer gets a better hammer at a lower price; it's *costed* at the lower cost; the salesman doesn't suffer; and the company absorbs the difference.

- *Garage Sale,* where a large quantity of dead material is collected in one location and advertised for sale to anyone that wants it (customers, competitors, employees, general public). If the public thinks they're getting something at "wholesale" prices, they'll buy stuff they don't even need.

- *Close-Out Merchandise Counters,* to encourage the impulse buyers and bargain hunters.

- *A Permanent Branch or "Store,"* operated by your company, with regular hours, and some form of advertising. Newly-identified deadwood flows regularly from all branches to the "store," so that the clientele find something "new" on nearly every visit. This concept can really pay off in a multi-branch network. The Coordinator approves material transfer into the store at full cost. At year-end, any profit or loss from the store's operation is shared proportionately on the basis of branch participation . . . the value of material each one sent in, etc.

- *Flea Market Sales Participation.* Your employees take turns hauling merchandise to area flea markets on weekends. The employee receives 25 percent of the receipts, as long as he sells items at or above pre-set amounts. You'd be amazed at the strange things that can be moved in these sales as "bargains."

- *Special Write-Off at Higher Than Cost,* when donating merchandise to organizations that qualify under IRS Code 170(e)3. In some cases, you may deduct up to 200 percent of cost. More about this in a minute.

- *Normal Write-Off After Charitable Contribution* to organizations such as hospitals, nursing homes, schools, Salvation Army, Goodwill, United Fund, Red Cross, etc.

- *Write-Off and Sale To Scrap Dealer.* You're lucky to get 10 cents on the dollar when you must resort to this step, but a dime is better than letting the material gather dust.

- *Write-Off and Haul To The Dump.* Nothing else is left, but you don't want to keep sitting on the junk at 30 percent carrying cost per year. Some distributors have found as high as 50 percent of their "book" inventory value actually to be worthless . . . because nothing was done about the absolute junk for 10 or 15 years. It was left on the books. If you get into that fix, you'd better hope the bank doesn't check your actual inventory value against loans they've made to you. They might just call your note.

- *Pray* . . . for a flood, earthquake, fire, tidal wave, invasion, or riot. These can solve a multitude of inventory problems, but don't do as some desperate distributors have . . . try to help the Lord out by creating a disaster of your own! This will result in an extended vacation at the government's request and expense.

There you have 'em . . . 19 unguaranteed ways to move out dead and slow-moving merchandise! I'll bet you have others that could be added to the list.

DEAD STOCK: THE PROFIT AND CONTROL SYSTEM CRIPPLER! 241

More about the Special Write-Off at Higher Than Cost

Are you familiar with IRS Code 170(e)3? This Internal Revenue code allows distributors to donate slow-moving and dead inventory to certain organizations and deduct up to 200 percent of the book value. Rather than attempting to explain the tax law here, I suggest that you contact the IRS, your own tax consultant, or the National Association for the Exchange of Industrial Resources (NAEIR) to get complete information.

NAEIR acts something like a clearing house by accepting your dead stock and then sending it on to some 2,500 organizations that qualify under the tax code. The material recipients pay NAEIR a fee to participate. Contact NAEIR at: 560 McClure Street; Galesburg, Illinois 61402. Telephone: (309) 343-0704. Ask for a packet of information about the tax law, the restrictions, and how to participate. Of course, you may well have local organizations that qualify. Contact the United Fund in your area, or just call any organization that you think might qualify. Ask if they know of IRS Code 170(e)3. If they answer "Huh?", hang up. The groups that qualify *know* that they do!

Getting the Boss Directly into the Act!

There's another very successful technique for large amounts of dead or slow stock you may have accumulated from one supplier. You'll need the direct help of your president, however. Here are the steps:

1. The list of material is compiled and given to the Boss. He contacts the *top executive* (Chairman, President, Division Manager but no lower) of the supplier and requests an appointment there at the supplier's home office. When asked "What do you want to talk about?", your president sidesteps by saying: "I'll tell you when we meet!" such a reply has ominous overtones (line to be dropped, etc.).

2. Your president travels to the supplier's home office, alone, at your company expense. He takes the material list with him.

3. When the meeting takes place, your Boss uses any one of several reasons why he needs "special dispensation" from the supplier to return the dead and slow stock without a restocking charge . . . even if the regular allowance for the year has been exhausted already or if the supplier has no return provisions at all. "We're opening two new branches this year, and to add the inventory we should, we need to clean our house elsewhere!" or "We've just bought out a competitor, and in the process took ownership of lots

of material. We need help elsewhere with slow stock on just a one-time basis!" or "We're going onto a new computer system. It's very expensive, and we need to return this material to begin this new system in a cleaner position and to help our cash flow . . . again, it's a one-time situation!" Any excuse like this is justification for the meeting.

4. Your president has made the trip at his expense. He came alone. The impression created is that this request he's making is very important . . . at least to him!

Two possibilities can result from this meeting of top executives:

1. Your president will leave with some kind of special return authorization. It may be permission to send back the entire list with no restocking charge. It may be a requirement to accompany the return with a dollar-for-dollar purchase order for other merchandise . . . or a 2-for-1, or 4-for-1, whatever can be negotiated.
2. He will be turned down cold. If that happens, however, you know exactly what your distributorship means to that manufacturer . . . zero! You should begin an immediate, intense search for a replacement product line.

In nearly every case, if you *do* mean anything to the supplier, their top executive will authorize special return provisions. That's why you must deal only with the supplier's top man. He made the rules. He alone can break 'em, and he *will* to keep your president happy! Everyone else must abide by the contractual material-return rules. No one else *wants* you to return additional stock. It could hurt their quota.

This technique works, but just remember to apply it only in the special cases where it fits: Lots of material involved from the one supplier; the request goes beyond the regular return provisions; and you still buy a significant amount from the supplier. Obviously, if you no longer buy much from the guy, he isn't likely to break his rules to help you out.

SUMMARY

This has been a long chapter, but dead stock demands more than a few words. At today's inventory carrying costs, it's deadly to profits to sit on your junk year after year in the flickering hope that someone will buy it eventually. It ties up cash that certainly could be put to better use . . . other new stock items that Sales needs desperately; new branches in new

DEAD STOCK: THE PROFIT AND CONTROL SYSTEM CRIPPLER! 243

markets; the chance to make acquisitions when the price and time is right; the need to increase pay scales to retain valuable employees; new trucks; warehouse additions; an up-to-date computer system; a trip to Hawaii; whatever . . . but any of these beats leaving the cash to gather dust on your shelves!

Dead stock can cause Management to try corrective action on inventory size in the wrong places. Sometimes an effective system might be discarded or modified because the inventory keeps going up, yet the system performs just as it should on the good material. Dead stock is the real problem. Decide now to work out your program and begin an all-out assault on this profit-drain.

16

BRANCH INVENTORY DISCIPLINES AND CONTROL

"Our new computer will make it so much easier to resupply our branches, keep track of what they have, and use our inventory investment more efficiently!" A terrific prophecy . . . and one that any distributor would reasonably expect to come true. After all, didn't he or she just spend a bundle on a new computer, or the new upgrade? The branch inventories have *always* been somewhat of a headache, but the new computer capabilities promise real improvements. Surely, for *this* kind of money, things should get better!

I wish it were always so. Unfortunately, it isn't. All too often, the inventory control system that worked just fine for the main warehouse begins to cause serious problems when applied to the branches. As many distributors have found, opening the first branch compounded their problems . . . hopefully, their profits too . . . but certainly their problems. When your inventory management is assisted by a computer, look out! The chances for a monumental foulup are increased significantly when branch inventories are added to the system.

Why? How? . . . and how can the problems be avoided? Obviously, that's what you're about to learn. A good percentage of my gray hair resulted from attempts to control branch inventories under a fully-integrated computerized system. Maybe you can avoid some of that gray before it should be there. As you'll see, some of the pitfalls involve common sense, but others are quite insidious. They're hidden and therefore doubly treacherous to profits. Some are caused by long-standing sales policies that should change . . . but won't unless top management keeps an open mind toward fresh new solutions.

NON-RECURRING TRANSFERS

The most dangerous aspect of branch inventories under an automated environment is how transactions are recorded when material is transferred from one company location to another. Why? Because many transfers are of the "non-recurring" type. Frank at Branch 1 asks good ol' Joe over at Branch 2 to help him out of a bind by transferring material that Frank is out of right now. Joe sends him whatever he can spare. He expects a return favor one of these days. Now what could be hazardous about that? All multi-branch distributors do this regularly. Sometimes, Joe's material is surplus and it's to the company's advantage for it to be transferred elsewhere. Where's the problem?

Recording Non-Recurring Transfers

When both branches had manual inventory recordkeeping systems, transfers like this posed no real difficulty. The next time Joe replenished the item, he ignored the "usage" represented in the transfer to Frank. Joe knew that the request was likely a one-time deal. Frank might not ever want any more of that item from Joe's stock . . . and so Joe made no provision, as he reordered, for a recurrence of Frank's need. Joe didn't "protect" for it happening again.

Now . . . both branches are computerized. The computer is programmed to record all outgoing transactions of stock material in the histories of items involved. It uses these histories to predict new expected usage rates which in turn set the replenishment controls that guide the buyers' decisions. The computer helps to protect for the expected "demand" against the inventory. Do you now see the problem? With such a system, the computer will record *both* recurring and non-recurring transactions . . . and then build up the stock to be able to handle them all in the future. The branch inventories move higher and higher as the transfer activity increases between branches. The more items move back and forth, the higher the inventories climb. The histories look OK; the computer seems to be using the histories correctly; but inventories keep spiraling upward. Disaster!

Avoid the Problem by Coding Transfers

You can avoid this calamity two different ways:

1. Decide on every transaction whether or not it's likely to recur and code it accordingly, so that the computer does or does not record the activity in the shipping branch's history.

BRANCH INVENTORY DISCIPLINES AND CONTROL 247

2. Assign every stocked item in every branch an "Authorized-Path-Of-Replenishment" code, which instructs the computer how to post the history for any outgoing transaction.

The disadvantage of the first method is rather apparent. It's easy to miss a non-recurring transfer and have the quantity wind up in the history. . . . and then there's the situation where a central warehouse supplies several branches' needs from inventory, and virtually 100 percent of all outgoing transfers *should be* recorded in the warehouse history of usage. Nearly all transfers are "recurring." It would be a nuisance to code each transfer individually.

First: Develop Your "Stock List"!

The better solution is to add information that allows the computer to process all transfers properly, posting or not posting them to histories without someone having to make a decision to each one. To begin, you'll need a very accurate list of the items stocked in each warehouse or branch. This isn't as simple as it sounds. Remember, you'll need the lists to measure service levels properly, so perhaps you've already done the work. If not, do it here.

What's "Stock" and What Isn't?

An item is not "stocked" in Branch 4 unless they offer it to customers from their own shelves. Often, a distributor considers an item to be stocked if it has been assigned an official part number and has a record established in the computer. One branch only may actually have inventory, but it's considered "stock" in the company . . . all locations. That's incorrect. Be sure your stock lists are made on a branch-by-branch basis.

There are other so-called "stock" items that shouldn't be listed. You've seen items that can't quite be classed as either "fish" or "fowl": One where computer records are maintained just to track sales (to aid a later decision on whether or not to stock it), to permit computerized pricing or quoting, to allow easier part-number-lookup, or for some similar reason . . . but there's zero stock in the warehouse.

Or perhaps your wierdo is like this: There are two dusty pieces of the product on the shelf, but customers never want just two. They order sets of ten. The dusty pair just sits, while you special-order (every time) what customers do buy! Such items are not truly "stocked." That's why the Stock List can be a study in frustration as it's worked out for a branch. It won't be easy.

Management must decide (finally) what each location *should* stock and what should be discontinued. Talk about some screaming and gnashing of teeth! "We've got to have *that* in stock! I know we're not selling any right now, but the customers will think we're going out of business if we don't have it on the shelf!" Hmmmm . . . so you want them for "show," right? Are you in show business or the profit-making business? You'd better decide! . . . another area where you'll need new levels of managerial intestinal fortitude (guts)!

"AUTHORIZED-PATH-OF-REPLENISHMENT" RULES AND CODES

Once the stock list is finalized, then *for each stocked item in each warehouse or branch,* the authorized path of replenishment is determined. For example, you might decide that all stocked items in the central warehouse are to be resupplied directly from the manufacturers. That's Replenishment Path 1. More decisions: Branch 1 is to replenish Item A's stock from the central warehouse. That's Path 2. . . . but on Item B, the branch is to be resupplied from Branch C, who acts as the warehouse for all locations (they're the only branch authorized to buy the product line or have the lion's share of sales, etc.) Item B is resupplied via Path 3 in Branch 1.

For every stocked item in every company location, the authorized replenishment path is determined. A code then goes into the computer files to designate the assigned path. OK, I admit . . . it's a nasty, time-consuming task to make the stock lists, decide the authorized paths, and then key the codes into the computer. You might be in the nursing home before you finish. But when completed, you never have to worry again about inventory "creep" (inventory creeping up all over your branch network) due to non-recurring transfers being recorded in history. This illustration shows graphically how the replenishment codes are developed:

A New Discipline: Stick to the Path!

Now a tough-to-enforce, but very necessary rule: The authorized replenishment path is the one preferred (by Management) for *that* branch to use to resupply *that* item every time! Sure, there will be exceptions and some that are encouraged by Management (use another branch's surplus). Generally, however, the branch is *NOT* authorized to get the material this time from the warehouse, next time from the manufacturer, and a third time from some other branch. They should stick to the authorized path of replenishment. Inventories will then be positioned properly

AUTHORIZED PATH OF REPLENISHMENT

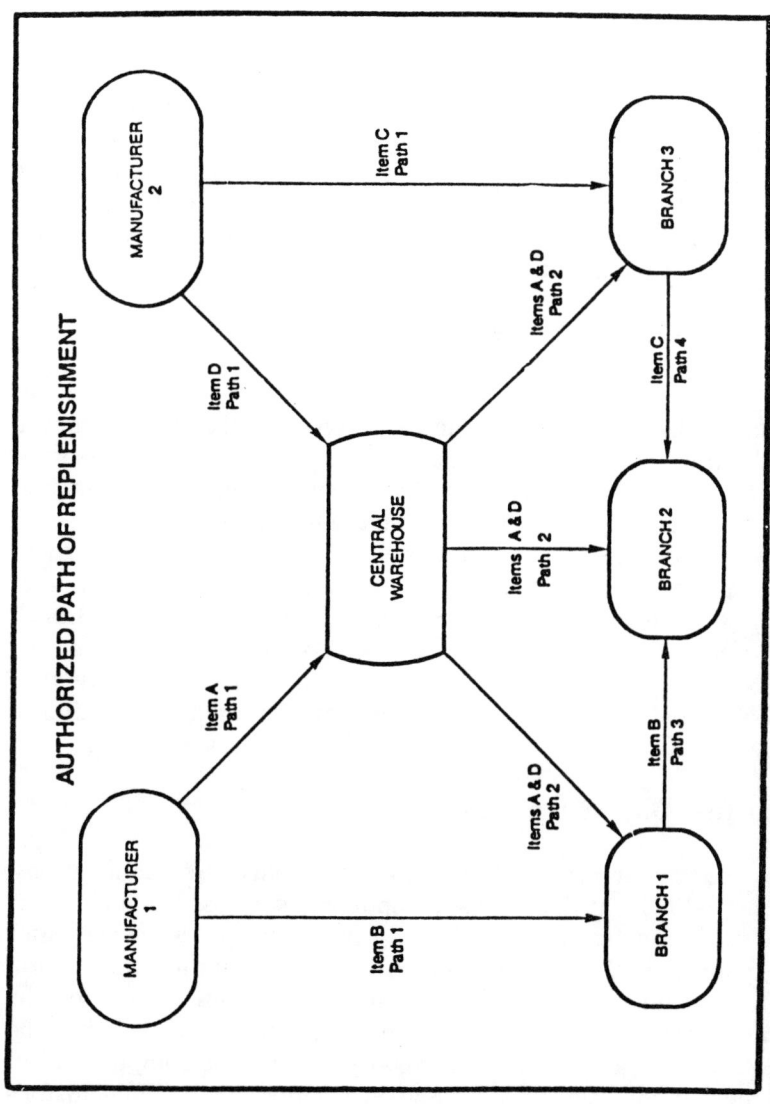

Determine an authorized replenishment path for every stocked item in every company location. A code goes into the computer files for every item in every branch to designate the assigned path.

to take care of their needs on the item. If the branch bounces around, getting it first here and there the next time, there's a serious risk of expanding more than one location's inventory to protect for their requirement.

When it's necessary to violate the authorized replenishment path on an item (and as I said, there are numerous times when it is necessary), the branch should do so only after informing the location set up to resupply them on the item. Why? It's obvious, isn't it? That location likely should make some adjustment in usage history, outstanding purchase orders, etc., since this usage they had anticipated from the branch was taken care of through another replenishment path.

Computer's Use of the Replenishment-Path Code

The computer uses the replenishment-path codes in this manner: When a transfer takes place between company locations, and the material moved along the approved replenishment path, the shipping location's history is posted. For example, when the central warehouse resupplies a branch as planned, the units are posted in the warehouse history for the item.

However, when a transfer resupplies a location (warehouse or branch) and the material moved outside of the authorized path, the computer *does not post the transaction in the shipping location's history*! If Branch 1 is supposed to be resupplied from Branch 2 on an item, but this time they transfer-in surplus from Branch 3 . . . the usage is *not* posted in Branch 3's history. The inventory must not be increased at Branch 3 to protect for a recurrence of the transfer. It was a one-time situation.

Use the Other Guy's Surplus!

Branches are encouraged, certainly, to use surplus in other locations. When material is identified by the computer as surplus, a branch needs no approval to transfer-in the stock. . . . but neither does the computer post the quantity in the shipping branch's history. Don't misunderstand. The *units* on hand in the shipping location are reduced, of course. The dollars move from one location's inventory to the other. . . . but the usage history isn't posted . . . that history used by the computer to set future ordering controls (as discussed in Chapter 6) . . . *that* history receives no entry.

No matter how much material moves between locations, the computer will not post non-recurring transactions inadvertently into branch histories. Recurring withdrawals only are posted. The replenishment-path code for each item controls how the computer records activity. If a branch is resupplied via the authorized path, then the computer records the usage in the history of the shipping location. When the material comes from somewhere else, the history is not posted in the shipping location. It's that simple. Do you have lots of transfer activity between branches? Then *be sure* your system handles this correctly. The more activity . . . the more potential "creep"!

RESTRICTIONS ON WHEN ONE BRANCH CAN USE ANOTHER'S INVENTORY

There's an old line of logic in distribution that goes something like this:

> Our inventory is for sale. It doesn't do us any good to have it sitting on one company shelf when a customer somewhere else wants the item. Therefore, any branch who has an item sold can have any other branch's inventory at any time!

Does this sound familiar? Is this rule in your company? Whew . . . I hope not! If you follow that logic . . . *DISASTER* in your inventory! In words of one syllable, *Don't Do It*! Although the reasoning appears sound; although it's premise is to serve the customers better, the actual result is extremely damaging to profit in a multi-branch network with well-balanced inventories.

Consider this scene: Jack, the manager in Dallas, does a fine job of controlling his inventory investment with the help of your company's new inventory management system that figures order points, EOQs, etc. He follows the rules; orders when he should; brings in economic quantities; and enjoys a profitable turnover rate on his inventory investment. Harry, over in Fort Worth, isn't nearly as conscientious. His first love is *sales* . . . so he runs a "hit-or-miss" operation relative to inventory.

One day, Harry gets a big order for one of his stocked items. . . . but he's out right now. He intended to order that manufacturer's line two weeks ago, but heck, he was busy making sales calls. There's no problem. He checks his computer terminal and sees that Jack in Dallas has just enough stock to fill the customer's order. Harry simply keys-in the transfer, it prints in Dallas, and because of the company rule (above), the material *must* be sent to Fort Worth or perhaps directly to the customer.

Everything's OK for about an hour. Then one of the Dallas customers calls to order the item. What does Jack tell her? Well, if he were brutally frank and told the whole story it would go something like this:

> Gosh, Anne, we're out of stock on that right at the moment. We just shipped all our material to another region to take care of customers over there. We should have more available in two weeks. Can you wait?

Customer's reply:

> Hmmm . . . let me see if I understand this. You've told me over and over that your company placed your branch and inventory here in Dallas to take care of my needs and those of other customers in this region . . . and now you ship all your stock somewhere else to take care of customers over there. I think I'll start doing business with a distributor who will protect *MY* needs rather than those in other regions!

The "Backlash" Effect on Inventory

What do you suppose ol' Jack will do the next time he replenishes that item? You guessed it . . . six carloads! He'll bring in a lifetime supply of that item (and all others as well). When you ask him, "Why aren't you following the new computerized inventory control system like you were?", what does he reply? "Are you kidding? The only way I can protect my customers is to carry a lifetime supply of *everything*! If I run too close, some jerk in another branch will steal all my stock." Backlash effect. Jack lashes back against "the system" to protect customers in his region.

The Reverse Reaction: "Let's All Play the Game!"

There's another course Jack might follow: He'll just play the same game as all those other managers who don't bother to control inventories. He won't keep much of anything on hand. When a customer orders, he'll search the branch network to see who's stupid enough to have any stock and transfer it in for the customer. Of course, the customers are nearly always told:

> Well sir, I don't have that item on hand right now, but I can have your order here by Wednesday. Will that be satisfactory?

Since the customers suffer when such games are played, this distributor becomes *very* vulnerable to competition who does furnish a solid array of merchandise off the shelf in the same locale.

With either a "Backlash" or "Let's All Play the Game" reaction, expand the results to 40,000 items scattered over ten company locations. Disaster with either one. With backlash, you can imagine the inventory buildup. It's massive! With games, you lose the customers in droves . . . but you can be sure the managers will take one course or the other. Would you sit still and keep following ordering rules that lead to stockouts? Neither will they.

BRANCH INVENTORY DISCIPLINES AND CONTROL

Well, When *Can* One Branch Draw Stock from Another?

Obviously, there's great opportunity in a multi-branch company to reposition inventory from time to time, take care of customers, and improve the overall use of inventory dollars. You just want to be sure that, in the process, no one gets hurt, retaliates with more stock, or cuts his own inventory to the bone and drives customers away. There are two basic rules to apply on transfers of material between branches:

1. Branch 1 can *always* have Branch 2 stock when the quantity desired is surplus in Branch 2.
2. When the quantity needed from Branch 2 isn't surplus, the requesting location receives the material (or some portion of it) *only* with Branch 2's approval.

Those two rules will keep you out of trouble but will move unproductive inventories to more profitable locations.

The Definition of "Surplus"

Surplus was defined in Chapter 12, but let's review:

$$\text{Surplus} = \text{Any amount of an item on hand that exceeds the } total \text{ of Line Point + Order Quantity}$$

or

$$\text{Surplus} = \text{Any amount on hand that exceeds the } maximum \text{ if a branch is on Min-Max Control.}$$

Line Points were discussed in Chapter 9. The Line Point sets the upper limit that qualifies an item as a candidate to be replenished when next a purchase order for the product line is being put together. Order quantities were covered in Chapter 10. The order quantity is simply how much is purchased at a time. The worst thing that could happen when an item is resupplied is to place the P.O. when the on-hand + on-order total is right at Line Point; sell absolutely zero during the lead time; and have the full order quantity arrive. So that's the maximum amount of allowable stock on an item: The full Line Point plus the full order quantity. Anything more than that is definitely surplus, and it would be advantageous (to the company) to move it.

The excess is "surplus," and can be withdrawn by any other branch without prior consent. Remember, I added an additional rule: The branch with surplus must pay the freight to get it to the other guy.

Great incentives! First, don't generate surplus in your location (by not following the system and reverting to SWAG)! If someone else catches you with it, you'll have to pay the outgoing freight. On the other side: Use the other guy's surplus. It costs nothing in freight to get it. Try these two rules to gain new popularity in your company . . . or perhaps achieve an involuntary move to a brand new career path . . . like writing books!

Make All Stock Visible . . . Surplus or Regular

A good computerized system makes all stock "visible" in all locations, whether it's surplus or not. The computer calculates the surplus amount (if any) to be displayed when an item's status appears on an inquiry screen or, as you found back in Chapter 12, on the Recommended Replenishment Action Report for other branches. The calculation takes place nightly, so the information is fresh.

Transfers for surplus quantities may be keyed directly from the requesting branch, to print on the shipping branch's equipment. . . . but when a "brother" wants stock that isn't surplus (needs a favor, a loan, to get out of a bind), then *that* transfer must be keyed by the shipping location, or at least controlled by a security code. That's Rule 2 above. "Sorry brother, but you can withdraw my regular stock only with *my* approval!"

Obviously, a manager helps out a buddy 90 percent of the time. He wants the same favor returned later . . . but non-surplus material goes out only with his approval. He can protect his customers. There's no need for excessive inventories or game-playing.

Don't Forget Basic Issues in the Heat of Battle

Just remember why you placed the branch in the locale you did: To take care of customer needs in *that* area! The inventory, when it's at proper levels, is there to take care of the local customers. Branches from other areas are trying to take care of the customers they serve . . . but they must not be permitted to strip away all the local stock to do so. Each location is responsible for service in *it's own locale,* and is therefore encouraged to do a solid job of inventory control. Management supports the effort by allowing each manager to retain a definite measure of control over his or her stock.

You're probably thinking: "This is all just common sense." . . . and of course it is. Still, it's surprising how many distributors today hold on to some vintage-1970 thinking. "Any sale is a good sale!" they say. It isn't. The successful distributors turn down business when it's not profitable.

BRANCH INVENTORY DISCIPLINES AND CONTROL

They find ways to service customers without risking the "rebound" effects discussed here which have led others into serious inventory trouble.

THE SLOW-MOVING STOCK ITEM . . . COMPANYWIDE!

We're not through with branch inventory problems. You may be sick of them by now, but there are additional hazards to bring to your attention. Next is the stock item that doesn't sell particularly well no matter where you find it in the company. Look at this picture. An item is stocked in the central warehouse and in each of three branches:

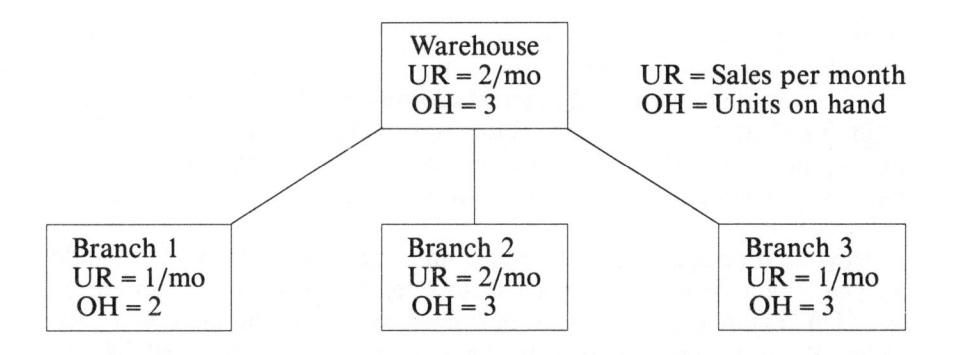

```
            Warehouse
            UR = 2/mo        UR = Sales per month
            OH = 3           OH = Units on hand

Branch 1           Branch 2           Branch 3
UR = 1/mo          UR = 2/mo          UR = 1/mo
OH = 2             OH = 3             OH = 3
```

The item doesn't do well anywhere, and the collective stock now on hand in all four locations is 11. The first question before proceeding: "Does this item deserve to be stocked *anywhere*?" Distributors are notorious for carrying items like this on the shelves for years, never generating enough profit to justify the inventory investment. We'll assume, however, that Sales is right about this one . . . we *must* offer it with a lead time shorter than would occur by ordering it from the factory for each customer.

Put All the Stock in the Warehouse. Carry Less!

Where should *all* the stock be located? Back at the warehouse. The branches keep none at all on their own shelves. When a customer orders, he or she is told: "We'll have it here tomorrow!" and that night a transfer brings the material out to the branch. Instead of 11 total carried year-round (at a 30 percent or better K cost), the network now supports only

4 or 5 units in stock. "Big Deal," you say. "This little critter costs $2.45, and you're worried that we'll carry 11 instead of 4?" Hmmmm . . . for one item, you're right. It's not important. What about 10,000 more just like it, scattered across three branches . . . this unimportant inventory excess repeated 10,000 times? . . . each with a potential inventory savings of 60 percent if only the main warehouse stocked them! Now the situation takes on a different tone, doesn't it? When Sales insists that a "dog" must be available on short notice, it's advisable to put *all the stock* in the central or regional warehouse. If you have more items or more branches, this inventory trap is not just serious . . . it can transform your company into a non-profit organization!

"Sounds Like a Contradiction Here!"

"Graham, you turkey, in the previous section you went on and on about not taking care of local customers from stock . . . and now you say it's OK to make them wait until the next day for a warehouse transfer!" Yes, I did. Yes, I do. The difference is the movement class of the items. Fast-moving items should be available to customers from local stock. Slower-movers, especially the real "dogs," are available . . . but with a one or two-day delay.

How mad does this make the customers? Not very. How mad would you be if you went to the grocery store for bread, milk, and imported Bolivian anchovies, but ran into this problem? Bread and milk, you need today. The anchovies are for Saturday night's party. The grocer tells you: "Gosh, we don't carry those anchovies, but stop by tomorrow evening and I'll have them here for you." You're furious, right? Shoot, no. You'd have been plenty mad if there were no bread or milk . . . but anchovies? You'd have been surprised if they had been on the shelf! Tomorrow is good enough. That's the way customers react to a quick . . . but not instant . . . performance on slow-moving items that they need infrequently.

DIFFERENT REPLENISHMENT CONTROLS FOR BRANCHES

Another common pitfall in handling branch inventories is to apply the same type of replenishment controls used by the central warehouse to resupply its stock. The main warehouse needs Order Points, Line Points, and EOQs. They have the double problem of longer lead times from the manufacturers and a requirement to purchase total-order quantities that will save freight or achieve some other unit cost discount.

BRANCH INVENTORY DISCIPLINES AND CONTROL

Now You Can Use "Min-Max" or "Order-Up-To"!

Branches, when supplied out of a central warehouse, usually have neither problem. They enjoy a very short lead time to get more of anything, and they don't have to order in large total quantities. Therefore, a branch often can be controlled effectively with the old "Min/Max" or "Order-Up-To" methods. When the stock drops to a minimum of two pieces of an item (for example), they "order up to" five. The calculations may be quite simple . . . often driven by how much space can be allotted to the item. The upper and lower control limits are set to avoid stockouts, stay within the (usually quite limited) warehouse space, and to develop a higher (than the warehouse) inventory-dollar turn.

The same formulas that are needed so badly for effective warehouse inventory management will cause serious problems if used to replenish most stock items in a branch. The reason? Formulas for Order Points and EOQs, for example, work well in a range of usages and lead times that could be considered "normal." Extremes in usage or lead time cause the formulas to misfire. Branch items with very short resupply lead times from a central warehouse are good examples of the low-end extreme.

A General Rule to Apply

When lead times are shorter than one week, use Min/Max. When lead times are longer than a week, use Order Points. A branch who does order directly from the manufacturer likely has lead times longer than one week on the items involved. For those items, Order Points and Line Points guide replenishment timing. The branch has the same purchasing restrictions faced by the central warehouse. Economic Order Quantities (EOQs) can be effective also for purchasing quantities. . . . but for other items resupplied out of the warehouse, those with a quick lead time of only a day or two, the branch should use Min/Max controls.

It's difficult to set down here the precise Min/Max "formula" to use. The right approach for a particular branch depends on how much space they have, the movement-class of items stocked in the branch, the "normal" lead time for resupply out of the warehouse, and the delivery they can expect when an emergency arises. Turnover goals are a consideration also.

Branch Inventory Turnover Rates

Branch inventories should turn faster than warehouse stocks. For most durable goods distributors, 5 to 6 pure turns (see Chapter 18) in a gross margin range of 20 to 30 percent will develop solid profits *in the warehouse*! . . . but those same margins might require 8 to 10 turns for adequate profits in a branch.

It's only logical. A branch receives the benefits of several corporate services, a large warehouse inventory, and special delivery conditions. Oh sure, they get hit with a "corporate services" charge each month, but in most companies this doesn't even approach the real costs. The branch *SHOULD* perform at a higher gross margin dollar-per-employee ratio and a higher inventory turn rate! For most items, they have no line buy to contend with, so they can replenish one item at a time. They can bring in one unit, two, or whatever, without a unit cost penalty . . . in fact, even low quantities like this still enjoy the volume discounts secured by the warehouse. It's logical that the inventory investment should turn more rapidly than the warehouse. The Min/Max controls reflect your company's branch turnover objectives.

A NEW METHOD FOR SETTING BRANCH REPLENISHMENT QUANTITIES

If you can establish the solid record accuracy discussed in Chapter 14, you may set branch stock items replenishment quantities under the "Push" system and develop as high as 12 turns on branch inventory dollars. Material for resupply is "pushed" out of the main company warehouse to those whose branches it supports. They do not request it. They receive replenishment stock automatically when the computer determines it's needed.

The first step employs the results of the stock item Classication exercise of Chapter 10. You'll recall that every item was assigned a class from 1 to 13, and that the classes were developed separately for each branch. If management now decides that a branch's inventory investment should turn 12 times a year, the individual classes must turn as follows:

Class 1	20 Times per year	Class 7	8 Times per year
Class 2	18	Class 8	6
Class 3	16	Class 9	4
Class 4	14	Class 10	3
Class 5	12	Class 11	2
Class 6	10	Class 12	1
		Class 13	0

If an item is Class 1 in the branch, it's replenishment quantity (when resupply is needed from the central warehouse) is 1/20th of a year's supply. A Class 2 item's quantity is 1/18th, etc. For the Class 1 item, the difference between Min and Max is 1/20th of a year's supply—easily calculatable. Example:

Monthly Usage = 100   Annual Usage = 1200
Class 1   Replenishment Quantity = 60
Difference Between Min and Max = 60

When the stock available-for-sale of this item reaches the Minimum (very similar to an Order Point: Enough material to last until the warehouse can resupply the item, plus a normal safety allowance), the warehouse ships 60 units to the branch. If the item had been a Class 7, the replenishment quantity would change to 1/6th of a year's supply, or 200 in the example above. If it were Class 4, then 1/12th of a year's supply (100) is pushed to the branch when the supply runs low.

The inventory-dollar turnover objective is forced on the branch. They receive smaller quantites on high-class items to force the dollars involved to turn faster. The branches SWAG would have requested transfers in much larger quantities on these popular items, but although smaller quantities are shipped by the warehouse more frequently (about every two weeks on a Class 1 item), good customer service is maintained. Each item's service control, the "Minimum," is recalculated monthly . . . more safety added to erratic items, etc.

Record Accuracy Is Mandatory

Don't even *think* about using this concept if the computer's records of stock available in your branches is poor! The Push System breaks down at once if a branch receives stock they don't need or isn't resupplied promptly on a very popular item . . . all because the records stink. The computer must have an accurate count of what's on the shelf.

HAND-TO-MOUTH ORDERING OUT OF THE WAREHOUSE

Having just convinced you to go for higher branch turns, now let's talk about carrying that too far. Yes . . . you should turn the total inventory-dollar investment in a branch rapidly, but not necessarily every stock item. The final pitfall about branches deals with "hand-to-mouth" replenishment out of the supplying warehouse.

Let's say you cannot move the stock of some slow-moving items back to the warehouse as suggested earlier. The salespeople would all have coronaries, develop high blood pressure, or at least, hemorrhoids. They threaten mass resignations if all those wonderful items are moved out of their local inventory. A few selected "dogs" must be offered off the shelf at branch level. If you fall too much in love with turnover, you may try to turn these dog items at the same rate as the fast-movers.

Don't do it! Be satisfied with three or less turns per year on any item that sells less than $20 at cost for the year. Don't push for six turns, or ten, on one like this. If you do, you'll wind up in the "Sell one, Order one, Sell one, Order one" cycle . . . which is OK on big-dollar-movement items but costly on the dogs, even in a branch. You'll work the warehouse staff to death. They'll have to fill, pack, and ship tiny quantities of two-bit items over and over . . . great turnover for the branch but a huge cost in the warehouse. Instead, the branch should order six months' supply or more on items like this if there's room to hold it. The Min's and Max's are set accordingly.

Be Careful How Warehouse Usage Rates Are Calculated

The warehouse, of course, must be able to handle withdrawals in these larger quantities (of slow-moving items). Warehouse usage rates should be based on how the branches order, *not how they sell*! I mention this, because some systems on the market total all *branch sales* rates to arrive at the usage rates used to establish inventory levels in the warehouse. That's one way to do it, all right, but it leads invariably to "hand-to-mouth" branch replenishment. That's all the warehouse can support . . . one or two at a time. The low branch sales cause a tiny support stock in the warehouse.

SUMMARY

Branch operations: A wonderful way to expand your business, enter new markets, provide opportunities for promising employees, test product lines, and get in a big mess with inventories! Five potential hazards were discussed in this chapter:

1. Helter-skelter transfers of material between branches, under no guidance or control, with the risk that non-recurring activity will be recorded and cause a massive inventory build-up all across the network . . . inventory "creep."

2. Executive edicts that smell of sales "domination," whereby one branch can rob another's stock if it's sold, resulting in branch

manager "backlash" or gameplaying . . . both leading to profit-drains: Unneeded inventory or lost customers.

3. Stocking too many slow-movers (companywide) at both branch and warehouse level, instead of carrying them only in the warehouse. Getting rid of the unproductive branch inventories requires Management to face-off with salesmen and make some gutsy decisions.

4. Applying the same replenishment formulas to a branch with no lead time or total-order requirement problems, as are necessary in the central warehouse where these purchasing restraints are a way of life. Use Min/Max for most branch items.

5. Hand-to-mouth branch withdrawals from the warehouse on the "dog" items Sales insists must be kept in stock locally. Forget the normal branch turnover objectives on such critters and bring in six months' supply or more at a time.

How's your headache? Doesn't it boggle your mind to dig this deep into the problems of inventory management in distribution? Branches! Who'd have thought you could get into so much trouble with their inventories? . . . but you *can*! Many distributors do.

There *really is* a lot more thought and consideration needed to manage a network of branch inventories effectively than most distributors have bothered to put forth in the past. As you've seen, there are some serious—and to a degree, almost hidden—traps waiting for the multi-branch company . . . particularly when the experience, knowhow, and common sense of long-time employees are replaced by a computer.

You *need* a computer! Make no mistake about that. If you're not fully automated by the 1990s, you'll be far behind the pack of competition. Computers do introduce, however, a new element into your business: Non-thinking, "just-the-facts, Mam" number-crunching. A great capability to process mountains of transactions and organize thousands of facts in a manner and at a speed no army of humans could approach . . . *but* requiring *very* detailed instructions and more thought as to what those instructions should be, than was necessary in the old days when you "programmed" humans instead of machines. Be certain your system includes the proper instructions about branch inventories! Your branch operations will pay off handsomely.

17

KITS, ASSEMBLIES, AND FAMILY-GROUPED ITEMS

When a distributor takes that giant step over to a computerized system, a problem surfaces that likely had been controlled in a satisfactory manner under the old manual system. True, it might not have been handled all that efficiently, but at least it was handled! . . . but now with the new computer, something goes haywire. You often run out of stock on items where it rarely happened before. The old procedures don't work very well or perhaps not at all! You'd like an example? The customer orders a "set," a "kit," or an "assembly." Chaos results. The new computerized system can't handle it.

Let's define those. A set, kit, or assembly is a product you sell but most likely do not stock in that configuration. A plumbing distributor's customer wants a tank and bowl set of a particular model and color. Usually, they're sold as a set . . . but the distributor has to stock them as individual items. Once in a while someone breaks one or the other during installation, and must replace it. The sets have a way of getting out of balance, and replacement tanks or bowls have to be bought from the manufacturer.

Perhaps it's a pump distributor who carries basic pump housings and numerous other components that allow the finished pump to be assembled in accord with customer specifications. This reduces the pump models he must carry in stock. It would be prohibitively expensive to try to stock completed pumps in all the different configurations a customer might need, so the plan is to assemble most pumps after a customer's firm order is in hand.

WHAT'S THE PROBLEM?

This all sounds routine, doesn't it? Almost every distributor has some variation of this stocking/ordering requirement: Installation Kits for large equipment that are stocked in component form; Filter-Regulator-Lubricator units that can be sold as left-hand or right-hand models and are configured after the customer's order is received. It's a common condition, so what's the big deal? Where's the problem?

The potential hazard here is in inventory and sales history recordkeeping, to assure that proper stock levels are maintained to sustain sales. Simply put, you are *SELLING* a part number you don't stock (in most cases), but reducing the stock levels of several other items you *DO STOCK* . . . which often can be sold to other customers just as they are. With the old kardex system, several notations told the clerk how to handle this. When a kit sold, the balances for all component parts were reduced. Now, with the computer and particularly in distribution where this *isn't supposed to be* a problem, the system designers may not have programmed this condition properly . . . and you can find yourself in a mess quickly!

WHAT'S THE CORRECT RECORDKEEPING PROCESS?

When a kit or assembly is sold, precisely what gets recorded in the sales history, and what components in what quantities are deleted from stock? Those are questions that must be answered *before* you start keying customer orders into your fancy, new computerized system. These are the questions to ask a turnkey package salesman as you evaluate the various products offered these days to distributors. Demand specific answers . . . not "Oh sure, we handle that!" Check the answers against the following guidelines.

Material Lists

Handling the Set/Kit/Assembly challenge effectively starts with some tedious data gathering. Obviously, each option in which a product can be sold has a list of components and quantities needed to deliver or package it in the manner specified by the customer. The first step is to *list all of these options* . . . yes, every single one . . . and assign a unique part number to each. And now (here comes the bad news), list every component and quantity required to assemble or package each sales option. In other words, you must create a "Material List" (the manufacturers call them "Bills of Material") for each sales option. For tank and bowl sets, the material lists are a snap, but for all the installation or repair kit options . . . whew, that could take some time! No argument about that. The job might require several man weeks or months, but you'll suffer for years if you try to avoid the task.

KITS, ASSEMBLIES AND FAMILY-GROUPED ITEMS

In a separate file in the computer records, each selling-option part number is entered, and tied to it is the list of components necessary to assemble or package that kit or configuration. A typical material list might look something like this:

Part Number 437JK   Installation Kit for Compressor Unit 437J

Consists of:

1	437J-MDL	Bracket
6	245986X	Mounting bracket
3	245708A	Brace
24	9000450	Spacer
24	9000500	Leveler
1	ADL-4	Hardware package
1	437J-I	Instructions

You sell several models of compressor units. Each requires some kind of installation kit, using many of these components or others from a total of 65 possible parts. The kits are put together *after* the customer specifies the exact compressor unit needed. . . . so for each kit, a material list is needed. The computer must be told what assortment of parts to take out of stock when a particular kit is packaged to accompany the compressor. Almost every one of the 65 components is used in several of the 16 kit options, and most are also sold individually. There are sales for these components other than when they go out as part of a kit.

In another situation, a particular pump configuration carries a unique part number, even though it's not stocked that way. The material list for that configuration shows the primary housing number *and* all other components and quantities needed to finish out the pump as the customer specified. The material list may go one step farther. It can even instruct the warehouse to change port locations, move a part to the right from the left side, etc., besides listing additional items to draw from stock.

What Happens When the Customer Orders?

Your sales catalog can show all the possible sales options, with a different part number and selling price for each. When the customer orders, the inside salesperson writes the part number on his or her paperwork, and that is keyed when the sales order is entered into the computer. Example: The order shows that the customer wants one 770-4 Tank and Bowl Set, Color White, which sells for $289.50. When the order prints, the warehouse copy tells the order-filler to pull the following:

1	Model 770-4T	Toilet tank, white
1	Model 770-4B	Toilet bowl, white

Each item is stocked and sold separately, in addition to being sold as a set. Each has its own unit cost. As soon as the computer accepts the set order from the customer, it *commits* the inventory (reduces the stock available to sell on each item) necessary to make up the complete product that was sold. The customer's copy of the delivery ticket and subsequent invoice can show all items in the set or kit (if that's what the customer wants), or just a single line entry:

    1   770-4 Toilet tank and bowl set, white $289.50

Your system should be programmed to allow this option in printing the delivery tickets, the invoices, or both. The "work copy" used by the warehouse to pull all the components need never be seen by the customer.

When the sale is invoiced, the computer removes the cost of each component from the company's total inventory value, costing-out the sale with a total for all items (including a labor charge when units must be re-configured or assembled from a selection of component options).

What About the Sales History?

Since each item in a set, assembly, or kit is inventoried separately with other usage besides that of the package, the sales history for each item shows usage when the set, etc., is invoiced that includes it. This sales history is used, of course, to establish correct replenishment-timing controls. When the stock available for sale (reduced when a customer's order is accepted) drops into the range between Line Point and Order Point, replenishment action is started. It's vital that *all usage,* kit or individual sale, be recorded in the computer's history for a component item. It's the component that must be replenished at the right time if future assembly sales are to be handled at a high service level.

Sales Information on Assemblies

The Sales Department, however, wants to know how many Model 770-4 Toilet Sets were sold, and to whom . . . so a special sales history also must be provided for each set, each kit, and each assembly option to show the sales in units for each on a month-by-month basis. Supporting detail identifies customers, dates, quantities, and sales order numbers. This information helps forecast anticipated future sales of sets, kits, or assembly options and, if you elect to use it, the anticipated usage of all components by "exploding" each sales option material list by the forecasted sales.

Just be careful *not to duplicate* a component's expected usage when employing this approach! Remember that the sales history for each component *already has* all withdrawals posted for set and kit sales. You could double-up the figures in error if you add the "exploded" material list quantities developed from set and kit sales forecasts. Only the new, or *extra* forecasted sales (beyond what the sales history now reflects) should be exploded. If a set or kit option sold 12 units last month and Sales forecasts 20 units next month (New business!) . . . *only the 8 extra units' material lists are exploded* to modify usage expected next month for components. Twelve units' worth of component usage are recorded already in the individual component histories. Complicated? A bit . . . yes, but unless you want SWAG to rule, and your warehouse to be bulging as a result, problems like this deserve much more planning and effort than distributors have put forth in the past. Mismanaged assets—not lost sales—continues today as the Number 1 cause of distributor failure. Remember that.

Producing Kits or Assemblies for Stock

Now, let's introduce another condition to make things a bit tougher still. To save time after a customer orders one of the more-popular kits or assemblies, you decide to make up some of these fast-movers ahead of time to try to keep a few in stock at all times. Using the earlier example of an installation kit, you find one ordered frequently enough to justify keeping some on the shelf already made up. Let's say that you set the Order Point at 1; the Order Quantity at 4 . . . arbitrary judgment (SWAG) admittedly, but these are the opening controls for the item. When the available-for-sale stock drops to one made up kit, you'd like the warehouse to withdraw enough components to make up four more.

Where before you had a "dummy" record file for this kit in the computer that showed part number, selling price and the sales history, now that file becomes a full-blown inventory record. You must know the warehouse location, official unit cost, the Order Point and Order Quantity just as for any other stock item. When the available stock drops to the order point of 1, it's not a purchase order to a supplier that's needed. Instead, it's a "work order" to your warehouse, instructing them to make up four more kits.

The Warehouse Work Order

The "Work Order" tells the warehouse how many kits to assemble and precisely how many of each component to pull from stock to get the job done. These four sets of components are "committed" immediately by the computer. When the work order is generated, the stock available for sale is reduced right then for all components involved. It might take the warehouse a week (it shouldn't but it might!) to get around to making up the kits. The component stock to be used is therefore *not available for sale*! It's been *committed* to the work order, just as for any other order requirement. You should "stage" the components rather than leaving them on the shelf. Remember Chapter 14. These components are no longer available for sale.

When to Record Component Usage for Work Orders

The sales histories for work order components show the withdrawals in the month the work order is generated. Recognize that this timing is different from the timing of posting for a regular sale. History is posted for a normal sale when the customer is invoiced (*STOCK AVAILABLE* is reduced when the order is taken—but *HISTORY* is posted at the time of invoicing).

Work order components are different. *BOTH* stock available and history are posted at the same time: When the work order is generated! The stock available of made-up kits is increased only when the warehouse reports the work completed, and the sales history for made-up kits is posted as with any regular sale: When the customer is invoiced.

Maintaining Matched Sets of Components

For some set or kit components, the distributor has an added objective: Try to maintain balanced sets of components at all times! To illustrate, let's return to the toilet tank and bowl illustration. The sets sell in scads to plumbing contractors, and a toilet bowl always requires a matching tank, etc. The bowls and tanks, however, are packaged separately and carry individual part numbers, while the set also has a part number for sales purposes. Once in a while, some turkey breaks either a tank or bowl (or claims it was broken when delivered), or simply has a need to replace one or the other. No one wants to break a set, of course, but to take care of an important customer we will do it. Now the inventory of tanks and bowls for this model and style is out of balance. On the next purchase order to the supplier, it's advisable to order a replacement bowl or tank . . . even though there may be an extra cost involved.

That's why it's necessary to establish individual component item records and usage histories even when the tank and bowl, for example, almost never sell apart from each other. It's the "almost never" that gets you. Once in a while, they *are* sold individually, and without separate stock records, a mess develops quickly. You may not recover until the day arrives that you must scrap-out a mis-matched (and now obsolete) tank!

KITS, ASSEMBLIES AND FAMILY-GROUPED ITEMS

With separate records for the components, and programming which ties them together in the computer's files, the "system" helps you stay in balance. If a tank and bowl set's inventory gets out of balance, the computer alerts you to buy the proper replacement unit on the *very next purchase order* to that supplier . . . regardless of whether or not the full set stock is in need of replenishment. You don't wait! The set is put back in balance at the first opportunity! The separate computer records for tanks and bowls, and a computer system programmed to identify mismatched sets, help avoid a costly scrap-out down the road . . . and perhaps a lost sale in the interim.

ARE FAMILY-GROUPED ITEMS RELATED TO THIS DISCUSSION?

Yes . . . and No. But first, let's define family-grouped items. These are items in your inventory that are sold separately. Usually, they're not components in kits or assemblies . . . but when you purchase them from your supplier, *the supplier* considers them as "families" and establishes special economic advantages if you'll order them grouped together. An example? You stock six sizes of one basic sprocket, out of some 75 total sprocket items on your shelves. The supplier's pricing offer is stated like this: "If you'll purchase 50 of the six items in this grouping, regardless of the quantity of each, I'll give you 20 percent off the entire 50!" You can order five of one size, 18 of another, etc. That doesn't matter, as long as the total for all six sprockets is 50. Unfortunately, your sales of the individual sprockets does not justify buying 50 at a time of any one of them by itself.

Now what? How do you program your system to assure that you get that 20 percent discount . . . but don't wind up with far more inventory than is proper for the slower-moving members of the grouping?

Family-Group Codes

Each size in the sprocket group has a separate inventory record, of course, in the computer files, but a "Family-Group" code is needed to tie the six together. When a stock item is not part of a family, this field in the record is blank . . . but for each of the six sprockets, the field might contain a "10," for example. This identifies each item as a member of Group Number 10. Other sprockets might be members of Group 20, etc. When any of the sprockets in Group 10 requires replenishment, you'll remember from Chapter 12 that the computer displays the item's condition on a Recommended Replenishment Action Report. Nothing new about that. What's different with family-grouped items is that the computer *displays the status of all other Group 10 members also, regardless of their condition in relation to Order Points or Line Points*!

In other words, if Sprocket 1 needs replenishment, the computer adds to the Replenishment Report the status of sprockets 2, 3, 4, 5, and 6—no matter what their situation. It's reference information only. Normally you do not want items to appear when they don't require replenishment action, but this is a special situation. You could blow a 20 percent discount or wind up with a huge stock of all six sprockets. Frankly, there's a little "line buy" within a larger one and special information should be provided to help out the buyer. He or she is given the status of the other five family items to guide a special decision (where it's practical) to purchase some of the others and meet the requirement for 50 sprockets.

The buyer views the entire family. Hopefully, he or she will select those items closest to Order Point to add to the P.O. . . . some educated SWAG . . . rather than bumping up the order quantity of the single item that must be replenished or trying to do the whole exercise from memory of the family. Such reference items, those not at Line Point, are not included in the line totals shown at the end of a supplier's products on the Recommended Replenishment Action Report.

You can see that the purchasing problem presented by families has some of the set/kit/assembly headaches, but the objective is to buy economically while avoiding inventory excesses . . . rather than to avoid stockouts or mis-matched components.

SUMMARY: AND YOU THOUGHT THE COMPUTER WOULD SOLVE ALL YOUR PROBLEMS?

Sets, Kits, Assemblies, Family-Grouped Items . . . those "fringe" areas in a distributor's operation that never caused much of a problem in the old manual environment when there was someone with 20 years' experience riding herd on each hazard. Today, the computer has been assigned the job—rightfully so—but something's been lost in translation. Often, we forget to tell the systems designers or programmers how to handle these conditions. . . . or we look at all the work required to build the material lists and say, "Shoot, we can't take the time now to do all that. We'll get to it later!" Take some advice from an old hand: Do it now!

Maybe you purchased your software or a turnkey package. When you were given that fantastic demo by the salesman, you were entranced by the bells and whistles of order entry, accounting gymnastics, and the flurry of report options. No one asked how the system handled kits. "Gosh, if it does all that neat stuff they showed us, it's bound to handle

KITS, ASSEMBLIES AND FAMILY-GROUPED ITEMS

kits correctly!" . . . or no one even thought to ask. Now, these problems are causing lost sales, unhappy customers, expensive inventory imbalances, or all of the above.

Well, that's OK. Everybody goofs once in a while—even consultants. (Heaven forbid! I *can't* be admitting that!) . . . but now it's time to get back in there with some reprogramming and fix these problems. Inventory Management, performed well these days, is *hard work,* and requires more planning, more thought, more skill to be applied than was necessary back in the "good old days" when margins were fat and sales increased 20 percent year after year.

Set, kit, assembly, family-group problems, and their solutions illustrate the new degree of sophistication a durable goods distributor must employ in the years ahead to remain profitable. Computers provide a wonderful range of new capabilities. You *must* upgrade your skills to assure that the computer works *for* . . . not against you! There are systems on the market that handle all these problems effectively. Look for one.

18

MONITORS, MEASURES, MODIFICATION, AND MOTIVATION

The planning's done; programming's over; training's behind you; installation's complete; system's in place . . . and you've aged only 40 years! Congratulations! You got off lighter than most people assigned the task of installing a new control system. Some have regular visiting hours at the institution to which they're now committed. Now, you have to *run this thing!* Now, you have to find ways to monitor what's going on, measure progress (or slippage), effect quick modifications when something goes wrong, and motivate inventory control personnel to superior performance.

THE NEED FOR "GAUGES" AND STEERING MECHANISMS

Automobiles have gauges and dials to help keep the machine running. The human body tells us by temperature and blood pressure when something isn't right. A functioning system needs gauges and monitors also . . . particularly a new Inventory Management system based on new philosophies. In Chapter 4, I warned about "Reverting," or falling back into old habits, and it's an ever-present danger with new procedures. The control system must therefore be monitored continually and consistently.

Just as your car has a steering wheel to assure that it goes where *you* want it to . . . your system needs ways to guide it back on course when a measurement shows that it's drifting or perhaps being moved in the wrong direction by someone who prefers SWAG. Let's talk now about monitoring methods, measurements, and modifications.

INVENTORY TURNOVER

One of the twin objectives of good inventory management is to provide the best turnover of dollars possible within the restraint of customer service goals. You remember that, of course. I harped on and on about it in the early chapters. Then it shouldn't be surprising that one of the key measurements of the system's performance is inventory-dollar turns.

Turnover is one of those words in the English language that, like the word "love," sure doesn't mean the same thing to everyone using it. Turnover has been measured and expressed so many ways that the numbers must always be qualified before accepted at face value. An executive reads in the trade journal that turnover averages 4.8 across distributors in his industry. His figure is 2.7. What does he assume? "Boy, we're terrible! Everybody else is doing a great job turning inventory dollars and we stink!"

As the old song says: "It ain't necessarily so." *Most* distributors do not measure turns correctly. The calculation includes numbers that are inflated, and the answer is inflated as a result. Since it's so easy to misfigure, let's start by defining turnover:

> Turnover is a measurement of *inventory-dollar use!* It expresses how many times per year the shelf inventory is "used." Turn results are good barometers of how effectively your "lumps" of inventory dollars have been employed . . . but can be very misleading when applied to individual item performance.

"Used" in the definition generally means sales. In a central or regional warehouse, it can also mean transfers-out to support satellite branches. In a location that does repair work, it includes the quantities of a product used to repair customers' equipment. You'll see in a moment why turnover can be misleading at item level. It's valid only to gauge the total company picture, branch inventory use, or product line performance . . . the "lumps" of inventory dollars.

The Turnover Calculation: Single Location

Two separate turnover formulas are necessary: One for a single location that has no formal responsibility to supply any other branch out of their inventory, and a second formula for the location that does. The single location formula:

$$\text{Turns} = \frac{\text{Annual cost of goods sold } \textit{from stock only}}{\text{Average inventory value across the year}}$$

MONITORS, MEASURES, MODIFICATION, and MOTIVATION

The Big Mistake in Computing Turns

Notice that qualifier: "From Stock Only." Since turnover measures inventory use, then transactions should be excluded from the calculation when the shelf inventory isn't involved. If you ship the merchandise direct from supplier to customer; if you bring it in special and deliver it immediately; if you run down to the supplier's local warehouse to pick it up; buy it from competition; transfer-in the material from another branch . . . *any method other* than using your own local shelf stock to take care of the customer . . . the cost of goods sold for those transactions should *NOT* be included in the annual total in the numerator of the formula.

Now do you see why turnover results are so often overstated? Distributors generally pull direct-ship's out of the calculation, but all that other stuff is left in. The degree of error depends on the percent of sales volume handled through these non-shelf-stock transactions. In the primary durable goods industries, actual turns average between 1.9 and 2.5 per year when all the fluff is removed . . . so don't feel so bad if you're figuring it correctly at 2.2, and the trade journal survey shows everyone else at 3.8. You can lie on the next survey like all of them did. Just don't lie to yourself!

Accountants sometimes don't understand the problem:

> Look Graham, all sales transactions process through the book inventory. The dollars go in when we purchase material of any category, stock or non-stock. Dollars come out when we sell it. That's certainly inventory turnover, so why the big deal about shelf stock activity only being included in the calculation?

I have no argument with accounting practice. Run the dollars through the books however you please, but segregate stock-sales activity on some report from non-stock. Otherwise, how can you ever measure the effective use of material sitting out on the warehouse shelves? If a high-enough sales percentage is the non-stock variety, but all sales numbers are mushed together, you can't! The real *inventory* dollar turn rate is inflated by all those *non-inventory* transactions.

How to Determine the Percent of Non-Stock Sales

"But our sales figures don't segregate activity that finely. How can we break out the true shelf-stock numbers and get an accurate turnover reading?" Here are the steps:

1. Find somebody in the company you don't like, because this is a nasty job. (Poor Agnes!)

2. "Agnes, I want you to take every sales order from last week, do a little research, and come up with some figures.
3. Look at each item on each order. If we took care of the customer by using shelf-stock, put a mark in Column A.
4. If we handled the transaction any other way, put a mark in Column B. These are the non-shelf-stock sales.
5. When you're through, calculate the percentage that all the As were of total line items sold that week."
6. Using Agnes' result, multiply that percentage against your total annual cost of goods sold for the year. The answer becomes the numerator for a true inventory turn calculation.
7. Repeat the exercise in about six weeks. (John, this time, because Agnes quit!) See if the percent of stock vs. non-stock activity changed. Usually, the two studies yield very similar results.

Agnes determined the stock-to-non-stock ratio for just one week of activity and that percentage was applied to all sales for a year. True, it was only a random sampling but John's repeat exercise verifies the validity nearly every time. Distributor salesmen are creatures of habit. They take care of customers in the same patterns from week to week. This little exercise allows you to develop a true inventory turn picture when the formal sales figures are all muddled together.

What's a Good Turnover Rate to Expect?

For the single location, a good turnover performance (measured correctly) is between 5.0 and 6.0 per year . . . provided your gross margins average in the 20–30 percent range. A few industries (paper, etc.) achieve higher numbers, but they have special conditions or must battle lower margin averages. The system outlined in this book will generate the 5.0 to 6.0 turns *IF* you do something about dead and slow-moving stock as suggested in Chapter 15. Dead material is usually the culprit when a distributor follows proven ordering controls but can't improve turnover significantly.

The Second Formula: Central Warehouses

Locations that must supply others from their inventory need a different turnover calculation:

$$\text{Turns} = \frac{\text{Annual cost of goods sold from stock} + \text{Stock transfers-out}}{\text{Average inventory carried across the year}}$$

MONITORS, MEASURES, MODIFICATION, and MOTIVATION

Stock-only transactions are still in view, but the central or regional warehouse gets credit for inventory "use" represented in material supplied to other branches. Part of the inventory was placed in the warehouse to supply the needs of satellite locations. Some distributors fail to put the transfers into a warehouse turn calculation, so it comes out too low.

Expect Better Turns in the Satellites

Chapter 16 explained why branches supplied from a regional warehouse should achieve much better turnover than the warehouse. Review that discussion if it's hazy now. Branches that buy little or nothing direct from suppliers have dramatic advantages in when and how they may replenish stock. The company has a right, also, to force higher turns there as partial compensation for corporate services that are never fully covered in a monthly fee. Satellite inventory dollars should turn 10 to 15 times per year, and branch replenishment-control calculations are structured to make this happen.

How Often Should Turnover Be Measured?

Turns for all company locations should be measured monthly. Frankly, it really doesn't matter if you elect to use End-of-Month inventory dollars in the calculation rather than the average across a year . . . but whichever you go with, *Be Consistent!* You're looking for trends. End-of-Month *or* Yearly Average inventory dollars reveal up or down trends if the same one is used in the formula each month.

Don't get overly excited (elated or depressed) about one turnover reading. Even when you're doing everything right, the month-by-month calculations show ups and downs. The *trend* should be upward! From quarter to quarter, year to year, there should be progress. One full turn improvement from one year to the next is wonderful. Chart the readings. Put them on a graph where it's easy to see how you're doing.

There are valid explanations for the up or down turns from month to month. Yours may be a highly seasonal business with low sales periods while inventories are building. Turns will drop off after receipt of a large shipment of fast-moving, big-volume product lines. You might make promotional purchases or buy heavy ahead of a price increase. Adding a brand new product line is detrimental for while if sales start slowly. That's why you study the trend. Turns should improve in spite of all these anchors if you follow solid replenishment rules and get after dead stock . . . but it won't happen overnight. Service is quickly corrected; not so with turns.

What's the Problem When Turnover Is Poor?

Turnover improvement is a slow process. If your true turns are 2.1, for example, it may require *three or four years* to move up to 5.0! Dead stock is a major contributor to lousy turns, and no matter how intensive your efforts, the junk doesn't vaporize. No matter how diligent you are with proven replenishment controls, a few items degenerate into the "dog" class. That's a characteristic of the distribution business. You do all you can to prevent or get rid of it, but a certain percent of the inventory investment will always be bad news.

There are trouble-spots to look for, however. Here are the areas to check when you see a questionable trend, up or down, in the turn rate:

- *Sales trend.* Obviously, if stock was purchased in anticipation of a high level of sales . . . and instead, sales fall off . . . the turn rate will dip rather quickly. Rather than waiting for the computer to "catch up" by working the reduced usage into the control calculations, the buyer inserts new controls on all affected products and freezes them for a month or two . . . then monitors the situation month to month. Is the sales dropoff temporary or permanent?

- *Unidentified seasonal items.* A big new product line contains a surprisingly large number of items that sell better one time of year than another . . . but no one knew it until you've been through one yearly cycle. Customers use the products differently than anticipated or a different mix of customers has developed. Turnover in the (unforeseen) off-season will nosedive.

- *Surprise purchases by management.* A Branch Manager decides to buy heavy in a big promotion offered by the supplier and loads up. He may or may not be authorized to do it, but either way, in a small branch the big order often has an alarmingly-negative turnover impact until the stuff sells off . . . and that can take several months.

- *Mis-coded sales.* Several large orders over an extended period, all coded incorrectly as stock, inflate the cost of goods sold numbers by which turns are computed. This usually happens when some customer repeatedly orders a very large quantity of one stock item with plenty of time allowed for delivery. The material is shipped direct from the supplier or purchased special to satisfy the requirement. Shelf stock is not used, so the transactions should be classified as non-stock for turnover purposes.

- *Management-directed repositioning of surplus.* Once in a while, the company benefits when all the stock of an item or product group is relocated to just one branch where it will sell eventually . . . even if

MONITORS, MEASURES, MODIFICATION, and MOTIVATION

it takes quite a spell. A large distributor with 10 or more branches should have a planned repositioning program moving stock like this almost every month. But be careful.

Sometimes, the accounting system has no provision to disregard the "you-gotta-take-it" stock when figuring turnover in its new home. The manager is upset; turns (one of his pay considerations) look bad; and he'll resist any further transfers. Correct that accounting.

- *Buyers reverting to SWAG.* After a new system has been in place for a while, buyers tend to drift back into old ordering habits. Truckload purchases are filled out by adding large quantities of the fastest-moving items. If turns begin to deteriorate on a product line, re-examine the buying practices. Are buyers overriding system recommendations without good reasons?

- *Duplicate product lines.* A salesman pressures the branch manager to "Put some of those ABC Manufacturing items in stock. Boy, we'll sell 'em like hotcakes!" Trouble is, the branch already carries the same items in XYZ brand. Too often, the available business for the products is now split between the two brands . . . not increased in total, but there's more inventory than before. Enforce strict rules as to when, what, and who can approve product lines that duplicate existing stock.

- *New branches.* The company's total turnover rate nearly always dips when a new branch is opened, unless an existing business is purchased. When you place a brand new inventory investment in some locale, the sales start slowly and then grow (you hope). During start-up, which could be as long as a year, sales do not justify the inventory investment. Be cautious with massive corrective steps in that first year.

- *Mergers or acquisitions.* When you buy out another distributor or merge businesses, the total turn rate usually drops significantly. The reason is basic: One or the other of the two companies likely wasn't doing all that great a job . . . or it would have continued as an individual entity. Time will be needed to work down the excess stocks that come as part of the package.

- *Consigned or protected stock for customers.* When you set material aside for just one customer . . . either in his warehouse or your own, the inventory dollars often turn at a less-than-desirable rate. You've committed the stock, but you still own it. You and the customer both know that no other customer can buy it. The customer has very little pressure to use the material. His needs are protected; he threatens to stop all purchases if you try to cancel the arrangement; and his volume is big . . . you wouldn't have agreed to the special stock if it weren't. Try to avoid such agreements. Getting out of them gracefully is tough.

- *Repair shop inventories.* You have a big repair business, with special personnel assigned in a separate area . . . and they set up their own special inventory. If the items stocked are truly unique to the repair work, so be it, but expect low turns. *Good* turns on repair part inventory is about 2.0 per year. Just guard against carrying the same item in both regular and repair stock!

This list isn't exhaustive. There are other factors that can contribute to lousy turns. You likely can add ten more of your own, but at least you have some places to look or plausible explanations when the Boss sees the month-end inventory figures, calls and says: "Get in here! We have to talk about this inventory *you're* supposed to be controlling with the help of our expensive new computerized system!"

TURN & EARN . . . AND SOME WRONG CONCLUSIONS

Before leaving the topic of turnover measurement, let's consider a popular spinoff called "Turn & Earn." The logic of the Turn & Earn concept:

> If the gross margin percentage on stock is low, you must make up for that with a faster turn of the inventory investment. When the GM percent is high, you can afford a lower turn rate.

Turn & Earn monitors the margin rates generated by Sales and then attempts to course-correct how Purchasing buys the products. There are times, I suppose, when that's wise to do, and I have no major complaint when management decides that a product line must turn eight times per year due to the low margins. However, there are dangerous aspects to Turn & Earn and disastrous results when the concept is applied at individual item level.

The dangerous facet is that T & E forces very uneconomical outgoing costs (Chapter 10) across a product line because of sales limitations. Net profit is *usually* maximized when Purchasing buys products in such a fashion that they all go out the warehouse door at the lowest total cost possible . . . and Sales sells each item for as much as they can. That principle is violated when Sales has trouble and Purchasing must try to do the adjusting.

Never Apply Turn & Earn at Item Level!

Completely ridiculous things can happen if T & E is applied as a driving control at item level. Consider a slow-moving item that sells only $15 at

MONITORS, MEASURES, MODIFICATION, and MOTIVATION

cost for an entire year . . . but the gross margin is also low . . . just 12 percent. Turn & Earn says: "Low margin; Turn the item faster," and so the buyer attempts to do that. He buys $2 worth of material at a time and achieves slightly better than seven turns. Wouldn't *that* be intelligent? Buy that little turkey seven times a year! Seven P.O.s; seven receipts; seven times to the shelf to put it away; seven invoices processed . . . mercy! Common sense tells you to buy the critter, if you must stock it, only once a year . . . even if Sales were *giving* it away.

Apply Turn & Earn (If at All) to Inventory "Lumps"

If you elect to use T & E as a measurement, keep the evaluations at company, branch, or product line level. Never draw a conclusion or adjust an order quantity because an individual item has a poor T & E performance. The EOQ discussion in Chapter 10 explained why it's profitable to buy six months' to a year's supply of over half your stock items. T & E might correctly suggest modification of the EOQ concept across an entire product line from top to bottom, but affecting individual items only slightly when small annual dollar-movement is involved. When Turn & Earn indicates an unprofitable line, it's probably smarter to drop it from stock than to start playing games on the Purchasing side. End of sermon. Let's talk now about Service.

SERVICE LEVEL

Good customer service is the other objective (with turnover) of a solid inventory management system, so service should be measured regularly. The problem is . . . it's much tougher than turnover to measure accurately. Turnover is easy to measure, hard to correct. Service is easy to correct, hard to measure. Why? Service evaluations are usually subjective . . . meaning that service is *perceived* to be good or bad, when reality might be something else. The reported figures are misleading.

Let's say that you've been reporting a 96 percent service level, based on orders taken and shipped. The salesmen, however, don't believe it. Customers complain that when they call for stock items, the telephone salesmen often try to talk them into substitutes because what they want isn't available . . . or they're promised delivery today and the stuff shows up tomorrow. Customers often hang up without ordering; have to accept an item they didn't really want; or get poor delivery. But who cares? Based on just the cold facts of orders actually recorded and percent of items shipped, the rate is 96 percent.

That's why it's tough to get the real picture on Service. I'll suggest a computerized measurement process, but recognize that the computer cannot reveal an absolutely true Service picture. Too many conversations and decisions occur before the computer touches a customer order.

Measure Service Only Against Stock Items

First, recognize this: Your service performance is measured only against those items you told customers to expect to find on your shelves. That may be 5,000, or 10,000, or 50,000 items . . . but think how many others they *could* order from you! If you counted all the items in each catalog for each manufacturer that you represent, whew, that might be several hundred thousand items . . . any one of which a customer could request. My point is simply that you should make no attempt to measure service performance on all those non-stock items. When a customer orders one, advise him what you must do to get it. Do as good a job as you can, but be certain the customer recognizes that you *don't carry that item on the shelf locally.* Service is measured only against the ones you do!

The Stock List

Which brings up good questions: Do you know; do your salesmen know; do your customers know the items stocked locally in each of your branches? Does the computer know? Is there a list of stock items for each company location? . . . or do you have many items that are neither "fish nor fowl"? You really don't carry any on the shelf, but there's a part number in the computer with a price, etc., so anyone viewing an inquiry screen might assume it's stocked. Even if a stock check shows none, a salesman (knowing the efficiency of your purchasing people) would figure that a big shipment *must surely* be on the way! . . . so what might the customer be told who wants to place an order? When will his order actually show up?

Maybe you carry two dusty pieces of an item on the shelf. They never sell, because these products are always bought in sets of six. How do you look if a new salesman tries to enter an order for six? Two are shipped; four backordered, and the customer is irate. You need an official stock list. Identify for the computer the items carried in stock at each company location . . . *before* making any attempt to measure service.

The Definition of Good Service

When one or more customers order 100 different items from the stock list, you should:

1. Fill at least 90 complete on your first attempt in the warehouse, with no backorders, no shortages.

MONITORS, MEASURES, MODIFICATION, and MOTIVATION

2. The customer gets the brand he requested if it's on the stock list. If you substitute on an item, even with his approval, you receive zero credit for that item.

3. If the customer ordered early enough to receive delivery today, and you promised it today . . . then even if he gets a full shipment tomorrow, you get no credit at all on the order.

Measure service weekly by tracking your performance on all stock items ordered during a week. It's a line-by-line, item-by-item measurement, with totals reported for the week. Look at the illustration which follows.

This measurement is for a regional warehouse that both sells to its own customers and takes care of satellite branches. During the week of October 21, the warehouse received 160 orders from customers with 482 stock items listed. Some items may have repeated several times,

SERVICE LEVEL MEASUREMENT
Illustration

Week: 10-21

Sales orders received	160	
Number of line items (stock only)		482
Transfer requests	72	
Number of line items (stock only)		216
(1) Total number of line items		698
(2) Number of lines filled complete		446

Calculation:

$$\frac{\text{Lines filled complete (2)}}{\text{Total no. of line items (1)}} = \frac{446}{698} = 64\% \text{ Service level}$$

This company is filling 64% of the "demand" against their *stock items* —represented in sales orders from customers and transfer needs to other branches. . . . the very purpose for which the inventory was established.

Admittedly, this measurement is quite harsh. It gives no credit for a line filled partially, as for example filling 82 out of an order for a 100 quantity.

It is however a defendable measurement. No one could argue that the figures are "padded". . . . and who's to say what negative impact a partial shipment has on a customer? Find out where you are under this measurement and then watch it improve as new controls are put in place.

but each occurrence is part of the 482 total. 72 transfer requests from the branches came in also, and those transfers needed 216 stock items. 698 times in total there was "demand" by someone (customer or branch) against material the warehouse stocks. 446 times the item was shipped in the right brand, at the right time, and in full quantity . . . a 64 percent service level.

For any one item, if the customer ordered 50 pieces and you ship 48, that receives no credit. It's not counted in the 446 total. Avoid using dollar totals as the measurement, since the results are skewed if you perform well on one high-dollar line item but poorly on a low-cost product. Dollarwise, you may score 90 percent on the order. Item-by-item, it's 50 percent. Remember, customers don't care how many dollars are involved when they order an item. Right then, that item is the most important product on their mind. If you told the customers that you stock it, you'd better perform! . . . so on an *item-by-item* basis, the goal is to perform *perfectly* on 9 out of 10 . . . 90 percent!

"Wait a minute, Graham!" you scream. "On that item where we shipped 48 out of 50 pieces, that customer may have wanted it for stock. We did pretty well. Why don't you allow any credit at all . . . kind of 'weight' our performance? Why is it all or nothing?" Hmmm . . . are you sure sure he wanted it for stock? Are you sure the customer wasn't inconvenienced or annoyed? Are you certain he isn't using some form of "JIT" (Just-In-Time) materials management system in his company, depending on a full shipment, and now must scramble in his production planning?

The System Recommended Here Develops 90 Percent Service . . . Measured Tough!

My 90 percent measurement is harsh, admittedly. You perform or you don't; it's black or white . . . gray performances get no reward, even though you may not have harmed that customer all that much. Today, it's hard to be sure, so I suggest a harsh measurement. Don't kid around or kid yourself on service . . . and the control recommendations in this book are designed to produce a 90 percent service level, measured the harsh way. By some of your old measurements, it could turn out 95 percent or higher. Keep in mind that you cannot get a pure reading on stock-item performance anyway. On what you can record, it's better to be tough.

Don't Treat Satellite Branches as Orphans!

In the service level illustration, transfer requests from branches were worked right into the calculation. If a branch asked for 30 pieces (for stock or whatever) and you ship 26 . . . no credit! Zero service performance on that item! "Boy, that's too much, Graham. You're getting ridiculous. If a branch wants stock and we don't send every piece, you say that's bad? C'mon . . . get real!" Well, let's consider some questions.

What's the regional warehouse for? . . . to take care of branch inventory needs, right? To allow a branch to bring in smaller quantities, carry a much lower stock, and yet enjoy competitive costs. What happens when they depend on the regional warehouse for resupply and are disappointed? . . . when they sense that the warehouse always takes care of its own customers first and they get the leftovers? They react, right? The branch starts going around the system, buying material wherever they can. When they do get material, it comes in bits and pieces . . . so they begin to order sooner and in larger quantities. Everyone involved . . . both in the warehouse and in the branches . . . works harder and less efficiently: packing/shipping/receiving/putting away little quantities. *YOUR INTENT,* and therefore a point to be measured, should be to resupply branches just as if they were customers!

The Computer's Job

Computerized service level measurement begins when the customer's order is recorded. Service levels each week are then based on:

1. The number of times stock items were ordered by customers.
2. The number of times a branch requested stock items that this location had been designated to provide.
3. How many times the quantities ordered were shipped complete
4. Subtract any computer-generated substitute line items, unless the customer's file and/or order heading code said that subs were OK.
5. Subtract line items canceled for any reason after order entry.
6. What was the delivery date promised (per line item)?
7. When was the merchandise shipped or delivered?

A perfect measurement? Heck, no . . . but it *is* a reading. If the measurement is consistent week after week, it's easy to see the progress or slippage. You could argue that it isn't fair to count as ordered but give no service credit for items canceled later by the customer. Remove that from the calculation if you like, but most cancellations after the order is once accepted are due to the distributor's inability to perform . . . the computer shows 18 in stock, the order-filler finds 10, and the customer says

"Forget it! You said you had 'em and I need the full 18. I'll get the stuff from your competitor!" . . . or "No, I don't want the 5 HP model. You said you could send the 7 HP. Just cancel. I'll get it somewhere else!"

The computer can't measure orders lost in initial conversations between customer and salesman, or substitutions worked out prior to order entry because a desired item isn't available. It can't identify an irate customer who expects delivery in the morning and the order shows up at 4:30 PM . . . but measure what you can and watch the trend.

What's the Problem When Service Is Poor?

Stockouts occur because the replenishment process isn't started early enough. You waited too long to reorder. It's as simple as that . . . but that's a bit like a doctor telling you: "You don't feel well because you're sick!" Obviously, you want to know the specific ailment and how to treat it. Here are checkpoints when something is amiss with replenishment timing:

- *Usage rates are too low.* The computer develops order-timing controls based on anticipated usage for the period just ahead. Most of the time, the past sales history is the source for the forecasted usage estimate. If the past is misleading as a guide for the future, the order point and line point will be off . . . perhaps too low. Stock then drops too low before the computer alerts a buyer to take action.

- *Control calculations are too old.* A very common mistake is to ride an order-timing control too long. The order point is left unchanged for six months, because the item isn't replenished. When the stock does run low and an accurate timing control is needed, replenishment occurs late. The old control is based on conditions over six months ago. *ALL* controls should be refigured each month by the computer, regardless of how far away an item appears to be from needing replenishment.

- *Lead times are old.* Supplier lead times are often the cause of late replenishment. Old delivery performances in the files are allowed to set order points. The suppliers then get in a crunch and lead times stretch out, but the timing controls are now too low. The average lead time for each stock item should be refigured with the initial receipt of that item on a new P.O. If there's been no delivery in six months, the computer lists the item for review when it gets within 30 days of Line Point (Chapter 9) . . . asking the buyer to recheck the lead time data and order controls *before* the stock gets any lower.

- *A recorded lead time is misleading.* One or both of the two lead times recorded for an item, from which an average is developed, are bad.

MONITORS, MEASURES, MODIFICATION, and MOTIVATION

The computer has averaged one delivery performance of 30 days, another of 1 day, for an average of 15. Likely, the 1 day is misleading. Material was purchased on an emergency basis from a local source. Chapter 7 explained how to screen out bad lead times.

- *Unidentified seasonal item.* A code is necessary to identify seasonal items, because the computer considers a different period from the past (Chapter 6) to forecast usage on a seasonal item than for a non-seasonal item. If the code is missing, incorrect ordering controls are in place as the season arrives. Result: Stockout.

- *The reverse: An item identified as seasonal that isn't!* Again, the wrong time period from the past is the basis for predicting the future. Sooner or later: Trouble.

- *Unusually large sale.* When a customer buys much more of an item than anyone has in the past, you can sail below the order point into instant trouble. One day, you're in good shape on the item; plenty of stock; no need to reorder. The next day . . . zap . . . no stock, or very little. A stockout is on you and can't be prevented, but the buyer should review the item immediately to determine what adjustments if any are needed in the replenishment controls (for next time). The current P.O. can also be expedited.

- *Review cycle/Order quantity imbalance.* You'll recall from Chapter 10 that an item order quantity should never be less (in months' supply) than the product line review cycle. If a product line is purchased just once a month, it's silly to order less than 1 month's supply of any item. You'll almost certainly run out in-between purchase orders. EOQ offers a profitable way to develop order quantities, but program the computer to check all answers against the product line Review Cycle. Adjust any EOQ to a minimum of Review Cycle × Monthly Usage Rate.

- *Lack of ordering disciplines.* Some buyers get lazy at times. Check frequently to see that purchase orders are entered within 24 hours after the computer prints a Recommended Replenishment Action Report (Chapter 12). A one or two-day lag in placing the P.O. on a fast-moving, short-lead-time item risks trouble and leads eventually to extra inventory (when the buyer applies SWAG later to compensate). Why risk either just because someone is careless?

- *Safety allowances below 50 percent.* Someone decides that slower-moving products shouldn't have the same stockout protection as the better items. It's OK to perform at a 70 percent or 80 percent service level on this "unimportant" stuff. Bad logic! Remember that a customer never orders a slow-moving or unimportant item. They're all Class 1 to him. If an item isn't worth 90 percent service, don't stock it! Offer it as a special only. Never place an item on the shelf and then, by setting a low safety allowance, determine to perform poorly. You can be sure you will! It's a self-fulfilling prophecy.

- *Inaccurate stock balances in the computer.* What difference does it make where the order point is set if you don't know how much stock you really have? Stockouts often occur even when fantastic mathematical gymnastics have been employed in the control calculations. The order point is 40; the computer shows 82 available for sale. True shelf quantity: 18. Big trouble looms just ahead. Chapter 14 explained how to keep shelf stock quantities in agreement with the computer numbers.

- *Programming errors.* It's one of the last places to look, but never discount completely that a (seemingly remote and unrelated) programming modification elsewhere in your system has fouled-up the way usage or lead times are captured, how controls are calculated, report timing, or how transactions affect stock balances. A change is made in the order entry program, for example, but now some infrequent stock item transactions are omitted from the computer's sales history. The error surfaces when you run out of stock . . . because new order-timing controls based on the history are too low.

As with poor turnover causes and corrections, this is not an all-inclusive list. You could likely add 15 more trouble-spots. These are just the major culprits I've encountered over the years.

SHOCKING THE SYSTEM WITH EXTRA MERCHANDISE

One of the problem areas above bears a little more discussion: "Instant Trouble" on a stock item . . . a total surprise . . . caused by any one of several situations. Often, it's a big sale that cleans out all the stock in one fell swoop. Perhaps a warehouseman opens ten boxes of fresh stock only to find hidden damage in all of them. None can be sold. The computer shows 82 in stock, but nobody can find 'em. They're probably out there somewhere, but from a customer-service standpoint you might as well have zero. Regardless of the cause, the result's the same: Instant trouble, and particularly so if the item is popular.

You may be able to scramble around and get in more material quickly with an emergency call to the supplier, an air shipment, an expensive fill-in purchase from a competitor, or some other way. You may not.

MONITORS, MEASURES, MODIFICATION, and MOTIVATION

If not and the item is popular, customers continue to order and backorders stack up.

An "Out-of-Rhythm" Problem

What happens when a replenishment shipment finally arrives? You guessed it . . . zap! Backorders eat up everything. You're right back in the soup. The pattern repeats again, and again. Each time material comes in, it barely touches the floor. Everything goes right to Shipping from Receiving and out on waiting orders. The item is badly out of rhythm . . . and it's a very serious situation. When a person's heart starts beating out of rhythm, it can be fatal if something isn't done quickly to restore the heart's regular beat.

The same thing is true here. If left unattended, this situation corrects itself . . . the hard way! Customers weary of having the item backordered every time they order it. They fix the problem. They stop buying it from *you!* The computer even helps to put you out of business on this product. As less and less sales are recorded, the replenishment controls drop lower each time they're refigured. The degenerating spiral is like an airplane in a tail-spin. If it doesn't pull out . . . goodbye Charlie!

Apply a Shock Treatment!

In the hospital emergency room, there's a standard procedure for the patient brought in with his heart beating irregularly. The attendants plop electrodes on his chest, back away, and hit the poor devil with big voltage. He bounces about a foot off the cart . . . but the shock often puts that heart right back in rhythm. It's discomforting for the patient, but what's the alternative? Death!

The sick, out-of-rhythm stock item needs similar emergency treatment. You must "shock" it with extra merchandise! When you see the in-out-in-out pattern repeat because backorders chew up stock as quickly as it comes in, place an order for *two or three times a normal replenishment quantity!* . . .enough to be sure that you can fill all backorders the next time and still be at least half way between Order Point and Line Point. The extra material should put the item back into a controlled situation. It's back in rhythm. You've "shocked" this item's system with extra material.

Expect Some Discomfort

There's discomfort involved. Likely you've lost sales somewhere through this mess, and they may not be recovered when the item pulls out of it's nosedive. You have to risk the extra inventory anyway. The buyer bird-dogs the item closely for the next several weeks or months and changes controls manually on this unstable critter for a while. The item requires more time, effort, and money investment than it did before it got out of kilter. That's the discomfort. The alternative? You can just let it die, lose the sales for good, and drop it from stock. Enough of these and your inventory problems disappear . . . along with your job.

Use Caution with Lower-Class Items

There are exceptions to the shock-treatment: The lower-class items (9s, 10s, 11s, and 12s discussed in Chapter 10) have *normal* replenishment quantities that represent from 9 to 12 months' supply at a time. When the first replenishment arrives for one of these items, chances are good that enough material will come in to take care of all backorders and still be well above Order Point. No additional "shock" is needed. If backorders *do* take all the incoming stock, the item is moving up in class. Besides shocking it with more inventory, the buyer should SWAG a new set of ordering controls and freeze them for a few months to see where sales will settle out.

OTHER WARNING SIGNS

In Chapter 7 under the "Master Inventory Record" discussion, two of the data elements recommended for each stocked item in each location were:

1. The date the item last experienced a stockout.

2. How many times a stockout has occurred over the last 12 months.

Excessive Stockout Incidence

Here's where the information is used. The computer isolates any item (with an order point other than zero) that has experienced _____ stockouts during the last 12 months with the most recent occurrence within the last _____ days. You fill in the blanks. Stockouts represent system or people breakdowns. A stockout is intentional for items with zero order points, but not for all others. If you last ran out of an important item 10 days ago, and it's happened 15 times in the last year . . . would you consider the item in or out of control? Review that item. Find out why the controls aren't controlling! Something's wrong. Don't just let the system plug along.

One-Time Stockout

You don't have to run out of an item several times before recognizing a problem. *One* stockout can be disastrous on some critical items! Develop "critical item" categories for each buyer or product group. If a stockout ever occurs on one of these items, the buyer fills out a little half-page form: What happened? Was some of the computer data incorrect or incomplete? Should any information elements be changed arbitrarily? Should controls be changed? Should the controls be frozen for a time to assure closer attention? Was this a one-time freak condition and no control adjustments are necessary? In other words, buyer, you *had better* be right on top of the situation when you run out of a Code 1 item!

THE INVENTORY "BUDGET"

"How much inventory will we carry if we do all this stuff you suggest, Graham?" . . . a question I'm often asked. Well, I can't tell you how much you'll carry, because I don't know how dedicated your efforts will be to get rid of dead stock. I have no idea where you'll fudge to play it super-safe on an item . . . or to get a cost someone says you must have to be competitive . . . or where you'll guess wrong in buying for a season . . . or fill in a truck with fast-moving items because that's quick . . . or fail to pull in surplus stock from another branch when you should. But I can tell you how much inventory you'll *NEED!*

Program this computation for each stock item in the central warehouse:

$$\left[\left(\frac{LP - OP + OQ}{2} \right) + SA \right] \times \text{Unit Cost} = \$\underline{\qquad}$$

LP = Line point   OP = Order point

OQ = Order quantity   SA = Safety allowance

The average inventory you'll carry for an item is half the difference between Line Point and Order Point; plus half the normal replenishment quantity; plus the full safety allowance. Multiply the answer in units times cost and you have the average dollar investment to expect. Example:

LP = 200   OP = 150   OQ = 300   SA = 50   Cost = $2.00

$$\left[\left(\frac{200 - 150 + 300}{2} \right) + 50 \right] \times \$2.00$$

$$175 + 50 \times \$2.00 = \$450.00$$

As long as the various controls and the cost remain as they are, $450.00 will be the average inventory carried for this item in this location. Just after a replenishment shipment, it's more. Just before receipt, it's less . . . but it averages $450.00.

Total the answers for product lines, for locations, for the total company, and you'll know how much inventory *is really needed!*

The Branch Formula

For a branch using Min-Max controls on items resupplied out of a regional company warehouse, the formula changes:

$$\left[\left(\frac{\text{Maximum} - \text{Minimum}}{2}\right) + \text{Safety Quantity}\right] \times \text{Unit Cost} = \$_____$$

A branch carries half the normal replenishment quantity, plus whatever safety pad, as an average inventory. That number multiplied by unit cost develops the average dollars carried in the item. Of course, for those items ordered directly from suppliers, the first formula applies . . . the one considering Line Points and Order Points. The "Authorized Path of Replenishment Code" (discussed in Chapter 16) tells the computer which budget formula to apply for each item.

Budget vs. Actual Reports

Once you know how much inventory is needed, it's compared to dollars on hand. Be careful about your conclusions. The budget formula develops averages for items and product lines. When a product line has hundreds of items on your shelves, the inventory total serves well as a guideline. If there are only 10 items in stock, the on-hand total can be far off the average—but still perfectly OK—right before or right after receipt of a replenishment shipment. So how is the budget number used? Program reports that compare the average dollars carried across a full quarter in a branch or product line to the budget. Now, it's averages against averages and the numbers can yield revealing conditions.

The Budget Represents "Utopia"

Recognize first that the budget represents a perfect situation . . . one that you'll likely *never* attain. It's the bull's-eye. It's a state of inventory perfection to strive for, even while knowing that few could ever achieve it. Then why compute it? . . . because it *DOES* reveal the dollars required in inventory to provide excellent service and turnover! "Required" is the key word. The budget total is what you really need to conduct your business. But it's still "utopia." Several conditions work together to keep a distributor's actual investment above the budgeted figure:

1. There's always dead stock around, for which no allowance is provided in the budget calculation.
2. It's often necessary to carry seasonal products over to the next season, even when you planned the purchases carefully. The season isn't as hot, or cold, or wet, or as long as last year . . . and sales just don't come off as planned.
3. New product lines are always speculative. You expect sales at certain levels; you stock for that; but a rather lengthy shake-down period is needed to find which items really sell, which don't . . . and during that period, the inventory is too high.
4. Pre-price increase purchases, or promotional buys, are often quite profitable. You'd be foolish not to participate with extra inventory, but the budget calculation has no provision for "Buy Low/Sell High" speculation.
5. Customers can exert tremendous pressure to carry special stocks just for them . . . perhaps even consigned in their location. Once committed like this, the distributor has little control over how the material moves.
6. Repair business or parts can be profitable gross margin sales, but the inventories involved usually turn slowly. The budget doesn't make special allowances.
7. Pre-season purchases often must cover your needs for the full season or item costs are prohibitive. Across an entire quarter, "Budget vs. Actual" on these product lines can look bad.

How to Use the Budget Figures

"Well then, the budget is really a waste of time," you say. No. It's still useful. The amount of dead stock in a product line or a location is calculatable (Chapter 15). Prepare a report which lists "Budget," "Actual" (Quarterly Average), and "Dead Stock." Ask the manager to explain the actual vs. budget variance that isn't covered by dead stock. Example:

Branch 2	Inventory budget	=	$228,000
	Quarterly average on hand	=	$416,000
	Identifiable dead stock	=	$ 61,000
	Unexplained variance	=	$127,000

"Mr. Branch Manager, please explain the $127,000 variance between what's really needed and what you've been carrying that isn't explained by dead stock!" It may be a combination of the reasons given earlier, but the manager *should know!* If he's in control of the company's investment in his location, that manager should be aware of the dollars needed to support each of the special conditions. Your programmers may be able to help him, by tracking what happens on specific items, so that the unit and dollar totals are visible for pre-season buys, special stock for customers, repair parts, new product lines, etc.

MOTIVATION . . . AN INCENTIVE PLAN FOR BUYERS

Distributors spend long hours of thought and planning on sales incentive and sales compensation. They want to be sure the sales force is motivated, challenged, and performances are measurable . . . but what about Purchasing personnel? They spend millions of dollars of company funds, can affect net profit drastically by good or bad performance, and they're paid a straight salary. Oh sure, there's the will-o'-the-wisp profit-sharing plan at year-end, but it's hard to see how day-to-day performance affects that much. Too many other economic factors drive those numbers. What about an incentive plan for buyers and purchasing managers? Let's motivate, challenge, and measure *them!*

Assign Responsibility, Measure, Pay . . . Based on Service and Turns

Since the two primary inventory objectives are to provide good customer service and good inventory turns, these two factors form the basis for incentives. The compensation plan for Purchasing, from Director through Buyer, should be based on performance against these two objectives. For this to work, however, several prerequisites are necessary that might not be present today:

1. You *can* measure turnover and service level, by product line, by location, and by total company!
2. Buyers . . . and thereby the Purchasing Director . . . do exercise control over the product lines. They decide when and how much to order; they have a voice in the decision to add new items to stock; they may recommend slow or dead items to drop; and they can reposition material from one company location to another when it better serves elsewhere.

   Purchasing personnel can impact directly what happens to service and turnover. They may be measured, therefore, against results in the two areas.

Turnover

When turnover improves one-half turn, from one six-month period to the next, without any dropoff at all in the service level, the buyer of that product line receives a bonus of $1,000 (for example). If service during the same period does deteriorate, no bonus is paid. It's easy to improve turns if service is allowed to suffer.

Service

The buyer receives a bonus of $1,000 if the service level weekly average, from one six-month period to the next, improves 5 percent . . . and there's no deterioration at all in the turnover rate. If turnover does drop, no bonus is paid. It's easy to improve service at the expense of turnover.

Combination

If, from one period to the next, *BOTH* service level and turnover come up in tandem 5 percent and one-half turn, the bonus is $5,000. This is the toughest to achieve, takes the most effort, and should receive the highest reward.

As stated earlier, the measurements are recognized as imperfect. The objective is to find a *consistent* measuring method on both turns and service . . . methods that always have about the same degree of inaccuracy because they're developed the same way, from the same data, every week or month. Even with erroneous numbers, the *relative position* from one quarter to the next is measurable. By refining the process, you'll find better ways to track each factor more accurately. Just remember . . . when a programming change alters the calculation striving for more accuracy, an adjustment factor must be applied as the new results are compared to last quarter's . . . or the buyers become discouraged. They'll think that the numbers are being manipulated to avoid paying bonuses.

Objectives of the Compensation Plan:

1. Buyers and/or the Purchasing Director become vitally interested in service and turnover results. They benefit financially when these improve, but learn the importance of progressing in both . . . not just in one at the expense of the other.
2. Buyers and/or the Purchasing Director seek actively to improve their Inventory Management knowledge and skills. They're no longer content to "order what we bought last time" based on

old-fashioned SWAG. They welcome the chance to work with data processing to upgrade the computer's capturing and use of lead times, usage, and calculation of effective replenishment controls.

3. Each assumes a new interest in "pruning" product lines of nonproductive stock items, sending lists regularly to Sales recommending "Do Not Reorder" reclassification.

4. Each becomes much more likely to consider interchangeable items in their own or another company location, when determining how best to meet customer demand. They go to Sales with requests like this: "May we use up our stock of Brand B on all orders for Brand A this next month? We're overloaded on B, but need to replenish A!" Sales may turn them down, but they ask!

5. Similarly, they develop a new interest in using surplus of an item that needs replenishment, transferring-in the stock from another company location, rather than ignoring it.

6. They seek an active voice in how and when new stock items are added that will be under their control . . . and during the first few critical months, they stay much more on top of which items sell and which don't!

7. They're keenly aware of stock return provisions and dates from the manufacturers, so as to make sure the company takes full advantage of these . . . rather than missing them on occasion.

SUMMARY

Since employees will always do more of what Management *inspects* than what they *expect,* it's vital to have measurements of a functioning Inventory Management system. Since the system is designed to provide good service and good inventory turnover, it's vital to measure performance against those two goals. Since people perform better when motivated, it's vital to offer financial incentives to the purchasing personnel, tying better results against their twin goals to better pay.

Turnover and Service are not easily measured with accuracy. Consistency is the key. The numbers may be partially "impure," not reflecting a 100 percent picture of true performance, but if the same factors are considered week after week, month after month, the trends are visible. The next key is corrective action. When a downward trend appears in Service or Turns, don't assume that it will smooth out on its own.

MONITORS, MEASURES, MODIFICATION, and MOTIVATION

Assume instead that something is wrong, spend the effort to find out what it is, and apply corrective action at once! I see poorly-performing systems all the time with glaring, obvious warning lights flashing for all to see . . . and nobody does anything.

When the "oil low" light appears on your car's instrument panel, you don't just say to yourself: "Oooh, how pretty . . . a little red light to decorate my dashboard for Christmas!" *YOU PULL OVER AND STOP THE ENGINE!* You know that if you don't, you could ruin the motor. Watch the warning lights for your inventory management system. Don't just keep on "driving" when one indicates a serious problem. Automobile systems fail; drivers sometimes do dumb things (not checking the oil) to help the failure. Computerized systems can drift off course also; experience hardware or software malfunctions; and all helped along by people not doing what they're supposed to do. Put your measurements in place, watch for the "lights," and take action when one glows red.

19

THE WRAP-UP

Whew! I'll bet you're as sick of reading all this stuff as I am of writing it. As my old friend Tom Reid says: "I feel like I've been rode hard and put away wet!" You probably do too. I hope, though, that you finished the book with one impression seared into your mind:

> Inventory Management, done well, requires more planning, more skill, more pure effort, more information, more computer involvement, more management support, and more gutsy decisions . . . than you had dreamed was necessary before you read it.

Remember? I warned about this early on. True Inventory Management results in great customer service and great use of the dollars invested. These two, in combination, lead to great profits. Trouble is . . . it's very difficult to achieve both at the same time. That's why all the planning, effort, skills, and support are needed. That's why a very capable computerized system must help out. That's why the president has to get involved in the dead stock program and have data processing report to him. That's why you must enforce tougher rules about putting new stock on the shelves and when branches can rob stock from one another.

IT'S TIME NOW FOR FILTERING

Every distributor who reads this book will not be able to use every technique or suggestion. You should now filter all you've learned through your company's "grid." What fits? What doesn't? What might be nice but the expense is greater than the benefits? What's essential? Just be careful that your grid isn't turned into fine mesh by comfortable old habits or organization . . . venerable old SWAG that you just can't bring yourself to part with . . . or a penny-wise/pound-foolish financial mindset.

Some Improvements Are Needed by Every Company

Every distributor would benefit from more accurate records (Chapter 14) and less dead stock (Chapter 15). If these two areas showed marked improvement, you could keep your records on the back of old envelopes with SWAG running rampant . . . and still make more money than today. Think what you could do if these improved and an effective system of controls replaced the SWAG!

Total-System Improvement Comes Gradually

Recognize also that great strides in Inventory Management are taken slowly. Your company didn't degenerate into a poor inventory position overnight. It happened gradually . . . over a period of years, as conditions changed but people or the "system" didn't! If you're now at 2.1 true turns, as the last chapter measures it, it may take up to *four years* to improve to 5.0 turns. It takes time to get rid of all the dead stock. It takes time to change habits, gain confidences, stop "playing it safe" with inventories, and evolve from a sales "dominated" company into one that's sales "oriented." It's tough to change the purchasing philosophy also . . . to break the old patterns where any cost was justified to avoid a stockout or to keep a salesman off your back.

Make a Beginning

But where will you be in four years if you don't start now? Yes, the work ahead is difficult. The hours might be long. A lot must be learned; many new skills mastered. New attitudes are required, and that may mean new people if some old hands can't adjust. If you look at all this and throw up your hands or start rationalizing a lack of action . . . then in four years you may not have to worry about the problem. It'll belong to the new owner or the bankruptcy court!

A GOOD WAY TO START

If you're the first in your company to read this book . . . and you like what you've read . . . pass it on to the Boss. If you're the Boss, let the Purchasing Manager read it; then the Data Processing Manager; the Sales Manager; and the Operations Manager. Talk over the concepts. Determine how well they fit you. Work out a plan to improve your system on a phased basis . . . not everything at once. What facets of your company, addressed in this book, are the weakest? Make improvements there first.

Are You Structured Properly . . . With Trained People?

How about your organization? Is it structured properly to achieve what needs to be done? Do you have enough people devoted to Inventory Management and Purchasing? Are they overworked? Underpaid? Do you have motivated warehouse people or are they just hanging around out there until they can find better jobs? Has all your training effort been aimed at Sales . . . very little at Operations or Purchasing?

The Need for Formal Training

An early step in your improvement program likely should be formal training in the various concepts, techniques, disciplines, and formulas you've just read. I offer two-day, in-depth sessions several times during the year. Contact me for a schedule at the number I'll provide in a minute.

The best combination of people to attend is (1) someone who can change the operating philosophy of the company . . . like the President, and (2) Others to learn mechanics . . . like the Purchasing Manager, Data Processing Manager, etc. The best results have been shown by companies sending teams made up like that. It does little good for a Purchasing Agent to get back home, explain (partially) some strange-sounding idea, only to have the Boss (who wasn't in the session) say: "Are you crazy? Graham couldn't have said *that*! You must have spent the entire time in the bar!" . . . and nothing results. You just wasted time and money.

THE SEARCH FOR A SYSTEM IS TOUGH

Often when tough questions are asked about the company's structure and operating methods . . . including the computer, the management team may feel that comprehensive changes are needed. The old system should be discarded in total for a fresh new one. Organizational changes are under your control directly, of course, so any moves there need first a decision . . . then time and money to implement. Computer system changes are tougher. You can consume many months searching for the right system, and if you look at enough . . . become more confused than ever. You can hire a firm to look for you, but that's *really* expensive. They first have to learn a tremendous amount about your company before even starting.

The Turnkey Packages

Today, there are a few excellent "turnkey" computerized systems available on the market that do most . . . from a hardware and software standpoint . . . of what's been suggested in this book. You purchase from one source the computer itself and all support equipment like disc drives, terminals, etc. The software comes in the deal . . . programs that bring to reality most of the features discussed. Finally, installation training and help is added to the package . . . people to show your people what to do and stick around until they can do it.

The term "turnkey" hints that all you have to do is "turn the key" and the system is running smoothly. Not so . . . I can assure you. Chapter 4 had plenty of warnings about changing systems and it's never easy. Still, if you're not already locked-in to a particular brand of hardware, or you're ready for a major upgrade, an effective turnkey package allows the fastest transition when you need nearly every improvement I've suggested.

There Is Good Software for Most Major Computer Brands

If you are locked into Honeywell, Unisys, Hewlett-Packard, NCR, DEC, IBM, Data General, Basic IV, or some other computer brand, you still don't have to program everything from scratch unless you want to. There are a few . . . I repeat . . . a *few* software packages (programs only) that fit most of the major computer brands and accomplish many of the system suggestions in this book. There are 500 others that don't . . . the "Me, Too" packages I mentioned in earlier chapters. Write for my list of the "white-hats" to 913 Loganwood in Richardson, Texas 75080 or call (214) 231-2215. The list is always changing. That's why it's not included here. If no one answers, I've been shot by one of those 500 "Me, Too" companies. Call the police.

GLOSSARY

Accumulative Purchase Order A special purchasing agreement with a supplier, wherein a few items are added to the P.O. each day or during a week. When a pre-set total order level is attained, the supplier issues an invoice. Often used in metroplex areas to purchase daily from suppliers' local warehouses.

Action Reports Reports that cause someone to take immediate *action* on all entries . . . as opposed to "reference type" reports that require extensive human-effort scanning, screening, and analysis before conditions are isolated for which action is needed. Also called "Exception Reports."

Alternate History Field (Duplicate Record) A second record of sales & transfers-out for a stock item during a given month of the past. The normal history field shows the actual quantity used. The alternate field has a modified figure: The Buyer-Analyst's estimate of what would have been sold had something unusual not occurred . . . a very large, one-time sale; an extended period without stock, etc. The alternate record exists *only* when the regular field's figure has been modified, but the alternate is the one used by the computer from then on to set future replenishment controls.

Arbitrary Controls Ordering controls set by human judgment and evaluation of conditions, rather than through the use of formulas and calculations of a computer. Many durable goods distributors should apply human-set controls on 10–20 percent of their stocked items.

Available-for-Sale Balance Merchandise on the shelves that is available for sale to the next customer or branch who wants it, as opposed to all the stock (the total on hand) within the four walls. The most important balance in an inventory management system, since it includes no stock that has been committed previously. The AVS balance triggers all stock replenishment action . . . not on-hand, and only the AVS balance should be on the shelves or regular storage area at the close of a business day.

Average Inventory Sometimes called the "Inventory Budget," it's the average number of dollars carried in stock on an item as long as the current ordering controls are in effect. Formula:

$$AI = \left[\left(\frac{OQ + LP - OP}{2}\right) + SA\right] \times UC$$

AI = Average Inventory OP = Order Point
OQ = Order Quantity   SA = Safety Allowance
LP = Line Point   UC = Unit Cost

Backlash See "Inventory Backlash."

Backorder A customer's need for material (stock or non-stock) that cannot be filled when the order is first received. The customer advises: "Ship as soon as you can!"

Backorder Record The computer's record of all backorders owed to customers, with the supporting detail. It should be complete enough and linked to other records in a fashion that permits the computer to print out backorders for immediate filling when the merchandise arrives from your supplier.

Batch A mode of computerized operation wherein newly input information is accumulated and processed all at one time . . . as opposed to "on-line" mode where each entry is accepted and processed at once by the computer. Batch systems update the computer's files only once or twice, etc., per day, posting many transactions in a "batch," rather than posting them one at a time all day long.

Bin Location The location in the warehouse, yard, mezzanine, or other storage area assigned to a stock item. It's recorded in the computer's files to assist in filling customer orders and in putting away stock. Often called "Warehouse Location."

Blanket Order A purchase order to your supplier or an order from a customer for a large quantity of material . . . but not all to be shipped at one time. The order may cover a long time period with portions of the material authorized for shipment on "Release Dates." Blanket orders are used to guarantee prices and material availability.

Block Method (Cycle Counting) A system of Cycle Counting that develops the best combination of results. Every item in a particular row or section of the warehouse is counted, regardless of how fast or slow-moving it is, whether or not it's an official stock item, or regardless of whether or not it belongs in that storage area. The method's advantage is in finding all unrecorded or misplaced items . . . thereby avoiding the annual physical inventory.

GLOSSARY

Branch Another company location with inventory.

Buyer/Analyst An individual assigned the responsibility for control (Service and Turnover) of a group of stock items. The job entails more than buying. He or she is also an "analyst," because several replenishment options should be explored ahead of just placing a purchase order. There are times as well, when information must be gathered, histories & conditions studied, to effectively set arbitrary controls.

Buying by Inventory Class A method of selecting the quantity of a stock item to purchase in accord with the item's ranking relative to other items in that company location. Each item is assigned one of 13 classes, based on how many dollars move through the inventory in a year.

Carton Quantities See "Standard Package Quantities."

Cash Sale Usually transacted in the Counter Sales area, it's a sale where merchandise is handed to the customer in exchange for some form of immediate payment.

Classification The data gathering, sorting, and analysis of stock items by a computer that results in 13 classes. The class then determines how many of an item (in that class) to buy. Class 1: 1 month's supply; Class 4: 4 months' supply; Class 11: 11 Months' supply, etc.

Committed Stock Stock material still owned by the distributor (not yet invoiced) but assigned to a specific customer's order or branch transfer. Generally, it's advisable to move it out of the regular warehouse storage area to a staging area . . . or at least mark it to show the commitment. Leaving it in with uncommitted stock invites trouble and makes cycle counting very difficult.

Commodity Item An item where manufacturer brand is not important to customers (black iron fittings, etc.). The item is often purchased from several suppliers, depending on who has the best price, and all stock stored together in the warehouse.

Computer An electronic information processing machine, capable of storing, screening, sorting, analyzing, transmitting, and otherwise manipulating vast amounts of information . . . within time frames far beyond human capabilities.

Controlled Demand See "Dependent Demand."

Conversion Factors Multipliers or divisors used by the computer to convert the quantity ordered by a customer or the quantity purchased from a supplier to inventoried units or to invoice in accord with industry practice. Conversion factors are common in paper, steel service, lumber, rubber products, as well as several other industries.

Cost of Carrying Inventory ("K" Cost Percentage) Hidden costs incurred when inventory is present: Storage Space, Taxes, Insurance, Obsolescence & Loss, Material Handling, the Cost of Money. Expressed as a percent, the cost is used in several calculations to aid "How Much To Buy" decisions.

Cost of Going Through the Replenishment Cycle ("R" Cost) Sometimes called the "Cost of Ordering," the "R" Cost represents how much your company spends each time you go through the cycle of replenishment on a stock item: Computer recordkeeping time, purchasing, expediting, receiving, paying the invoice. For most distributors, it's between $4 and $6 and is used in the EOQ calculation.

Counter (or Sales Counter) An area for walk-in customer service. Can generate expensive sales if average-order size is low, the sales process is slow, or if it serves low-profit customers only.

CPU Stands for "Central Processing Unit." See discussion under "Mainframe."

CRT Stands for "Cathode Ray Tube," an early descriptive name for the terminal screens used to input information, make inquiries, or receive displays into or out of the files stored in a computer.

Customer The "life-blood" of a distributor's business . . . and every distributor should be customer oriented. It's vital, however, to avoid becoming customer "dominated."

Customer Record A file in the computer containing all the pertinent facts a distributor might need about a customer. Through programming, the file is linked to other records in a manner that allows the computer to access the information quickly.

Cutoff An interruption in the flow of paperwork and material, during which a count of stock on the shelves can be compared to the computer's figures. With effective cutoff, adjustments to the computer files are inserted without error.

Cycle Counting A partial inventory of the warehouse performed each morning or evening after achieving a cutoff in the flow of paperwork and material. The objective is to find only the stock available for sale in the regular storage area, count it, and make adjustments as required to the computer's records. Cycle Counting is the single most important activity to assure effective physical control.

D Class Item Under the old "A-B-C-D" classification system for inventory, D class material includes the dead or very slow-moving stock

GLOSSARY

items. For most distributors, it's the item that sold less than $10 at cost during the previous 12 months.

Data Processing See "EDP."

Dating A supplier's special offer which allows the distributor to receive merchandise now, but pay for it much later. A very common practice with seasonal products. Distributors are encouraged to take delivery far ahead of the actual selling season because the supplier postpones the payment-due date for 90 days or more. The vital fact to keep in mind: The distributor still picks up all elements of the inventory carrying cost ("K") except the Cost of Money.

Day's-Work-In-A-Day An operating philosophy that promotes stock record accuracy. Each person who performs a function affecting the accuracy of shelf-vs-computer counts (keying orders, filling orders, receiving, material putup, processing of returns, etc.) must complete all required activity before leaving each day . . . so that there is no paper or material "float" at day's end.

Dead Stock Same as "D" Class item. Stock determined to be a noncontributor to sales, or that sells slowly . . . but does not justify an investment in inventory. Such items are candidates to be discontinued as "stock" and disposition made of anything on hand.

Dependent Demand Usage of a component that is "dependent" on the production schedule of the assembly or end product of which the component is a part. Dependent demand is *very* rarely present in a pure distributor's business, but some inventory control philosophies offered to distributors today (DRP, etc.) are based on the concept. Unless you control to some degree how customers may order, DRP is out of its element.

Direct Shipment Sometimes called "Drop Shipment," it's a customer's order that goes directly from your supplier to your customer. The item does not actually pass through the distributor's inventory, although the dollars are posted in and then out by Accounting.

Discount A money-saving purchasing opportunity the supplier offers a distributor if he will buy a higher quantity of a single item, buy a large-enough total order, buy ahead of the season, during a promotion, or in advance of a price increase.

Disposition Coordinator (For Dead Stock) The person assigned the responsibility by Management of coordinating the Dead Stock Program's Identification & Disposition phases . . . assisted by a team of executives appointed by the President.

Disqualification (of History) Determining that a stock item's Sales and Transfer history may be misleading as a reflection of what to expect in the time just ahead. The computer often can identify unusual conditions, insert a flag in the item's history, and thereby "freeze" the ordering controls until instructions are provided by a human.

Distributors Companies that do not manufacture or change the configuration of material purchased for the purpose of resale. Their role is to perform functions the manufacturers cannot accomplish . . . reach wider and wider market & geographic areas, contacting levels of potential product users that would be unreachable for the manufacturer. Some distributors also perform "processing" steps. (See "Processor")

Distribution Requirements Planning (DRP) An inventory management concept evolving from "Material Requirements Planning" (MRP). DRP replaces Order Points and EOQ's with different order timing & quantity methods, but requires at least some elements of dependent demand be present. Since dependent demand is extremely rare in the pure distributor's environment, DRP is not recommended.

Drop-Ship See "Direct Shipment."

DRP See "Distribution Requirements Planning"

Duplicate History Field See "Alternate History Field."

Economic Order Quantity (EOQ) One of the formulas for determining how many to buy of a stock item when replenishment is needed. The formula balances the cost of carrying inventory with the cost of going through a replenishment cycle . . . thereby developing the lowest possible "outgoing cost."

EDP Stands for "Electronic Data Processing," which describes what a computer does. In some companies, EDP or the shortened form "Data Processing" is also the name given to the department responsible for programming and/or operating the computer.

Equivalent History Used to develop expected usage rates on seasonal items, it's the period from last year's history that corresponds to the months just ahead. If today is March 1st, equivalent history is last year's March, April, May, June, July, and August.

Exception Principle Displaying or printing out only those conditions that are exceptions . . . that should receive attention or action, as opposed to reporting every item or condition in a category. Example: Reports that show only items requiring replenishment action, instead of "Stock Status Reports" that show every item in a product line.

GLOSSARY

Expedite Report An example of the exception principle above. Open purchase orders with your suppliers are called out for expediting action *only* when the item(s) involved meet pre-set conditions. Expediting becomes a productive, manageable function.

Expediting Follow-up activity after a purchase order has been placed with the supplier. It's necessary only when the unexpected occurs, but provides the "recovery" capability that must be present in any system to develop excellent customer service.

Exponential Smoothing A complex mathematical method which tries to "smooth" out unusual fluctuations in a stock item's usage history. More weight is given to recent months; less weight as you move back in time. Several options may be selected as the smoothing factor, as the formula attempts to predict usage to expect next month. Not recommended.

Field The location for information storage in a computer's internal files. The term can apply also to the space allotted on a display screen or printout where specific information appears.

FIFO The "First-In/First-Out" accounting and costing method. The unit cost (incoming) of the oldest material on hand is used to value each sale or to value the inventory.

FISH A spoof of FIFO, LIFO, etc. Stands for "First-In . . . Still-Here!"

Flag A warning code, or even a total "roadblock," which causes the computer to omit some regular step entirely or move to alternate programming. Flags may be inserted by the computer itself, or by a human, when dangerous conditions are encountered.

Float (Paperwork or Material) The Number 1 cause of poor physical control. Customer orders are keyed-in but not filled by quitting time; material is posted as received but not put away, or put up but not posted; material is taken from the shelves without paperwork. Result: The computer's count never agrees with what's actually on the shelf.

"Found" Item A non-stock item that appears in the warehouse, can be sold immediately, and you do not want to make it an official stock item. Requires a special order entry code.

Future Order A customer's order entered much earlier than needed, with instructions to ship the merchandise on a specific future date. The customer wants guaranteed delivery because the date is critical, but future orders for stock material present unusual programming & processing challenges if inventory imbalances are to be avoided.

GIGO An old, overworked catch-phrase which means "Garbage In—Garbage Out!" Still, its message for all employees is worthwhile: Accurate, complete, timely data must be fed to a computerized system if the potential benefits are to be enjoyed.

GMROI "Gross Margin Return On Investment," an effective measurement of a product line's profit productivity, considering what the sales force sells it for, weighed against the inventory investment. GMROI should be used to decide to stock or to discontinue stocking a line . . . but *not* to modify how the items are replenished!

Hardware The equipment (central processing unit, disc drives, printers, terminals, etc.) that comprise a computerized system, as compared to the instructions (software) that cause the computer to function in a desired manner.

History The record of units sold or transferred out month by month, back for a minimum of 13 months on each stock item in each company location that carries it.

History Disqualification See "Disqualification."

Incoming Cost The price paid per unit to a supplier for a stock item . . . the cost as the material comes "In" the warehouse door. It should include freight when the inbound transportation expense equals 15% of the price paid to the manufacturer.

Independent Demand Stock item usage that is totally independent of any other factor . . . as opposed to "dependent" demand which derives from controllable conditions. Manufacturers enjoy dependent demand on components where usage is tied to the master production schedule of end products. Distributors must prepare for independent demand from their customers. Order Points & EOQ's work best for independent demand . . . DRP for dependent demand.

Information Management System Often abbreviated "IMS," it's a valid description of a computer's function . . . and thus the term may become the name of the department responsible for the computer. Summarizes the end result of effectively combining hardware, software and people.

Input The act of giving information to a computerized system (or any system) . . . and the name for the information fed in.

Inquiry A request for the computer to retrieve and make available specific facts stored in its records. Quite often, the term applies to the use of a CRT or terminal as the request is keyed-in.

GLOSSARY

Integrated System Computerized file structure, operating system, and programming that integrates the file storage and use of information. A new record being formed (customer sales order, etc.) draws many elements of data from existing files (customer record, inventory master file, etc.). There's no need to re-input the information.

Interchange Another brand of a stock item that may be sold interchangeably, with a high degree of customer acceptance. To avoid problems, it's recommended that interchanges recorded in the computer files be 100% functional substitutes . . . not upgrades.

Interchange File A form of "artificial intelligence" provided by the computer to make Inside Telephone Salesmen appear brilliant, even if their actual product knowledge is limited. Product numbers from competing brands; obsoleted or superceded numbers; even customers' own part numbers are added to the Interchange File over a period of years. A customer can provide almost any product number in ordering or inquiring . . . and the computer interchanges at once to the one you stock or can supply.

Inventory One of the major assets of a distributor. It's the stock in which his dollars are invested.

Inventory "Backlash" A very human, psychological reaction by a branch manager when all his stock is (by executive edict) sent to fill a customer order in another location. He must load up on nearly all stock items as protection for his own customers. Solution: Permit the manager to protect his non-surplus stock. It ships elsewhere only with his approval (which he grants nearly every time to encourage a return favor).

Inventory Budget See "Average Inventory."

Inventory Class A categorization of stocked items based on how many dollars move through the inventory in a year. Set by the Classification exercise, an item's class may be used (as an option) in the calculation of order quantity for stock replenishment.

Inventory Control A function or a department with this goal: To provide the best customer service possible through the use of inventory . . . but to accomplish it with the most practical turnover of inventory dollars. True control (or lack of it) results from the buying decisions on stock material.

Inventory Correction The only activity open as an option when Inventory "Control" is performed carelessly, by someone untrained, or in a sales-dominated company. Control is exercised when material is purchased for the first time or replenished. When that's done badly, the only thing left is correction.

Inventory "Creep" A slow, but continual increase in inventory across a multi-branch network as the computer records non-recurring transfers in shipping branch histories. The computer calculates higher controls to raise the inventory levels . . . protecting for a recurrence of one-time situations. A very serious problem to recognize and prevent through effective programming.

Inventory Management A term used interchangeably with "Inventory Control," but in some companies it embraces inventory-related functions beyond stock replenishment: Dead Stock Disposition, Stock Repositioning, Decisions On New Stock Items, etc.

Inventory Manager One of several titles that might be assigned to the individual responsible for Inventory Control/Management functions. Others: Inventory Control Manager, Materials Manager, Purchasing Manager.

Just-In-Time A very popular inventory concept now with distributors' customers. The objective is to develop inventory plans and sources that deliver needed merchandise "just-in-time" . . . thereby reducing the inventory levels the customer carries. Tremendous pressure is exerted on the distributor to perform at very high service levels.

Kan-Ban The Japanese version of "Just-In-Time" inventory planning . . . from which the new concepts have evolved.

Kardex A brand of inventory recordkeeping equipment used for many years in manual systems. Its use was so widespread that "Kardex" became synonymous with manual equipment of any type or brand.

Keying Using the keyboard of any device (usually a CRT or terminal) to input information for the computer's records. When the system is "On-Line" or "Real-Time," the data is accepted by the computer immediately after the keying step is completed.

Lead Time The total time required to replenish a stock item, from the date that a need to replenish is noted through all the steps of purchasing, transport, receiving, put-away . . . to the date that the computer's records show more stock available to sell. For the Order Point calculation, however, lead time is from date of order to first receipt (and recording) of an item on the P.O. Each item has its own lead time.

LIFO The "Last-In/First-Out" accounting and costing method. The incoming unit cost of the newest material on hand is used to value all sales of a stock item until that layer of stock is exhausted. Then the next-oldest stock's cost is used, etc. The term applies also to a year-end technique for saving taxes which values inventory at unit costs from some earlier year.

Line Buying The distributor's unique purchasing restraint which requires an assortment of the supplier's product line to be ordered (rather than one item at a time) to qualify for a discount: 10% off the entire purchase, freight paid, etc.

Line Point The replenishment-timing control set higher than the Order Point on all stock items in a product line where Line Buying is required. The Line Point establishes the upper limit for an item to be included in the purchase order: On Hand + On Order must be below the Line Point. Computer-calculated Line Points help remove the guesswork on which items to buy, which to omit when building a "carload" purchase.

Line Review Cycle See "Review Cycle."

Locator System The plan and number/letter designations for all material storage areas. Aisle, row, shelf, drawer, section, mezzanine, yard, or floor area identifications to guide stock put-away, customer order-fill, and cycle counting.

Mainframe The central processing unit in a computerized system. There may be many devices connected to the mainframe, such as printers, tape or disc drives, terminals, or even smaller computers . . . but the main unit that does all the heavy processing work is called the "CPU" or Mainframe.

Manual Records Records of sales, transfers, purchases, receipts, and stock on hand maintained on hand-posted cards (like a Kardex system), as opposed to a computer-posted recordkeeping system.

Manufacturer One of several names for the supplier of goods to a distributor. The producer of those products the distributor sells. Alternate names: Vendor, Supplier, Source.

Master Inventory Record The computer file that contains "everything you need to know about a stock item anywhere in the company!" The record may be quite large if several branches carry the same item in stock.

Materials Manager One of the alternate job titles for the Inventory Manager . . . but this particular one is more often found in manufacturing.

Maximum An ordering control often used for stock in a branch when resupplied from one of the distributor's master warehouses. When available stock reaches the "Minimum," an amount is ordered to bring the balance up to the "Maximum." Min/Max controls are used in place of Order Point/EOQ since the branch may order one item at a time, has a very short lead time.

Minimum The order-timing control under a Min/Max system. Used in place of an Order Point, since the branch enjoys a very short lead time for resupply of the item from a master warehouse within the company.

Material Requirements Planning (MRP) The manufacturer's method for providing raw materials & components at just the right time in his production and/or assembly process. A complex computerized ability to order exactly the required quantities of each component so that production is uninterrupted. An approach to the same concept (DRP) has been offered to distributors, but is not recommended. MRP and DRP both require "dependent" demand. Distributors experience independent demand.

Next Cost (To Be Paid) The price per unit to be paid for a stock item on the *next* purchase order to the supplier. Price changes announced by the manufacturers are keyed at once into the computer files . . . for future quotations, or to enable the computer to price-out future purchase orders, check vendor invoices, modify systems contracts as soon as the agreement permits, etc.

NIFO "Next-In/First-Out" . . . a controversial modification to the LIFO accounting and costing method. You should get approval from your auditors and IRS before adopting NIFO. It may well be illegal, since it raises current inventory values to prices you have not yet paid.

Non-Recurring Transfers Inter-branch movement of material on a one-time or "Buddy-Helping-Buddy" basis. Should *NEVER* be posted in the shipping branch's usage history! Inventory levels should not be raised (with the computer's help) to protect for non-recurring demand.

Non-Significant Part Number A part numbering scheme that simply assigns a designation to each item in inventory . . . without regard to the item's category, dimensions, use, etc. The opposite of a "Significant" number which attempts to describe the item within the construction of the part number scheme.

GLOSSARY

Non-Stock Item An item offered for sale by a distributor on a special-order basis. The item may or may not be part of a product line the distributor is authorized to sell, or one where other items are offered from stock. For most distributors of durable goods, non-stock items comprise about 30% of the total sales volume. Where technology is higher in the products, the non-stock percentage will also be higher.

Obsolescence One of the risks (and costs) incurred by carrying inventory . . . stock that cannot be sold because of better products on the market, lower priced items, or changes in technology or style, etc. Obsolescence is one of the annual costs considered in the Cost of Carrying Inventory ("K") calculation.

O.E.M. "Original Equipment Manufacturer." Someone who uses a distributor's material as part of the product he manufactures.

On-Line System An interactive computerized system, which may also be called "Real-Time." Information fed into or requested from the computer files is processed immediately, and the file is updated or facts displayed at once.

Operator A term that could mean many things, but with computers it refers to the individual who "operates" any piece of equipment: The main computer itself, terminals, printers, tape or disc drives, etc.

Ordering Controls Controls to guide the "When To Order" and "How Much To Order" decisions when replenishing a stock item: Order Points, EOQ's, Minimums, Maximums, arbitrary levels, etc.

Ordering Cycle See "Review Cycle."

Order Point The lowest order-timing control for most stock items (Highest: Line Point). It may be calculated or set arbitrarily, but it establishes the lowest amount of stock to have on hand + on order when starting the replenishment cycle. Used with independent demand and when buying under lead times one week or longer.

Outgoing Cost A hidden (but the most important) cost in relation to a stocked item . . . the *total* cost an item has accumulated when it finally leaves the warehouse on the way to a customer. Included are the costs paid to the supplier, replenishment-cycle cost, and cost of carrying the inventory investment. The outgoing cost is minimized when EOQ's are purchased.

Overflow Stock Excess stock of an item that will not fit into the assigned warehouse location(s). If handled improperly, overflow stock is often the cause of inaccurate records or lost merchandise.

Overflow Stock Tags A manual method used by warehouse personnel to keep track of secondary storage locations for overflow stock. Tags are placed at the primary location to show where to find additional material, and other tags placed on the overflow stock indicating where the primary stock is. Helps order-fillers and cycle counters.

Packaged System A total "package" of computer programs offered for sale or lease, that performs most of the functions a distributor needs. Like all other products, there are very good, average, not-so-good, and awful packages on the market.

Part Number In a computerized system, the part number has the same function as a street address for an individual . . . the location where information is stored. A well-planned part numbering scheme makes it easy to accept customer orders, key them into the system, and track what happens. Today, many distributors are adopting the manufacturers' part numbers as their own, to avoid the "lookup" step at order entry or for stock inquiry.

Physical Control One of the major foundations on which an effective systems rests: The degree of accuracy between quantities out on the warehouse shelves and what the computer says is there . . . as well as the ability to *find* stock when you need it. Poor physical control undermines all other aspects of Inventory Control. Calculated controls are no better than SWAG; people all through the organization compensate for the inaccuracies with extra stock.

Physical Inventory An annual, periodic, cyclical, or emergency count of stock in the warehouse to verify records, to determine financial value, or to help track down the cause of suspected problems. A full-warehouse or full-company physical inventory is often required by auditors at fiscal year end.

Picking Ticket A computer-prepared copy of a customer's order (or transfer) to guide warehouse orderfilling and shipping activities. Often shows the storage location, and may be "zoned" with items grouped together by aisle or warehouse section.

Prevention (Of Dead Stock) An ongoing, first-phase of an effective Dead Stock Program. New, tougher attitudes are needed in those "up-front" decisions that add new stock items or lines. Distributors need management-approved plans for dealing with pressure from customers, their own salesmen, and from manufacturers to add new stock items.

GLOSSARY

Primary Storage Area   One spot in the warehouse, recorded in the computer's files, where you could go and always find at least some quantity of an item . . . or be told (by an Overflow Stock Tag) where material can be found. When a primary location is assigned to an item, it's advisable but not necessary that all the stock be kept there at all times.

Prime Rate (Of Interest)   The commercial lending rate for funds to finance inventory, accounts receivable, new buildings, equipment, or any other need for cash. The Prime Rate is set by major banking institutions and impacts almost every cost of doing business.

Processor   As a business category, the Processor does not manufacture basic materials, but does alter the configuration. Examples: Steel Service Center that cuts material to customer specs; Rubber products distributor that slits a roll; Fluid Power distributor that assembles a unit ordered by a customer from numerous stock components. Special programs are needed for proper inventory control, billing, etc.

Programmer   Anyone with the skill to prepare instructions that cause a computer to perform one or more of the functions of which it is capable.

Programs   Instructions, prepared in special forms and languages, that a computer can accept, interpret, and execute. See "software."

Protected Stock   Material set aside for just one customer, in an attempt to guarantee a 100 percent service level on the items involved . . . a very expensive inventory to carry and administer. Such customer agreements are often initiated by your own salesmen as a hedge against poor control of regular stock.

Purchase Order   The distributor's official agreement to buy merchandise from a supplier. The contract may be written and mailed in, or simply verbal in person or by phone.

Purchasing   The activity or department involving the commitment of company funds to merchandise from sources outside the company. On stock items, it's at the moment when purchasing decisions are made that Inventory "Control" is exercised. If done badly, only Inventory "Correction" remains!

Purchasing By Inventory Class   See "Buying By Inventory Class." An optional method of determining quantities to order that avoids the EOQ calculation but achieves some of the EOQ benefits. Be sure to note that the "Class" method generates 1 less turn of inventory per year (total across all items) than does EOQ.

Qualification (Of History) See "Disqualification."

Random Storage Method (In Warehouse) Putting incoming stock anywhere it will fit in the warehouse and recording the location in the computer. The same item can be in several spots. Not recommended for durable goods distributors. Requires that all stock items use the same amount of space, the same cube, etc.

Real-Time System See "On-Line" System.

Receiving The activity or department involving the check-in of merchandise arriving from manufacturers, other branches, competitors or returned from customers. *The single most-important* warehouse activity, where physical control begins, but an area rarely manned with the experience or afforded the importance it deserves.

Recommended Replenishment Action Report The most important report generated by a computerized inventory management system. It's a list of all stocked items in a category or product line where the on-hand + on-order total is below Line Point, Order Point (or Minimum in a branch). Under the exception principle, items appear *only* if replenishment action is needed.

Replenishment Cycle The process by which a continuity of supply (and good service) is guaranteed on a stock item. For purchased material, the cycle includes triggering the "Buy," placing the order, expediting if needed, receiving, putting material away, paying the invoice, and posting all records. The "R" Cost, used in the EOQ calculation, is developed to consider the cost of going through the replenishment cycle.

Replenishment Options Methods . . . including purchasing . . . that make provisions to meet anticipated customer demand for a stock item. An effective Buyer/Analyst considers several other options: Transfer-in of surplus; use of interchangeable items; substitutions; A decision to offer the item on a special-order basis only . . . all ahead of the most costly option: A new purchase order.

Reserved Stock See "Protected Stock."

Response Time The time required for a computerized system, with related communications equipment, to reply to a request for information or to accept new data into its files. Response time, measured is seconds, relates to on-line, interactive systems.

GLOSSARY

Review Cycle The frequency with which a product line is purchased when the supplier offers a total-order discount. In an effective system, the Review Cycle is calculated (rather than the result of guesswork) and becomes the planned frequency for a computer-scan of all items in the product line . . . to find the proper candidates for replenishment. The Review Cycle is also part of the Line Point calculation.

Safety Allowance A measured amount of "pad" incorporated into an Order Point calculation to protect for a reasonal variance in anticipated usage or lead time when next replenishing a stock item. The pad is actually needed only half the time, so (although absolutely necessary for good service) it becomes a fixed asset that turns zero times per year. Set it through proven principles and not guesswork!

Sales-Dominated Distributor Describes almost every distributor in years past . . . where the environment was "any sale is a good sale" and "do whatever the customer asks (as regards inventory)!" The business changes of recent years dictate a sales-oriented, but not sales-dominated approach, if a distributor is to survive and prosper.

Sales Order Record The computer file containing all pertinent information in a customer's order. The record is maintained on-line until all items have been delivered or cancelled and the customer has paid the invoice(s).

Seasonal Items Products that sell much better in one time of year than another. Generally, it's an item where 80 percent of the annual sales volume falls in six (or less) consecutive months. The computer is programmed to look back at the "equivalent" sales history from the past to develop usage predictions and to set replenishment ordering controls for both seasonal and off-season periods.

Secondary Storage Area A second assigned warehouse location for one stock item (in addition to its primary location). Sometimes recorded in the computer, but often handled by warehouse personnel by using Overflow Tags.

Service Level Measurement of an inventory system's effectiveness against one of its two primary goals: Service and Turnover. Considering stock items only, what percent of the line items on customer orders were filled complete on the first attempt, no backorders, no shortages, no substitution, and delivery within acceptable timeframes?

Service (Repair) Item A stock item that supports major units sold earlier. Service part inventories generally turnover more slowly than regular items and may be continued on the shelves even when little or no sales activity is recorded. Many service parts require replenishment ordering controls to be set arbitrarily.

Sequencing Number A computer's special internal numbering scheme employed to position one item relative to another when displaying information on reports or screens. It permits item insertion or rearrangement without a need to change part numbers. For this reason, it's a good idea *not* to use item part numbers as the sequencing numbers.

Sheet-To-Shelf Counting A very common, but incorrect, method of counting items in the warehouse for the purpose of verifying the computer records. The counter is provided a list of items to count; he or she finds these in the warehouse and counts them; the records for these items are verified/corrected. Does not find items out of place, lost stock, material covered up, or material no one knew was stocked.

Shelf-To-Sheet-Counting The proper way to count stock in the warehouse. The counter covers a "Block" of space, looking first to see what's on the shelf or in the area. Counts are recorded on a preprinted list, but items are added if not listed, material moved if out of place. The shelf-to-sheet technique, when used under a well-planned cycle count program, can help a distributor avoid the annual physical inventory.

Shocking The System Special corrective ordering action for an item that experiences repetitive stockouts . . . and customer backorder accumulations deplete each replenishment shipment immediately. The item receives a "shock" of extra material (twice or three times the normal quantity) to return it to a controllable pattern.

Ship-Complete Order A customer's order carrying instructions not to deliver anything until all items are available, even though some may be stock and others non-stock. It's recommended that such orders be "staged" in a designated material accumulation area (bin, shelf, floor section, etc.) with care exercised to *protect* the staged merchandise. Otherwise, stock available today will be missing when the non-stock items finally are received.

Shrinkage (Shortage) Disappearance of material from inventory. One of the hazards and costs of carrying stock. The cause may be theft or an innocent (but still expensive) mishandling of paperwork. Usually discovered during a cycle count or a year-end physical.

Significant Part Numbers Part numbering schemes which attempt to categorize or describe each item within the framework of the part number itself: The first two digits designate product group; the next two the supplier; the next two the product type; final four digits the dimensions, etc. Significant numbering plans often break down for lack of sufficient open numbers when a group of new items must be inserted into the scheme.

Silent Partners From an inventory standpoint, those persons who steal merchandise. Management's task is to make it as difficult as possible for theft to occur, and to let all employees know that you *take it seriously!*

SKU Stands for "Stockkeeping Unit," or the number of stock items times the number of company locations that carry each one. 10,000 items, each stocked in 5 branches, are 50,000 SKU's. An important consideration in planning the computer and file size your system will require.

Slow-Moving Stock Stock that's only slightly above the "Dead" class. It sells, but far short of the amount that justifies a continued inventory investment.

Software Coded instructions prepared by humans to guide the specific steps, sequence, and timing of a computer's work . . . as compared to "Hardware," which is the actual equipment that performs the work.

Staging Areas Storage areas in the warehouse (aisles, racks, shelves, bins, floor sections, etc.) set aside for accumulation of material for customer orders of the "ship-complete" type, "tag & hold" orders, weekly branch replenishment shipments, etc.

Standard Package (Carton) The quantity of an item packed normally by a supplier in a box, carton, bundle, or on a roll, reel, or pallet. Purchased quantities (for stock) should always be rounded-off to the nearest standard package as part of the computer's calculation. Some suppliers add a charge to supply nonstandard quantities.

Stock Item Material offered to customers from a distributor's inventory . . . as opposed to the much larger array available only by special order from the suppliers. In most durable goods industries, stock items comprise about 70 percent of a distributor's total sales. Turnover should be calculated considering *stock sales only!*

Stock List The array of items designated as "stock" in each company location with inventory. The management objective: Maintain a continuity of supply on these items that develops a 90 percent service level and about 5 to 6 turns per year. Surprisingly, many distributors have no such official list.

Stock/Non-Stock Sales Profile The percentage of sales generated from shelf-stock, as compared to sales of non-stock items . . . in total for the company, for a branch, or for a product line. Often a good measurement of how well customer demand is being met locally, under the restraint of inventory-dollar use. In most industries, a 70/30 stock-to-NS profile is a desirable goal. With high-technology products, the ratio moves down around 50/50.

Stockout Running out of stock before replenishment material arrives. If sales are lost or customer backorders build up, a stockout represents a system failure, but it can be a planned condition for items with zero order points or for seasonal items at the close of a season.

Stock Status Reports A reference-type report that can be useful if prepared for backup or general information duty . . . but dangerous for use in preparing stock replenishment orders. All items in the branch or product line are listed, showing the status of each compared to current controls. It's too easy for a buyer to add items to an order that should not be purchased now, and to omit others that should. Instead, use an exception report for buying.

Supplier A manufacturer, broker, warehouse, or any other source from whom a distributor buys merchandise. Other terms: Vendor, Source.

Surplus Stock Any quantity on hand in excess of Line Point + Order Quantity in a warehouse or the "Maximum" in a branch. If replenishment were triggered on an item at Line Point (the highest allowable condition), and the full order quantity arrived before even one unit sold, then the combination (LP + OP) would be on hand and thus represents the maximum allowable stock. Anything more is definitely surplus.

SWAG "Scientific, Wild-Ass Guessing," an overused technique that guided many distributors' buying practices for years. It *does* have proper times and places for use, however. Stock items with conditions to defy any formulized approach need ordering controls set by SWAG . . . educated guesswork!

Systems Contract (Systems Selling) An agreement between a distributor and customer granting the distributor exclusive rights to all

GLOSSARY

the business on a specific list of items. The time period, prices, and quantities are set by the contract terms. The benefits: Locks up a segment of the customer's business; guarantees pricing and delivery for the customer. Can be very expensive to administer.

Tag & Hold Order A customer's order tagged with his name, P.O. number, etc., with instructions to gather all items and hold them . . . until the customer notifies to deliver or until some other special condition is met. Example: Plumbing contractor asking the distributor to gather tubs, tanks and bowls, lavatories for an apartment complex job (some special-ordered) and hold the items until construction begins.

Terminal Normally a CRT device that communicates with a computer, to provide new input or to retrieve and display information from the files.

Turn & Earn Another measurement (like GMROI) of product line, branch, total company profitability. Concept: Low margin on a line/turn the dollars frequently; High margin/lower turn rate allowable. Be careful to apply T & E to "lumps" of inventory but *never* to an individual item!

Turnkey Package A Hardware/Software/Installation package offered by an outside firm. Supposedly, all the distributor need do is "Turn The Key" and they're up and running on the new computerized system. It's not that simple, but Turnkey packages (if well developed) do allow a quicker implementation of complex systems, touching almost every function in the company, than will occur with any other approach.

Turnover Rate (Turns) Measurement of an inventory system's effectiveness against one of its two primary goals: Inventory-Dollar Use and Service Level. Five to six turns per year is good in most durable goods industries, if gross margins average 20-30 percent. Remember to exclude from the calculation any transactions that did not use shelf-stock to meet customers' requirements.

Unit Cost The official value placed on one unit of a stock item when it enters inventory and when it leaves. Used to value inventory and to cost sales and transfers.

Unit of Measure Generally, the lowest unit of a product that a distributor will sell . . . EACH, BOX, POUND, FOOT, COIL, etc. The Unit of Measure should be the stockkeeping unit expressed in the computer's figures of on-hand, on-order, backorder, etc., as well as the normal unit of sale and pricing. It may not be the unit purchased from the supplier. Example: Buy coils but sell by the foot.

Unit-Record Equipment Data processing equipment of the 1950's and early 60's, designed primarily for accounting applications. By today's standards, very slow and inefficient.

Unusual Order Any sale (or transfer-out) of stocked material so large that a human decision is needed on whether or not the sale will recur . . . before the history is used to estimate future usage and inventory levels raised to protect for higher demand in the months ahead.

Up-Front Inventory Decision The original decision by Management, Marketing, Sales, Purchasing, a Branch Manager, a salesman, or anyone to add new items to the "stock" category, thereby committing new funds to inventory. Such decisions often are due to pressure from customers, sales, suppliers, or the desire to enter new markets. No longer can they be made by whims or pure speculation. Need for "commitment" and accountability for inventory requires tougher attitudes.

Usage Rate The rate of anticipated usage (sales + transfers-out) for a stocked item in the period just ahead . . . expressed as so many units per month. It may be developed from the computer's recorded history or set arbitrarily. Usage Rates form the basis for replenishment control calculations, which in turn generate the service and inventory turnover results. A *very* important data element!

Usage-Value The number of dollars of an item moving through the inventory in a 12-month period. The first step in "Classification," it puts all items (expensive or cheap; fast or slow-moving) on one basis for effective comparison. Formula: Units sold (or transferred-out) in last twelve months times unit cost.

Vendor See "Manufacturer" or "Supplier."

Vendor Record The computer file containing all pertinent facts about one of the suppliers. Linked to other files through programming, the Vendor Record provides information quickly when other one-time files are being built (purchase order record, etc.) and to answer inquiries.

Warehouse Location Another name for "Bin Location." The storage location in the warehouse, mezzanine, yard, counter area, etc., assigned as the primary location for each stocked item. Recorded in the computer and printed on sales order and transfer picking tickets, as well as Receiving's paperwork to guide stock putaway.

Will-Call Order The customer calls with an order and these instructions: "Get it ready, and I'll be by to pick it up!" Presents inventory (and possibly service) problems if he's slow in coming or fails to show at all. Material accumulates in the Will-Call area and is unavailable for sale to anyone else.

INDEX

A-B-C Item Classification, 152–153, 306–307
Accountants, 275
Accounts Payable, 41, 94–95
Accounts Receivable, 200
Accumulation-Time-Protection Stock, 138–140, 148
Accumulative Purchase Orders, 41, 109, 303
Accuracy, Stock Record, 14, 25, 205–222, 259, 288, 300, 316
Acquisitions (Other Companies), 279
Action Reports, 17–18, 177–197, 199, 303
Agreement, Distributor/Supplier, 228–230
Alternate Brands, 185–187
Alternate History Record, 79–82, 303
Arbitrary Controls (Human-set), 87, 126, 150, 267, 303, 320
Artificial Intelligence, 24, 311
Associations, Distributor Trade, 10, 239
Assemblies, 263–269
Assemblies, Built to Stock, 267–268
Auditors, 215–216, 314, 316
Authenticity, 230
Authorized Path of Replenishment, 247–250, 292
Automatic Receipts, 41
Available-for-Sale Balances, 13, 37, 180, 191, 201, 209–213, 216–217, 259, 266–276, 288, 303, 306
Average Inventory, 156–157, 168, 291–294, 304
Average Lead Time, See "Lead Time, Average"

Backup Reports, 199–200
Basic IV Corporation, 302
"Bass-Ackward" System Selection, 7, 9–10
"Backlash" Effect, 17, 252, 261, 311
Backorders, Customer, 30, 41, 220, 289–290, 304
Backorders, Supplier, 189–196
Backorder Record, 304
Bar Coding, 4, 60
"Bass-Ackwards" System Selection, 7, 9–10
Batch Mode, 13–14, 304
Bin Locations, 219, 304
Bills of Material, 264
Blanket Orders, 109, 227, 304
Block Method (Of Cycle Counting), 213–215, 304
Branches, 15–17, 68–70, 117, 126–127, 183–185, 245–261, 274–275, 277–279, 284–285, 292–294, 305, 314
Branch Inventory Turnover, 257–259, 277
Branch Zones, 184–185
Broken-Package Charges, 150, 321
Budget, Inventory, 291–294, 304
Budget vs. Actual Reports, 292–294
Buffer Inventories, 43, 79, 87, 99, 111, 123
Buyer/Analysts, 14–15, 17–18, 78–80, 82, 85, 96, 129, 133, 135, 142, 150, 152, 165, 172, 178–180, 185–187, 190–191, 194, 197, 201, 204, 208, 281–282, 286, 290–291, 294–296, 303, 305, 318, 322
Buyer Incentives, 294–296

INDEX

Buying Ahead of Price Increases, 165–174
Buying by Inventory Class, 152–156, 177, 305, 317
Buying for Promotions, 174–175
Buying in the Last Column, 139–142, 157
Buying Target, Total Order, See "Purchasing Target"

Carton Quantity, See "Standard Package Quantity"
Carrying Cost, See "Cost of Carrying Inventory"
Cash Sales, 305
Cash "Traps," 238
Classification, Inventory, 152–156, 229, 258, 305, 311
Classification Frequency, 154
Classification Steps, 152–153
Classification Method Turn Rate, 155
Class (Inventory Movement), 101, 180, 229, 305, 311
"Close-Out" Sales Campaigns, 239
Codes, Family Item, 269–270
Codes, Line Item Handling, 29, 32, 34–35, 107–108
Codes, Purchase Order Handling, 41, 109
Codes, Replenishment Path, 248–250, 292
Codes, Sales Order Handling, 35
Codes, Surplus Stock, 107–108
Commitment, Customer (For Stock), 227, 324
Commitment, Letter of (Salesman), 228, 324
Committed Stock, 38, 209, 211, 215, 220–221, 266–267, 279, 305
Commodity Items (Generic Items), 32, 305
Compensation Plan, Purchasing, 294–296
Compensating (For Poor Records), 25, 208, 218, 316–317
Components, Assembly or Kit, 264–269
Components, Matching Sets of, 268–269
Competitors, 2, 99, 141, 239, 261, 275, 286, 288

Complementary Products, 28
Completing Items, 28
Computer Project Cycle, 49
Computers, 1, 3–6, 9–22, 33–36, 45–58, 61–63, 75, 99–111, 204–205, 234, 245, 261, 263, 270–271, 278, 280–282, 285–289, 297, 301–302, 305
Consigned Inventories (Customers), 279, 293
Contract, Manufacturer/Distributor, See "Manufacturer/Distributor Agreement"
Controlled Demand, See "Dependent Demand"
Contributions, Charitable, 240–241
Conversion, System, 45–57
Conversion Factors, Unit, 305
Coordinator (Dead Stock Program), See "Dead Stock Coordinator"
Coordinator (System Conversion), 56–57
Cores and Warranties, 4
Corporate Services Charge, 258
Cost of Carrying Inventory ("K"), 91–94, 144–148, 166–170, 228, 306–307
Cost of Replenishment Cycle ("R"), 94–96, 144–148, 306, 318
Cost of Ordering, See "Cost of Replenishment Cycle"
Cost, Item Unit, See "Unit Cost"
Counter (Sales Counter), 220, 306
CPU (Central Processing Unit), See "Mainframe"
Credit limit, Customer, 103, 200
Credits, 211, 221
Creep, See "Inventory Creep"
Critical Item Categories, 291
CRT (Cathode Ray Tube/Terminal), 20, 27, 99, 106, 306, 312, 323
Customers, 2, 17, 20, 23–27, 29, 33–39, 45, 103–105, 114–115, 123, 143, 179, 190, 194, 204–205, 220, 222, 224, 226–228, 230, 233, 239, 247, 251–252, 254–255, 263, 265–266, 271, 278–279, 281–282, 284–286, 288–289, 293, 296, 306
Customer Part Numbers, 27
Customer Record, 103–105, 285, 306

INDEX

Customer Service, 113–142, 206
Customer Service Manager (Supplier), 195–196
Cutoff (Paperwork and Material), 212, 217–218, 306
Cycle Counters, 211, 213–217, 219
Cycle Counting, 14, 209–218, 220, 222, 306, 320
Cycle Counting Corrections, 215
Cycle Counting Gap, 212, 217
Cycle Counting List, 213
Cycle Count Item Quantities, 216

"D" Class Items, 152–153, 306–307
Dangerous Product Lines, 137–139
Data General Corporation, 9, 302
Data Processing Department, 62–63, 296, 299, 308
Data Storage, 89–112
Dating, 109–110, 307
Day's-Work-In-A-Day, 210–212, 216, 218, 222, 307
Deactivated Stock Record, 182–183
Dead Stock, 2, 19, 151–154, 207, 223–243, 276–278, 291, 293–294, 299–300, 307
Dead Stock Coordination, 234–238, 307
Dead Stock Coordinator, 235–238, 307
Dead Stock Disposition Alternatives, 238–242
Dead Stock Disposition Program, 153, 223–242
Dead Stock Disposition Team, 235, 237–238
Dead Stock Identification, 230–234
Dead Stock Prevention, 226–230
Dead Stock Store or Branch, 240
Demand Buy, 141
"Demand" Sales History Posting, 81
Dependent Demand, 117, 127, 307–308, 310, 314
Digital Equipment Corporation (DEC), 9, 302
Direct Shipments, Customer Orders, 39–40, 109, 275, 278, 307
Discounts, Item Quantity, 156–159
Discounts, Supplier, 129–134, 138–140, 307
Discounts, Total-Order, 132–134, 162–165

Disqualification (Sales History), 75–87, 308
Disqualification Rules (History), 77, 82, 86
Disposition Steps (For Dead Stock), 235–242
Distributed Processing, 14
Distributor/Supplier Agreement, 228–230
Distributors, 1–7, 9, 27–28, 43, 45, 47, 59–64, 118–119, 129, 143, 150, 161, 169, 194, 207, 221, 223, 226–227, 230, 234, 238, 245, 247, 252, 254–255, 261, 263, 270–271, 274–279, 285, 292, 294, 299–301, 308
Distribution Requirements Planning (DRP), 117–118, 190, 307–308, 310, 314
DNR (Do Not Reorder) Warning, 122, 182, 296
Dominant-Customer Stock Items, 82–83
Drop-Shipments, See "Direct Shipments"
DRP, See "Distribution Requirements Planning"
Dummy Assembly/Kit Records, 267
Dummy Inventory Records, 19
Dummy Part Numbers, 18, 31
Duplicate Product Lines, 279
Duplicate Sales History, 79–82, 303

"Early Warning" Expediting, 192
Economic Order Quantity (EOQ), See "EOQ"
EDP, 308
EDX, 110
EOQ, 139, 146–152, 177, 257, 281, 287, 306, 308, 315, 317
EOQ Calculation, 92, 96, 147–149
EOQ Exceptions, 149
EOQ Formula, 147
EOQ Rounding Rules, 150–151
Equivalent Sales History, 74, 308, 319
Exception Principle, 179, 308
Exception Reports, 17–18, 99, 179–194
Exceptional Usage, 12, 77–80
Expedite Report, 192–194, 309
Expedite Report Timing, 191–192

Expediters, 194
Expediting Function, 95, 189–196, 309
Expediting "Ace," 194–196
Explosions, Material List, 266–267
Exponential Smoothing, 70, 190, 309

"Fair-Game" Stock, 16
Family-Grouped Items, 269–270
Family Item Codes, 269–270
Field, 309
Field/Tent Syndrome, 5–6, 9–11
FIFO (First-In/First-Out), 309
FISH (First-In/Still-Here), 309
Fixed-Length Records, 101
Fixed Stock Item Information, 100
Flags, Usage History, 13, 77–78, 85, 87, 122, 135, 309
Flags, Lead Time, 99
Flea Market Sales, 240
Float (Paperwork or Material), 210–212, 218, 307, 309
Forecasting Usage, 65–68, 72–74
Foundations, System, 207, 234
"Found" Items, 108, 309
Four Stages (Of System Conversion), 46–52
Frankenstein Monster, 64
Freeze, Ordering Control, 80, 83–87, 126, 135, 150, 278, 290–291, 308
Frozen Controls, Temporary, 84–85
Frozen Controls, Permanent, 84–85
Frozen Control Warning Report, 85–86
Future Orders, 37–38, 309

Gap, Cycle Count, 212, 217
Garage Sales, 239
Generic Items, 32
GIGO (Garbage-In/Garbage Out), 310
Goldfish (Size K Cost), 92
Goodwill Industries, 240
GMROI, 310, 323
Great White Shark (Size K Cost), 92
Gross Margin Return On Investment, See "GMROI"

Handling Codes, Purchase Order, 41, 109
Handling Codes, Sales Order, 35
Handling Codes, Sales Order Line Item, 29, 34–35, 107–108

"Hand's-Off" Managers, 50–51
Hand-to-Mouth Ordering, 259–261
Hardware, Computer, 310
Harvard Business School, 3
Hewlett-Packard, 9, 302
History Flags, See "Flags, History"
History (Sales and/or Transfers), 69, 75–82, 108, 180, 186, 234, 246, 250, 264, 266–268, 286, 288, 310
Holding Cost, See "Cost of Carrying Inventory"
Honeymoon Stage (System Conversion), 46–47
Honeywell Corporation, 9, 302

IBM Corporation, 9, 302
Identification (Dead Stock), 230–234
Incentives, Buyer and Manager, 294–296
Incoming Cost, 129, 144–145, 147, 156–157, 159, 162, 165, 310
Independent Demand, 117–119, 127, 310, 314–315
Inflation, 2–3
Information Classifications, 90
Information Management System, 310
Input, 140, 310
Inquiry Definition, 310
Inquiry Phase (Of Ordering), 20, 24
Insurance (On Inventory), 93
Integrated System, 311
Interchanges, Stock Item, 26–27, 182, 296, 311
Interchange File, 26–27, 311
Inventory Analysis Report, 19, 231–233
Inventory "Backlash," 17, 252, 261, 311
Inventory Budget, 291–294
Inventory Buffers, See "Buffer Inventories"
Inventory Carrying Cost, See "Cost of Carrying Inventory"
Inventory Control Function, 311
Inventory "Control" Applied, 114, 177, 224, 230, 311, 317
Inventory "Correction" Applied, 114, 177, 224, 230, 311, 317
Inventory Class, 101, 180, 229, 305, 311
Inventory "Creep," 22, 248, 251, 260, 312

INDEX

Inventory Management Function, 37, 59, 312
Inventory Management Training, 301
Inventory Manager, 312
Inventory Philosophy Changes, 46, 54, 56–58
Inventory Shrink, See "Shortage"
Inventory "Tracking," 14–15
Inventory Turnover (Rate), See "Turnover Rate"
Inventory Write-Off, 240
"IQ" Capability, See "Query" or "Report Writer"
Internal Revenue Service (IRS), 241
IRS Code 170(e)3, 240–241
Item Family Codes, See "Family Codes"

"Just-in-Time" Control (JIT), 117, 284, 312

"K" Cost, See "Cost of Carrying Inventory"
K Cost Calculation, 93
K Cost Calculation, Shortcut, 94
Kanban Inventory Control, 117, 312
Kardex Systems (Hand-Posted), 1, 4, 9, 130, 183, 201, 246, 263–264, 312
"Kardex" Inquiry, 78, 102, 201
Keying Function, 312
"Kiss" Principle, 121
Kits and Kitting, 263–269
Kits, Definition, 263

Last-Column Buying, 139–142
Last-In/First-Out, See "LIFO"
Lead Time, Average, 38, 98, 191, 286
Lead Time Calculation, Computer, 97
Lead Time Definition, 96–97, 312
Lead Time Exceptions, 98–99
Lead Time Exception Report, 99
Lead Time Records, 97–98
Lead Times, Supplier, 38, 96–99, 191, 255–257, 286–288, 312
Lead Time Trash, 98–99, 286–288
LIFO (Last-In/First-Out), 3, 312–313
Line Buying, 116, 129–142, 144, 270
Line Buying Definition, 313
Line Item Detail Information, 107
Line Item Handling Codes, See "Handling Codes, Sales Order Line Item"
Line Points, 18, 131–142, 171–172, 174, 177, 188, 209, 224, 253, 257, 266, 270, 286, 289, 291–292, 313
Line Point Formula, 131–132
Line Review Cycles, See "Review Cycles"
Line Point Recalculation Frequency, 135
Locator Systems, Stock, 219, 313
Lost Sales, 24, 81, 192, 267, 269, 271, 289
Low-Sales Stock Items, 86–87

Mainframe, Computer, 313
Management Information Services, 62–63
Manual Records, 313 (Also See "Kardex")
Manufacturer Record, 102–103, 324
Manufacturers, 313 (Also See "Suppliers")
Manufacturer/Distributor Agreement, 228–230
Master Inventory Record, 99–102, 313
Matching Component Sets, 268–269
Material Handling Expense, 92–93
Material Lists, 264–270
Mathematicians, 75
Materials Manager, 313
Material Requirements Planning (MRP), 117–118, 308, 314
Matrix Pricing, 104
Maximums, 5, 117, 184, 253, 257–261, 292, 314
Measurements, System, 273–294
Menu-Driven Systems, 20
Mergers, 279
Merrifield, Bruce, 238
"Me, Too" Systems, 5, 7, 11–12, 22, 24, 51, 302
Microfiche, 199–200, 204
Minimums, 5, 16–117, 131, 184, 253, 257–261, 292, 314
Misunderstood Aspect (Of Inventory Management), 113–115, 143
Modified Sales History, See "Duplicate Sales History"
MRP, See "Material Requirements Planning"
Monitoring, System, 273–294
Monthly Usage, See "Usage Rate"

INDEX

NAEIR, 241
NCR Corporation, 9, 302
Negative Stock Balances, 218
Negotiation, Supplier, 123–124, 203, 229–230, 241–242
Negotiation, Computer System, 55–56
Next Cost to be Paid, 314
NIFO (Next-In/First-Out), 314
Non-Profit Organizations, 90, 139, 144, 157, 162, 256
Non-Recurring Sales, 78–79
Non-Recurring Transfers, 16, 68, 183, 246–250, 312, 314
Non-Significant Part Numbers, 314
Non-Stock Items, 18–19, 28–33, 220, 234, 278, 282, 315
Non-Stock Item Control, 30–31, 220
Non-Stock/Stock Item Percentage, 275–276, 315, 322

Obsolescence, 93, 151, 268, 315
O.E.M., 315
"Oh, Well" Stage (Conversion), 51–52
On-Line Systems, 13–14, 312, 318
Operations Manager, 235–236, 300
Operator, 315
Options, President's, 139–140
Options, Replenishment, 182–189, 318
Ordering Controls, 15, 57, 115–160, 315
Ordering Cycle, See "Review Cycles"
Order-Filling, Customer, 219, 285, 313, 316
Order Points, 15–16, 83, 115–125, 209, 224, 257, 266–267, 270, 286–292, 315
Order Point Exceptions, 125–126
Order Point Formula, 119
Order Quantities, 113–115, 136, 143–160
"Order-Up-To" Controls, 5, 257
Organization, Corporate, 61–63, 299, 301
Out-of-Rhythm Items, 289–290
Outgoing Cost, 114, 144–147, 159, 162, 165, 177, 280, 308, 315
Outgoing Cost Calculation, 145
Overflow Stock, 219, 315
Overflow Stock Tags, 214, 219, 316–317, 319

Packaged Systems, 316
Parris, Dr. Dan, 158
Part Numbering Scheme, 32, 314, 316, 321
Part Numbers, 26–27, 32, 282, 316, 320
Path of Replenishment, 247–250, 292
Physical Control, 14, 205–222, 234, 309, 316
Physical Control Definition, 206, 316
Physical Distribution, 118
Physical Inventory, 31, 40, 209, 213, 215, 220, 304, 316
Picking Tickets, 27, 35–36, 205, 316
"Pick-Up-on-the-Way" Sales, 40–41
Piranhas (K Cost), 91–92
Planning, Corporate, 59–60
Pre-Price-Increase Buying, 165–174, 293
Pre-Price-Increase Formula, 169–170
President, Distributor, 9–10, 21, 48–51, 54–55, 61–64, 96, 114, 130, 133, 137, 139–142, 195, 203, 207–208, 224–225, 231–232, 234–238, 241–242, 296, 299–301
President's Options, 139–140
President's Priorities, 225, 235, 237
Prevention (Of Dead Stock), 226–230, 316
Price Increases, Supplier, 165–174
Prices, Special Customer, 27, 104
Primary Storage Area (Stock), 219, 317
Prime Rate (Of Interest), 3, 93, 317
Principles, Inventory Management, 54, 71, 156, 161–162, 177, 201, 224
Priorities, President's, 225, 235, 237
Processor (Business Type), 317
Programmers (Systems Designers), 2, 38, 52, 73–76, 100, 101, 104, 117, 189, 203, 216, 264, 269–270, 287–288, 292, 294–295, 317
Programs, Computer, 3–7, 10–12, 270, 297, 301–302, 306, 310, 312, 317, 321
Promotions, Supplier, 65, 71, 109, 174–175, 277–278, 293
Protected Stock, 24–25, 65, 122, 126, 222, 233, 279, 293–294, 317
"Pruning" of Product Lines, 296

INDEX 333

Purchase Order Header Codes, 41, 99
Purchase Order Header Screen, 99
Purchase Order Heading Information, 109
Purchase Order Inquiry Screen, 20
Purchase Order Records, 108–111
Purchase Orders, 41, 135, 317
Purchase-Order-Accumulation-Time Stock, 138–140, 148
Purchasing Ahead of Price Increases, 165–174, 293
Purchasing Department, 95, 224, 236, 280–282, 294–296, 301, 317
Purchasing Department Incentives, 294–296
Purchasing by Inventory Class, 152–156, 177, 305, 317
Purchasing for Promotions, 174–175, 293
Purchasing Manager, 180, 235, 294–296, 300–301
Purchasing Target, Total Order, 132–134
"Push" System (Branch Resupply), 258–259

Qualification (Of Sales History), See "Disqualification"
Quantity Discounts, See "Discounts, Item Quantity"
Query, 21–22, 67, 104, 201-204
Query Restrictions, 21, 201–202
Quotations, 24, 42, 104–105

"R" Cost, See "Cost of Replenishment Cycle"
R Cost Calculation, 95
R Cost Calculation, Shortcut, 96
Random Storage Method (Warehouse), 318
Real-Time Systems, 13–14, 312, 318
Rebates, 4
"Rebound" Effects, 255
Receipt, Automatic, 41
Receiver Cycle Count Method, 215
Receiving Department, 219, 318
Receiving Function, 1, 19, 28, 30, 33, 41, 95, 111, 211, 219–220, 289, 309, 318
Recommended Buy Report, 179

Recommended Replenishment Action Reports, 18, 154, 179–189, 254, 269–270, 287, 318
Record Accuracy, 14, 25, 205–222, 259, 288, 300, 316
Record Design, 96–111
Recovery Capability (Expediting), 190, 309
Recovery Room Stage (Conversion), 47–51
Recurring Transfers, 16, 247
Red Cross, 240
REDINET, 110
Reference Information, 199–201, 270
Reference Inquiry Screens, 200–201
Reference Reports, 178, 199, 303
Reference Sales Orders, 38–39, 210–211
Reid, Tom, 299
"Remember-to-Ask-About" Items, 28
Reorder Cycle Count Method, 215
Reorder Points, See "Order Points"
Repair Parts, See "Service Parts"
Repetitive Usage, See "Usage, Repetitive"
Replacement Cost, See "Next Cost to be Paid"
Replenishment Controls, 15, 57, 115–160, 223–224, 246, 256–260, 266, 277–278, 287, 324
Replenishment Cycle Definition, 318
Replenishment Options, 182–189, 318
Replenishment Path Codes, 248–250, 292
Replenishment Timing, 115–116, 129, 313
Report Generator, See "Report Writer"
Report Writer, 21–22, 201–204
Reserved Stock, See "Protected Stock"
Resolution Phase (Conversion), 51–52
Response Times, 21, 202, 318
Restocking Charges, Supplier, 229–230, 236, 241
Return on Added Investment (ROAI), 169–170
Returns, Stock (From Customers), 68, 211, 220–221
Returns, Stock (To Suppliers), 236, 239, 241–242, 296

INDEX

Reverting, 54, 121, 273, 279
Review Cycles, 18, 132–142, 151, 163–164, 177, 180, 287, 319
Review Cycles, Seasonal Line, 133–134
Review Cycle Formulas, 132–134
Review Cycle Interruption, 141–142
Review Cycle Monitoring, Correction, 136–137, 189
Review Frequency (Product Line), See "Review Cycles"
ROAI, See "Return on Added Investment"
Robbing Stock (Committed), 35
Robbing Stock (From Other Branches), 16, 251–252, 260
Robbing Stock (From Complete Units), 209, 221
"Robot" Purchasing Syndrome, 152
Rolling-Average Usage-Rate Computation, 72, 75
Round-the-Clock Operations, 217–218

Safety Allowances, 69, 119–125, 191, 287, 291, 319
Safety Allowance Computation, 120–122
Safety Allowance Check, 124
Safety Stock, See "Safety Allowances"
Sales-Dominated Distributors, 2, 115, 143, 300, 311, 319
Sales Management, 233–237, 248, 256, 266, 296, 300
Sales-Oriented Distributors, 2, 115, 143, 300, 319
Salesmen, Inside (Telephone), 4, 20, 23–26, 28, 40, 200, 208–209, 215, 218, 220, 265, 281, 311
Salesmen, Outside, 19, 23–25, 31, 66, 78–79, 130, 140, 142, 157, 165, 172–173, 185–187, 190–192, 203, 208, 216, 220, 227–230, 234, 259, 261, 278–282, 286, 317
Salesmen, Supplier, 123–124, 196, 203, 216, 220, 229
Salesmen, Computer Systems, 52, 88, 202, 204, 222, 264, 270
Sales, Non-Recurring, 78–79
Sales-Order Entry, 28–29, 35, 38, 111

Sales-Order Heading Information, 106, 285
Sales-Order Inquiry Screen, 20
Sales Order Records, 32, 105–108, 319
Sales Orders, 29–30, 40–41
Sales Order/Line Numbers, 20, 29–30, 110
Sales-Oriented Distributors, 2, 115
Sales, Unusual, 12, 77–80, 287–288, 324
Salvation Army, 240
Samples, Inventory, 209, 211, 221
Scheduled Orders, 109
Scientific, Wild-Ass Guessing, See "SWAG"
Seasonal Items (Seasonality), 65, 71, 73–74, 88, 133–134, 164, 277–278, 287, 291, 293, 307–308, 319, 322
Seasonal Items, Definition, 73, 319
Seasonal Line Review Cycles, 133–134
Secondary Sales History, See "Duplicate Sales History"
Secondary Storage Area, 319
Security, Warehouse, 220
Sequencing Numbers, 320
Serial Number Tracking, 4
Service, Definition of Good, 282–283
Service (Repair) Parts, 75, 209, 211, 221, 233, 280, 293–294, 320
Service Level, 87, 113–128, 206, 224, 259, 282–288, 294–296, 319
Service Level Measurement, 122, 206, 282–284, 296
Service Level, Universal, 125
Sets, See "Kits"
Sheet-to-Shelf Count Method, 215, 320
Shelf Life, 164
Shelf-to-Sheet Count Method, 214, 320
Shocking the System, 288–290, 320
Ship-Complete Sales Orders, 34–35, 211, 320
Shortage, Inventory (Shrink), 40, 93, 151, 320–321
"Show" Stock, 230–231, 248
Shrinkage, Inventory, 40, 93, 151, 320–321
SIC Codes, 103
Significant Part Numbers, 314, 321

INDEX

Silent Partners, 321
Silver, Alan, 169–170
Single-Customer Stock Items, 82–83
Six-Month, Rolling-Average Method (For Computing the Usage Rate), 72, 75
Sixty-Day Reminder (Ship-Completes), 36–37
SKU, 100, 321
Slow-Moving Stock, 207, 239, 255–256, 259–261, 276, 287, 321
Slow-Moving Stock Positioning, 255–256
Smoothing Factors, 70, 309
"Snapshot" Inquiry, 102, 200–201, 204
Software, Computer, 3–7, 10–12, 270, 297, 301–302, 306, 310, 312, 317, 321
Special Prices (To Customers), See "Prices, Special Customer"
Speculation with Inventory, 79, 162, 170–172, 293, 324
Split-Delivery Purchase Orders, 109
Staging Areas, 35–36, 38, 210–211, 220, 268, 320–321
"Stand Alone" Items, 131
Standard Package (Carton) Quantity, 100, 150, 154, 321
Stock Item Definition, 321
Stock Item Handled as Non-Stock, 33–34
Stockkeeping Units, 100, 321
Stock List, 247–248, 282, 322
Stock/Non-Stock Profile, 275–276, 315, 322
Stockouts, 13, 15, 76, 80–82, 119, 130–131, 205, 207, 252, 257, 263, 270, 286–288, 290–291, 308, 322
Stock Status Reports, 17, 178–179, 199–200, 322
Sub-Divided Product Line Offers, 134
Substitute Items, 27, 209, 239, 281, 283, 285–286
Superseded Part Numbers, 26
Superman, 64
Supplier Record, 102–103, 324
Suppliers, 3, 185, 191, 195–196, 224, 228–230, 239, 241–242, 256, 269, 277–278, 282, 286, 288, 322

Surplus Stock, 13–14, 107, 180, 183–185, 187–188, 248, 250, 253–154, 278–279, 291, 296, 322
Surplus Stock Code, 107–108
Surplus Stock Definition, 183–184, 253, 322
Surplus Stock Planned Repositioning, 278–279
Surplus Stock Transfer Rules, 184–185, 253
Surplus Stock Warning, 187–188
Surprise Stock, 24
SWAG, 1–2, 5, 10, 14–15, 17, 46, 54–55, 66, 70, 74, 77, 111, 121, 131–132, 142, 150, 152, 156, 159–160, 165, 172, 184, 208, 254, 259, 267, 270, 273, 287, 290, 296, 299–300, 322
SWAG Definition, 322
System Degeneration, 52–54
Systems Contracts, 84, 122, 126, 172–173, 233, 314, 322–323

Tag & Hold Sales Orders, 34–37, 323
Taxes (On Inventory), 93
Team, Computer/Human, 12–13, 197
Team, Computer Planning, 61
Team, Dead Stock Disposition, 235, 237–238
Team Sent for Formal Training, 301
Team, System Installation, 55
Telemarketing, 4, 60
Telephone Salesmen, See "Salesmen, Inside"
Terminals, Computer (Screens), 20, 27, 99, 106, 306, 312, 323
Texas A&M University, 4, 65
Total-Order Discounts, See "Discounts, Total-Order"
Tracking, Inventory, See "Inventory Tracking"
Tracking, Non-Stock Item, 29–30
Training, Formal Inventory, 301
Transaction Stream, Daily, 215
Transfer History Records, 16, 69, 126–127
Transfers, Branch, 15–17, 68–70, 106, 187, 211, 239, 245–255
Transfers, Branch (Coding), 246
Transfers, Branch (Non-Recurring), 16, 68, 183, 246–250

Transfers, Branch (Recurring), 16, 247
Transfers, Branch (Rules), 54, 253
Trash Lead Times, See "Lead Time Trash"
Trash Stock Item Records, 31
Trend Percentage (Seasonal Item), 74
Turn and Earn Measurement, 280–281, 323
Turnkey Packages, 264, 270, 302, 323
Turnover Definition, 274, 323
Turnover Rate (Turns), 25, 113–115, 120, 130, 133, 137, 139, 148, 151–155, 169, 176, 179, 188, 223–224, 251, 257–261, 274–281, 294–296, 300, 323
Turnover Formulas, 274, 276
Turnover Measurement Frequency, 277

Uncommitted Stock, See "Available-for-Sale Balances"
Unisys Corporation, 9, 302
Unit Cost, 101, 156, 323
Unit Cost, Net, 157–160
Unit of Measure, 1, 100, 213, 221, 323
United Fund, 179, 240–241
Unit-Record Equipment, 324
Unusual Sales Orders, 12, 77–80, 287–288, 324
"Up-Front" Inventory Decision, 226, 316, 324
Upgrades, Computer System, 61, 245, 296, 302
Upgrades, Personnel, 217
Upgrades, Inventory Skill, 3, 271
Upgrades, Stock Item, 27, 311
Usage, 65–88

Usage, Erratic, 122–123
Usage Lumps, 67
Usage, Non-Recurring, 68
Usage Rate, 12, 72–73, 88, 122, 286, 324
Usage, Repair Part, 68
Usage, Repetitive, 68
Usage, Transfer, 68–70
Usage-Value, 153, 324

Value-Added, 4, 27, 43, 123
VanDeMark, Bob, 190
Variable-Length Records, 101
Variable Stock Item Information, 101
Vendors, See "Suppliers"
Vendor Record, 102–103, 324

Warehouse Security, See "Security, Warehouse"
Warehouse Space, 93
Warehouse Stock Locations, 219, 304, 324–325
Warning Report, Frozen Control, See "Frozen Control Warning Report"
Will-Call Sales Orders, 211, 325
Workman, Dr. Mike, 4
Work Orders, Warehouse, 267–268
"Wow" Stage (System Conver-sion), 52
Write-In's, Physical Inventory, 31
Write-Off, Inventory, 240

Zero Stock, 192, 247, 287
Zero-Turn Inventory, 120, 137–139, 148
Zones, Branch, 184–185